Institutional Theatrics

performance works

SERIES EDITORS
Patrick Anderson and
Nicholas Ridout

This series publishes books in theater and performance studies, focused in particular on the material conditions in which performance acts are staged, and to which performance itself might contribute. We define "performance" in the broadest sense, including traditional theatrical productions and performance art, but also cultural ritual, political demonstration, social practice, and other forms of interpersonal, social, and political interaction that may fruitfully be understood in terms of performance.

Institutional Theatrics

Performing Arts Policy in Post-Wall Berlin

✦

Brandon Woolf

NORTHWESTERN UNIVERSITY PRESS
EVANSTON, ILLINOIS

Northwestern University Press
www.nupress.northwestern.edu

Printed in the United States of America

10 9 8 7 6 5 4 3 2 1

Library of Congress Cataloging-in-Publication Data

Names: Woolf, Brandon, author.
Title: Institutional theatrics : performing arts policy in post wall Berlin / Brandon
    Woolf.
Other titles: Performance works.
Description: Evanston, Illinois : Northwestern University Press, 2021. |
    Series: Performance works | Includes bibliographical references and index.
Identifiers: LCCN 2020056751 | ISBN 9780810143555 (paperback) |
    ISBN 9780810143562 (cloth) | ISBN 9780810143579 (ebook)
Subjects: LCSH: Performing arts—Government policy—Germany—Berlin. |
    Theater and society—Germany—Berlin. | Berlin (Germany)—Cultural policy.
Classification: LCC PN2044.G4 W66 2021 | DDC 792.0943/155—dc23
LC record available at https://lccn.loc.gov/2020056751

In memory of
Marvin Perlowin,
Vera Cohen,
and
Traute Petereit,
whose *freie Geister* inevitably run through these pages

CONTENTS

ACKNOWLEDGMENTS

Institutional Theatrics would not have been possible without absolutely unwavering avowal and expansive support from a vast array of institutions and individuals on both sides of the Atlantic. It is an honor to begin this book by expressing my immense (perhaps immeasurable) gratitude to all of them.

I begin with the network of organizations that more than generously funded my work as I lived in and moved between Berkeley (three years), Berlin (six years), and New York City (four years). At University of California, Berkeley, I am deeply appreciative to the Graduate Division, the Program in Critical Theory, the Department of German, and the Department of Theater, Dance, and Performance Studies. Thank you to the Fulbright Foundation, the DAAD, as well as the Berlin Program for Advanced German and European Studies, the Institute of Theater Studies, and the International Research Center for "Interweaving Performance Cultures" at the Freie Universität Berlin. At New York University, I have been so generously supported by the College of Arts and Science, NYU Skirball, NYU Center for the Humanities, and most especially, the Department of English. The gracious encouragement and assistance from the staff at each of these places warmed my heart at every turn. Special thanks go to Mary Ajideh, Claudia Daseking, Robin Davidson, Lissette Florez, Karin Goihl, Alexandra Guillen, Paget Harris, Holger Hartung, Armin Hempel, Jaysen Henderson-Greenbey, Grace Leach, Alyssa Leal, Kate Mattson, Mary Mezzano, Patricia Okoh-Esene, and Bennett Williams.

This book began as a dissertation at UC Berkeley, where I had the incredible privilege of studying with, working for, and always learning from wonderful teachers. Heartfelt thanks to Judith Butler, Brandi Wilkins Catanese, Abigail De Kosnik, Peter Glazer, Yvonne Hardt, Robert Kaufman, Angela Marino, Freddie Rokem, Kaja Silverman, and Linda Williams. I was so fortunate to have a dissertation committee that remained such committed and enthusiastic readers, advice givers, critics, and supports—in spite of my great distance from California much of the time. Thank you to Martin Jay for his ever-discerning eye, his encyclopedic further-reading suggestions, his thick and timely manila envelopes of helpful comments and critique, and for my first extended foray into the world of Adorno. Thank you to Catherine Cole for her always-incisive professional advice, her lived model of self-reflexive organizational reorientation and leadership, and her warm and welcoming open-door policy to discuss most anything. Thank you to Tony Kaes for so many inspiring and multihour conversations, for all the Berlin theater adventures, and for his consistent generosity of spirit and profound kindness. And I want extend my deep gratitude to Shannon Jackson, who was much more than an adviser along the way—she has been a mentor and a guiding force. I feel so very lucky to be the recipient of her generosity, her insight, and her inspiration.

My research consisted of what felt like constant movement between the theater, the library, the archive, the classroom, the demonstration, the living room, the park, the canal, and the café in a Berlin that continued to reveal itself anew with the help of a giant cast of loving guides. Thank you to Hans-Thies Lehmann and Helene Varopoulou for inviting me into their home for tea, theory, and politics, for trips to the theater, for their seemingly limitless Rolodex, their mentorship, and their embrace. Thank you to Matthias Warstat, Christel Weiler, and Erika Fischer-Lichte for inviting me into (and extending my time with) the theater studies community at FU Berlin, and to Evelyn Annuss, Peter Boenisch, Adam Czirak, Kristin Flade, Julius Heinicke, Ramona Mosse, David Savran, and Florian Thamer for the always provocative and productive conversations while there. I owe so much to the staff at the archives of the Akademie der Künste, Berlin, and especially to Sabine Zolchow, whose patience never waned as she helped me navigate the history of theater *nach der Wende*. Thank you to Benjamin Foerster-Baldenius, Elke Knöss-Grillitsch, Sean Patten, Aenne Quiñones, Berit Stumpf, and Sarah Waterfeld for making so much time to talk to me about their inspiring projects. And a special thank-you to Alex Karschnia for his energy, curiosity, commitment, and friendship.

Since arriving at NYU in 2016, I have benefited from many forms of generosity from across the university. I am grateful to John Archer, Tom Augst, Richard Halpern, Wendy Anne Lee, John Waters, and the rest of my colleagues in the English Department for welcoming me into the fold at 244 Greene Street. And thank you to Gwendolyn Alker, Sebastián Calderón Bentin, J de Leon, Erin Mee, Robert Vorlicky, and Alisa Zhulina for inviting me into NYU's broader theater and performance community. Without the gracious mentorship and boundless generosity of Una Chaudhuri and Patrick Deer I would be lost. I owe a great deal to Jay Wegman for his warmth and his endless enthusiasm for big new ideas. And Julia Jarcho, somehow our paths have continued to cross, and I am just so grateful for her brilliance, her friendship, and her baked goods.

Most humble thanks to Nicholas Ridout and Patrick Anderson for including this book in their Performance Works series. Trevor Perri, Maia Rigas, and the rest of the team at Northwestern University Press have been so generous and skilled in shepherding the project through production. I am very thankful for Michael Gnat and his truly unbelievable patience and precision while copyediting. Thank you to the two anonymous readers who provided succinct and very necessary feedback. The photos interspersed throughout the book appear thanks to the generosity of Thomas Aurin, David Baltzer,

Sonja Gehrke, and Hans Jörg Michel. Matt Cornish's sage advice and exhaustive knowledge of the German theater panorama improved this manuscript (and other projects) in innumerable ways along much of its journey. And for very early guidance and encouragement down a road whose undulating path I never could have foreseen, thank you to Lydia Goehr, Julie Stone Peters, Martin Puchner, and Randall Stevenson.

I also want to acknowledge the editors and publishers of journals who gave me the opportunity to refine some of the ideas included in this book. The introduction was developed in part from an article titled "Putting Policy into Performance Studies?" that was published in *Performance Research* 20, no. 4 (2015): 104–11, doi:10.1080/13528165.2015.1071047. Likewise, sections of chapter 2 appeared in "Frank Castorf's Art of Institutional Dis/avowal: A Volksbühne Elegy," *Theatre Survey* 59, no. 2 (2018): 249–64, reprinted here with permission.

At every turn, and on many different levels, I was so very lucky to assemble the most loving multitude of caregivers, supporters, inspirations, and friends who became family. This growing group of saving graces attended more than generously, from near and far, to so many needs, wishes, and dreams. I live in gratitude for each and every sofa, smile, space, thought, concern, cash infusion, song, meal, beer, ear, whiskey, hug, and so much more.

From my time in the Bay Area, I feel so very fortunate for Sima Belmar, Marc Boucai, Brandon Chalk, Jonathan Combs-Schilling, Kristin Dickinson, Kate Duffly, Stefano Gargiulo, Amy Ruth Hale, Bernhard Haux, Chris Hebdon, Beth Hoffmann, Lasse Landt, Ariel Osterweis, Nina Billone Prieur, Kelly Rafferty, April Sizemore-Barber, Joanne Taylor, Alfie Turnshek-Goins, and Scott Wallin, as well as Larry Bogad, Mandy Cohen, Alex Dubilet, Ashley Ferro-Murray, Jessie Hock, Danny Marcus, Caitlin Marshall, Jessica Smith, Morgan Wadsworth-Boyle, and the rest of the tactical comobilizers behind UCMeP.

In Berlin, I could never have dreamed of being taken in, even adopted, by Abby Anderton, Jashen Edwards, Paul Flaig, Alberto di Gennero, Janek Jonas, Joy Kristin Kalu, Tina Kettering, Benjamin Kiesewetter, Dagi Kiesewetter, Johanna Kiesewetter, Marcela Knapp, Deborah Metternich, Moshe Perlstein, Carolin Philipp, Jan Philipp, Jonas von Poser, Carina Sarstedt, Jan Strobl, Martin Urmann, Katrin Wächter, Hans Zwemke, and all of those who filtered in and through that alternative reality that was SHAKESPEARE IM PARK BERLIN.

In New York (across the years), I owe more than a great deal to Faraaz Ahmed, Frank Angones, Tal Beery, Nicole Bryant, Phil Coakley, Lee Sunday Evans, Adam Gidwitz, Neal Gruer, Eden Kasle, Julia Kelly, Dan Kluger, Andrew Lyman, Jess Mezei, Adam Mitchinson, Ronit Muszkatblit, Sean Nuttall, Nick Renart, Jacob Silberstein, Betty Springer, Scott Statland, Kathryn Struthers, Andrea Timpone, Cody Upton, Anja Westray, and Nick Westray. I am also deeply indebted to the communities of the Drama League, LABA:

A Laboratory for Jewish Culture, University Settlement, and Target Margin Theater, who have welcomed my artistic explorations into their spaces.

And for loving friendship, collaboration, inspiration, heartfelt criticism, and awakening that extended in, through, and beyond this manuscript in ways that exceeded my wildest imagination, I will never be able to offer enough thanks to Katrin Beushausen, Shane Boyle, Maxwell Flaum, Ben Gassman, Dennis Johannßen, Sylvie Levine, Lauren Mancia, David Max, Peter Remmers, and Stew.

For my family, too, there are not enough words. I am so grateful to have been welcomed with such acceptance to join the ranks of Familie Lorenz (Ulla, Sven, Leonard, and Henri), Familie Keppler (Anja, Sven, Junia, and Maja), and Familie Petereit-Ludwig (Tanja, Christoph, Emma, Hannah, and Jonna). I have so much love, appreciation, and gratitude for my mom, Ivy Woolf Turk; my dad, Louis Woolf; Richard Turk, Amanda Turk, Josh Turk, Bobbi Perlowin, Merrie Bernstein, Eric Bernstein, Karen Present, Alison Weinflash, and my superhero sister, Kelly Woolf. Tina Petereit, my wife and my partner, I just hope you know how much I *schätze* your love, laughs, patience, and enduring commitment to coconspiring A.Z. And to our daughter, Thalia, your musings and light fill my days.

Introduction

✦

Arts of Institutional Dis/avowal

Putting Performance into Policy Studies

Whoever speaks of culture speaks of administration as well.
—Theodor W. Adorno, "Culture and Administration" (1959)

Who would've thought that in the 21st century the fate of a
theater could trigger a public policy debate?
—Evelyn Annuss, "On the Future of the Volksbühne—
Failure Is an Option" (2018)

July 20, 2017. The air was thick with anticipation. A caper was afoot. My
friend Katrin and I ate our dinners quickly. We pushed our bicycles through
Berlin's Mitte neighborhood toward the Volksbühne theater on historic
Rosa-Luxemburg-Platz. I had it on good authority that an occupation was
planned. As we approached the immense building, however, things looked
quiet. And quite strange. The massive iron Robber Wheel, or *Räuberrad*, that
bedecked the theater's front lawn since 1994 had been removed in protest a
few weeks earlier. For the past twenty-five years, this sculpture had served as
an insignia and metaphorical calling card for knaves, tricksters, and thieves
of all sorts to make themselves at home at the Volksbühne. Under the impas-
sioned leadership of East German enfant terrible Frank Castorf, this people's
stage proffered a consistent challenge for a new generation of artists and
audiences alike to rethink the theater's social function in reunified Germany.
But the Castorf era came to an unexpected end: it was announced in 2015
that Chris Dercon, a curator at London's Tate Modern museum, would be
the Volksbühne's new director as of September 2017. No one could have predicted that this "confused"[1] policy decision would provoke such an explosive
scandal. Recent weeks leading up to the end of the 2016–17 season were
filled with a dramatic hubbub of activity, day and night: standing-room-only
showings of repertoire mainstays, protests against the new administration,
international headlines, emotional goodbyes, widespread lamentations
of a broken cultural policy system, a healthy dose of nostalgia, and wild

celebration. But tonight, there were no crowds. The lights were dim. And a detail of security guards patrolled the premises.

Surprised to see these men in uniform outside the theater, Katrin and I debated whether we should spark up a conversation with one of them. He looked rather bored, and as there was nothing doing, we walked over and said hello. The guard told us he was part of a private security service hired by the theater to be on alert in case anyone tried to enter the historic building without permission. If so, he and his colleagues had been instructed to call the police. They were on particularly high alert this evening because—so he had heard—an occupation had been announced on the internet. With typical Prussian brusqueness and a thick *Berliner Schnauze* dialect, he explained that he found the entire situation a bit comical. Apparently, there was some hoopla among people who worked at the theater. Some folks were set to lose their jobs under the new leadership. Others were nervous about the prospect of outsiders occupying the space. He giggled at the thought of protesters leaving piles of shit on the doorstep of the theater to show their disdain and disappointment. And he found it utterly ridiculous that anyone would openly announce plans for an occupation online. But he didn't mind the work, he said. He had been out of a job the previous week. And he was happy to have one this week.

As I write these paragraphs a few years later, I am still struck by this encounter. My central task in the pages that follow is to investigate theater's changing role in a changing society by examining intersections of performance and policy. Indeed, one of the broader claims I make is that theater and performance provide us with means—artistic, theoretical, political—to reimagine institutions of public life. And yet as the above anecdote makes clear, as soon as a member of public life is thrown—perhaps unwittingly—into conversations about cultural policy, something feels askew. There is something grounding—humbling even—about a perspective that couldn't care less about the dramatic intrigues that constitute much of this book. The security guard's perspective from the literal front lines serves as a kind of limit or check on my own propensity (some of the protagonists of this book might call it an *American* propensity) for naive optimism. Indeed, the theater is a place of work. And that work has become increasingly precarious in Berlin and beyond. This anecdote serves as a reminder that as much as this book looks to the theater as a space and practice of possibility, we must also—at the same time—reckon with it as a site of that possibility's foreclosure.

The Dercon Debacle

In the end, there was no occupation that evening. As it turned out, members of the theater's technical team objected to plans for a July occupation. They were too tired after the weeks of closing Castorf festivities, and though many

The Robber Wheel (*Räuberrad*) on June 20, 2017, ten days before it was removed in protest against the new Dercon administration. Photograph copyright © Brandon Woolf.

were openly against Dercon's appointment, they could not support an occupation that would keep the theater open into the summer months. It would be their responsibility to stay in the building, make sure it was safe, and prevent damage. They just weren't prepared to work (for free) during their much-needed holiday.[2] The occupation would have to be delayed—until September 22, when the Volksbühne was occupied by a broad coalition of artists, activists, students, scholars, employees of the theater, longtime fans, and other community members. Explicitly calling their action an act of interdisciplinary performance, over the next six days the occupiers sought to rework the space of the theater. By critically reactivating the massive public infrastructure of the Volksbühne—making use of every room in the building—their occupation sought to perform modes of collaborative institutionality aimed precisely at addressing and urgently rethinking just how public culture might be organized differently in Germany. The idea, according to Sarah Waterfeld, one of the organizers, was to "collectively develop a new concept for the state-subsidized stage that could be transferable to other spheres."[3]

What were they protesting specifically? On the one hand, the occupation was perhaps the most visible instantiation of a massive public controversy—and in some cases panic—over Chris Dercon's appointment as successor to Frank Castorf. Many critics saw the selection of a London-based museum curator as director of an experimental Berlin theater, with radical left leanings to boot, as a "flagrant violation"[4] of the Volksbühne's iconic aesthetic and political identity. Other critics saw Dercon's appointment as an even broader attack on, and "systemic crisis"[5] for, the German theatrical landscape writ large. Is the German-speaking world, they asked, still committed to maintaining its unique albeit highly costly theater system—grounded historically in large ensembles, extensive repertoires, and full-fledged state support?[6] Or has the time come for the German theater to justify its activities economically and compete in an innovation-based global network of private and third-sector-driven creative industries? Must Germany, in other words, embrace the trend toward fewer production facilities in exchange for a growing number of touring and guest performance venues?[7]

Chris Dercon's answer: yes, absolutely. Even though Berlin already has a number of these kinds of presenting houses, Dercon's concept for the "new" Volksbühne was a complete reorientation of the German *Staatstheater*, or state-stage. No more ensemble. No more repertoire. No more *Intendant*, or artistic director responsible for maintaining the unique artistic vision of the house *and* directing on its stage. Instead the theater would become a project-based platform for an international lineup of interdisciplinary guest artists, a revolving door of en-suite productions curated by a committee of "experts." Text-based drama and theater were almost entirely eliminated from Dercon's proposed program and subsumed by a range of high-profile dance, installation, participatory, and digital performance works. Indeed, Dercon expressed his disdain for the tradition of auteurist German *Regietheater*, or director's theater, of which the Volksbühne is emblematic: "I just cannot stand to see Macbeth wearing Burberry, eating *Buletten* [Berlin-style meatballs], and drinking a glass of vodka. I mean, it has nothing to do with theater. If that is theater, then I can't stand it. I really can't stand it. I get an allergy."[8]

Central to Dercon's vision was an expansion of the new Volksbühne brand beyond the Mitte neighborhood in which it is located through the activation of two former aircraft hangers at the historic Tempelhof airfield in south-central Berlin. This enormous new multidisciplinary exhibition and performance hall, which Dercon claimed would secure Berlin as a global cultural metropolis, fit neatly with the larger urban planning initiatives of Berlin's incumbent mayor, Michael Müller. Berlin should no longer be a "poor, but sexy" center for modern bohemians—per the ironic slogan coined in 2003 by its former mayor, Klaus Wowereit. Rather, Müller wanted to establish a new urban center for creative industries, and Dercon's expansion of the Volksbühne into the not-yet-gentrified district around Tempelhof could begin a twenty-year process of profitable urban development: "Art as Social Work and City-Making," as Dercon put it.[9] The final step of Dercon's reorientation of the state-stage was economic. Since Berlin's public coffers couldn't accommodate the additional five million euros per year Dercon required, he planned to secure adequate funds through corporate sponsorships and commercial rentals.[10]

For those of us based in the United States—whose jaws might drop at the very thought of a robust system of centralized funding for the arts—the demand that theater institutions justify their bottom lines and secure always-limited funds from any source possible is rather standard. The US performance economy knows very little about ensemble, about repertoire, about coordinated cultural policy programs at the municipal, state, and federal levels. But in Germany, this particular brand of institutional disavowal, so eager to rethink "big" government and its long-standing swath of accompanying infrastructures of support in the arts sector for a more flexible model, is still highly controversial in many camps. Indeed, in Germany, *Kulturpolitik*—and the often-tenuous relationships between state and market, between modes of social organization and artistic production that it encompasses—is still very much up for debate. For many of the Volksbühne's proponents, the Tate Modern—a colonial-era power plant turned corporate tourist attraction—was a terrifying adversary most unwelcome in Berlin. Dercon knew full well his proposals would cause a stir.[11] And they did. Preceding the theater's occupation, the outcry in print and social media was immense. Many stalwarts of the German theater lamented that someone who lacked theater experience—or even any real interest in the theater—would transform perhaps Germany's most important state-stage into an empty "event-shed."[12] Two hundred staff members, freelance artists, and technicians affiliated with the Volksbühne published an open letter stating their lack of confidence—and worries that most of their jobs would be made redundant.[13] What use is there after all for builders, designers, and makeup artists if the season consists of an ever-changing lineup of guest performances produced elsewhere? This letter was followed by an online petition—which garnered more than forty thousand signatures—criticizing Dercon's appointment as an "inappropriate top-down decision" made by party politicians behind closed doors without public support.[14] And when heaps of feces began to be delivered daily in front of his office, Dercon questioned whether he should consider leaving Berlin.[15]

While much of the anti-Dercon rhetoric remained theater-centric at first, it quickly became clear that the criticism was aimed at something much broader: the future of Berlin. As the occupiers asked in their online invitation—which the security guard rather glibly mocked—"In what kind of city do we want to live? Under what circumstances do we want to work? . . . Who will we allow to determine our lives? The theater has become a symbol of urban development."[16] Indeed, in the long wake of German reunification, Berlin emerged, now quite famously, as a paradise for the "weird and wacky,"[17] as "Europe's Capital of Cool."[18] Since living was cheap—as the city had not yet undergone the postindustrial transformations of other European capitals—Berlin became an offbeat mecca for a lively, postpunk subculture.[19] At the same time, tourism boomed beyond the wildest of expectations,[20] and an influx of mobile young urban creatives, or Yuccies,[21] cemented Berlin as a center of unbridled energy for a "new spirited"[22] start-up culture—with English as the dominant language. As Peter Boenisch notes, since the 2008 financial crisis, the split between these two groups has grown increasingly present—and divisive.[23] To make matters more contentious, building has boomed, and many apartments have been renovated by international developers and are being rented through Airbnb, or sold with high price tags to investors from around the globe. As a result, gentrification hit big—particularly in the areas of Mitte and Prenzlauer Berg around the Volksbühne. Whereas these were some of the poorest neighborhoods in the city in the 1990s, they are now Berlin's most expensive districts.[24] Very much in line with these developments, Berlin has solidified its standing as a coveted zone of artistic "freedom" for an international jet set of art-world elites—many of whom have fled other cultural hubs and taken up residence in what is now considered the "new" Paris, the "new" London, the "new" New York. According to Klaus Biesenbach, former director of New York's MoMA PS1, Berlin is "the most liberal, artist-friendly place I have ever been."[25]

Although he strongly objects to being labeled a *neo*liberal,[26] Dercon's new Volksbühne made productive use of just this kind of language: he jettisoned the politically charged "am Rosa-Luxemburg-Platz" from the theater's name and inaugurated in its place a "theater without borders" that "reflect[s] on the contemporary," in which "artists from Berlin, Europe and the world are invited to contribute to an ever-evolving urban society" in order to promote a "vision of an open, cosmopolitan community."[27] Less generously stated, as Sven Lütticken recapitulated the occupiers' critique, Dercon inaugurated a brand of "homogenized global art-in-general that . . . serve[d] the city's event-culture—rather than serving the city's residents and reflecting the fundamental hybridity for which the Volksbühne is known."[28] With their occupation, the activist performance artists sought, so they claimed, to establish "free spaces" and "collective structures" based on "respectful coexistence, acceptance and tolerance": "We are not the Berlin of city marketing, investment incentives, performance rivalry, of social marginalization, of deportations and gentrification."[29] In other words, the occupiers sought to perform a very different mode of "Art as Social Work and City-Making." The plan, according to Sarah Waterfeld, was to present an open, heterogenous, and ever-expanding program of performance works in each room of the theater, accompanied by public discussions about how the theater should be collectively organized and administered going forward. More than three thousand people helped organize the action in advance, and during the six-day occupation thousands more moved through the space in the hope of collectively creating new "spaces of possibility."[30] The priorities of Dercon's "open, cosmopolitan community" became clear, however, when on September 28, a squadron of over fifty riot-clad police officers arrived to clear the theater forcefully at the behest of the Berlin city government.

We see, then, that the extended outcries over and actions against Chris Dercon and his proposals for a new Volksbühne were much more than a

Occupation of the Volksbühne, September 2017. Photograph copyright © David Baltzer / bildbuehne.de.

Co-organizer Sarah Waterfeld during the Volksbühne occupation, September 2017. Photograph copyright © David Baltzer / bildbuehne.de.

quibble about the aesthetic proclivities of a new theater director. Indeed, the Dercon debates extend way beyond the Volksbühne's stage and call into question the priorities of Berlin's cultural policy. As Dercon himself explained, "The rage has less to do with me personally than with the state of theater today, and its future. Of course, German theater is very important, but the audience, the public, has changed. Berlin today is a cosmopolitan city, and to come to terms with this fact is not easy for the German theater."[31] *Institutional Theatrics* tracks both the challenges and opportunities of this coming to terms in the decades since German reunification. This book examines the steady proliferation over the past thirty years of agendas to disavow and even dismantle the long-standing tradition of state-subsidized theater in Berlin, even as the German capital worked to redefine itself as a global arts epicenter. I claim that these varied stages of disavowal—these crises of cultural policy—provoked a range of performative arts of dis/avowal on and off the stage that worked to forge new relations between performance and the institutions that house it. By focusing on the restructuring of Berlin's major public theater infrastructures as well as the interdisciplinary performance practices that responded to these shifts, I argue that cultural policy must be thought of as a performative practice of infrastructural imagining, not just as an administrative agenda for divvying and delegating funds. Furthermore, understanding performance as itself a form of policy can help us understand the ways artists engage systems of state support as the means of enacting their undoing.

Theater in Crisis in Post-Wall Berlin

Despite the great fervor of the most recent Volksbühne controversy, public debate about the state of the state-stage has a long institutional history in Berlin. I begin with the recent Dercon debates in order to emphasize that many of the questions that constitute contemporary cultural policy discourse first emerged after the fall of the Wall, as Berlin was thrust (and thrust itself) into a new era. Throughout the Cold War, on both sides of the Wall, legislators, arts administrators, and artists across both Germanys maintained dogged commitments to national traditions of public support for the arts. As Traute Schölling explains, "Regardless of their antithetical socio-political structures and ideological aims during the previous forty years, both states were committed to a common German tradition: the responsibility of the state to support culture."[32] Theater subsidies in the formerly western Federal Republic of Germany (FRG) were higher per capita than any other country in the world.[33] Centralized support for the theater in the formerly eastern German Democratic Republic (GDR) was also quite substantial.[34] Accordingly, the reunification treaty, signed in August 1990, made an explicit commitment to maintaining the continuity of cultural life in the newly unified nation, committed in other words to the continued relevance of the German *Kulturstaat*, or Culture State—with a capital "C."[35] Article 35 of the treaty read:

> During the years of division, art and culture were—despite differing developments in the two German states—a basis for the ongoing unity of the German nation. They represent an independent and indispensable contribution to the process of German state unity on the road to European integration. A united Germany's position and prestige in the world depends not only on its political weight and economic achievements, but also on its importance as a cultural nation. . . . The fulfillment of cultural tasks, including the financing, must be secured in such a way that the protection and support of culture and art falls to the new states and cities according to the division of responsibilities defined by the Constitution. . . . To compensate for the consequences of Germany's division, the Federal government may help finance in the transition individual cultural projects and institutions in order to maintain the cultural infrastructure.[36]

This explicit legislative commitment proved harder than expected to maintain. According to the West German constitution, or *Grundgesetz*, approved in 1949—and amended to include East Germany in 1990—the individual German states were responsible for subsidizing art and culture.[37] In line with the agreement to fold the former GDR into the West German system, the responsibilities of all formerly East German cultural institutions passed from the central government to the newly formed state governments. Reunification proved incredibly expensive, however, and the German states—especially those in the East—faced enormous deficits and major unemployment in the years after reunification, brought on by the largest economic recession since the 1970s.[38] Anticipating the potential lack of funds to support the expanded cultural sphere, the new federal government committed to a temporary sum of transitional and explicitly federal subsidies: in 1991, the commitment was for 900 million DM for the preservation and promotion of culture; this sum decreased each year until the federal aid expired at the end of 1994.[39] This federal commitment ultimately proved inadequate to ameliorate the rising deficits and infrastructural uncertainty that ensued—in the arts landscape and beyond.

Due to its unique status as city, state, and future capital of the new German nation, Berlin became the focus of much cultural political attention. Berlin, 1989, was a city wrought with the weight of twentieth-century Europe: a metropolis long divided, working to reinvent itself explicitly as the center of the reunified *Kulturstaat*, as literal and symbolic meeting point of East and West. Though Berlin received some additional funding from the temporary federal fund due to its exceptional status, the newly reunified city found itself responsible almost overnight for an unprecedented number of state-funded cultural institutions from the East and the West, an overabundance that was particularly pronounced in the performing arts. From the former West: the Deutsche Oper (and Ballet), Theater des Westens, Staatliche Schauspielbühnen (or State-Stage Complex, which included the Schiller Theater, Schlosspark Theater, and Studio Theater), Schaubühne am Lehniner Platz, and Freie Volksbühne, in addition to the partially subsidized Grips and Hebbel Theaters. From the former East: the Staatsoper and Komische Oper (both with their own ballet troupes), Metropol-Theater, Friedrichstadtpalast, Deutsches Theater (and Kammerspiele), Berliner Ensemble, Maxim Gorki Theater, Volksbühne am Rosa-Luxemburg-Platz, Kabarett-Theater Distel, Theater der Freundschaft, Staatliches Puppentheater, and the Theater in the basement of the recently closed Palast der Republik, the East Berlin community center and seat of the former East German Parliament.

To make matters more complicated, the city's rapidly changing arts landscape was also mediated by an emerging agenda of (nascently) neoliberal urban development, supported by the party politics of Berlin's Grand Coalition government, which catalyzed a slew of heated cultural policy controversies about the future of the state-subsidized arts, with an intense focus on Berlin's pressing theater situation. In the immediate context of reunification, cultural political authorities working on behalf of the Grand Coalition launched a sustained critique of the state-stage's infrastructural stagnation. They argued that state support and enduring security facilitated intransigent inflexibility, bureaucratic malaise, and an abuse of privilege through rapidly expanding administrative and technical apparatuses and outdated federal and municipal budgetary laws. In the interest of creativity, then, austerity was deemed necessary to relieve the city of its high cultural expenditures by transitioning toward private initiatives attuned to the benefits of a consumer-oriented theater model and a commercially driven box office.

There was a first round of debates, cutbacks, and administrative adjustments in the early months of 1990. But the ensuing years of what many have since labeled the first Berlin "theater crisis"[40] saw a series of truly dramatic shifts: the dismantling of a number of long-standing theater institutions, the advent of new institutions, and the refunctioning of older institutions with new purposes and orientations—both aesthetic and political. These institutional transformations were also the sites of and catalysts for Berlin's reemergence as a vibrant center of experimental theater and performance over the next thirty years. *Institutional Theatrics* examines this extended period of precarious adjustment of, at, and in the theater—this "coming to terms"—in order to provide critical traction to the complex operations of *performing arts policy*.[41] In a series of case studies of performance *as* institutional analysis, the book traces the fraught history of a Berlin caught uncomfortably between the shrinking welfare state theater and the emergence of an "alternative" ethos of self-administering and project-based creativity. In other words, the book historicizes the conditions of possibility for the most recent theater crisis at the Volksbühne by tracking an extended set of performance-based responses to a persistent set of policy questions: in a city struggling to determine just how neoliberal it can afford to be, what kinds of performing arts practices and institutions are necessary—and why?

To address these questions, *Institutional Theatrics* charts an approach for thinking in new ways about the relations between art and the infrastructures of its support. The central methodological argument of the book is that aesthetic formations cannot be separated from institutional and broader social formations. Indeed, I argue that formal experimentation, both onstage and off, is a vital strategy for making sense of theater in imminent crisis. In the specific context of German theater studies, or *Theaterwissenshaft*, my attention to the successive crises in Berlin responds directly to recent calls by both Christopher Balme and Peter Boenisch for "institutional dramaturgies"[42] committed to a "sharper institutional dimension of theater research and analysis in order to better understand the changing role and cultural relevance of theater in present-day (Western) Europe."[43] Further, my focus on policy expands upon recent efforts to unsettle an anti-institutional prejudice that has haunted theater and performance studies.[44]

In the next section, I explicate the ways my notion of *institutional dis/avowal* is implicitly embedded in a history of contentious conversations about culture and administration. As my rather polemical subtitle to this introduction suggests, I enter these discussions by revisiting another set of cultural policy debates that arose in the annals of cultural studies also in the 1990s. I argue that Tony Bennett's controversial claim—that we *put* policy into cultural studies—unintentionally invites us to examine how "policy" itself continues to serve as a generative term to unravel binarizing and suffocating logics of state subsidy versus neoliberal reform, bureaucracy versus flexibility, overabundance versus austerity, artistic freedom versus, well, artistic freedom. By tracking a critical genealogy of these so-called policy debates, I contend also that we move beyond a mere acknowledgment—or avowal—that arts of institutional thinking are essential in and for theater and performance studies. Indeed, the conceptual framework of institutional dis/avowal takes seriously the seemingly paradoxical circumstance in which artists who receive public support make use of it to avow the administrations that govern while simultaneously performing their transformation. This methodological examination of artistic critique as institutional overhaul sets the stage for the complex intersections of performance and policy in post-Wall Berlin.

Staging the Cultural Policy Debates

In April 1990, an international crowd of almost a thousand scholars gathered for a weekend-long conference at the University of Illinois at

Urbana-Champaign. Among those poised to present papers that weekend was Tony Bennett, whose provocative policy polemic would raise eyebrows. Indeed, Bennett's "Putting Policy into Cultural Studies" catalyzed a set of heated cultural policy debates that polarized interdisciplines in the critical humanities for years to come.[45] As Bennett explained, he was interested in a radical reappraisal of the underlying theories and political orientations of cultural studies. Specifically, Bennett took issue with the preponderance of neo-Gramscian thinking, which, so he claimed, committed a generation of scholars to "too automatic a politics" and a romance of resistance indifferent to the specific institutional conditions that give rise to particular kinds of political situations and "regulate different fields of culture."[46] Instead, Bennett called for an explicitly pragmatic agenda for cultural studies—one that, in his most sardonic articulation, insists that we abandon the "heady skirmishing with postmodernism" and the "sleuth-like searching for subversive practices just where you'd least expect to find them."[47] In Toby Miller's more reserved recapitulation, Bennett called upon those he termed "left" cultural theorists to abandon their penchants for "public resistance in favor of a more measurable and measured influence inside the apparatuses of the state."[48]

In Bennett's admittedly idiosyncratic view, Michel Foucault's writings on governmentality demanded "a revised understanding of the relations between civil society, culture and the state which allows culture its autonomous spheres and forms of action."[49] Unlike Gramsci's centralized flows of hegemonic ideology, says Bennett, Foucault does not rely on a notion of centralized power. Rather, governmentality is characterized by a diversity of means of social management that exceed state action. Culture, Bennett insists, is one of those regulating technologies that shapes social relations and organizes human conduct.[50] Culture is, in a certain sense, already cultural policy. For this reason, Bennett suggests that "an engagement with policy issues needs to be seen as a central component of the practical concerns of cultural studies."[51] Further, he stresses that a policy-oriented cultural studies would "begin to think [of] the possibility of a politics which might take the form of an administrative program, and so to think also of a type of cultural studies that will aim to produce knowledges that can assist in the development of such programs rather than endlessly contrive to organize subjects which exist only as the phantom effects of its own rhetorics."[52]

Bennett's proclivity for disciplinary institutions and administrative programs—in addition to his flagrant diatribe against the "contrived appearance of ineffable complexity"[53] that, in his mind, characterizes much social theory— evoked strong reactions. Even if one were compelled by Bennett's particular reading of Foucault, why should cultural studies become cultural policy studies a priori? Why should cultural critics become bureaucrats? Fredric Jameson was only the first to excoriate Bennett for his "anti-intellectualism," his "obscene . . . proposals," his "misplaced advice," his "remarkably misleading" tone, and his overall "ignorance."[54] What followed were years of adamant debate, resulting often in the most starkly polarized positions: policy versus cultural criticism, top-down versus bottom-up practices, reformist versus revolutionary politics, and contextualist versus textualist emphases.

In a peculiar turn, this was also the criticism that Bennett himself hurled back at debate participants in his book-length intervention in 1998. Surprisingly—and without much explanation—Bennett condemned his many "real and substantial"[55] critics for their own propensities toward binary thinking and their failure to demonstrate adequately a more productive permeability between policy and critique. Although he continued to lament the "serious . . . blockages to an adequate engagement, both theoretical and practical, with the horizons of policy,"[56] Bennett suddenly dashed the air of exclusivity, of strict either-or, from his vocabulary and hinted instead that there must be a mutual imbrication of seemingly contradictory perspectives—although he provided little methodological help. In an even more unusual move, Bennett claimed that the penchant for polarity on the part of his critics—and perhaps himself—was in fact an extension of, and could therefore be blamed on, Theodor W. Adorno's infamous meditations on the inherently "contradictory tensions between culture and administration"[57] from his 1959 radio lecture of the same title—with which I began this chapter. Bennett accused Adorno of first formulating and then sustaining the irreconcilable antinomies that came to constitute, as Oliver Bennett put it later, the "torn halves of cultural policy research."[58]

Tony Bennett's invocation of Adorno is powerful precisely for its productive misreading. Indeed, Adorno's analysis provides the very tools necessary to unsettle the overwhelmingly stagnant binaries that Bennett accuses him of fixing in the public imaginary. Rather than explicating an impenetrable set of opposites, Adorno's mode of negative dialectical argument provides methodological insight into the ways a more *critical* policy studies could—and should—explore the nuanced entanglements of policy and critique that Bennett and many of his critics failed to demonstrate. Further, Adorno begins to articulate the radically different kinds of institutional practices and programs enabled by embracing such tendentious interdependencies.

Bennett focuses the bulk of his critical attention on a later moment in "Culture and Administration" in which Adorno "opens a perspective for the protection of cultural matters from the realm of control by the market," by turning to the "ignominious figure of the expert"[59] as a potential foil to the reified logics of administration that, for him, constitute the culture industry. In his attempt to imagine what kinds of historical actors may advocate for this perspective, Adorno postulates a Benjaminian critic "whose task it is to uphold the interest of the public against the public itself."[60] Here Bennett digs in his heels, as he has little patience for what he considers to be Adorno's blatantly elitist commitment to "men of insight,"[61] to the "aesthetic personality who alone is able to act in the sphere of administration in the name of values which exceed it, a lonely historical actor destined to be lacerated by the contradictions he seeks to quell in culture's favour."[62]

It is a shame, however, that Bennett pays almost no attention to Adorno's broader discussion about the nature of policy itself. Although Adorno's "expert" language and its classed, raced, gendered, and abled entailments are troubling, his unfortunate wording does not pervade the essay in its entirety, nor does it theoretically exclude more radically inclusive formulations. Committed to his negative methodology, Adorno does not posit a lone elitist who proceeds from a "position of transcendence in relation to its object."[63] Rather, Adorno's critic must critique, even protest against, those most pervasive institutions, just as they reflect the institution's "objective substance."[64] Elsewhere, Adorno remains open about the kinds of critics and the arts of critique that may prove useful in exposing the ways culture and administration enact their own interdependence. Indeed, Adorno works consistently to demonstrate how a more critical cultural policy can only be thought immanently from within the very material and always heteronomous ranks of the publics in which it is invested. He insists, "Cultural policy would not misunderstand itself as godwilled; it would not blindly endorse faith in culture, blind to its entanglement with the social totality—and for that very reason truly entangled—it would find a parallel in the negative naiveté involved in accepting administration as faith."[65]

Adorno's position is one that *already* accommodates and challenges Bennett's. Adorno is certainly aware of, and dialectically obliged to consider, the most pragmatic horizons of policy, and he takes seriously the suggestion that we begin, as Bennett puts it, "talking to . . . what used to be called the ISAs [ideological state apparatuses] rather than writing them off from the outset."[66] In the opening half of the essay, Adorno examines how all artists and their modes of production are deeply reliant on the material and financial supports of the varied administrations in which they are enmeshed: "The appeal to the creators of culture to withdraw from the process of administration and keep distant from it has a hollow ring."[67] Indeed, Adorno obliges himself to interrogate closely a version of Bennett's later claim that "we can now, without regret, treat culture as an industry,"[68] even if Adorno's version of no regret more closely resembles the "urge to release the safety catch on a revolver."[69]

Even more interesting, however, are the ways that Adorno begins to imagine alternative possibilities for administration itself. He is interested in thinking through, and again dialectically obliged to think through, what cultural policy may entail if it were to exceed increasing normalization—to which Bennett seems to have already subscribed. Adorno is interested further in thinking through what kinds of institutions and administrative programs this different mode of policy may enable. Here he begins to sketch, albeit tentatively, what I call a negative art of institutional dis/avowal. This is a practice or "dialectical idea of absorbing that which is spontaneous and not planned into planning, of creative space for these factors and of a strengthening of their possibilities."[70] In this moment, Adorno alludes to the ways an institution might embrace its own determinate negation. He gestures toward an institution that is itself obliged to reckon with the concrete particulars of its own contradictions, to reckon also, in other words, with its own inherent proclivity for spontaneity, processuality, even instability. In a move, then, beyond a unilateral critique of the reified tendencies of administration, and at the same time, in a move beyond the sphere of idealist autonomy that Bennett associates with his thought, Adorno sketches the broader entailments of a critical cultural policy. This alternative institutional orientation—one of dis/avowal—would necessarily attend to the more "pragmatic" considerations of deutsche marks, pfennigs, nuts, and bolts, while *also* proliferating practices and programs that move beyond obduracy or entrenchment and that call urgent attention to the institution's own inherent penchant for "renounc[ing] itself."[71]

Policy and Performativity

Ten years after Bennett's inaugural polemic, Toby Miller and George Yúdice shifted the discursive terms of the debates with the publication of their book *Cultural Policy* in 2002. On the one hand, their volume directly challenged Bennett's dismissal of the "committed norms of cultural studies,"[72] thus taking up Angela McRobbie's urgent call for a new cultural policy "agenda"[73]: "Our book seeks, in other words, to articulate knowledge with progressive social change, with social movements as primary *loci* of power, authorization, and responsibility. More conventional research articulates knowledge with social reproduction, with governments as primary *loci* of power, authorization, and responsibility. Whereas our project is concerned with transforming the social order, the alternative seeks to replicate it—a struggle between cultural policy as a transformative versus a functionalist sphere."[74] While Miller and Yúdice stress the importance of "committed" scholarship, their project also engages with Bennett by focusing critically on the specific institutional conditions that give rise to particular political situations and regulate different fields of culture. Specifically, they argue that an appraisal of the *performativity* of policy is necessary to account for the complex interplay between the "transformation" and the "replication" of institutional matrices already in place and at work. In his solo project on the increasing *Expediency of Culture*, published just the following year, Yúdice makes a similar claim: "The very term [cultural policy] conjoins what in modernity belonged to emancipation on the one hand, and to regulation on the other."[75] In line with his larger argument diagnosing how culture has become a central resource in the globalized, post-Fordist market economy, Yúdice sees policy as a necessary consideration *and* intervention at a time when—as was already the case in Article 35 of the German reunification treaty, for instance—"culture is being invoked to solve problems that previously were the province of economics and politics."[76]

In place of Adorno's "administration" and Bennett's take on "governmentality," Yúdice describes a performative "field of force generated by differently arranged relations among institutions of the state and civil society, the judiciary, the police, schools and universities, the media, consumer markets, and so on."[77] The varied national—and sometimes multinational—intersections of these institutional frames compose a performative matrix of comportment and knowledge production. For Miller and Yúdice, then, cultural policy must be conceived in terms of performativity because, in part at least, it is "dedicated to producing subjects via the formation of repeatable styles of conduct, either at the level of the individual or the public."[78] Cultural policy, they continue, "always implies the management of populations"[79] through suggested forms of normalized behavior, which have varying degrees of performative force depending on the context, "enjoining [for example] universal adoption of bourgeois manners or stratifying access to cultural and other material resources on the basis of other demographic categorizations."[80]

In his lengthy exposition of Judith Butler's early work, Yúdice also reviews how her theory of performativity was devised precisely to contest these constraining frames. He recapitulates the ways in which her politics of "disidentity" emerges from and plays within the sovereign aims and representations of the institutional regimes of power, discourse, and culture. Here, however, Yúdice raises his most fundamental objection. Questioning the efficacy of Butler's theory, he asks just how she proposes actually to confound those most powerful and normalizing institutions. "Deconstructive analyses . . . work quite well for texts but seem powerless before the operations of the institutions that exert regulatory force over texts."[81] He continues:

> Butler's contention that the "turning of power against itself to produce alternative modalities of power, to establish a kind of political contestation that is not a 'pure' opposition," . . . has yet to be elucidated at the level of institutions and their effects. . . . To the degree that Butler imagines "democracy" . . . to inhere in such forms of gender trouble, and more generally, cultural trouble, she is caught up in the very fantasy that she aims to elucidate.[82]

For Yúdice, cultural expression is by no means a sufficient strategy against the ubiquitous condemnation to perform. In an age of expedience, in which culture functions as a technology of biopower on a global scale, "there is little to be gained by deploying identity or disidentity if there is no juridical or other institutional uptake."[83]

For this reason, Miller and Yúdice turn to policy as a means of both participating in and intervening in culture. In one of his clearest articulations of the importance of this kind of explicitly institution-based thinking, Yúdice explains (albeit in the form of a disclaimer): "It is beyond the scope of this chapter to elaborate on the premise that there is no outside of institutionality and that it will not do to expect an external force—the real—to solve the problems of an institutionally bound practice."[84] To work against the institution, in other words, is "another way of allowing that institution to frame the understanding of the practice and to seek to incorporate it."[85] Instead—and this is the methodology Yúdice invokes in his book's final chapter on the international inSITE triennial festival—it is necessary to understand, and to critique discursively, the inner workings of the institutional matrices that enable or performatively shape acts of culture. But in addition to this understanding, Yúdice claims that it is also essential to embrace, work for, and participate in the institution itself in an effort to modify it from within:

> inSITE . . . makes visible and palpable how the cultural economy functions. But what do we do once we see how it functions? Critique of this venue will not produce the disalienating effects believed to ensue from the uncovering of ideological structures and processes characteristic of ideology critique. Nor will we get in touch with our phenomenological body or have a limit experience. What inSITE calls for, in my view, is to become a user, a col*la*orator who intervenes in order to have the labor expended recognized and compensated. Venues like inSITE become important sites for the reformulation of cultural policy in a post-Fordist, globalizing world, not from the vantage point of a government agency, foundation or university office, but by engaging as an archaeologist-practitioner in the process.[86]

Yúdice insists that we understand arts institutions like inSITE as complex systems of laboring bodies and infrastructural supports. And the task of a critical policy practice is both to expose the supporting structures upon which those bodies depend to do the kind of work they do *and* to engage those supports on behalf of the workers who make them possible.

For some critics, Miller and Yúdice end up sounding more like Tony Bennett and less like Judith Butler than perhaps anticipated. Peter Osborne, for example, is frustrated with what he reads as Miller and Yúdice's resigned endorsement of "actually existing politics" and accompanying reduction of policy to an advocacy program for better working conditions. "How," Osborne laments, "did the path that Yúdice and others set out on in their desire for a cultural studies linked to a transformative left populism come to terminate in the sorry state of a cultural theory dedicated to legitimating an emergent political-administrative status quo?"[87]

My sense, however, is that Osborne oversimplifies Miller and Yúdice's analysis, which, in certain moments, is interested in more than a simple avowal of the way things are. "Cultural policy," they claim, "refers to the institutional supports that channel both aesthetic creativity and collective ways of life."[88] And while policy is often associated with highly deliberate and determined institutional practices, they explain that it is also "often made unwittingly, through the permeation of social space by genres that invoke 'a particular kind of organization of audience' that may maintain or modify ideological systems . . . on an *ad hoc*, inconsistent basis."[89] In this iteration, which seems to glance in Adorno's direction, policy is not a completely bound and determined activity. Rather, it is also something that can happen in action, inadvertently, "'on the run,' in response to unpredictable pressures."[90] It is a practice of participation and intervention within the institution that is uniquely poised to help participants rethink how the institution itself is organized. The performativity of policy, then, also becomes an enabling paradigm, one that takes hold institutionally and—at least potentially—performs a negative mode of dis/avowal.

Interestingly, while Miller and Yúdice are critical of Butler for her presumed lack of institutional uptake, these more Adornian moments in their meditations on policy begin to sound something like Butler's own recent recontextualizations of her performativity theory from the perspective of contemporary social movements. In this newer writing, Butler draws explicit connections between her earlier work on gender and her subsequent work on precarity. "If performativity was considered linguistic," Butler asks, "how do *bodily acts* become performative?"[91] Although she is operating in a context outside the so-called policy debates, Butler makes it quite clear that critics like Miller and Yúdice have misread one of her central interventions by relegating her project to a merely discursive exercise. Butler insists instead that "there can be no reproduction of gendered norms without the bodily enactment of those norms" (31). And elsewhere: "Performativity is not only speech, but the demands of bodily action, gesture, movement, congregation, persistence, and exposure to possible violence" (75). Indeed, for Butler, performativity functions precisely as a mediating term between language and body, both of which—and this is central for her—are interdependent and infrastructurally supported acts:

> It is not, then, exclusively or primarily as subjects bearing abstract rights that we take to the streets. We take to the streets because we need to walk or move there; we need streets to be built so that, whether or not we are in a wheelchair, for instance, we can move there, and we can pass through that space without obstruction, harassment, administrative detention, or fear of injury or death. If we are on the streets, it is because we are bodies that require public forms of support to stand and move, and to live a life that matters. (137–38)

It seems, then, that Butler would agree with Miller and Yúdice that there is no outside of institutionality. Indeed, bodies depend upon varied forms of social and institutional support, and this most fundamental state of interdependency comes into highest relief precisely as it is disavowed by the very infrastructures upon which it relies—for employment, education, healthcare, shelter, mobility, freedom of expression, dare we say art-making. "This produces a quandary," Butler claims, in an articulation that reminds us also of Adorno's inescapable yet constitutive tensions: "We cannot act without supports, and yet we must struggle for the supports that allow us to act or, indeed, that are essential components of our action" (72). Here Butler works explicitly to elucidate a contemporary politics of performativity by means of destabilizing acts of institutional dis/avowal. She proposes a practice of "acting together that opens up time and space outside and against the established architecture and temporality of the regime, one that lays claim to materiality, leans into its supports, and draws from its material and technical dimensions to rework their functions" (75). Here Butler also implicitly refunctions Miller and Yúdice's dialectics of "replication" and "transformation," of "regulation" and "emancipation," for now the platform of politics itself is front and center on the policy agenda as neoliberalism "reconfigure[s] what will be public" (75).

Performance as Policy

In a 2012 keynote coperformance at New York's Museum of Modern Art (MoMA), Butler further recontextualized her thinking in order to reexamine ways that performance itself might be understood as performative. In doing so, Butler explicitly expressed her debt to, or interdependency on, the work of her coperformer, Shannon Jackson, whose ongoing project demonstrates the different ways the interdisciplinary art of performance both relies upon and mobilizes a diverse set of interdependent bodies, objects, and social institutions. In her 2011 book *Social Works*, Jackson enumerates an "infrastructural politics of performance,"[92] which calls into question a long-standing and widespread "mistrust of 'structure,'" of institutions, of bureaucracy, and of policy, not only in "neoliberal . . . circles but also [in] avant-garde artistic circles and critical intellectual ones where freedom was increasingly equated with systemic *in*dependence."[93] Instead, Jackson's work exposes the complex matrix of interrelated social institutions—both material and immaterial—that enable and also constitute the work of performance. As Butler explained at MoMA, "I take from Shannon the importance of the following question: how do we understand that mode of performance art that imagines it is without any need of infrastructure in a time when the destruction of social and economic infrastructure seems to be happening all around?"[94]

During the MoMA coperformance, Jackson claimed that she is interested additionally in the ways these acts of critical exposure may also constitute a "performance-based institutional reimagining."[95] But once we recognize performance—as I agree we must—as a set of interdependent and infrastructurally supported acts, how are we to understand such practices of "reimagining"? Jackson's explicit preference involves modes—or arts—of what she calls "infrastructural avowal":

> I am most interested in social practices that provoke reflection on the non-autonomy of human beings, projects that imagine agency not only as systemic disruption but also as systemic relation. Through social art projects that provoke a reflection on the opportunity and inconvenience of our enmeshment in systems of labour, ecology, able-bodiedness, social welfare, public infrastructure, kinship and more, expanded artworks might induce a kind of "infrastructural avowal," that is, an acknowledgement of the interdependent systems of support that sustain human beings, even though we often feel constrained by them.[96]

Institutional Theatrics shifts its focus beyond practices that work to induce such acknowledgment. Post-Wall Berlin is exciting—and inspiring—for me because of the preponderance of practices that provoke reflection on the ways performance itself questions, critiques, and even fundamentally challenges the institution *as* its way of acknowledging—of dis/avowing—the interdependence so central to Jackson's argument. To phrase it differently: in light of the preceding analysis—and especially in light of Butler's toggling of transformation and replication, of emancipation and regulation, even of disruption and relation—I find myself most drawn to performances that lean on and into systems of support as the *very* means by which they seek to rethink, confound, destabilize, disrupt, even undo them.

Stages of Dis/avowal

In the chapters that follow, I bring these overlapping conversations to bear on the undulating set of institutional avowals and disavowals that constitute the German theater's "coming to terms" over the past thirty years. Indeed, Butler and Jackson's reworking of Miller and Yúdice's reworking of Adorno and Bennett serves as a methodological kernel—or specter—as I explore Berlin-based instances in which performance functions as a performative art of policy. We will see also that these different stages of institutional dis/avowal assume diverse forms (and degrees of "success"), and that they employ very different vocabularies depending on the concrete particulars of the institutional context. For this reason—and this was a methodological priority for me throughout the process of writing—I have endeavored to allow the performance sites themselves to dictate (and produce) the theoretical vocabularies required for their own immanent analysis. Each chapter, then, consults a quite different set of interlocutors from an array of disciplines in order to chart the fundamental imbrications of performance and policy, of art and infrastructure, of stage and state.

Though each of my four central cases engages a particular set of institutions, performance pieces, policy puzzles, and theoretical questions catalyzed by the costly processes of German reunification, the chapters also progress chronologically and build upon one another thematically in order to narrate the dramatic reimagining of Berlin's theater and performance landscape since the end of the Cold War. As a means of demonstrating the book's methodology of conceiving aesthetics and infrastructures, performances and policies together, one chapter in each part narrates a particular policy problematic in order to understand the performances that were staged in response and as proposed solutions; the other chapter in each part close-reads a single performance as the key to unraveling the policy problems bound up within the staging itself.

Part 1, "State-Stages," focuses, in different ways, on the infrastructural impact of reunification on the state and municipal stages, *Staatstheater* and *Stadttheater*, in the former East and West. Chapter 1 examines the controversial closure of the three-stage State-Stage Complex, or Staatliche Schauspielbühnen, the largest and most expensive theater venture in former West Germany, which included the iconic Schiller Theater. This unexpected decision by the Berlin Senate in June 1993 catalyzed a dramatic series of structural debates about the status of the state-subsidized theater in Berlin and the future of German cultural policy writ large. The first chapter also functions as a contextual companion to this introduction. The public conversations that culminated in the closure of the complex in 1993 and the performances that were staged in protest serve as a heuristic for a more detailed historical conversation about the origins of the state-stage and its—sometimes self-imposed—floundering in the face of the new Berlin government's emerging neoliberal agenda of urban development in the early 1990s.

While the debates sparked by the closure of the State-Stage Complex certainly raised important questions about the future of a reunified German state-subsidized theater ecosystem, from the perspective of the former East, the controversy was also, in many ways, a highly bourgeois and western drama. Chapter 2 focuses on two prominent former East Berlin state-stages that underwent major infrastructural and aesthetic adjustments in the mid-1990s: the privatization of Bertolt Brecht's Berliner Ensemble and Frank Castorf's rise to prominence as the new *Intendant* of the Volksbühne am Rosa-Luxemburg-Platz. By means of an analysis of Castorf's recent engagement with Brecht's *lehrstück* and its accompanying theory, I argue that Castorf worked explicitly to refunction Brecht's hopes for a very different kind, or art, of public—and publicly supported—theater in reunified Berlin.

The second part of the book shifts focus by considering projects that reckon with the precarious future of the state-stage through very different practices of dis/avowal—practices that try, in different ways, to "free" themselves of this one infrastructural model in search of others. In other words, part 2, "Free-Scenes," tracks the emergence of the heterogeneous assortment of performance practices and organizational structures that constitute Berlin's independent or so-called free-scene (*freie Szene*), again in both the former East and West.

After its closure in 1990, the Palast der Republik quickly emerged as one of Berlin's most controversial sites of contested memory. The subsequent decision to raze the Palast and to rebuild the Prussian Imperial Palace (Berliner Stadtschloss) in its stead catalyzed heated architectural and city-planning debates and protests in the early 1990s that continue into the present. Chapter 3 examines a series of interdisciplinary performance experiments within the shell of the former Palast just after the millennium, which set out not only to critique its destruction but also to investigate collectively the possibilities for a radically public and entirely temporary performance institution in the newly gentrifying center of reunified Berlin. I argue that this durational initiative, titled Volkspalast (People's Palace), attempted to enact a "spectral" mode of institutional disappearance, exploring various ways that arts infrastructures in the burgeoning free-scene might remember and reimagine civic space.

Chapter 4 focuses on the ways "alternative" works of free-scene theater set themselves apart (or not) from the aesthetic and labor configurations and funding structures of the state-stage. To address these questions, I turn to the popular Hebbel am Ufer (HAU) performance complex—a center for Berlin's free-scene—and a performance at HAU by andcompany&Co. titled *The (Coming) Insurrection according to Friedrich Schiller*. I examine how this performance both traces and stages an infrastructural politics of Berlin's free-scene by offering a critique of the recent mobilizations on its behalf. I argue further that andcompany&Co.'s performance exposes the complex ways in which HAU dis/avows the steadily increasing precarity of a project-based and mobile performance economy by providing a bastion for artistic laborers in search of a secure home base.

Finally, *Institutional Theatrics* concludes where it began (as does this introduction) with a more thorough analysis of—and additional questions posed by—the recent controversies at the Volksbühne. Did Chris Dercon's appointment mark a final stage of disavowal and Berlin's ultimate embrace of itself as a postindustrial European capital of global capital? Or do the ongoing mobilizations and cultural political conversations on behalf of a "new" Volksbühne provide continued evidence (and hope) for dis/avowal as a performative strategy for rethinking Berlin's public institutions?

After we finished speaking with the security guard, Katrin and I mounted our bikes and set out for home. As we made our way down Rosa-Luxemburg-Straße and toward the bright lights of Alexanderplatz, we speculated aloud about how the situation at the Volksbühne might resolve. I had no idea yet the role this rather odd encounter—and the Chris Dercon situation as a whole—would come to play in my ongoing thinking about this book. I had no idea that Dercon's tenure would last only seven months before he would be fired by the new culture senator. I had no idea that René Pollesch—a staple of Castorf's Volksbühne—would be the next in line to take the reins. I return briefly to the security guard again here because our innocent yet unexpectedly provocative conversation is indicative of the joys, quandaries, challenges, and surprises of composing a history of the present. Although I couldn't have predicted the outcome that night on Rosa-Luxemburg-Platz, the occupation that looms above aligns with one of the analytical strands of this book: the investigation of performance's potential to utilize the public institutions of its support to reimagine those very institutions from within. The looming security crackdown, on the other hand, aligns with another concomitant strand, one that reckons with the increasing precarity of Berlin's (and the larger, global) performance economy. As I discovered along the way—and as I demonstrate in the pages that follow—these strands constitute the entwined logics of institutional dis/avowal.

Part 1

✦

State-Stages

Chapter 1

✦

"Is There a Cultural Policy?"

Debating the Demise of the State-Stage Complex

But the verdict of this epoch does not, by any means, seem to be going in favour of art. . . . [A]t the present time material needs reign supreme and bend a degraded humanity beneath their tyrannical yoke. Utility is the great idol of our age, to which all powers are in thrall and to which all talent must pay homage. Weighed in this crude balance, the insubstantial merits of Art scarce tip the scale, and, bereft of all encouragement, she shuns the noisy market-place of our century.

Since no good State should be without its *Constitution*, it is legitimate to require one for the Aesthetic State too. No such is as yet known to me.

—Friedrich Schiller, *On the Aesthetic Education of Man* (1795)

The Robbers

June 21, 1993. All eyes were turned toward a remote guesthouse deep within the quiet Grunewald forest, where the Berlin Senate convened for its 111th meeting. On that fateful Monday—which some would soon sardonically call the "night of the long knives"[1]—members of the Senate locked themselves behind closed doors and sat around a conference table covered in mountains of files, half-empty coffee cups, sandwiches, and plates of assorted cookies to debate the inevitable austerity measures to come.[2] The economics were grim: a daunting deficit of just about eight billion DM for 1994.[3] Speculation ran deep: What would the Senate decide? Who would bear the brunt? "Secret! Senate Cuts!" reported the evening daily.[4] The legislators deliberated through the night into early Tuesday. For seventeen hours they went without sleep. But by midday on June 22, all was signed; by midday on "black Tuesday,"[5] the stage was upset.

Enter Ulrich Roloff-Momin, Berlin's senator for cultural affairs, for a typical midday press conference, but this time with most unexpected news. Very matter of fact, he began with a proverb: "Horror without end is always worse than an end filled with horror."[6] Pause. Silence. Next sentence—somber, straight-faced, but sure of himself: "At the start of the next season, the operations of [Berlin's] State-Stage Complex will cease."[7] Another pause, waiting for some reaction, but there was none. He repeated the news: "Cease at the start of the next season." Pause, again. Just what did this mean? Clarification: after an evening performance on July 4, 1993—in just twelve days—the largest and most expensive theater complex in all of Germany would be forced to close its doors.

The justification was clear: Germany's new capital city was in major debt, and it must cut costs. Berlin's mayor, Eberhard Diepgen, was adamant that Berlin must ensure its future survival: "That's why we must disconnect the IV drip. That's why the yearly debt must be cut down. This is certainly very painful in many areas. It is also painful for those who must make these decisions."[8] The economics of the Staatliche Schauspielbühnen Berlin—which included the flagship Schiller Theater, the Schiller Werkstatt (Studio) Theater, and the Schlosspark Theater—were certainly painful, and the numbers staggering. In 1992, the three-theater complex racked up 47,520,317.98 DM in expenses, and only brought in 3,840,858.31 DM in revenue. Berlin's public coffers were left to pay 43,679,459.67 DM. The shortfall to be covered by subsidy in 1993 was a similar 41,374,000 DM. By June 1993, the theater was already running a 28,425,000 DM tab for the 1994 fiscal year.[9] In 1991, it was calculated that each ticket purchased at the Schiller Theater cost the state 288 DM, making it by far the most expensive theater in town.[10] "We have to make decisions today," Diepgen persisted, "that will provide us, also after 1994, with the necessary latitude to make decisions for social justice, economic revival, as well as cultural and scientific diversity."[11] He continued, "Our children will not forgive us if we spend today what they will need to survive tomorrow."[12] The mayor signed off on the official Senate decision immediately:

a. The state of Berlin is not in the financial position to continue to operate all state theaters.

b. The operations of the State-Stage Complex . . . will cease at the end of the 1992/93 season. The Department for Cultural Affairs will manage the inevitable contractual obligations with the artistic and other staffs; this includes the establishment of a compensation plan, and overseeing the transfer of employees into other work situations within Berlin.

c. The Department for Cultural Affairs will immediately draw up proposals for the future use of these venues and submit them to the Senate no later than the end of 1993.

d. The Department for Cultural Affairs will immediately prepare a presentation that lays out the financial implications of these structural measures.[13]

The Senate's decision to close the State-Stage Complex was, in fact, part of a much larger cost-saving measure, or *Sparpaket*. The BVG metro system would face cuts, as would Berlin's three universities. The Senate also decided to close the Staatliche Kunsthalle (State Art Gallery) and the Berliner Symphoniker orchestra, among other smaller arts institutions, which would yield—they hoped—64 million DM.[14] But it was the theater in particular that made the front and opinion pages that day: "Cultural kamikaze act!"[15] "Cultural-political assassination!"[16] "Unbelievable!" "Brutal!" "A false decision!"[17] Many of the complex's 550 workers heard the announcement for the first time over the radio during their lunch breaks. Without any warning, they had lost their jobs.[18] Soon after Roloff-Momin's press conference, the office of the culture senator posted a matter-of-fact letter to Volkmar Clauß, the artistic and managing director of the theater complex: "Dear Dr. Clauß: In reference to today's discussion, I instruct you, regarding the impending closure of the State-Stage Complex, from this moment on, to take on no more financial commitments that will extend beyond this season. In the interest of a cost-effective closure of this institution, I request that you coordinate with my office on any necessary legal business that extends beyond this period. Yours sincerely."[19]

Throughout the afternoon, hundreds of actors and employees gathered outside and in the lobby of the Schiller Theater. Black flags of mourning hung from the roof. Theater students bedecked the lawn in front of the theater with symbolic headstones and wooden crosses. Notes (and telegrams) of condolence and support flew in almost immediately from the whole German-speaking theater world and beyond. From Hamburg: "Dearest Colleagues, we are united with you in protest."[20] From Vienna: "Dilettantism, provincial thinking, nepotism, and great negligence."[21] From Munich: "We must find a way to convince the Senate that its decision was wrong."[22] From Teatro di Genova. From Teatro Stabile del Veneto. From Teatro di Roma. From the National Theatre in London. In his first public response, Volkmar Clauß declared: this "panic-ridden decision" is "inimitable in the postwar German cultural scene."[23] Boris Wendt, spokesperson for the Schiller Theater, followed suit: "The perversity lies in the fact that no one consulted us, no one talked to us, no one warned us. . . . We understand that there are problems, but their solution lies in making structural changes to the entire theater scene, not in wiping out the largest and most legendary theater in the country."[24]

The shock ran so deep that the Schiller ensemble canceled their performance of Schiller's *Don Carlos* scheduled for that Tuesday evening. And though Martin Olbertz did not have the opportunity to grace the stage as the Marquis of Posa, Rodrigo's hopeful idealism seemed to motivate those theater workers, cast members, and spectators alike who "took to the streets"[25] to voice their grievances: "Oh give us back what you have taken from us. / Be strong, and bountiful, let happiness / Flow from your fingers."[26] A long procession of cars, led by a Schiller Theater truck, made its way eastward though the streets of Berlin, through the Brandenburg Gate, honking, screaming, lights flashing. When

Schiller Theater supporters protesting onstage in East Berlin, June 1993. Photograph copyright © David Baltzer / bildbuehne.de.

Schiller supporters banged on the doors of the formerly eastern Deutsches Theater in the middle of the evening's performance, audience members looked alarmed. But as the crowd rushed into the theater space, chanting and crying, they were greeted ultimately with applause, enthusiasm, and support.[27]

On Wednesday, the Schiller remained occupied all day long. As an act of consolation, Roloff-Momin announced that he would join protesters at the theater. His efforts were unsuccessful, however, for the Schiller was brimming to capacity with the most hostile of crowds. As he entered the space, the cat-calls clamored: "*Raus! Raus!*" (Get out! Get out!). Amid whistles and shouts, Roloff-Momin took a seat in the center of a long white table under the pro-scenium arch. Hunched behind large microphones, he worked to explain—to no avail—that he had fought for a "two-year reprieve,"[28] but that in the face of such a large deficit "I could not say 'no.'"[29] "I was the only one in this city who, until the end, publicly fought for [the complex]. But in the bud-get deliberations, I had no tailwind."[30] The protests were "understandable and correct," he continued, but they came "late, all too late, and directed to the wrong address."[31] As Roloff-Momin fidgeted nervously with his pen, it was Volkmar Clauß's turn to speak. "We have only two questions," Clauß began. "First, do you take back your decision to close this theater? Second, if not, when will you resign?"[32] Accompanied by cheers from the crowd, Clauß walked angrily to the side of the stage. "Mr. Roloff-Momin, you have already left us in spirit. Now please do the same with your body."[33] And with that,

Clauß turned off the overhead lights. As the crowds rushed out of the theater, cheering, Roloff-Momin was left alone, center stage, in the dark, looking none too happy. And the TV cameras were rolling.

What was it they captured on tape? Theater artists emerging as performers in an expanded political arena? Politicians defending their policy decisions on the (state) theater's stage? Just what are the roles and responsibilities of cultural politicians *and* theater artists in performing arts policy in Berlin? And to what address *should* questions about structural changes to the entire theater scene be directed? Roloff-Momin provided a most concrete answer: "In this situation, the culture senator cannot escape the objective restraints and say to his colleagues, 'You go ahead and save money, I'm going for a coffee.' "[34] Elsewhere, he claimed, "We didn't make this decision in order to send a message, but because there was no alternative."[35]

This chapter has three interrelated tasks. The first is to explore the infrastructural preconditions of Roloff-Momin's claim. What, in other words, were the "objective restraints" and the political assumptions that provoked the culture senator's grim outlook for the future of the State-Stage Complex? And just how grim was his position really? In fact, Clauß's flip of the light switch marked the end of just the first of a great number of public spats in the aftermath of the Senate's decision. In the days and months that followed, many arguments were staged both for and against the closure of the State-Stage Complex. The chapter's second task is to track how these varied public performances (texts, interviews, discussions, debates, protests, legal proceedings, etc.) help us address a broader structural conversation about the shifting state of the state-stage amid the shifting realities of postreunification Berlin. How, to phrase it somewhat differently, might we understand the so-called theater crisis as part of, even representative of, intersecting processes of neoliberal urban development after the fall of the Wall? Finally, this opening tale of intersecting institutional avowals and disavowals functions as both a springboard and a strategic counterpoint—a site of dis/avowal—for the chapters that follow. Though the policy debates-cum-performances on the stage of the State-Stage catalyzed an important series of structural conversations in Berlin and beyond, my third task is to demonstrate that most of the participant-performers were, in the end, unable or unwilling to engage in a more critical art of institutional reimagining. Instead, cultural politicians and theater artists alike found themselves caught upholding the very structures they were endeavoring to undo (or vice versa), and therefore united, at least in part, in facilitating the expediency of the theaters' demise.

Naive and Sentimental

The State-Stage staff clicked into overdrive almost immediately, working day and night to launch the largest protest movement on record at that time against the closure of a theater.[36] Resolutions went to press: "We play on. We will not desert this theater."[37] Requests for donations, petitions to sign, calls for solidarity: "We call on the public, the media, and theater colleagues to partner with us against the Senate decision. . . . We ask all workers in the German theater to join in immediate acts of solidarity."[38] Invitations went out to theaters across the reunified nation and across the world: "To all theaters: We will not accept the intended closure of the State-Stage Complex in Berlin, which was decided without any preliminary discussions with those involved. We will continue working! If it is possible to wipe out the largest German theater . . . , this signals a devastating future for all German stages. Fight with us to reverse this decision, and come to the Schiller Theater to protest."[39] By Friday morning, June 25, almost every newspaper in Berlin ran announcements: on Saturday night at 11:00 P.M., after that evening's scheduled performance, a "Night of Solidarity" would convene. The following day at noon, there would be a public forum in the foyer titled "Is There a Cultural Policy?" And the main event would take place on Sunday at 3:00 P.M.: "Solidarity of the German Theater with the State-Stage Complex." "The Berlin culture scene bubbles," announced the *Morgenpost*.[40] And though all remaining performances sold out almost immediately, the lines at the box office continued to grow.

Many of Germany's cultural elite flocked to Berlin and joined in protest for the "Long Night" at the Schiller Theater. More than fifty directors, dramaturgs, and artistic directors from around the country were in attendance.[41] The theater was "besieged" by more than three thousand people—way over capacity—coming, going, shouting, chanting, singing, and dancing. All guests that Saturday evening were greeted by long banners hanging on the front of the building: "HERE WE PLAY ON!"[42] Many visitors had already bedecked themselves in T-shirts proclaiming, "Schiller Must Stay!"[43] As samba music filled the foyer, a young man held up a picture of Schiller with a caption that read, "If Schiller only knew, he'd puke for sure."[44] A little girl held a sign addressing the mayor: "Herr Diepgen, when I grow up, I too would like to go to the Schiller Theater."[45] Posters hung from the balconies: "Roloff-Momin = Schiller *Robber*!"[46] Actress and singer Georgette Dee addressed Diepgen and Roloff-Momin in her own way with a special rendition from Brecht and Weill's *Happy End*: "You talked a lot, Momin; it was all lies, Momin; just take that Diepgen out of your mouth."[47] Brecht was all over the lobby that night; two red flags framed a standing placard that read: "If an injustice occurs in a city, there must be an uproar. And if there is no uproar, it is better that the city goes down in flames before nightfall!"[48]

The pledges of solidarity continued. The Thalia Theater in Hamburg closed down for the weekend. All artistic directors from North Rhine-Westphalia vowed to boycott: they would not play in Berlin until the Senate decision was reversed. Choreographer Pina Bausch canceled her upcoming engagement at the Volksbühne. At 3:30 A.M. (9:30 P.M. eastern daylight time) the phone rang. Edward Albee was on the line: "Fight for your theater! Theater makes

The Schiller Theater, June 1993. Photograph copyright © Thomas Seufert / bildbuehne.de.

people laugh, it makes them cry; theater is life. When theaters close, humanity dies."[49] By the time of Albee's phone call, the petition against the Senate decision had already garnered twenty thousand signatures: "This sudden, inhuman decision by the Berlin Senate is not just an attack on the cultural landscape of the city but also an attack on the fundamental values of its people. . . . We therefore ask you to demonstrate as loudly as possible with actions and petitions against the decision."[50] Very early in the morning, Clauß took the Schiller stage, welcomed by a still-boisterous crowd. Over the din, he hollered, "Our approach can no longer be soft and timid. We are no longer an opposition, we are now a resistance."[51] As the newspapers clarified, this was "no gala, but an action":[52] "An ecstatic union of theater and audience, of a city and its artists, of high and popular culture."[53]

In the meantime, the culture senator and his department worked hard, both in print and on television, to cast a wide net of responsibility. He explained that he had repeatedly appealed to the various Berlin artistic directors and asked whether they would prefer a number of smaller cuts across the board or just one large cut. "For years, all the artistic directors have insisted urgently that they cannot cope with more cuts to their individual houses."[54] Next, Roloff-Momin criticized the decline in quality of the State-Stage's offerings. Since the mid-1970s, he explained, the complex had been consistently stricken with artistic stagnation and changed leadership repeatedly. This resulted in a severe reduction in attendance. As he repeatedly emphasized, the Schiller consistently played to only 55 percent capacity. In their "obituary"

"Night of Solidarity" at the Schiller Theater on June 26, 1993. Photograph copyright © David Baltzer / bildbuehne.de.

for the theater, titled "Adieu, Dinosaur," the *Frankfurter Allgemeine Zeitung* endorsed Roloff-Momin's diagnosis, making clear that the theater was dead long before the Senate's decision to "kill" it: "One cannot look back fondly on a single production from recent years. There is no inspiration, no excitement, no bliss, but also no harm in this house. You would always leave a performance with the feeling of having dedicated a few hours to a nice, mediocre experience. By the next morning, everything was wiped from your mind."[55]

As might be expected, there were angry retorts from the Berlin acting community against this mode of argument. Susanne Böwe, a young actor in the Schiller Ensemble, objected, "What right do politicians have to assess the quality of a theater or of its actors? Are they experts? Do they go to the theater regularly? . . . That's where it begins to become dangerous. For there begins, as I understand it, a kind of political censorship, which I thought we had really left behind."[56] The *Morgenpost* subsequently ran excerpts from reviews of past productions, both positive and negative, to demonstrate the subjectivity of the quality question. And on the attendance issue, Volkmar Clauß published an open letter in the *Tagesspiegel*, landing a quick jab back at the culture senator:

> Correction: The Schiller Theater holds a capacity of just under 1000 (996 to be exact), far more than other theaters in town. The attendance numbers are just a few percentage points lower than the

smaller stages (8% in comparison to the Deutsches Theater). The number of visitors (this past season, it was almost exactly 200,000) was much higher than those of the Deutsches Theater. Figures are not everything in the art world, but what are we to make of a culture senator who denies them, or does not know anything about them? It is simply bewildering.[57]

Roloff-Momin responded strategically by expanding the scope of his arguments beyond the mere tit-for-tat: "One should definitely not close theaters, but one must, if one's hands are tied, close one theater in order to save the others."[58] He pushed the argument farther, claiming that with this single cut he was able to ensure the "health" of the rest of the Berlin theater community: "I had to make the decision in order to secure the other twenty-one theaters for the next five years."[59] The closure of one theater, he insisted, is hardly a "demolition" of the theater landscape, though it is most certainly a shame: "It hurts me too. I understand the protests and the reactions of horror."[60] But Roloff-Momin continued to emphasize the upsides: "Berlin's cultural offerings are the richest of all European metropolises."[61] And indeed, the numbers were most impressive: 39 theaters, 21 of which were supported by state subsidy; 7 orchestras, 3 operas, 167 museums, 400 art galleries, 500 independent or "free-scene" theater groups, 264 libraries, 127 cinemas. In June 1993 alone, there were 327 theater productions, 100 children's shows, 18 cabaret acts, 320 films, 300 music events, and on and on.[62] What the culture senator never explicitly discussed, however, were the structural and political preconditions behind the austerity thinking that fueled many of his "no alternative" arguments. In other words: though the hints were there—in the language of "quality," of "attendance," of a "rich" metropolis—Roloff-Momin did not, in these early days at least, fully acknowledge the new Berlin government's shifting priorities; priorities that did not neatly align with the "fundamental values" of a fully state-supported theater landscape.

So just where did all the city's debt come from? And what were the larger—and longer-term—implications of these fiscal woes for the overall "health" of the new capital? Certainly, the fall of the Wall in November 1989 and the speedy unification of the two German states over the course of the following year catalyzed a series of unprecedented economic and social transformations. As a result of this "sudden acceleration of history," Claire Colomb explains, Berlin was "abruptly confronted with the urban economic and political problems which other Western industrialized cities had faced since the 1970s under the pressures of globalization, European integration and structural economic change: rapid deindustrialization, shift towards a service- and knowledge-oriented economy, rising unemployment and welfare expenditure, pressures for the transformation of the role of the local state and for cuts in public expenditure."[63] All these challenges were magnified by the increasing pressure to prepare the city's infrastructures to become the unified capital once again. In former West Berlin, decision makers had to face the gradual phasing out of federal subsidies that had supported the city—due to its "exceptional" status—throughout the forty years of the Cold War. These subsidies would cease in 1994 and lead ultimately to a 30 percent net reduction in the city's overall budget between 1993 and 1994.[64] In the former eastern end of town, the sudden integration of the failed state-socialist system into a relatively market-oriented one proved incredibly expensive and resulted in both increased unemployment (and a steadily declining GDP) *and* increased welfare expenditure. The merger also led to an ostensible doubling of many of the city's public institutions, including libraries, universities, operas, and theaters.

Berlin's first unified elections in December 1990 also marked a definitive shift in the city's program of urban governance. On December 2, the center-right Christian Democrats (CDU) won the election with 40 percent of the vote; the centrist Social Democrats (SPD) were close behind with 30 percent.[65] The two winning parties quickly formed a Grand Coalition—under the leadership of Mayor Eberhard Diepgen—which would govern Berlin for the next decade. The political priorities that united the Grand Coalition were clear and explicit: to respond to all the above-mentioned challenges of reunification by transforming Berlin into a European—or even better, a globally competitive—post-Fordist metropolis. As Colomb explains further, "The new mayor of Berlin explicitly advocated the shift to a new entrepreneurial urban politics, which would prioritize the attraction of external capital, investors and labour force to the city. This was accompanied by a discourse on the necessity and ineluctability of the so-called process of 'metropolization' or 'catching up modernization,' . . . i.e. the conversion from an industrial city to a service metropolis of global status."[66]

This shift toward an explicitly entrepreneurial—or emerging neoliberal—agenda was immediately evident in the Wild West economic policies and accompanying real estate building boom actively promoted by the Grand Coalition from its very first days in office. An intricate system of new laws, direct subsidies, and tax incentives to benefit developers and real estate (and other) companies was quickly put into place to stimulate rapid urban development. The 1992 Investment Priority Act, or Investitionsvorranggesetz, for instance, enabled investors with "convincing investment concepts" to buy a property despite an existing restitution claim and to compensate the alleged owner later (or not). Another new federal law, called the Regional Development Act (Fördergebietsgesetz), granted large tax breaks to developers who erected new buildings in Germany's eastern states. This incentive, combined with the new city government's belief that office buildings were a sign of economic promise, fueled the construction of a large supply of retail and office space in former East Berlin. Within just a few years, a slew of multinational corporations and other investors were lured to Potsdamer Platz, Alexanderplatz, Friedrichstraße, and other former eastern development sites.

Ultimately, however, the new supply proved too great: nearly seven million square meters of office space were built in Berlin during 1990–98, and much of it remained unoccupied—contributing to a real estate market crisis later in the decade.[67] As Stefan Krätke writes, "Besides corruption and murder within the professional real estate scene, the Berlin government proved to be highly talented and creative in developing particular instruments to prevent any public control of the project developments in central parts of Berlin's City-East."[68] These instruments—with their accompanying tax write-offs— contributed significantly to Berlin's rapidly mounting debt, which would reach 40 billion euros by 2001 and 55 billion by 2004.[69]

A significant portion of this debt was the direct consequence of corruption orchestrated by members of the Grand Coalition government throughout the course of its tenure. Krätke continues, "We might say that Berlin's economic policy in the 1990s is an outstanding example of 'worst practice' urban governance, since it has led to a financial crisis with truly catastrophic effects."[70] These "worst" practices came into highest relief with the exposure of the Berlin banking scandal in 2001. It turned out that, throughout the 1990s, the city government itself participated in a number of large-scale speculative real estate investments through a public-private financial corporation called the Bankgesellschaft Berlin. In 2001, it was announced that the Bankgesellschaft—which had become one of Germany's largest banks and employers—was in need of a substantial capital infusion because of major losses from a series of these failed investments. Due to worries about EU intervention, and since the city owned 56 percent of the bank, legislators agreed on an expensive bailout package. To make matters even worse, it also came to light that politicians from the CDU had played a substantial role in the more-than-questionable management and creative accounting of the bank. Finally, to add insult to sustained injury, the city government voted not to close the failing Bankgesellschaft but instead to approve a 35-billion-euro risk-shield law, or *Risikoabschirmungsgesetz*, which transferred the financial risk of the Bankgesellschaft's outstanding speculative investments onto the city and its citizens. In spite of the intended "shield," the overall financial losses from the banking scandal amounted to somewhere between 20 and 30 billion euros and ultimately fueled the collapse of the Grand Coalition later in 2001.[71]

In the face of this history yet to come, it is interesting to return to 1993, just a few days after the Senate's decision that there was no alternative but to close the State-Stage, as Mayor Diepgen delivered his midyear address on the financial health of the new capital and the general state of its union. In the face of the Grand Coalition's shifting concerns, Diepgen's words take on a quite particular timber:

> Those who do not fast today will be hungry tomorrow. . . . As painful as many cuts . . . may be, an intensified need to set priorities can also be an opportunity to think things anew. A weak Senate would have

distributed the necessary cuts, like a lawn mower, equally among all stakeholders. And in the end, all would have had too little to live and too many would have to die, without regard for their profitability, their reputation, or their popularity.[72]

Likewise: "A unified Berlin is more than the sum of its parts; it is more effective, more efficient. Not all institutions are required twice. One or the other will have to be 'liquidated,' and not only in the East."[73] Though Diepgen never addressed the closure of the State-Stage explicitly, he argued that the ongoing discussions about the organization of the Berlin theater landscape required "more practicality" in general. And what was it Diepgen had in mind—practically speaking? Although he insisted that the "most important task of Berlin cultural policy [wa]s to consolidate and preserve the city's diverse and rich cultural traditions,"[74] it soon became clear that he imagined a different financial structure for the complex of state-stages writ large—featuring much less "state" involvement. Diepgen continued:

> To fund the rich theater and orchestral landscape, a unique financial concept for the theater was adopted in Germany, in order to give the Berlin stages and orchestras the opportunity to do business independently and over the long term and in particular to set their own prices. The privatization concepts that are already completed or being developed—for the Berliner Ensemble, Friedrichstadtpalast, and Metropol-Theater—also promise more personal responsibility, independence, and long-term security.[75]

This was not the first time Diepgen emphasized the benefits of a private, consumer-oriented theater model. Indeed, back in 1991, as all three formerly eastern state-stages were facing privatization—in the form of a *Gesellschaft mit beschränkter Haftung* (GmbH), or limited-liability company—Diepgen touted the importance of a commercial theater that catered exclusively to its audience. His prime exemplar was producer and entrepreneur Friedrich Kurz, who founded the Neue Flora Theater in Hamburg and became famous throughout Germany for his successful transatlantic transfers of Andrew Lloyd-Webber's *Cats* and *Phantom of the Opera*. Diepgen praised Kurz's desire to transform the old Wintergarden *variété*-theater, on (formerly eastern) Friedrichstraße, into a hotel-restaurant-entertainment complex. These were just the kinds of "responsible" 400 million DM investment initiatives essential to the "long-term security" of the "new" Berlin. To supporters of the state-stage, Diepgen's penchant for the boulevardization—even Americanization—of the German theater was by no means uncontroversial. The *Tagesspiegel* critically queried, "Why, especially now, is the mayor calling public support into question? As if the sudden appearance of businessman Friedrich Kurz serves as an alibi for cultural policy to reduce both its responsibilities and spending. The opposite is true. The for-profit competitor must not have it so easy in Berlin: I came, I saw, I conquered. His triumphal march at the cost of sensibility would be a defeat for Berlin."[76]

This criticism of the new government's efforts to relieve the city of its admittedly high cultural expenditures via private initiatives was a common and rather foreseeable position in response to the Grand Coalition's emerging priorities in the early 1990s. What could not have been foreseen, however, was the extreme dearth of good sense that the city government would exhibit in its use and abuse of more "flexible" business models like the GmbH. These inherent dangers came to light in the scandal that emerged around the bid to hold the 2000 Olympics in Berlin. In the concluding sentences of his June 1993 address, the mayor spoke with great excitement about the city's application to host the Games:

> Berlin has prepared an excellent hosting concept as part of its official bid. The plans for sporting facilities and apartments, infrastructure and media establishments meet the highest standards. Individual construction projects, such as the Velodrome and the Olympic Stadium, have already begun. . . . Planning for the Olympics is meaningfully linked to rebuilding the capital. The Olympic Games in Berlin are thus not only a unique event for all sports fans but an important program for the development of Berlin's economy and infrastructure. A reunified Berlin thanks the world and presents itself as a cosmopolitan and tolerant German capital in the center of Europe.[77]

The Olympics were the perfect infrastructural medium to attract external investment, demonstrate global competitiveness, and mobilize large numbers of people and sums of capital for structural renewal in the early years of the Grand Coalition. Early in 1991, the Berlin Senate founded Olympia GmbH, a limited-liability corporation funded primarily with public monies, in order to prepare the official bid to host the Games and eventually (or hopefully) to oversee the entire planning process.[78] Claire Colomb notes:

> The reason for the choice of a private law company was outlined clearly in the official document for the bid: "the bid to host the Olympic Games can only be successful if it is backed by an organization specifically set up and suitable for this purpose which can act *flexibly* and *independently outside the public administration*." . . . This demonstrates the government's intention to short-circuit the standard procedures applying to the activities normally performed in-house within the Senate, which are subject to parliamentary scrutiny.[79]

Over the next three years, the organization of just forty-five employees officially spent an exorbitant 60 million DM drafting the bid document. These numbers were by no means firm, however: other estimates went as high as 86 or even 250 million.[80] When Berlin lost the bid to Sydney in September 1993, a giant corruption scandal unraveled as Olympia GmbH was forced to close up shop. Though the GmbH status permitted (or even encouraged) opacity regarding the use of public funds, the scandal revealed a complex and far from kosher system of contracts and excessive allocations between the GmbH and other purely for-profit entities, and a highly symbiotic relationship—read: wining, dining, gift-giving, and a buy-off campaign—with Berlin's mass media complex. Andrew Jennings reported that the GmbH served as "an Olympic washing machine through which tax payer's [sic] money [was] redirected into the pockets of the private sector."[81]

In light of this persistent political tomfoolery, then, one of the satirical placards hanging in the Schiller lobby during that long night of solidarity in June 1993 proved more prescient than its author could have anticipated: "Politicians can make theater on their own, so why do we still need theaters when there are parliaments, city halls, and ministries?"[82] Nevertheless, the festivities at the State-Stage continued well into broad daylight. At 6:00 or 7:00 A.M., the crowds retired for only a brief respite, as many would return for Sunday's full program of events. At noon, four artistic directors from various theaters—Volkmar Clauß, Jürgen Schitthelm, Frank-Patrick Steckel, and Jürgen Flimm—as well as two well-known critics, Peter Iden and Friedrich Dieckmann, assembled as a panel in the lobby of the Schiller to raise a question that would become a guiding thematic for subsequent discussions in the weeks and months to come: "Is there a cultural policy?" In these earliest articulations, however, those asking the deceptively simple question did not pay much attention to its inherent complexity. As Klaus Pierwoß, the chief dramaturg from the Gorki Theater, later reported, this introductory event amounted to little more than a rather one-dimensional—naive and sentimental—pointing of fingers at the standard targets, namely Roloff-Momin and his Department for Cultural Affairs. A properly functioning office, the panel insisted, would never have permitted such a perversion of policy. But, as Pierwoß adeptly argued, this kind of singular interpretation of the question "Is there a cultural policy?" neglected its much wider scope—neglected *both* the complex political motivations (and machinations) in which the Senate's decision was embedded *and* the complex infrastructural dynamics of the state-stage itself. He warned just how dangerous it would be to scapegoat Roloff-Momin and anoint him as the one player poised to perform policy properly. As Pierwoß explained, "The theater people, who rightly complain that they are more and more the objects of political decisions and not working partners with politicians, have only negatively reproduced this lack of cooperation by keeping to themselves."[83] Indeed, no cultural or other politicians were invited to participate in these inaugural discussions at the Schiller. "Without a coming together of politicians and theater people," Pierwoß continued, "a structural reform of the theater will not occur."[84] Martin

"Is There a Cultural Policy?" event in the Schiller Theater foyer on June 27, 1993.
Photograph copyright © David Baltzer / bildbuehne.de.

Linzer, editor of the (formerly eastern) magazine *Theater der Zeit*, issued a similar critique:

> Demonstrations and media attention are important, but solidarity rallies with sappy, sentimental appeals, Brecht songs and chants are, in the end, only insider events that help us to relieve our conscience and go home again peacefully, after we have made sure to be seen. . . . [I]f none of the Berlin artistic directors has an answer on how and where to make cuts, then it is not the culture senator who needs to resign, in spite of the nonsense for which he is (and should be) accused. . . . [I]f all those responsible parties do not quickly join a roundtable discussion to talk about long-overdue structural reforms, then yes, they have no right to complain about any closures.[85]

At 3:00 P.M., all those gathered in the foyer filtered into the Schiller auditorium, and the panel members were joined by a number of other artistic directors, most of whom had been there the previous evening. While this next event began to address, to some extent, Pierwoß's and Linzer's call for an accounting of the broader infrastructural situation, those gathered under the proscenium were not yet fully prepared to examine their own critical positions as players on the policy stage. It was August Everding, president of the German Theater Association, or Deutscher Bühnenverein, who best articulated, and also represented, the complexity of the problems at hand. In fleeting moments, Everding did stress the necessity of a move beyond claims of solidarity toward a committed and enduring "structural debate" about the ways public culture is organized. "We must all, theater people and politicians alike, stop the tearful recriminations, . . . and we must begin the concrete reform of our theaters."[86] He continued, "Of course, there are substantial reasons—and the German Theater Association, too, knows that the structure of the theater must change." Everding briefly mentioned abandoning certain "habits" that had become too expensive; he alluded to his own ongoing negotiations with various unions to "tidy up" old and restrictive wage agreements. In these few moments, he seemed adamant about reimagining ways cultural ministers, politicians, trade unions, theater leaders, performance artists, and community members might begin to think and work together to envision new models for the state-stage. "We do not run our theaters in an ideal world," Everding insisted. "Unfortunately, our theater system is a mirror of our society. But who, if not we, is able to change it?"

In many, if not most, other moments, however, Everding moved away from this self-critical approach and instead reinforced the kinds of polarizing logics—of state-stage versus the state, of critical culture versus administrative policy—so worrisome to Pierwoß and Linzer. "The occasion that has brought us together is not a pleasant one. It is a frightening one. Yes, I say, scandalous." Or: "If this disastrous decision is not rectified, it indicates the bankruptcy of a directionless cultural policy in the history of German theater." Or: "Any real city has independent groups, . . . private theater, national and international guest performances, . . . Theatertreffens and other kinds of festivals. But from Rome to San Francisco, from Sydney to Amsterdam: what don't most cities have? . . . I'm talking about our ensemble and repertory theaters, which are the envy of everywhere else in the world." Eliminating state-stages was, simply put, not an adequate solution, Everding insisted, since *this* form of theater is "a public responsibility, one that requires public financing." In these moments, then, Everding revealed his unshifting political priorities as the chief representative of the German Theater Association—notorious "stalwarts of the existing system"[87]—as well as his proclivities for and historical understanding of the kinds of theater institutions that are, and should remain, public goods. Everding concluded his remarks with one of his more eloquent, albeit most sentimental, articulations:

> When culture falls away, there is room for violence. But when there is nothing left, there is also nothing left to reform. When still more commercial amusements infiltrate, as is already the case in another theater in this city, . . . then we can no longer speak of the theater as "moral institution." It was none other than the namesake of this house that laid this claim. And that was no old-fashioned, conservative instruction. Properly understood, it is a deeply progressive one—still.[88]

The Stage Considered as a Moral Institution

The protests did not conclude that Sunday evening. On Tuesday, June 29, more than three thousand Berliners congregated for a demonstration in front of the Rotes Rathaus, Berlin's city hall, equipped with banners, signs, kettledrums, trumpets, and New Year's Eve–style noisemakers. The crowds whistled, yelled, sang, and banged, with the hope that their calls might penetrate the red-brick facade and the offices of the mayor and other members of the Senate located within. Volkmar Clauß emerged out of the crowd, looking rejuvenated by the weekend's excitement, microphone in hand and ready to address the *Volk* gathered before him. The purpose of this protest, he explained, was to ask the mayor and the Senate to abandon their plans for closure and instead to convene a *Sondersitzung*, a special Senate session, to discuss the "basic structure of theaters in the capital city." Clauß continued, "A fundamental reform that incorporates the financing system, the operating models of the theater, and their mission can only be achieved by collaboration between political decision makers, the German Theater Association, and the theaters themselves."[89] Inspired to some extent, it seems, by Sunday's discussions on the Schiller stage, Clauß suggested reframing the Senate's decision as something more than an "unprecedented act of violence."[90] Instead, he suggested that the question of closure—and the accompanying question: Is there a cultural policy or not?—be expanded to include a broader-sweeping and quite necessary infrastructural analysis of the state of the state-stage itself.

In the days that followed, counting down anxiously to July 4, other members of the theater community echoed Clauß's shift in defense tactics beyond, again, the merely polarized tit-for-tat. In an open letter organized by the (formerly western) magazine *Theater heute*, for instance, forty-eight of Germany's leading theater critics signed the following statement:

> Theaters, especially in Germany, are part of the bourgeois culture out of which, to say the least, parliamentary democracy emerged. . . . Instead of frantic either-or decisions, the current crisis should be used to change the defunct structures of the theater to allow for more creativity, which hopefully costs less money. To this end, the existence of all the theaters must first be secured, so that this necessary debate can proceed in a climate of mutual respect.[91]

Theater critic Hartmut Krug also diagnosed the urgent need for debate, albeit in a more cutting tone. "For years," he explained, "a magic word has haunted the German theater landscape without much consequence: 'structural change.' Everyone talks about it; no one says exactly what it means; and no one implements it."[92] But, Krug persisted—almost as if he were responding to Everding directly—there is an ideological danger in entering such debates with a view of the "theater as a moral institution," a danger in

Protest in front of the Rotes Rathaus, Berlin's city hall, on June 29, 1993. Photograph copyright © Thomas Seufert / bildbuehne.de.

holding tight to the theater "as the last bastion of cutting, critical culture."[93] Krug went on to claim that "those fiercely *moralizing* theater people" had refused to confront their drastically changing material realities. Instead, he argued, they have "fled toward the haven of a 'critical' stage reality," within which artistic directors "are more concerned with the size of their company car than they are with fighting for better policies and structures for their bloated theatrical institutions."[94] Perhaps it was Benjamin Henrichs who best captured the nuance of the varied (and often competing) calls for so-called structural debate: "The Berlin 'assassination' (perpetuated by the thunk of panic) could be something like the saving, illuminating catastrophe for the subsidized German theater."[95] In turn, Henrichs attempted to repurpose that "dinosaur theory" used to justify the closure of the State-Stage, since, as the argument went, the theater was blind to its inevitable extinction. Instead, as Henrichs argued, in the face of its demise "we must behold our rich German theater [as] an endangered wonder of the world: we can still marvel at its innumerable treasures, but we must also finally confront its monstrosities without fear."[96] On the one hand, as he pushed the metaphor even farther, the State-Stage-osaurus was "something of a hapless giant, stricken with plague: by the ugliness of German postwar theater architecture; by the proliferation of a swollen management and technical staff; by the aging and slowly pet-rifying ensemble; by the helplessness of its artistic directors; and of course, by the cluelessness of Berlin's reigning cultural policy dilettantes—especially the confused terminator, Roloff-Momin."[97] On the other hand, however, as Henrichs was at pains to assert, the looming alternatives, which both welcomed and hastened the dinosaur's expeditious demise, were also gloomy. After its extinction, he concluded, the "amusement [or Jurassic] park of commercial theater and private sponsorship" will be all that remains: "Beloved television actors, bon vivants of the *Boulevardtheater*, and frivolous musical poppets. Cultural policy (and culture senators for that matter) will no longer be needed—and the theater can be released into the custody of the municipal tourist offices."[98]

In light of these urgent calls for sustained and interdisciplinary structural debate as an evolving defense tactic for State-Stage supporters (and state-stage supporters more broadly), it became more evident that the "theater crisis" was not solely a crisis of the Berlin government's evolving neoliberal priorities. In fact, state-stages across Germany also worked hard to perpetuate an air of indispensability—especially in light of the changing governmental agendas postreunification. My task in the rest of this section, then, is to explore the infrastructural prehistories that both illuminate the necessity of such structural discussions and simultaneously undermine the novelty of these calls for sustained self-criticism. In what follows, I work to defamiliarize the Senate's decision to close the State-Stage *as well as* the sense of astonishment among the many who, aghast, protested against the decision. This I do by situating both within a longer set of ongoing discussions about the state-stage as public good, or *öffentliches Gut*. By tracing the legacies and historical undulations of the development of both state and municipal theater in Germany, I try to make sense of the sliding scales and critical lacunae at play between "old-fashioned" and "deeply progressive," between moral institution and commercial fancy, between artistic freedom, "encrusted"[99] bureaucracy, and bourgeois decadence.

Christopher Balme complicates the common assumption that the state-stage-cum-moral-institution has functioned as a—if not *the*—central ballast of the precious *Kulturstaat* since the golden age of German idealism. Instead, he argues that, "contrary to popular belief," the vast system of state and municipal theaters, which became a standard fixture in Germany over the past century, is actually a relatively recent development.[100] Indeed, many—including those authors of the reunification treaty—who like to invoke the "culture nation" as an essential component of Germany's "position and prestige" tend to forget that things were once quite different.[101] Balme writes:

> The current municipal theater structures, within which there is a consensus that certain forms of theater and music are considered public goods, did not hatch from the egg already intact, but they are instead the result of historical development processes stretching back about a century. They are not much older than the first German unification (in 1871) and probably have, so I argue, a lot to do with the cultural

struggles and the social legislation of the Bismarck era and the increasing social-democratization of German society. That in the US, for example, one speaks of the Western European system of cultural subsidy as part of the welfare state . . . may sound a bit strange to German ears but certainly is not devoid of a certain justification. . . . A century ago, however, Germany was quite far from regarding its theaters as public goods.[102]

In fact, it was not until the period between the First and Second World Wars that most of the financial and other infrastructural responsibilities for Germany's theaters were taken over completely by the states and municipalities. And interestingly, it was the Nazis who completed the job: they fully communalized all of the nation's stages before having to close them all down again as the war effort intensified in 1944.

As Balme suggests, the "genesis and eventual stabilization" (65) of the theater system resulted from the convergence of three intersecting factors. The first of these was certainly the evolution of the notion of *Kulturstaat* in post-Enlightenment art-historical and aesthetic-theoretical discourses and its subsequent political mobilization by Otto von Bismarck and company. The second was the rapid urbanization of German society in the second half of the nineteenth century, which resulted in a building boom of still-extant cultural buildings (such as theaters, museums, and zoos) and a simultaneous shift in public opinion about the city's obligation to provide for its citizens. The third factor was an ongoing series of heated and strikingly familiar debates, largely after the turn of the century, about the function of theater itself: should theater be understood primarily as a for-profit "business" or as a form of "culture" (Balme, 65)?

One of the more interesting historical ironies is that the predominant business model for theaters in Germany throughout the second half of the nineteenth century was indeed a private model. The expansion of German cities—small and large—accompanied by the legislative introduction of free trade throughout the country in 1871, facilitated a rapid proliferation of theaters funded by entrepreneurs seeking a profit and hawking the motto "For every city, a city-stage" (Balme, 68). For example, although Berlin had only six theaters in 1869, there were several dozen by 1900, all of which were operated privately, with the exception of two court theaters.[103] The most common financing structure and organizational model for these new stages was the joint-stock corporation (*Aktiengesellschaft* [AG]). But times proved hard: as any American reader would attest, the for-profit theater business is a fickle and expensive beast. And as Balme explains, "Despite such impressive buildings, where one could watch Schiller, Goethe or, more often, [Lehar's] *The Merry Widow* every night, the institution of the municipal stage stood on shaky ground. Economically, most cities had created an institution that was no longer commercially viable" (71). At the start, most German municipalities served as just one of many investors in these burgeoning private ventures: those legislators overseeing the public coffers hoped to earn some profit on the back end by waiving rent for the land on which the theaters were built and sometimes even covering the heating and electrical expenses (Balme, 68). As time progressed, however, and theater managers found themselves deeper in the red, the cities and states began assuming increased responsibility for keeping the flailing businesses afloat—in the form of what began to look a lot like direct subsidy. As it turned out, Diepgen's presumed trifecta of "personal responsibility, independence, and long-term security"[104] did not cohere all that neatly in those early days of theater entrepreneurship.

After the turn of the century, an extensive series of public structural debates commenced about the necessary reformation, even complete over-haul, of the theaters—which, by that point, were no longer a bargain for any municipality but had become a pricey and constant line item. It was Lud-wig Seelig who first articulated the idea (in 1915 and again in 1918) of the complete communalization of the municipal and state-stages. Seelig argued that the widespread private joint-stock tenancy system, which was no longer really a private system, had become unsustainable. To make matters worse, he continued, the local governments were already meddling constantly in the organizational leadership of the theaters while refusing to take any official responsibility for the effective management of the institutions. Instead, Seelig proposed a model that resembled the current state-stage system, in which the municipality would be the sole supporter of the institution: there would be a fixed annual operating budget, which would curb any potential loss, and the theater's organizational structure would be integrated into the city or state administration. Seelig had the unique opportunity to begin actual-izing his proposals after the First World War, when he became the official theater adviser for the Prussian Ministry of Culture—before being forced into exile by the Nazis. The process was a slow yet incremental one: by 1930, there were twenty state-stages, fifty-nine municipal stages, thirty-five private theaters, and a great number of other institutions with mixed financial struc-tures (GmbHs, AGs, etc.; Balme, 74–75).

Many of Germany's 262 theaters were badly damaged—and 98 were decimated—during the Second World War. Most of the country's theatrical ensembles were also destroyed, as hordes of their artists were sent to prison, forced into exile, or worse. Within months of the Allied victory, however, a number of theaters began housing performances once again, and before long, many began the slow process of reconstruction. By 1949, the restoration of the theater as a central public institution was in full effect—in both the East and the West. In the Federal Republic, for instance, the seventy-eight state and municipal stages received more than 63 million DM in public subsidy—which was a very hefty sum taking into account the 10:1 rate of exchange with the reichsmark. After the founding of the FRG, the theaters received approximately half of the total subsidy apportioned for culture. This liberal allocation was justified by the claim that state and municipal theaters proved useful as quite capacious employers, providing a form of public service, of *öffentlicher Dienst*, in times when work was scarce. In both the East and West, theater artists, technicians, and administrators signed generous wage agreements that provided long-term, sometimes even lifelong, job security and benefits.[105]

As the story goes in some cases, generous support and enduring security also facilitated intransigent inflexibility and the abuse of privilege, especially in the Federal Republic. Slowly, some of the newly communalized theater infrastructures began to perpetuate their own petrification via enormous administrative and technical teams, overly firm union regulations and strict divisions of labor, rigid allocations of internal funds due to the strict federal and municipal budgetary laws, and an increasingly static repertoire of classics and light comedies. The reports were legendary: severely bloated institutions with hundreds of employees, many holding tight to their coveted tenure status, "sitting in dusty offices covered in cobwebs and doing little or nothing except waiting to retire."[106] By 1980, Arno Paul and Martha Humphreys were already speaking about a system in crisis and the desperate need for infrastructural adjustment across the board:

> In the last 20 years, talk of a "theatre crisis," often similarly judged by external factors, has replaced references to the theatre miracle. . . . The main targets of criticism are the ostentatious cultural palaces with their enormous technical and administrative systems. It is evident that the massive structures and their heavy-handed, complicated organization impede any vital dialog between art and society and that the constantly increasing expense in personnel and materials are in disproportion to the social significance of theatre art.[107]

Or, a few pages later: "With some polemical exaggeration, the present theatre system in the Federal Republic could be called a prolongation of court theatre. . . . Whether this condition can or should be maintained is altogether doubtful. The lobby still exists, though. It permeates all political parties and opinion-forming organizations and is strong enough to repel isolated structural criticism even from its own ranks."[108]

In many ways, then, the State-Stage Complex epitomized the shifting priorities of the (western) state-stage itself, from proudly "progressive" symbol in a divided land to inflated instantiation of infrastructural stagnation. The original Schiller Theater, which opened in 1907, was destroyed in an air raid in 1943. After the war, the structure was completely redesigned and reconstructed—as was its organizational infrastructure. In 1951, the new State-Stage Complex, with the Schiller as its flagship space, opened its doors with great pomp and circumstance and an inaugural production of Schiller's *Wilhelm Tell*. Boleslaw Barlog, the new *Intendant*—and the theaters' most successful—hoped that *Tell* would help a shattered public reconceive its understanding of some version of "national unity"[109]—at least in West Berlin. Under Barlog's leadership, the State-Stage Complex became home to many internationally acclaimed directors: Gustaf Gründgens, Jürgen Fehling, Fritz Kortner, George Tabori, Hans Neuenfels, Hans Hollmann, and Peter Zadek, to name a few, all directed on the Schiller stage. Perhaps most notably, the State-Stage became a home for Samuel Beckett in Germany, producing *Waiting for Godot* (1953), *Endgame* (1957), *Krapp's Last Tape* (1959), and *Happy Days* (1961). Beckett even directed his own "landmark" production of *Godot* at the Schiller in 1975.[110]

While State-Stage supporters might have been justified in claiming, which they surely did, that the Schiller Theater under Barlog helped to "write German theater history after 1945,"[111] these same supporters were loath to admit that the complex had long since fallen upon hard times. Already in 1987, critic Michael Merschmeier penned a dooming diagnosis: "Here we had a gigantic production machine for highly heterogeneous theatrical venues, and a diffuse audience that was supposed to be entertained by the same actors, directors, and dramaturgs. These contradictions did not produce creativity, instead they absorbed it."[112] In a desperate effort to rejuvenate the complex in 1990, the city hastily appointed a four-headed directorate—comprising Volkmar Clauß, Alfred Kirchner, Alexander Lang, and Vera Sturm—but by 1993, after a great deal of infighting, Clauß was the only one who remained. All the while, fixed costs soared to unprecedented heights. In 1992, the complex paid out 16,739,232.97 DM to artistic personnel and 14,363,012.08 DM to technicians and other staff members.[113] As Lothar Schirmer later recollected, "Wasteful extravagance was the hallmark of theater work at the State-Stage Complex for years. We all remember Peter Zadek's production of *Everyone Dies Alone* [*Jeder stirbt für sich allein*], for which the Schiller Theater was reopened on January 8, 1981, after a long conversion that cost 8.1 million DM."[114] Zadek's justification for his creative decisions was simple: "That's the beauty of subsidized theater. We can even afford this scale of expenditure. On the free market, such a production would be unaffordable. We have these big stages; we should be allowed to put them to use."[115]

The Drive to Play

As July 4 drew closer, the nervous energy was publicly palpable. *Die Zeit* likened the Senate's decision and its aftermath to a root canal gone awry: "Frenetic pain and hysterical convulsions."[116] By July 3, the public petition against the Senate decision had garnered more than forty-one thousand signatures. In a survey published in the *Tagesspiegel* on July 4, 1,688 people wrote the newspaper to express their dismay over the closure.[117] Anyone who wanted to make a donation to support the theater could transfer money via bank wire to account number 1614301000.[118] There was also a permanent donation bin in the Schiller lobby, which was never empty in the days leading up to the final performance of the season. Inspired by this great show of public support, the leadership maintained a consistent position: the operations of the State-Stage Complex will not cease; *Wir spielen weiter*, we play on—even after July 4. To mark the end of the season and launch the summer's unofficial protest program (*Widerstands-Spielplan*),[119] the theaters' staff planned yet another party.

On the evening of July 4, thousands of eager fans stood outside the front doors of the Schiller Theater during the completely sold-out performance of Coline Serreau's light comedy *Rabbit Hare (Hase, Hase)*, pleading with the ushers to open the doors and let them in to watch. Six television crews were positioned inside to capture what could be the final performance at the Schiller. Just before 10:00 P.M., the curtain fell and the actors bowed and bowed and cried and bowed to standing ovations that lasted much longer than normal. As the applause dwindled and the crowd exited to meet the eager group outside in the lobby, the also-doomed Berliner Symphoniker took the stage. More than three thousand people celebrated in the theater proper, in the foyer, and on the lawn late into that evening of American independence. Director Einar Schleef rehearsed his then nascent but soon much-lauded production of *Faust* on the front steps. The beer and champagne flowed generously.[120] Actors and audiences, young and old, came together in celebration and hope. And though the threat was aired, the police did not clear the Schiller, even though the space remained occupied long after the curtain fell.

Early the next day, July 5, the complex leadership officially announced the details of the upcoming protest program. The Schiller Theater would not close its doors for a summer break, as was the usual procedure, nor close its doors for good, in accordance with the Senate's mandate. Instead, the space would remain open, unofficially. The staff and ensemble—those who chose to participate—would continue to work through the summer without pay. Early the following evening, Bernhard Minetti—at eighty-eight, the most senior actor in the Schiller ensemble—played to an absolutely packed lobby on a makeshift stage. He was backed by large black flags with white writing: "No to the Senate decision!" "Theater makers against cultural cuts!"[121] As August Everding characterized the goings-on in the Schiller foyer, "I did not understand the reactions of some of my colleagues, who said we will protest now instead of play, or we will no longer play in Berlin. Refusal is nonsense. Now we must play twice and three times, day and night. We must prove that the people are interested in the theater."[122] And the audiences did continue to flock. More than sixty thousand spectators attended the twenty-seven performances staged in the foyer of the Schiller over the next five weeks.[123]

These performances, however, were only the first, and perhaps even the least consequential, of a number of strategies staged by the State-Stage that contentious summer as a means of protesting against but also actively interrogating the Senate's decision. In addition to the performance series in the foyer, the broader protest program consisted of three other interrelated initiatives:

1. a legal suit filed by State-Stage advocates to question the legislative validity of the Senate's mandate to cease operations;
2. a second "performance" series that staged explicit cultural policy conversations on the Schiller stage—conversations that would explore different infrastructural models for the state-stage more broadly; and finally,
3. an attempt by the complex's own staff to articulate a new and concrete reform strategy for the State-Stage, one that might, so they hoped, serve as a schema for wider-reaching systemic overhaul.

The goal of this protest program was to move beyond merely naive optimism and sentimental calls for solidarity. Rather, in these proposed performances, the State-Stage team seemed adamant about reimagining the ways cultural ministers, politicians, trade unions, theater leaders, performance artists, and community members might think and work together to envision and materialize new models for the state-stage. In certain, albeit rare, moments, even Roloff-Momin and Volkmar Clauß seemed to find some common ground. The culture senator argued, shifting his own rhetoric yet again, that "the structures of the state-stages are moldy and must be changed." "We must move away from artistic bureaucracy [and indefinite tenure]," he added.[124] Clauß was finally poised to agree—to some extent: "The theater operates like any other public service organization. Labor [union] contracts apply to the gravedigger and the actor alike. They take no account of the specific operations and needs of the theater. Thus, the apparatus has become bloated."[125] Even the ever-optimistic August Everding changed his tone in the face of the State-Stage's shifting strategy: "Who is to blame? Of course all of us: the clueless culture politicians and the incompetent artistic directors, the feeble composers and those who pocket exuberant [artistic] fees, the malicious critics and the comfortable audiences."[126] As would become clear in the performances that followed, however, this seemingly advantageous shift in rhetorical strategy proved much harder to substantiate in sustained infrastructural practice.

On Tuesday, July 27, the Verfassungsgericht, or Constitutional Court of Berlin, convened to adjudicate the legitimacy of the Senate's decision from June 22. On behalf of the State-Stage, members of the two minority political parties—the libertarian Free Democratic Party (FDP) in consort, interestingly enough, with the Alliance 90/Green Party—had previously petitioned the high court to suspend the closure of the complex. The court agreed to hear the motion, and oral arguments began at 11:00 A.M. on the sixth floor of Hardenbergstraße 21—just a few blocks south of the Schiller Theater.

The questions on the table were weighty: Does the Senate, a small group of legislators appointed by the mayor, have constitutional authority to make budgetary decisions without a more expansive debate and subsequent vote by the Abgeordnetenhaus, or Berlin Parliament? Does the Senate have the power to close a state-stage and nullify state contracts? Or is this too a question to be decided on the floor of the Parliament? Peter Raue, lawyer for the FDP, insisted that the Senate had indeed overstepped its bounds. Proceeding with "rhetorical brilliance"[127]—Roloff-Momin said it himself—Raue explained that the Parliament had approved a budget for 1993–94. The Senate's decision to close the theater complex, he continued, would subsequently and significantly affect that budget due to all the open contracts and other expenses entailed by closure that would have to be paid off. Then came the controversial legal claims: "It is illegitimate for the Senate to appropriate funds for the liquidation of the theater without the involvement of the Parliament and interested parties."[128] All changes to the budget must be voted on by the Parliament. Therefore, the closure of the theater should be delayed, at least until the Parliament had the occasion to vote on the proposed budgetary changes. And time was of the essence, Raue continued with subjunctive urgency: if the theaters were to close, and the Senate's decision were later overturned by the Parliament, the theaters would already be "unrevivably dead"[129]—all State-Stage ensemble members and employees already would have started looking for jobs or been lured away by other theaters. Roloff-Momin and the Senate's attorney did not have many new arguments with which to counter. They maintained the line that Mayor Diepgen had touted since late June: "If the Senate overturns its decision . . . than its very capacity to act is called into question."[130] A great deal of time and energy had been spent on this particular decision, they continued, and there was no stipulation in the 1993–94 budget that required the Senate to maintain the State-Stage Complex. Therefore, they insisted, the Senate had full authority to make this kind of budgetary decision. It need not submit its decision to a parliamentary vote.

While careful to avoid all bleeding-heart-style arguments, for this was certainly the wrong address for such tactics, the plaintiff's call for a reevaluation of the Senate's authority implicitly underlined the State-Stage's broader call to expand the bounds of (and possible participants in) the emerging structural debates about the whole state-stage complex in Germany. Transferring the debates to the floor of the Parliament would at least facilitate, so it was hoped, the possibility for a larger contingent—across party lines, albeit still within the standard "representative" channels—to shape these conversations in a more substantive way. Further, and perhaps more radically, the plaintiff's call also implicitly questioned whether it was possible to perform cultural policy outside the bounds of the Senate's (i.e., the Grand Coalition's) particular policy agenda. On July 29, seven judges in dark violet robes sat behind a long wooden table looking out on an over-capacity crowd. They had come to a decision: the Senate did, in fact, require the cooperation of the Parliament in budgetary matters of this kind.[131] The Parliament would resume its work on September 2, and the State-Stage Complex would have a reprieve until the Parliament voted for or against closure.[132] *Officially* speaking, the Constitutional Court opted not to address the plaintiff's questions in their implicit complexity. Indeed, as Chief Justice Finkelnburg stressed repeatedly, the court did not intend, in any way, to comment on cultural policy matters.[133] "We had to rule not on the Schiller Theater," he explained, "but on the rights of Parliament. We emphasized this again and again: it is only about that—no matter where the hearts of the individual justices lie."[134] Yet, even though the court emphatically maintained that its decision had absolutely nothing to do with the state of the complex itself, the State-Stage staff knew it had won a strategic victory: they had bought themselves some time.

Over the next five weeks, before the Parliament reconvened, the theaters' team would attempt to reconceptualize the way the State-Stage Complex and state-stage system as a whole could survive moving forward. As Clauß announced in *Der Spiegel*, "Of course we are rehearsing for the first premiere of the season, but at the same time we are also working on a new, slimmed-down concept for our theater. The Senate's ludicrous decision has one upside: it is finally time to think about reform."[135] On August 12, the Schiller announced optimistically that the new season would open on September 3—one day after the eagerly anticipated Parliament meeting—with a repertory production of *A Midsummer Night's Dream*. *Don Carlos* would follow on the 4th, *Hase, Hase* on the 5th, *As You Like It* on the 6th, and a new production of *Antigone* on the 8th. But even more urgent was the announcement that a protest-program redux would continue on the Schiller stage. Beginning at 8:00 P.M. on August 19, the State-Stage would sponsor a series of interdisciplinary policy discussions, debates, lectures, and readings. As the official description read:

> There will be a continuation of the public debate about the theater, its structures, its cultural role, and its self-image. In lectures and papers, different theses and viewpoints on the current situation of the theater and the State-Stage controversy will be discussed. In this lecture series, distinguished speakers from the arts and theater scene will have a chance to speak, and there will also be literary readings and film screenings. . . . Answers must be sought and solutions proposed.[136]

This was "a concrete chance to fight,"[137] Clauß explained, a chance for the theater itself to stage its version of a "structural debate"[138] on the Schiller stage. Gerhard Ahrens, another of the Schiller's artistic managers, complemented Clauß: "We are making an argumentative discussion program, in order to intervene in the [ongoing] debate. We have invited presenters who can lay out a blueprint for the discussion that is independent of the specifics of the house. This is meant to be controversial. . . . We want to lead an argumentative discussion that is free of self-pity."[139] In the administration of these performances, then, the State-Stage designated its space as one capable of and primed for these explorations. By means of the protest program, the theaters' team also designated their stage as a space where one was permitted—even encouraged—to hope that performance itself might induce its own institutional reorientation beyond the conceptually predetermined present.

The reality of the protest program, however, was that much of the content presented was not all that hopeful, nor all that reorienting. Some of the performances were, simply put, completely tangential: Peter Wapnewski somehow found himself onstage talking about Virgil and the rest of the history of Western literature, or so it seemed;[140] Rolf Hochhuth quite predictably advocated a return to the "author's theater."[141] Some of the performances seemed to reify the logics of Grand Coalition governance and austerity thinking that the protest program sought to critique. Ivan Nagel, for example, caused quite the stir in his emphatic reprisal of Roloff-Momin's cut-here-to-save-there approach. Ivan Nagel already was a controversial figure in Berlin, both as a theater critic and as Roloff-Momin's go-to "theater expert." In the spring of 1991, the then newly appointed culture senator commissioned Nagel and three other colleagues to pen a series of expert "Considerations on the Berlin Theater Situation" in the wake of reunification.[142] While this public document expressly issued a "radical plea for the preservation of the Berlin theater landscape,"[143] it also generated a great deal of heat for its earnest and detailed appraisal of every individual performance institution and its often controversial proposals, which, the authors claimed, "require[d] courage to try out different forms of theater production and theater subsidy."[144] As the *Morgenpost* put it, "With his often provocative mode of delivery, his ironic tone and intelligent parentheticals, Ivan Nagel does not make many friends."[145] So when he stepped onto the Schiller stage on August 20 to ask—purposely refunctioning Roloff-Momin's language—"Is there an alternative?" he must have expected a critical response to his emphatic "no." Nagel began, "I would not be standing here if I did not hope that the Schiller Theater would survive these bitter weeks and months. What I have to say is hard. It would be a disgrace to speak ill of a dead man in his own house. On the contrary, it is compulsory to tell the truth to a sick person. For no seriously ill patient will get well without a rigorous diagnosis and an even more stern treatment."[146]

Most troubling about Nagel's diagnosis, however—and in stark contrast to the "Considerations" document from 1991—was his uncannily uncritical alignment with Roloff-Momin: first the quality argument, then the lack of attendance, then the lack of press, and finally a nod to the bloated administration and ensemble. Since he was an invited guest at the Schiller, however, he explained that he would not fully endorse the culture senator's "treatment" plan. In turn, he offered two other controversial suggestions: the first was that the State-Stage could streamline its expenditures by closing only one of its theaters, the Schlosspark, which would yield 15 to 17 million DM in his calculations. But before the audience could respond to that recommendation, Nagel laid out his second, self-titled "gruesome proposal."[147] The only way to save the entire State-Stage, he claimed outright, was to close another (albeit eastern) state-stage: the Maxim Gorki Theater. Though Nagel's "frivolous horse trade"[148] raised many eyebrows and vicious retorts—especially from those in the former East[149]—his newest considerations, which read more like reprises (and reprisals), were not given much explicit consideration in the days and discussions that followed.

Some other conversations did garner sustained traction, however. In the days after Nagel's political "karate chop," three other artistic directors—Nele Hertling from the Hebbel Theater Berlin, Tom Stromberg from the Theater am Turm (TAT) in Frankfurt, and Jürgen Flimm from the Thalia Theater Hamburg—took the stage to make "stimulating suggestions" about their "successful" experiences with "programs and working structures quite different than the highly subsidized [state-]stages."[150] Hertling, Stromberg, and Flimm were invited to brainstorm infrastructural suggestions that had not yet received much attention but would soon become a central focus: a move away from the current state-stage structure in favor of renewed exploration of a publicly subsidized albeit private model, in the form of the GmbH. While the Hebbel, TAT, and Thalia operated with very different aesthetic missions—the Hebbel and TAT were emerging epicenters of the burgeoning independent or free-scene, whereas the Thalia produced a repertoire with a fixed ensemble—all three artistic directors spoke highly of the benefits of the limited-liability company for theater production. Hertling explained that the unique mix of international guest performances and self-produced touring productions with "free" groups, for which the Hebbel had become well known, could function outside the economic strictures of the state-stage only with a small team of permanent employees permanently supplemented by freelancers. Tom Stromberg also emphasized the greater flexibility of smaller teams with whom, he explained, experiments were possible without years of planning.[151] Of the three presenters, Flimm was the most adamant about the viability of the GmbH as a solution to the state-stage dilemma.[152] As he explained, the model permits greater flexibility, aesthetic experimentation, and a reinvestment of profits, since the theater's income does not flow directly into the state coffers. Contrary to Nagel's suggestion, Flimm argued that the GmbH was the " 'only *alternative*' to bring costs down to a sustainable level."[153] "Why not bring together a few directors and actors and suggest to the culture senator that they should take the Schiller Theater into their hands . . . at their own risk and expense?"[154] There must be personal risk and personal investment, Flimm persisted. His suggestion—which in hindsight reads as a historical reversal—was that the state still hold a significant stake in the company; it would pay for basic costs, building maintenance, and a modest annual production budget. But in the end, he claimed, it should be up to the artists—and not the state—to determine "how many dark nights they can afford, how much vacation, how much equipment, how much *l'art pour l'art*, how much risk, how much 'committed art,' and how many commitments."[155] The theater's revenue would depend directly on how the artists in charge answered these questions.

As the countdown to September 2 continued, the language of GmbH-ization increasingly infiltrated the heated State-Stage debates. In an interview for *Neue Zeit*, which coincided with the protest program, August Everding balked at the very idea: "[It] is certainly incontrovertible: the German ensemble and repertory theater will continue to be paid by the public sector. Privatization is nonsense."[156] But was Everding hoping, grasping too tightly in unrealistic intransigence? Was the fate of the State-Stage to be the same as the Berliner Ensemble, the Friedrichstadtpalast, the Metropol-Theater, and so many other institutions reckoning with the realities of this "new" business model? Had Everding misunderstood just how the GmbH would function as more than *mere* privatization? And was this other model really pernicious enough to deserve such a vitriolic response? Certainly, no one—except perhaps the mayor himself—could have predicted the scandalous storm that would unfold around Olympia GmbH just a few months later. In the meantime, however, the State-Stage team took Hertling, Stromberg, and Flimm's suggestions to heart.[157] In an interview in the *Berliner Zeitung*, Clauß was emphatic: "New legal structures must be created. State and municipal theaters should be operated as state-supported GmbHs. Contracts could be worked up that make sense for the theater. This would not lead to material disadvantage for employees and would make the theater—as an organization—more effective. But the politicians and the unions cringe at such changes in the public sector."[158]

On Thursday, August 26, Clauß and other members of the theaters' leadership hosted a press conference to announce the results of their third ongoing initiative: the details of a "two-stage plan" for reforming the State-Stage Complex. At the start, Clauß stuck to his evolving position that structural debates about the state-stage—and the traditional bounds of cultural policy more broadly—must both accommodate the views of, but also expand beyond, the Department for Cultural Affairs: "We very much hope that [this proposal] can make a concrete contribution to the discussion going on in the policy-making bodies about the continued existence of the theater."[159] Clauß continued, "Cuts in the culture budget are possible without threatening the existence of Berlin's cultural offerings. This would require, however, a fundamental willingness to reform the ruling cultural policy. If we continue to refuse this [reform], the continued dismantling of culture is foreseeable."[160] In this introduction to the two-stage plan, Clauß seemed poised to address some of those complicated questions that the Constitutional Court had postponed for another day. He seemed poised, in other words, to propose a new plan for the State-Stage that would reflect, at least in part, the infrastructural analyses and critical cross-disciplinary conversations so central to a rethinking of the state-stage more generally.

It quickly became clear, however, that in spite of the team's hard work and effective rhetoric, it was not in fact prepared to confront—and even cringed in the face of—these larger questions. In a surprising if not reactionary move, Clauß returned (with some degree of self-awareness) to those narrower pro and con arguments from late June: "The essential structural reforms of the theater will not be achieved by the folly of closure. Quite the opposite: closure reinforces the remaining structures by [mere] redistribution [of funds]. They are helpless participants in maintaining the status quo."[161] And yet, as Clauß maintained, he was unable to focus on broader questions of reform: "This proposal provides no universal answers to the structural issues of publicly subsidized theaters," he explained. "It is based on the specific case of the State-Stage Complex."[162] In other words: the new plan was a strategic attempt to cut expenditures in order to swing the parliamentary vote and prevent closure in the short term. It was a strategic attempt to engage in a kind of policy making that nodded toward those expanded bounds, toward the necessity of large-scale structural debate, and toward more experimental modes of institutional dis/avowal, but one that ultimately remained entrenched in its own highly politicized and most obdurate status quo.

Clauß went on to present an articulate and detailed proposal to "reform" the State-Stage Complex—where "reform" was understood primarily as "cut costs." The reform would proceed in two phrases. In the first, to be executed in 1994, he proposed reducing the size of the artistic and technical staff: one stage manager, twenty-four stagehands, six electricians, and one lighting designer would be let go; the number of invitations to guest artists would be reduced; the salary structures for upper management would be reviewed; spending on decorations, costumes, and programs would be reduced; the cleaning of the building would be contracted out; and house staff would be reduced by providing lockers instead of a coat check. Instead of the repertoire system at the Schlosspark, a "block system" would be introduced: no more than three productions would play at any given time, and each would play up to ten times per month. The main stage would be used only in the final two weeks of rehearsals before a premiere and in other exceptional cases. This would permit a reduction in technical staff. The Studio Theater would feature only five performances per week and be closed the other two days. This first phase would yield approximately 4,825,600 DM in savings.[163]

In 1995, the second phase would begin with the conversion of the three theaters—the Schiller, Schlosspark, and Studio—into a state-supported GmbH. In spite of this more significant infrastructural experiment, however, the team's plan did not offer a simultaneous and sustained rethinking of the kinds of best practices that such a transformation would both entail and enable—most likely because, as Flimm had explained, this new business model would not result in immediate savings but only open up a long-term possibility of increased revenue.[164] The second phase would continue, then, with another reduction of artistic and technical staff—ten ensemble members, seven artistic assistants, and additional technical workers would be let go. The Titania Palast rehearsal stage—a drain on resources—would be closed, and a building would be erected in the Schiller parking lot to serve as a rehearsal space. Other plans to cut costs and supplement revenue included renting out all three stages during the summer months; the joint purchase of essential materials for all of the stages; a centralized ticketing system for all theaters; and even selling gourmet food in the foyer of the Schiller Theater. Phase 2 would yield approximately 6,652,000 DM in savings, increased to 7,073,000 DM once the parking lot rehearsal space was completed.[165] And with that, the proposal was packaged and sent off: to Roloff-Momin, Diepgen, the other senators, the press, and most important, the members of Parliament, who would reconvene in less than one week.

The Aesthetic State

The finalized proposal marked the end of what—this time around at least—had been a very short period in which broader discussion of institutional dis/avowal seemed possible. As the final countdown to September 2 commenced, a most hyperbolic tone accompanied a return to more static positions: either for or against. The local newspapers weighed in: "Never before has the conflict between theater people and politicians in this city been so tense."[166] "Since June 22, 1993, the theater city of Berlin has been in an ongoing process of self-mutilation. We must all be careful that it does not become a hara-kiri that extends far beyond the theater."[167] "The Senate's decision is forcing members of Parliament to make possibly the most momentous cultural policy decision of the postwar period."[168] Ultimately, neither State-Stage supporters nor detractors were able, in these final days, to look far beyond the fray in order to engage in a sustained art of institutional reimagining. Instead, the interested parties (and parties) fell back on, for the most part, polarized political viewpoints—state versus state-stage, flexibility versus bureaucracy, austerity versus overabundance, and so on—which the previous calls for structural debate had worked, if ever so briefly, to interrogate and even untangle. The return of this art of discussion—or lack thereof—was only exacerbated by its transfer to a very different stage: namely, the floor of the Parliament.

On September 2, 1993, the Berlin Parliament convened at its newly remodeled building, just off Potsdamer Platz. Members of Parliament filtered slowly inside the great stone structure—studded with Corinthian columns—and convened in the highly charged plenary room. Five concentric circles of tables and chairs formed an amphitheater in the round. After the legislators took their assigned seats alongside other members of their parties, Parliament president Dr. Hanna-Renate Laurien of the CDU opened the proceedings. The Parliament had many issues to discuss after its long summer holiday. But finally, halfway through the day's session, the State-Stage arrived on the docket, and President Laurien explained that each political party would have fifteen minutes to state its claims. As was expected, CDU and SPD representatives of the Grand Coalition recited those stock arguments proffered by Roloff-Momin and Diepgen in the previous months. State-Stage advocates—FDP, Alliance 90/Green, and the leftist Party of Democratic Socialism (PDS)—returned, as they had early on, to those tit-for-tat retorts supplemented both by overwrought claims about the destruction of the entire German theater landscape and what by now seemed to be fairly hollow calls for sustained structural debate.

Amid their deployment of these familiar strategies, however, State-Stage supporters did demonstrate a small—albeit fleeting—degree of self-awareness about the ultimate futility of the tired strategies of polarized party politics. Dieter Klein, from the PDS, exclaimed, "The siege mentality of the Senate and the coalition parties on this issue . . . has nothing at all to do with the art of government."[169] Carola von Braun from the FDP agreed: "We appeal to everyone—especially the members of the Grand Coalition—to venture into a joint effort to try to open a new way." "I urge my colleagues of the Grand Coalition," she continued, "give yourselves, this Parliament, and the Berlin theaters a chance! Do not let the extraneous arguments of coalition tactics dominate when it is about the future of public theater. That is not worthy of a capital city."[170] Of course, this mode of argument could be, and indeed was, read as a creative tactic on the part of minority parties: guilt as last resort. Uwe Lehmann-Brauns of the CDU worked hard to draw attention to this strategy. "I ask you to refrain from dramatizing the situation," he exclaimed. "We have a Senate proposal, which comes from an austerity decision. This is all in order, and we as a Parliament have to rule on it. Whoever speaks in this context of a coalition crisis does not know what they are saying, because there is no talk of theater closings in the coalition agreement."[171]

No decisions were reached in the plenary session that day. Once all parties had spoken and been given a brief time to respond, President Laurien took the floor again. A vote on the issue would be delayed until the next Parliament meeting on September 16. In the meantime, the issue would go before two committees for further discussion-cum-party-posturing: the Committee for Cultural Affairs on September 13 and the Budget and Finance Committee on September 15. Over the following days, the State-Stage season would open as planned—with champagne and Shakespeare, Sophocles, and Schiller himself. By September 11, the petition against closure had garnered sixty-five thousand signatures.[172] Though the wait was prolonged, however, there was not much hope left. The committees met as prescribed by Dr. Laurien, but the boardrooms remained sites of entrenched party politics. In both meetings, representatives of the Grand Coalition confirmed their unequivocal intention to vote for the State-Stage's closure in the meeting of the main house on the 16th.

On September 16, 1993, after almost three months of protest, performance, and policy debate, members of Parliament convened for the last time to vote on the Senate's decision from June 22—but not before one final and rather naive showing from State-Stage supporters. More than fifty actors and other employees gathered in the hallway in front of the plenary room. Everyone was in uniform: an artsy black block, with sunglasses, black baseball caps, and megaphones. The protesters formed a gauntlet of bodies through which every member of Parliament had to march to cast a vote, a formation in which the polarizing demarcations were made clear: the enraged "theater people" would berate their "politicians" on their way into the chamber. Roloff-Momin was not exempt: as he walked through with his typical shiny sports jacket, wire-rimmed glasses, two briefcases, and a frown, he was greeted with catcalls, boos, curses, and a number of TV cameras. As the hubbub grew, President Laurien phoned the police for help removing the protesters. Before long, thirty officers arrived to break up the crowds, who would not stop shouting: "Pigs!" "Schiller-killers!" Of course, the daily rags blew up the confrontation: "Riot in Parliament"; "Actors storm the Parliament house."[173] The *Morgenpost*, which had been supportive of the State-Stage all along, was not prepared for this kind of sentimentality: "On the stage of democracy, would-be revolutionaries and vulgar people also have their place. But the Parliament must not be one of those places. Artists must maintain a sense of self-control, even in moments when desperation is understandable."[174]

Once all members had walked the gauntlet and found their seats in the main hall, President Laurien began:

> Ladies and gentlemen! I declare open the 52nd meeting of the Berlin Parliament. I would like to make a statement: We are an open house to which visitors will always have access. Civil-looking people, not equipped for a demonstration, entered the House. They then grouped in formation and suddenly appeared up here. They denied the members of Parliament access in an unbelievable way, and they berated the members with evil, fascist language. . . . Let me state that one can indeed disagree. But hindering the members from performing their duties is unacceptable! . . . I will omit the insults—of which "hog" was the friendliest. I also noticed that the television [crews] took great pleasure in recording this protest group. Well, there will now be order.[175]

And order is precisely what followed. Each party was given a brief opportunity to speak before the vote. The Grand Coalition voiced condolences about the difficulty albeit necessity of the decision. The formerly eastern PDS spoke of the necessity of future debates. And Albert Eckert of the Alliance 90/ Green Party resigned himself to Beckett:

> HAMM: It's the end, Clov, we've come to the end. I don't need you
>   any more.
> CLOV: Lucky for you.
> HAMM: Leave me the gaff.
> CLOV: I'll leave you.
> HAMM: Before you go . . . say something.
> CLOV: There is nothing to say.[176]

The silent vote was decisive: 135 for closure, 56 against closure, 15 abstentions.[177] As Brigitte Fehrle of the *Berliner Zeitung* reported, "What have we learned in the fight over the Schiller? That in the face of the 'Grand Coalition,' the Parliament does not have much to say. Within two months, members of Parliament transformed from recalcitrant nay-sayers to resigned yea-sayers. What began with great pathos ended in humble consensus. Members of Parliament submit to the Senate decision. That is democracy turned upside down."[178] Later that evening, Volkmar Clauß appeared on the stage of the Schiller during the final curtain call of that evening's *Antigone*. Hands on hips, looking first toward the balcony, then into the orchestra, slumped, defeated, with a despondent cast of actors behind him, he announced the decision to the crowd. Silence. There was nothing to say.

A few days later, the final decision was announced: the State-Stage would play through the month and close its doors on September 30. Roloff-Momin invited all employees to a—this time—private gathering at the Schiller for anyone with additional questions or concerns. Speculation ran deep in the media as to what would come of the three theater spaces in the months to come.[179] Regardless, the State-Stage team was determined to go out in style: they planned another massive—and surely expensive—gala for the closing ceremony. Free beer for everyone. A live video feed to accommodate the twenty-five hundred people who had come to bid farewell but could not fit into the main house. There was a twenty-minute ovation after the evening of performance. Roses flew through the air. The Schiller house band played on the Studio stage as fireworks lit the sky. And finally, as the sun rose, the technical staff wrapped the entire building in a very large, continuous piece of black aluminum foil. The only color remaining was a banner streaming across the rotunda, which read most indignantly, "Here stands the theater of the Grand Coalition."[180]

Chapter 2

✦

Frank Castorf's *Lehrstück*

Refunctioning Brecht's Institutional
Legacy at the Volksbühne

Nothing less than a change of the theater's function as a social
institution was required.
　　　　　—Bertolt Brecht, "Die dialektische Dramatik" (1929)

We will build dialectical institutions, which are mutable and
exhibit irreconcilable opposites.
　　　　　—Bertolt Brecht, "Dialektische Planung" (1952)

Tonight's performance takes place backstage.[1] Streaming in from the bar in the foyer, the audience is invited up a few stairs, across the apron, and under the proscenium arch. We are ushered through the flap doors of a giant, red, circus tent that has been erected inside the heart of this giant state-stage. Every plush seat in the auditorium remains empty tonight. Instead, we filter into white plastic lawn chairs grouped together on either side of the large oval room; a runway divides the space in two. Straight ahead, marking the far end of the aisle and extending laterally across the whole space, stands a giant wall of fluorescent tube lights, glowing a bright, fiery yellow and casting the entire room in ominous orange silhouette. A five-piece chamber ensemble is gathered around a baby grand just in front of the light wall. Across the runway, a chorus of twelve performers sits in two rows surrounded by other audience members. Three performers, the "leaders" of the chorus, sit casually in the first row of chairs, and two other performers sit further back, closer to the door, blending in with the audience members still finding their seats. A sixth performer, the "crashed pilot," stands directly behind the piano, against the wall of the tent, isolated from the rest. All performers are dressed in royal blue jumpsuits—they could be flight suits or janitorial uniforms or perhaps both. Strategically positioned—or exiled—in the last seat in the house, closest to the door, sits a life-size puppet with long hair and glasses, turned away from the light wall and the seated performers. The puppet is a spitting image of Frank Castorf, the director of tonight's performance and the longtime artistic director of this theater, the Volksbühne am Rosa-Luxemburg-Platz.

Audience members take their seats. The first bars of Paul Hindemith's intimate and haunting score fill the room. The doors to the tent are closed. And the chorus stands and sings in slow, harmonic unison, as the lyrics appear on two electronic LED ticker displays mounted on either side of the tent: "Ages long all things fell in a downward direction / Except for the birds themselves. . . . / Our artless invention took wing / Pointing out the possible / Without letting us forget: / The unattainable."[2]

To Brecht and Castorf insiders alike, these opening moments might seem familiar—albeit in different ways. While the red tent setup does not reenact the staging conceits from the premiere of this "People's Oratorio"[3] in Baden-Baden on July 28, 1929, the backstage setting, the projection screens anticipating filmic material, and the use of a mixed ensemble of veteran performers and an amateur choir are reminiscent of the original dramaturgy. The spatial divide of the runway underlines Brecht's original staged division between producer and receiver, between apparatus and listener, and the mixed placement of performers and spectators throughout the room underlines the ways Brecht hoped to blur and shift these stratified relations by means of the performance itself. Neither does the red tent setup precisely reenact previous Castorf productions, though certain set pieces and faces are strikingly familiar. The wall of light was conceived for his staging of Gerhard Hauptmann's *The Weavers* (*Die Weber*) in 1997. The puppet first appeared on a paisley sofa next to an Eric Honecker puppet in the final scene of his production of Arnolt Bronnen's *Rhineland Rebels* (*Rheinische Rebellen*) in 1993. And some of the performers in this arrangement have been with Castorf since his start as *Intendant* of the Volksbühne in 1992.

Originally titled *lehrstück* (with a lowercase "l"), the piece was written in collaboration with Hindemith as a companion to *Lindbergh's Flight*, a Brecht, Hindemith, and Kurt Weill collaboration, which premiered one day earlier at the same Baden-Baden festival in 1929. Picking up textually where *Lindbergh* leaves off, *lehrstück* considers the plight of an unknown pilot injured in a crash, whose appeal for help prompts a series of "inquiries" about the nature of help itself and the significance of individual life and death. These performance experiments, the first of the *Lehrstücke*, or learning plays, marked the start of a sustained artistic, theoretical, political, and institutional exploration—for Brecht, for his collaborators, and later, for scholars and interpreters of their work—of the potential uses of and relations among theater, music, new media (namely, radio), and their apparatuses of production, distribution, and consumption. Brecht's subsequent revision and publication of these performance pieces as *The Baden-Baden Lesson on Consent* (that last word sometimes translated as *Acquiescence*) and *Lindbergh's Flight: A Radio Lehrstück for Boys and Girls* in 1930 also marked important moments in the ongoing development of, and controversial debates about, his *Lehrstück* theory, which continued throughout his life and beyond.

What, then, is a Brecht-Castorf insider to make of the first lines sung by Castorf's choral ensemble? "Unattainable. Unattainable. Unattainable. Unattainable." The chorus repeats the word four times at the end of the opening stanza—each time, as the score prescribes, with a slow, "very broad,"[4] dramatic tonality. One might notice that Castorf has chosen, in these first moments at least, to work with the text of the original *lehrstück* performed in 1929—he has also titled the evening simply *Lehrstück*—and not with the revised and more widely circulated *Baden-Baden Lesson on Consent* of 1930,[5] in which Brecht substituted the words "not-yet-attained" for "unattainable." Brecht's substitution, some would argue, suggested the emergence of a decisive artistic and political strategy in place of the impossibility of, or resistance to, this kind of conceptual predetermination and programmatic politics. In Stephen Hinton's (Hindemith-centric) estimation, for instance, Brecht's 1930 revisions "sought completely to radicalize the content of the original, calling for political action and change, augmenting its structure, and substantially reducing its musical portion, . . . effectively suppressing the work's musical origins and revising its ideological function in line with his [Brecht's] more recent ideas about didactic theater."[6] Although I return to Hinton's claims about the nature of Brecht's revisions later in this chapter, the word substitution in the 1930 revision does seem to indicate a discursive shift away from an experimental and improvisational approach, one less convinced of concrete answers to difficult questions. It indicates a shift away from the utopian impulse inherent in working toward that which cannot be attained and instead implies a solution that has—simply stated—not yet arrived but is most certainly achievable, even anticipated, nonetheless. At first glance, then, Castorf's allusion to the earlier draft draws our attention to his own penchant for, or at least interest in, the experimental, the improvisational, the utopian impulse of the impossible, and the inherent dangers of the programmatic, especially in the realm of politics.

But Castorf's staging is in no way a simple, unmediated restaging of *lehrstück* as originally intended in 1929—whatever that might mean. Later moments in the performance do stage parts of the revised 1930 text. Other moments comment, sometimes directly, sometimes obliquely, on the tension between the aesthetics and politics of the two versions. Still other moments—as many have come to expect, love, and hate from Castorf— extend, even explode, beyond the text and the score into other realms, some of which are well-established components of his own repertoire, some not. So what is at stake in these opening moments? Why has Castorf chosen to enter what John White calls the "minefield"[7] surrounding Brecht's early *Lehrstück* theory? Is it even possible, White asks skeptically, to reconstruct Brecht's "putative theoretical position out of a series of inconclusive fragments"?[8]

One would be hard pressed—and this is certainly not my intention in this chapter—to argue that Castorf is interested in putative reconstructions of any kind, be they artistic, theoretical, or political. I do want to suggest, however, that Castorf stages a highly mediated reflection on the continued relevance of Brecht and his learning plays. He invites us to revisit Brecht's critical meditations on (technological) progress, on the role of the individual (artist) in society, on the possibilities of collective action, on a (state) theater for new audiences, and on the tensions between the cautionary tale and the utopian-revolutionary impulse. I argue further that *Lehrstück* provides a heuristic to revisit Castorf's outspoken meditations on these subjects and to reflect upon the continued relevance of his artistic, political, and institutional projects. This production, in other words, presents a self-reflective and provocative lens through which one can revisit (though not necessarily reconstruct) Brecht's *Lehrstück* theory and understand the ways in which Castorf put that theory to use at the Volksbühne in Berlin.

A one-to-one Castorf-Brecht conjunction is by no means immediately apparent. Many critics actually consider the two aesthetic approaches incompatible, like "fire and water."[9] Laura Bradley, for instance, claims that "postmodern directors—like Frank Castorf—presented their work as a reaction against Brecht's political theatre of reason."[10] Similarly, Dirk Nümann finds it self-explanatory that Brecht's "theater model . . . should actually be among the favorite enemies of a disciple of deconstruction, who is so skeptical of progress and enlightenment thinking."[11] Throughout his career, Castorf has remained ambivalent toward Brecht. In certain moments, he cites Ionesco's critique of the purely rational and didactic Brecht who wants to "progressively shape society."[12] In other moments, he "feel[s] close" to a Brecht who "wanted more good sport at the theater; wanted to bring more life, more contingency, more disorder into a hermetically sealed communication process."[13] Sometimes Castorf pledges allegiance to the emotional authenticity of sense-memory one finds in Stanislavsky. Sometimes he sides with Brecht's critique of the "as-if."[14] Sometimes Castorf works to overcome the apparent tensions by framing his own work as striving toward both "extreme construction *and* extreme psychological authenticity."[15] And in other moments, Castorf pushes outward at the possible oppositions by periodizing Brecht's aesthetic development.[16] In some of these moments, he detests all things preformulated, detests the fable as road map, and like the "young, nondidactic Brecht,"[17] the "incurably, erotomaniacal lyricist,"[18] the "Dadaist"[19] Brecht, Castorf praises "the fight, . . . the surprise, the honesty, and also the endangerment of self."[20] On other days, Castorf is less thrilled by the younger "wild phase" plays but is excited by the plays with "allegoric clarity" or even the purportedly "orthodox"[21] ones, namely the *Lehrstücke*.

For most of his incredibly prolific career as a director, Castorf has been reluctant to stage too much Brecht. As a dramaturg and budding director in Senftenberg in the late 1970s, he worked on *He Who Says Yes / He Who Says No* (*Ja-Sager / Nein-Sager*), another of the *Lehrstücke*. In 1984, during his tenure as artistic director of the theater in the small East German city of Anklam, his production of *Drums in the Night* was shut down by the local

Party leadership shortly before its premiere. Castorf directed a production of *Mr. Puntilla and His Man Matti* as a guest in formerly western Hamburg in 1996. His reign as *Intendant* of the Volksbühne remained relatively Brecht-*frei*—with the exception of two productions by guest directors. That is, until 2006. Beginning that year, the fiftieth anniversary of Brecht's death, the typically unsentimental Castorf staged four "early" plays in five years: *In the Jungle of the Cities* (2006), *He Who Says Yes / He Who Says No* (2007), *The Measures Taken* (2008), and finally, *Lehrstück* (2010).[22]

Although Castorf was *the* dominant figure of the German (and perhaps broader European) theater in the 1990s and early 2000s, critics widely acknowledge that this stardom has "distinctly faded" in recent years.[23] None of his productions was invited to the Theatertreffen festival between 2004 and 2013, after almost a decade of consistent invitations. And though he did receive invitations in 2014, 2015, and 2018, many agree that his work has "increasingly run out of control . . . becoming ever less coherent."[24] Critics and audiences alike often greet his premieres with annoyance, or worse yet, with ambivalence, claiming that the work has become "repetiti[ve]" and "thoroughly predictable."[25] His four Brecht productions at the Volksbühne proved no exception. *Jungle of the Cities*, for example, was panned as a familiar and redundant "jumble of contemporary slapstick and political finger-wagging."[26] Rüdiger Schaper writes that the production was little more than that "anarcho-shit from the day before the day before yesterday," consisting mainly of the "reminiscences of a director."[27]

Schaper understands Castorf's reminiscence and redundant citations of earlier work to be indicative of his ongoing "artistic crisis."[28] Peter Laudenbach draws a similar conclusion in his review of *Measures Taken* from 2008: "The only question raised by this evening is just how far Castorf's self-demolition . . . will stretch."[29] In spite of the great fanfare sparked by the end of his tenure at the Volksbühne, his more recent pieces have also received tepid responses: "As always with Castorf, by the end you are only waiting for it to be over."[30] But have all things really fallen in such a "downward direction"? While one would be hard pressed to disagree fully with the critical claims of stagnation, I want to read against the grain of this widespread critique of redundancy and repetition as artistic crisis. Instead, I want to question the significance of Castorf's choice to revisit Brecht *and* an earlier incarnation of himself in *Lehrstück*. Without placing too much analytical emphasis on periodization, I wonder: Why did late Castorf return to early Brecht *and* early Castorf? Did late Castorf choose to look backward to reimagine what the future might hold? Perhaps late Castorf's return to early Brecht and early Castorf was somehow reminiscent of a late Brecht lamenting (and dreaming) in his journal about his own possible future: "Our performances in Berlin have hardly any echo at all. . . . Our efforts might be completely meaningless unless our mode of playing can be taken up later, that is if their value as teaching material is eventually realized."[31]

I claim, then, that *Lehrstück* provides a productive opportunity to reread Castorf's Volksbühne as a project of institutional dis/avowal. While I too aim to present a mediated reflection on the relations between Brecht and Castorf, between the *Lehrstück* project and the Volksbühne project, the parallels are provocative from the outset. The Volksbühne, like the *Lehrstück*, critically explores what it means to think about—and operate—a public (state-supported) *Volks* or people's theater. It explores radical notions of education, communication, technological innovation, and collective labor. Both projects understand themselves as theater for a new audience, also always calling into question just what is meant by the "audience." Both evoke a troubled history of order, discipline, and submission—on both Right and Left. Both foreground, as well, their experimental and improvisational form, which resists the production and reception of stable meaning. Like the *Lehrstück*, the Volksbühne proudly presents its contradictory, antagonistic, even morally nebulous nature. And like the Volksbühne, the *Lehrstück* challenges widely accepted relations between theater maker and theater audience, between producers and their means of (cultural) production, between aesthetics and its supporting apparatuses, between culture and policy. Finally, both projects serve—as Brecht stated near the end of his life—as "limbering-up exercises for . . . good dialecticians." [32]

In his 1959 study, *Brecht, a Choice of Evils*, Martin Esslin recounts a short, albeit epic anecdote about home decorating. Later in life, once he was reestablished in East Berlin, Brecht asked one of the set dressers at the newly established Berliner Ensemble to help him hang some window curtains in the study of his retreat in Buckow. When the gentleman hid the wire for the curtain behind an ornate oak pelmet, Brecht was—allegedly—taken aback: "'Fischer,' he said to the man, 'you are covering up the technical apparatus. One must be able to see how things work.'" [33] Esslin's poignant tidbit is demonstrative of the Brecht many know and love: a Brecht whose aesthetic innovations reveal the theater's technical and institutional enmeshments through varied acts of *Verfremdung*. And of course, this act of revelation served as a cutting critique of, and a call to arms in, a "real" social world obscured by ideological illusion.

But there is a question that is less often addressed in post-Brecht studies, one that Castorf-via-Brecht (and Brecht-via-Castorf) helps us to explore. Just what is the relationship between a theater aesthetic that exposes and critiques the structures of its support and a theatrical institution with similar goals? In other words, how—if at all—do Brecht and Castorf hope to *refunction* the theater apparatus itself, to transform the theater *as* public and state institution, *as* a complex and interrelated set of supporting structures that extend beyond *and* behind the proscenium arch? Finally, how does Brecht and Castorf's theorizing about the theater as public institution necessitate continued reflection on the bounds of cultural policy, on the complex mediations between the state and the state-stage? In this chapter, I approach these questions through Castorf's engagement with Brecht's understanding of the theater apparatus and his influential notion of *Umfunktionierung*—often translated as "refunctioning" or "functional transformation." Ultimately, I argue that Castorf explicitly refunctioned Brecht's meditations on the possibilities of a *Lehrstück* theory in order to imagine, and subsequently enact, a new kind of public—and publicly supported—theater in post-Wall Berlin. All this began in Baden-Baden. And it was *umfunktioniert* on Rosa-Luxemburg-Platz.

✦ ✦ ✦

As twelve members of the chorus take their seats, the three chorus leaders jump to their feet, hurry around the seated musicians, and climb atop the piano lurching suddenly toward the crashed pilot and shouting, most accusatory, over the piano's sharp staccato. "Fly no longer. . . . / The lowest piece of earth / Is now high / Enough for you. / Lie there still and be / Content. / Not high above our heads. / . . . Tell us who you are."[34] The three then march calmly back to their places, grab their plastic chairs, and move to the center of the aisle, commencing an extended, and unexpected, sequence of slapstick-style pratfalls: sitting forcefully on the chairs, flipping over the backs, tipping over, rolling to the side, breaking the chair legs in the process and trying to balance unsuccessfully. Eventually, the three regain composure, and the crashed pilot introduces herself, staring at the chorus across the aisle, her (clearly trained) operatic soprano filling the entire room with a very different timbre, asking, almost begging, to be heard. "I had been seized with the fever / Of building cities, and of oil. / And all my thoughts were of machines and the / Attainment of ever greater speed. . . . / But I beg you / To come to me . . . / And to assist me, for / I do not wish to die."[35] The chorus remains seated and, most calmly, in an almost robotic unison that underlines the stark difference in the sound of the "two" voices, asks its three leaders "whether we should assist him." But immediately—with a different frenetic energy this time, more like aggressive, inebriate fans at a college football game, shouting, clapping, chanting, hustling around the room, kicking their chairs—the three leaders protest and encourage everyone in the room to repeat, "Why should we now assist him? / He has not given us assistance."[36] The three tire themselves out eventually and regain composure yet again; as they collect pieces of their plastic chairs, now scattered around the room, the two other performers, seated amid the audience, jump to their feet and testify in unison, succinctly clarifying the pressing question of the evening and the guiding thematic of many of Brecht's *Lehrstücke*: "Across the body of the dying man the question is considered: whether men help each other."[37]

This is a question that would remain on Brecht's mind, in different valences, for many years to come: What are the dialectical relations between the individual and the collective, between the "you" and the "us," between the subjective and the intersubjective (and the objective)? When does spontaneity endanger doctrine and vice versa? Is subjective violence justified to bring

The three chorus leaders lurching toward the crashed pilot in Bertolt Brecht's *Lehrstück* (music by Paul Hindemith, directed by Frank Castorf) at the Volksbühne am Rosa-Luxemburg-Platz, which premiered on October 5, 2010. Photograph copyright © Thomas Aurin.

about objective revolutionary change? This line of inquiry was most certainly controversial from the start. And it would grow ever more controversial and multilayered as the years unfolded and the political and theoretical contexts shifted dramatically. In the context of the late and highly volatile Weimar Republic, the question carried its own baggage in light of the nascent Communist, Social-Democratic, and extreme right-wing parties in Germany. In the National Socialist context, the "well-disciplined conformist"[38] carried another connotation. In the eyes of a Committee on Un-American Activities, collectivism was cause for major trepidation. And in the burgeoning, pseudo-Stalinist East German state, "conscious, rational self-sacrifice"[39] had its own unique resonance. Brecht spent a lot of time and ink navigating these changing political landscapes and—his own understanding of—the shifting meanings of and uses for his work. *The Measures Taken*, for example, another of the *Lehrstücke*, was banned by the Nazis, but Brecht refused to lift the ban after the war—he did not want to see the play performed.[40] Yet in this same postwar period, he also spoke "without hesitation" about *Measures Taken* as a "form of the theater of the future."[41] The debates and uncertainties about the politics inherent within, or called for by, the *Lehrstücke* continued—and still continue—after Brecht's death: *Measures Taken*, for instance, would not be performed again until 1997.

In the context of a newly reunified German state after 1989, individuals and collectives garnered yet another sweeping range of politicized and polemicized connotations, from so-called Right and Left, former East and West alike. And in the context of Berlin's rapidly changing arts landscape—and emerging cultural policy aporias—the *Lehrstück*'s guiding thematics took on a most explicit infrastructural dimension: Which institutions would be left to "die"? Which would receive "help"? Who would provide this help? And on what grounds? In chapter 1, I reviewed some of these pressing questions and the ways in which Berlin's post-Wall cultural policy (and the fate of its state-stages in particular) was mediated by an emerging neoliberal agenda of urban development and a commitment to a particular brand of Grand Coalition party politics. The debates that emerged around the closure of the State-Stage Complex serve as a crucial backdrop here.

From the perspective of the former East, however, the dramas staged around the demise of the State-Stage Complex showed a distinctly "western" tenor. And while many members of the formerly eastern theater community stood in solidarity with the complex, their perspectives were certainly different from those of their formerly western compatriots. Castorf, the newly appointed artistic director of the Volksbühne, explained at the time, "I often go to the Schiller Theater, but in this bourgeois crowd, I feel rather uncomfortable."[42] The space, he continued, is particular to West Berlin's cultural life, and for "traditional bourgeois citizens it is a bitter loss." But he emphasized, "If it closes now, the West will finally realize that the present is really nothing like before 1989."[43] From a formerly East German perspective, that present was quite grim indeed. The processes of reunification decimated the GDR's vibrant performance panorama. Theaters in the former East closed in droves, and many ensembles scattered—or fled to the former West for higher-salaried jobs (or any jobs at all). For Berlin's formerly eastern state-stages—Berliner Ensemble, Volksbühne, Maxim Gorki Theater, Deutsches Theater, Komische Oper, and Staatsoper—speculation ran deep in the early 1990s. Which theaters would survive the crisis? Which would be forced to close their doors? Which would be forced to adopt entirely new artistic or infrastructural models? To the looming question, "Is there a cultural policy?" Castorf proclaimed in one interview after the other, "It is like Russian roulette."[44]

From the perspective of formerly eastern theater makers like Castorf, survival was also multivalanced and much more than a question of funding. What would it mean to speak of a formerly East German *state* theater in the context of the newly reunified German state? What would it mean to continue to speak of the formerly East German state theater as public project, as collective project, as *Volks-* or people's project, as ensemble? What role would Brecht continue to play in the theatrical—and institutional—aftermath of reunification, with his divergent meanings for East and West? In the early 1990s, the Berliner Ensemble and the Volksbühne am Rosa-Luxemburg-Platz emerged as paradigmatic sites to pose, consider, and debate these questions.

Both institutions had helped define the tradition of political theater in Germany in the twentieth century. The hallowed halls of the Volksbühne provided a theatrical home for the likes of Max Reinhardt, Erwin Piscator, Benno Besson, Heiner Müller, and many others. The Berliner Ensemble—established by Brecht and Helene Weigel in 1949—cemented Brecht's legacy with a slew of landmark, or *Modellbuch*, productions before his premature death in 1956. The ensemble also trained and inspired a generation or more of influential Brecht "disciples" like Peter Palitzsch, Carl Weber, Manfred Wekwerth, and Ruth Berghaus. By the early 1990s, however, both theaters found themselves in crisis, highly uncertain if—and if so, how—they would survive moving forward. The history of "bizarre episodes"[45] that constituted the crisis at the Berliner Ensemble after reunification has been well documented.[46] In what follows, I sketch out only a few moments of that history as a necessary counterpoint to the Volksbühne's dramatically different trajectory (one that has received much less attention, especially in English)[47] and its dramatically different attempt to reimagine what a formerly eastern theater could mean in the newly reunified, albeit dominantly western, Berlin Republic.

Vicious power struggles for succession ensued at the Berliner Ensemble after Brecht's death in 1956—a sort of "backstage . . . War of the Roses."[48] Ultimately, Manfred Wekwerth emerged as chief director under Helene Weigel's leadership from 1960 to 1969. He fell out with Weigel prior to her death in 1971, but he returned as artistic director of the ensemble in 1977 and remained at the helm until 1991. Wekwerth's highly orthodox understanding of Brecht's Marxism and of Brecht's hopes for the BE's social mission in the GDR resulted in a particular aesthetic and political orientation:[49] "Theater should be 'utilizable' for accomplishing the current political tasks of socialist development. Anarchistic or accidental theatrical interventions should be eliminated as much as possible. To achieve this, theatrical representation must be 'uniformly organized.'"[50] As a result, Wekwerth's leadership of the ensemble was criticized as perpetuating a "museum"-like[51] ossification of Brecht's oeuvre, very much in line with the ossified "realist" agenda of official GDR cultural policy. Some would go so far as to say that the ensemble under Wekwerth was little more than "a party organ in the East."[52]

It came as little surprise, then, that the Berliner Ensemble would have to undergo a period of "ideological cleaning"[53] after the Wall came down. Matthias Langhoff, in an open letter to culture senator Ulrich Roloff-Momin, wondered how the ensemble might, as Martin Linzer summarized it, "break free of entrenched institutional thinking."[54] We must "found the Ensemble anew," argued Langhoff, "to revive the idea of a theater that questions the usual way theatrical life is conducted, through its alternative working methods."[55] As the editorial pages of the *Frankfurter Allgemeine Zeitung* reported, "The Berliner Ensemble, under [Wekwerth] is now nothing more than a well-known monument to the GDR. . . . As it is, it must not remain—that was one of Bert Brecht's favorite ideas."[56] In spite of Wekwerth's forward-looking and long-overdue attempt to revise his program for the BE in 1990,[57] Roloff-Momin demanded that he step down in June 1991 to make room for a new "political and cultural vision."[58] According to Roloff-Momin, the ensemble must again become "a place where the process of German development will be reflected and where contemporary German theater, as in Brecht's time, can find a home."[59]

Roloff-Momin's proposed solution and desired process were, as one might suspect, in line with a different brand of party-line institutional thinking. In early 1992, it was announced that the Berliner Ensemble would become a GmbH, or limited-liability corporation, led by a "Gang of Five"[60] partners responsible for both the artistic and economic well-being of the ensemble. The Senate would continue to subsidize the company to a large extent, but the financial and budgetary structures of the former state-stage would shift dramatically, with a new focus on maximizing profits—or at least breaking even. As a private enterprise, the partnership could reduce the size of the company without old GDR labor union rules taking effect: the BE would be trimmed from 280 to 70 or so employees.[61] The repertory system would also be limited drastically in exchange for a new, American-style, en-suite block system, in which the directors would each be responsible for one production per season that would run for a few weeks. Each director would work predominantly with a discrete group of actors—mostly guest performers hired just for that production—thus eliminating the need for an ensemble as such.[62] To complicate matters further, thus feeding the ongoing racket about "privatization," Brecht's daughter—the executor of his estate—entered into long debates with Roloff-Momin and company about the conditions under which the family would grant the "new" Berliner Ensemble permission to produce Brecht's valuable intellectual property.[63]

The installation of the rotating artistic committee—the Gang of Five—only fed the media frenzy about the "permanent crisis at the BE."[64] Heiner Müller, Peter Palitzsch, Fritz Marquardt, Peter Zadek, and Matthias Langhoff were, of course, star directors in their own right. And in spite of the epic failure of the multiheaded directorate at the State-Stage Complex, Roloff-Momin's office touted the BE's restructuring as an opportunity to "bind the best German-speaking actors, directors, and playwrights within a new theater center."[65] However, most members of the press—and the theater community at large—had pressing objections to an "'old men's club' or a group of 'retirees,'" who shared "no visible artistically coherent philosophy" and would draw exorbitant salaries as well as additional fees for each production.[66] The former East German *Neue Zeit* newspaper exclaimed, "The . . . design can therefore only mean one thing: an elaborate cover-up of the fact that they failed to find a leader and a concept for the future of the Berliner Ensemble."[67] And the reviews were even less generous: Palitzsch's "painfully faithful and boring" premiere, Marquardt's "flop," Zadek's "laughing stock."[68]

Much more interesting, though, were the tense dynamics that emerged from within the new leadership itself. Heiner Müller and Peter Zadek locked horns almost immediately over political differences. Zadek, outspoken and combative, accused Müller of trying to turn the BE into an "Ost Theater," an East theater.[69] As a Jew from the former West, Zadek was disturbed by the pessimism, cynicism, depression, and "in-your-face"[70] nature of the East German theater aesthetic, which presented a "cold, humorless, anti-human atmosphere."[71] For Zadek, Einar Schleef, Frank Castorf, and Müller himself were representatives of the "new German nationalism,"[72] "a new face of fascism."[73] Zadek even insisted that these supposedly left-wing artist-intellectuals were anti-Semites in disguise. Müller, whose diagnosis of the situation was more controlled, understood this conflict with Zadek as a "reflection of the unification process," a realization of just how different things were—still.[74] One by one, the members of the directorate began to withdraw, and once Zadek stepped down in early 1995, only Müller remained—determined, in spite of his declining health, to shepherd the Berliner Ensemble (and Brecht's legacy) in a new direction.

In the short time between his emergence as the sole leader of the BE and his death later the same year, Müller began to explore just what Brecht's "Ost" ensemble could still mean and still do in a reunified Berlin, and how this new orientation would not only demand that "Brecht's texts be both read and heard anew,"[75] but also demand a reengagement with Brecht's lifelong penchant for experimentation, for *Versuche*. In turn, both Schleef and Castorf were invited to direct at the BE during the following season, and Müller went to work on what would become his landmark staging of Brecht's gangster parable, *Arturo Ui*. Alongside—and essential to—this investigation of the potential of a post-Brechtian theater in post-Wall Berlin, Müller also began to explore different infrastructural possibilities for the ensemble, possibilities that embraced—and attempted to install—a kind of infrastructural uncertainty, instability, chaos even. Ute Scharfenberg recounted:

> Unlike Zadek, Müller consciously attempts to disrupt the conventional structures of the subsidized theater system, to organize disruptions. He places hope in the creative energies that originate in chaos, in disaster, in the unplanned. . . . The attempt to find the most widely open form of organization for the Berliner Ensemble finds expression in the fact that the Berliner Ensemble no longer has a distinct bureaucratic apparatus. The current operations of the Berliner Ensemble may seem chaotic from the outside. Nevertheless, one must endure the current dissolution of the rigid modes of organization without becoming nervous. Heiner Müller proceeds from the idea that "we . . . will not find a common conception." "Maybe this is the most interesting thing; the Berliner Ensemble is an East-West stage, dissent is scheduled."[76]

Unfortunately, Müller passed away in December 1995, only midway through his first solo season and in the midst of another major administrative scandal: a drawn-out fight with playwright Rolf Hochhuth, who had bought the Theater am Schiffbauerdamm and was threatening a "hostile takeover" of the ensemble.[77] Müller's death marked the end of the critical investigation at the Berliner Ensemble of the possibilities of an Ost Theater and of Brecht's continued relevance for reunified Berlin. But related versions—even more radical versions—of these aesthetic and infrastructural investigations continued and, indeed, gained incredible traction in the work of Frank Castorf, the newly appointed artistic director of the Volksbühne.

In the early 1970s, the Volksbühne am Rosa-Luxemburg-Platz, under the leadership of Benno Besson, emerged as one of the most important theaters in Germany. After Besson's departure in 1974,[78] however, the theater was plagued by one interim directorship after another, accompanied by plummeting audience numbers and harsh reviews as the "worst"[79] ensemble in the city. This "unsupportable situation"[80] made the Volksbühne a prime candidate for closure after reunification, alongside the (western) Freie Volksbühne and the State-Stage Complex.[81] However, at the behest of Ivan Nagel and his three colleagues, Roloff-Momin considered a different approach for the Volksbühne in those early days after reunification. In their infamous "Considerations on the Berlin Theater Situation" Nagel and company recommended

> that the city of Berlin (with the same courage it displayed in 1970, when it took in Peter Stein and his ensemble) give the Volksbühne on Luxemburgplatz to a troupe of young artists, preferably with an ex-GDR core—a group dedicated to making its own theater. The sociocultural shock and confusion of our times could translate themselves in Berlin—into a new, illuminating, and provocative theatrical gaze. The troupe of the Volksbühne East would need approximately the same amount of funding that the Volksbühne West has been receiving—perhaps less in the first two years. By the end of the third year it would be either famous or dead; in either case, further subsidies would not be a problem.[82]

"Famous or dead": an ultimatum sure to make headlines—and it did. For Nagel, there was only one director in town who could attempt to reenvision a distinctly *eastern* Volksbühne within the landscape of the "new" Berlin.[83] There was only one "play-defiler," "*Altterrorist*," "leftist ayatollah"; only one "manic, pathological *Schmuddelfink*, gaunt eclectic, hooligan, a[nd] primal-scream-therapist";[84] only one "theater-terminator and drama-detonator"; only one "wrecker and destroyer," "enfant terrible and clown-king";[85] only one "charlatan of the demise or prophet of the beginning"; a "poseur, a bully, a moralist."[86] In other words, for Nagel, there was only one suitable candidate to lead this young, ex-GDR troop: Frank Castorf—the "cowboy from Prenzlauer Berg."[87] And the culture senator heeded the advice.

Castorf inaugurated the new Volksbühne on October 8, 1992, with a motto that would dictate (or at least color) the thematics and methodological bent of this first season and many seasons to come: "From the Seventh of October to the Ninth of November." October 7 marked the inaugural day of the German Democratic Republic in 1949, and November 9 was the day the Wall came down in 1989. But Castorf's invocation was much more than an uncritical commemoration of the GDR or an attempt simply to revive some bygone brand of Ost Theater, of theater as it purportedly had been in the former East. Sometimes referred to as *Schicksalstag*, or that "Fateful Day," November 9 also bore witness to some of the most significant events in twentieth-century German history: the demise of the German monarchy and the declaration of Karl Liebknecht's failed "Free Socialist Republic" in 1918; the Beer Hall Putsch, which marked the emergence of the Nazi Party in 1923; and Kristallnacht in 1938. Castorf's invocation was also much more than a call for simple, unmediated comparisons among revolutionary socialism, national socialism, "real existing socialism," and socialism's subsumption by global capital. Instead, he was interested in and committed to an immanent analysis that mandated a deep and thorough engagement with the complex relations (and contradictions) among these movements, their ideas, their historical figures, and their artistic outputs. For Castorf, there is no "right" message, no hard distinctions to be made between past and present, between good and evil. Rather, as Siegfried Wilzopolski understands Castorf's approach, "[He] does not recognize theater as a means of solving problems. On the contrary, theater amplifies problems and destroys every alternative. . . . Theater doesn't resolve contradictions; it intensifies them beyond acceptable limits."[88]

The Volksbühne programmed eight premieres that first season, four directed by Castorf: Shakespeare's *King Lear*, Arnolt Bronnen's *Rhineland Rebels*, an adaptation of Burgess's *A Clockwork Orange*, and Euripides's *Alcestis*. Each play, claimed Castorf, could be reread from the perspective of an immanent "left critique of a left Utopia."[89] And the results were fiery: "Beer spills, potato salad flies. . . . Joy through strength!"[90] "On the stage, without regard for the plays, excrement is openly and diligently secreted and genitals are presented with dedication."[91] "Irritations, amalgamations, role play, small fights in over-the-top costumes."[92] "Castorf's obsessions are not ideas but what is left over: crap, junk, garbage."[93] "Mannerist, hyperrealistic, decadent, nihilistic, exactly the opposite of everything else."[94] A "theater hostage crisis."[95] In concert with chief designer Bert Neumann and chief dramaturg Matthias Lilienthal, Castorf also programmed a diverse auxiliary program to accompany and augment the productions in repertoire on the main stage. "Where the dramaturgy departments of other theaters usually strive for a so-called coherence of content," Thomas Irmer remembers (citing Lilienthal), "in which supplementary programs are brought in connection with [the theater's] productions, the mise-en-scène of the Volksbühne as 'total event' ['*Gesamtereignis*'] consciously aimed at openness and at the offer to leave it to the 'recipient' to construct potential connections."[96] Concerts, symposia, films, lectures, political meetings, and "café hangs" filled all rooms of the massive building until the wee hours of the morning. There was a youth theater—without pedagogical guidelines. There were performances administered by the homeless. There were brawls between skinheads and *Autonomen* ("autonomous" antifascists). There was a left-wing hunger strike. There was football, rock 'n' roll, and lots and lots of beer. Lilienthal explained, "In place of intelligibility, the Volksbühne proposed fragmentation, dictatorship in the place of democracy, irony and trash in place of political correctness, in the place of acquiescence came provocation, in the place of understanding came strangeness."[97]

Castorf's explicitly Ost Theater, then, was no mere (n)Ostalgic derivative.[98] When asked if he mourned the loss of the GDR, his response was quick and to the point: "No, for God's sake. . . . [T]he GDR perished very logically in its own decadence."[99] The East German state was a "colossus of nonmovement,"[100] he argued, a "still and stinking body of water"[101] paralyzed by doctrine. "Finally, it could not go on any longer, because there was no more fresh blood, no more wind, no oxygen left in that stinking swamp."[102] And "when I look to Bonn now," Castorf exclaimed glibly in reference to the former capital of West Germany, "I see this again"—the same penchant for doctrine, for inflexibility, for stasis, for homogenization, and for totalizing "appropriation"[103]—only now sanctioned by a new republic. For Castorf, then, the project of the Volksbühne was not to embody or restage the "typical" GDR state-stage but rather to "release the potentialities of this state."[104] And though those potentialities were most certainly varied along the political spectrum, for Castorf they also stood in critical tension with the agendas of Berlin's Grand Coalition government—itself another instance, he explained, of entrenched institutional thinking. As Castorf liked to say, there was something profound about the artist's capacity as political actor, a capacity for shock, within the GDR's totalitarian system; this is something he desperately missed in the reunified Germany.[105] For this very reason, as soon as he moved into his new office on Rosa-Luxemburg-Platz, Castorf infamously hung a large framed portrait of Stalin on the wall. Next, he erected three massive letters—"OST"—at the building's highest point, perched prominently for the whole town to see, to encourage—or demand—that a new (re)public engage the many associations that word might evoke. "The Volksbühne is important because it *is* a GDR institution that survived," Castorf explained. "But we do something that the GDR, as a state, did not do."[106] Namely, "I want to open up a window through which a clear, cold wind blows, which brings with it a bit of disorder to stuffy Berlin."[107]

To return, then, to that provocative vocabulary from the *Lehrstück*, the crashed pilot can be understood, at the outset, as standing in opposition to the totalizing collective agendas of the Grand Coalition *and* the former GDR leadership. The pilot's crash serves as an allegory—or wish fulfillment—of the failures and dangers of a politics "seized with the fever / Of building cities, and of oil," be they in the former East, former West, or the newly reunified republic. At certain moments, the chorus provides an outlet to dream of the forgone possibilities of collectivism in its different iterations. And at others, the buffoonish and slapstick-laden chair debacle from the "leaders" serves as a critical reflection on both Honecker's "real existing" regime and Mayor Eberhard Diepgen's plans for "staging the new Berlin."[108] Castorf has never been shy about stating that he opposes the totalizing collective agendas of both the former GDR leadership *and* contemporary party politics. "I am marred by the GDR," he claims. "All that [i]s interesting for me [i]s movement."[109] This "movement," always frenetic, always energetic, spectacular even, is one in which individual and collective, capitalist and socialist, past and present collide, always also externalizing this collision in "hysterical eruption."[110] Lilienthal explains, "The Volksbühne 1992 was above all an adventure playground. The uninstitutionalized moment after the fall of the Wall made everything possible. . . . It was a utopian moment, in which hierarchy seemed to be abrogated. . . . What came to pass was a trashlike reenactment of a recently destroyed history."[111] This reenactment was inextricably bound with a trashlike imagining of a future that was not yet determined. But in the present moment, the results were in—and well within the bounds of Nagel's three-year asymptote: Frank's "postsocialist gambling joint," his "ruffians' playground," his "blood-and-testicle-temple"[112] had arrived, indeed exploded, on the scene as the "most controversial and exciting stage in Germany."[113] Before long, the Volksbühne team installed the massive Robber Wheel sculpture on the front lawn, thus calling upon—and challenging—all Berliners to engage the new social function of the theater standing before them in all its delinquent knavery.[114]

✦ ✦ ✦

The musical inquiry—or tribunal—persists among the chorus and its leaders: Explorers kept exploring. Inventors kept inventing. Philosophers kept philosophizing. But all the while "the price of bread did not get cheaper." "Poverty and need increase within our cities." "Long years have passed since / anyone knew what a man is."[115] Some insist—chorally—that the pilot, the exemplary bourgeois individual, should therefore be left to suffer: "Tear up the pillow, throw the water away."[116] Others have not yet decided whether she should receive assistance. All of a sudden, on the final note of an inquisitive-sounding musical passage—a "melody of surprise"[117]—the fluorescent light wall is switched off, and the room takes on a distinctly different ominous glow, with the stark white light and long shadows of a prison cell or interrogation chamber. Two of the leaders turn to the third and ask—breaking for the first time this evening with Brecht's text: "And you, comrade? The glass of water?"

Without hesitation, the third raises a large jar of water high above his head and, with a steely, confident glance at his "comrades," empties the water onto the floor. The other two leaders turn to one another, aghast, and shout in unison, "He is going to take over the leadership of the Party." Again. "He is going to take over the leadership of the Party." With feigned innocence, standing tall and most stately, the third calmly responds, "No. That demands the involvement of everyone. I am of the smallest dimension [*die kleinste Grösse*]."[118] Read: I am the least significant element. Without pause, one of the two more paranoid leaders spins around, pointing his finger upward; an idea has occurred to him. With the air of an academician, he launches back into a Brecht text—but a text of a very different sort: "Experiment [*Versuch*] number seven, *The Baden-Baden 'Lehrstück,'* is a further essay in the *Lehrstück* genre following *Lindbergh's Flight*." As he continues, his tone and gestures become harsher; he is now a most disciplinary political organizer: "On its completion the piece turns out to be unfinished. . . . The work is printed here because, when all is said and done, its production creates a collective apparatus." He then remembers, most dismissively, to add, "For some parts of it there is a musical score by Paul Hindemith."[119] The metatheatrical lecture-cum-indoctrination continues—still in haunting shadow—but he now draws our attention to the revisions Brecht made in his 1930 publication of the play: "Not-yet-attained. Not: unattainable. Do you understand?" Yes, they understand, bowing to one another, becoming more "fanatical," and simultaneously more comical, now. One mechanically regurgitates that with which he has been indoctrinated: "Lenin proceeded from the endless possibilities of human understanding, not from the unattainable." Another responds, relieved, "Gott sei Dank [Thank God]." The other sputters in response, loud and nasal, without hesitation: "Marx. Sei. Dank!"[120] Pause. The three leaders bow again and march, regally, down the runway and out of the tent as the musicians resume Hindemith's score.

Castorf breaks here, for the first time this evening, with his presentation of the text and music of Brecht and Hindemith's original *lehrstück*—the version that premiered in Baden-Baden in 1929. In doing so, he explicitly highlights a major tension that colors the production and reception history of *lehrstück*—namely, between Hindemith and Brecht's divergent understandings of the work's intended *Gebrauchswert*, or use value. In 1930, Brecht began to compile and self-publish a series of "experimental" writings—performance pieces, theoretical explorations, commentaries, and so on—which he titled *Versuche*. The seventh *Versuch* volume contained a revised version of *lehrstück*, loaded with a good deal of newly devised scenic material and other structural and wording changes, and retitled *The Baden-Baden Lesson on Consent*. Brecht made—and published—these changes after his collaboration with Hindemith had come to an end; the new texts therefore had no music beside them. In Castorf's sudden break with the 1929 text, however, he does not opt to stage Brecht's revised 1930 text, in which the chorus provides a decisive answer, namely "no," to the question "So does one man help another?"[121] Instead,

Lehrstück: "Marx. Sei. Dank!" Photograph copyright © Thomas Aurin.

Castorf moves away from the revised text entirely ("And you, comrade?"), and he inserts a text that highlights the act of revision itself, in turn asking that we consider the theoretical implications of Brecht's revisions and his tenuous relations with Hindemith.

Klaus-Dieter Krabiel argues (alongside Stephen Hinton) that Hindemith and Brecht maintained very different ideas about the primacy of text and music, as well as about the ultimate political goals—and intended "use"—of musical performance. As a "full-blooded musician," Krabiel claims, Hindemith was much less interested in literary content, and he "wanted to know nothing of the music's political charge. . . . The only aim of his [score] was to enable a collaborative musical practice."[122] Hindemith saw the piece and its performance as a vital contribution to the burgeoning *Gebrauchsmusik* (community or utility music) movement in Germany.[123] These trends, which were popular in youth music circles, had also gained popularity among artists in the avant-garde. The movement advocated a departure from the more traditional bourgeois music institutions and their virtuosic, pedagogical practices, and instead focused on the virtues and accessibility of community and amateur music. In his introduction to the original piano-vocal score, published in October 1929, Hindemith explained that the size and composition of the orchestra were left fully to the "director's discretion. The purposely vague division of the score into high, middle, and low voices enables the conductor to allocate them according to the wishes and capabilities of the performers and the limitations of the room."[124] These specifications, Hindemith continued, were a direct reaction against theater or concert performances in which the performers' central task was to "entertain or instruct" an audience:

> Since the only purpose of a *Lehrstück* is to bring everyone present into the performance of a work and not directly to arouse artistic impressions in others, the form of the piece should be adapted as far as possible to the actual aim. The order in the score should consequently be regarded as a suggestion rather than a command. Cuts, additions, and changes in the running order are permissible. Whole musical numbers can be omitted, as well as the dance, and the clowns' scene can be shortened or left out entirely. Other musical pieces, scenes, dances, or readings can be introduced, if these are felt to be necessary and not clashing in style with the rest.[125]

Accompanying his publication of the revised text as *The Baden-Baden Lesson on Consent*, Brecht responded to Hindemith's preface, claiming that some of the composer's erroneous ideas were based on a "misunderstanding" of the work's intended goals.[126] "Even if one expected . . . that certain formal congruencies of an intellectual nature came about on a musical basis," Brecht explained, "it would never be possible for such an artificial and shallow harmony, even for a few minutes, to create on a broad and vital basis a counterbalance to the collective formations which pull apart the people of our times with a completely different force."[127] While he did not object to an understanding of the piece *as* experiment, Brecht argued that Hindemith had not grasped the full scope of the structural problems, those other "collective formations" of capital, that he hoped to engage with *lehrstück*. For Brecht, performance itself has a much grander social and political capacity than one of "purely musical *form*";[128] collaborative (or collective) music making was *only* one tactic in a larger, more complex arsenal. In Hinton's highly polemical appraisal, "In dispute was the nature of the 'use' being proposed and the type of community that the new 'utility' art should serve. By way of making its voice distinct, the [L]eft replaced the neutral notion of *Gebrauchswert* (use value) with the ideologically more colored criterion of *Kampfwert* (the value of didactic art in the service of a specific political struggle). Traditional aesthetic values had to yield to the requirements of agitprop."[129]

While Krabiel and Hinton are certainly right that Brecht's ideas about the possibilities for the *Lehrstücke* were very much in flux in 1929, 1930, and beyond[130]—as were his political commitments[131]—it is far from clear that Brecht's intentions for *The Baden-Baden Lesson on Consent* can be reduced to *mere* agitprop. Rather, Brecht's break with Hindemith marked the start of a productive and provocative period of thinking and writing in which he begins to explore more deeply and comprehensively the workings and limitations of those "collective formations," those "ponderous apparatuses"[132] of capitalist (and cultural) production, and the ways performance itself—and the *Lehrstücke* as case in point—might play a crucial, even *useful*, role in the "functional transformation" (*Umfunktionierung*) of those apparatuses. It was in this most productive and provocative period, then, that Brecht began to rethink the theater's function as a social institution.

As a way into these institutional dimensions of Brecht's work—and toward an unraveling of the agitprop critique—I find it helpful to consult Walter Benjamin's theoretical reflections on his new friend's work from this period.[133] Long before critics like Hinton, readers of Benjamin began to worry that essays like "The Author as Producer" from 1934 were tainted by an undialectical commitment to a pseudo-Leninist politics, due to the effects of a dreadful "Brechtian sun" hovering above its "exotic waters."[134] Benjamin's interest in Brecht—his "Brechtiania,"[135] as Maria Gough puts it—had little to do, however, with an uncritically predetermined and merely programmatic political agenda. In fact, Benjamin was frustrated by the popular, albeit vulgar, temptation to substitute "propaganda" for art.[136] He was frustrated by the simple, unmediated binaries of commitment and autonomy, of content and form. For Benjamin, mere discursive *Tendenz, Engagement*, commitment (to the Party) was insufficient, even "counterrevolutionary."[137]

Ironically—in light of Brecht's hallowed place in the halls of "political" theater—it was indeed Brecht whom Benjamin consulted to transcend the limits of mere aesthetic commitment. As a first step in the argument, and in a vein quite similar to the argument his friend Theodor Adorno would pose about "commitment"[138] many years later in 1961, Benjamin (citing Brecht's *Versuche 2*) explained that the "bourgeois apparatus" is remarkably capable of assimilating political content.[139] Many artists imagine "that they own an apparatus that actually owns them," wrote Brecht:

> They defend an apparatus over which they no longer have any control—which is no longer, as they believe, a means for the producers, but has turned into a means directed against the producers, in other words against their own production. . . . This apparatus, however, is determined by existing society, and only assimilates whatever keeps it going in this society. We could possibly discuss any innovation that does not threaten the social function of this apparatus, namely evening entertainment. But what cannot be discussed are any innovations that might press for a change in its function and so would reposition it in society, for instance by linking it up with educational establishments or major organs of mass communication.[140]

For Brecht, "apparatus" is a broad term that includes aspects of the means of cultural production—everything from the technical tools to the institutions that house, promote, and organize production; sometimes "apparatus" is even used to designate the entire cultural complex writ large.[141] Benjamin-via-Brecht explained that artists must first acknowledge their lack of control over the means of cultural production; they must be careful not to *supply* the apparatus. Instead, and this is the second phase of the argument, they must work to *change* it—specifically by engaging with the means and *thereby* the relations of production. Benjamin famously wrote, "Rather than asking, 'What is the attitude of a work *to* the relations of production of its time?' I would like to ask, 'What is its position *in* them?' This question directly concerns the function the work has within the literary relations of production of its time. It is concerned, in other words, directly with the literary *technique* of works."[142]

Here Benjamin suggested a fundamental "functional interdependence"[143] between an artwork's social and political tendency and its technique, or in other words, between its various commitments and its formal engagement with the apparatus. Like Brecht's apparatus, Benjamin's technique operates as a pivot between artistic and social production; questions of progressive technique are not limited to traditional understandings of formal artistic innovation—montage, for example. Rather, technique mediates between the various *means* of production at the artists' disposal, be it on the level of stylistic originality, technological possibility, or institutional orientation, *and* in the spaces between. Thus, two years before his famous pronouncements about the possibilities of "politicizing art,"[144] Benjamin explained that the work of art is no longer only intended, as Brecht put it, to represent "'individual experiences,'" but rather is aimed at "'certain institutes and institutions.'"[145] The work of art should achieve "organizational usefulness."[146] The work of art should work toward—here he invokes Brecht's provocative vocabulary— "functional transformation"; it must strive to transform the "forms *and* instruments of production."[147] For Benjamin, Brechtian "functional transformation," then, provided a means to rethink the relations between art and the social world, because—for Benjamin—formal, *technique-al* questions are already questions about the state (of the) apparatus. Revolutionary artists, then, are charged not merely with the task of taking a political position for or against but, contrary to Hinton's claim, also with considering just how their work might *formally* "refunction" (again, *Umfunktionierung*) the various social institutions, or apparatuses, in which they are already enmeshed.

Benjamin-via-Brecht's analysis here is by no means uncontroversial. To begin with, their ideas about just what such desired *functional* transformations should look like are not fixed. In certain moments, both Brecht and Benjamin seem committed to a "complete break with past modes of production."[148] Benjamin espouses the necessity of "freeing the means of production" and changing the apparatus "to the utmost extent possible . . . in accordance with socialism."[149] A like-minded Brecht, at moments, is adamant about erasing the possible contradictions between producers and the means of production. As Roswitha Mueller notes, Brecht seems confident in "the appropriation of the apparatuses by the producers, to achieve control over their means of production, [even though] the *Threepenny Opera* trial had demonstrated the difficulties of such a project."[150] In other moments, however, the language of "functional transformation" seems less concerned with fundamental "breaks" and much more interested in "formal . . . experiments"[151] with, or "innovations"[152] within, the contemporary apparatuses of production. In these moments, Brecht speaks of "new uses of existing [but] unused apparatuses,"[153] in which "a collaboration develops between participant and apparatus";[154] he speaks of "battles *for* the modern institutions and apparatuses."[155]

Brecht's seeming willingness here to embrace, or to collaborate with, the current modes and technologies of capitalist production certainly makes him vulnerable to a certain brand of critique: Is it really possible to rely on a (state) apparatus to support and enable (artistic) work that is fundamentally opposed to the operations of that apparatus? Mueller argues, "It seems that here Brecht is giving in to the same theoretical fallacy that allowed the introduction of Taylorism in the Soviet Union under Lenin. Brecht's at least partial belief that advanced modes of capitalist production foreshadow socialist practice was supported by the avant-garde's love affair with technology and the latter's ability to intervene rationally in the mystification of social processes."[156] Maria Gough—who carefully unpacks the theoretical foundations of and turns within "The Author as Producer"—makes a related argument that Benjamin's (and Brecht's) rethinking of artistic commitment as a question of technique "draws upon one of the most fundamental, and controversial, aspects of Marx's theory of history."[157] She continues, "The basis for Benjamin's belief . . . is a technologically determinist reading of the contradiction of productive forces and relations. In other words, in his producer essay, Benjamin implicitly vests explanatory primacy in the productive forces, technique being chief among them. In doing so, his essay engages in an affirmative reading of one of Marxism's most enduring controversies."[158]

My concern in this chapter is not to adjudicate long-standing debates about whether Benjamin and Brecht have read Marx and Lenin properly. Rather, most important for me here—and what seems most important for Castorf—are the ways in which Brecht and Benjamin underline the fundamental (albeit tenuous) imbrications of the artistic and the infrastructural; they underline the ways in which aesthetic concerns are already institutional, and in which institutional concerns are already aesthetic.[159] Further, such an engagement with Brecht and Benjamin also reveals the tenuous imbrications of those already existing (bourgeois) apparatuses of production and the refunctioned apparatuses in question, or in other words, the tenuous imbrications of the attained, the not-yet-attained, and the unattainable.

Brecht's *Lehrstücke* are aesthetic-cum-institutional experiments that explore the bounds and potentials of these intimate coimbrications. In other words, the *Lehrstücke* are attempts to explore how the refunctioning of certain "aesthetic" practices also entails a refunctioning of the theater as institution, which in turn entails—so is the hope—an even broader "societal refunctioning."[160] In the 1929 *lehrstück*, Brecht is working to understand how a "direct collaboration between theatrical and radio performances"[161] could prompt a radical reappraisal within both media—and in the space between—of the structural relationships among the state, the artist, and the audience. As Mueller explains further, in a helpful précis:

> Brecht's *Lehrstück* experiments fall into the same period when his radio theory was written. . . . [His] opposition to the political institutions of radio and their unilateral distribution of programs has its correlative in the total abolition of the conventional actor/audience structure in theater. Just as the actors and audience are encouraged to take charge of the text, to criticize and change it, the listeners are called upon to appropriate the apparatuses for their own needs and interests. Brecht's complaint about the eclectic and random selection of programs distributed by the dominant media originates in his demand not only for new topics to be discussed, but also for an examination of attitudes and new behavior, the promotion of which is precisely the aim of the *Lehrstück*.[162]

The 1929 *lehrstück*, then, works to refunction both theater and radio as apparatuses of multidirectional communication and not merely unilateral distribution and consumption. This is at the root of Brecht's break with Hindemith: simply moving *out* of one's former bourgeois digs would not do the trick. Rather, it is by means of this "re-functionalization,"[163] this deep engagement *with* the apparatus and battle *for* the institution, that *lehrstück* works both to mediate *and* foreground the tensions between those so-called antinomies of bourgeois (aesthetic) experience—form and content, producer and consumer, performer and spectator, individual and collective—in order to rethink, and re*work*, varied infrastructures of "public life."[164] "Should you consider this utopian," Brecht quipped, "then I ask you to reflect on the reasons why it is utopian. Whatever the radio sets out to do, it must strive to combat the *lack of consequences* that makes almost all our public institutions so ridiculous."[165]

Castorf has indeed engaged in sustained reflection, and *Lehrstück* provided him with an opportunity to revisit his own explicit refunctioning of Brecht's argument. "I believe . . . that we can refunction [*umfunktionieren*] the flaw that we all have in the areas of administration and organization into a virtue," he claimed.[166] And for Castorf, the apparatuses and administrations in question were, of course, those of the state-stage, the *Staatstheater*. While he admits that the state-stage system is laden, if not burdened, with what he calls "feudalistic structures,"[167] he also understands these structures, at least as a starting point, to be the theater's strength. But how? "The [state] subsidy system has the great advantage that we are economically independent," he explains. "This is a crazy privilege. We do not need to beg for grants from Mercedes or Hoechst."[168] Political *independence* via financial *dependence*? At first, one suspects a most twisted logic. But for Castorf, the subsidy system—*as* feudal system—secures the theater as an "elite island of resistance"[169] against "capitalist efficiency"[170] and the kinds of political "straightforwardness" and tactical "systematic thought"[171] that accompany it. "*Especially* if you are funded through tax money," Castorf claims, "you have the duty to be subversive. You have to be ungrateful."[172] As he had previously stated, "All theater lives on subsidies. When these cease to exist, then the differentiated cultural offerings that were previously on offer will no longer be feasible. If we abandon the [state] theater, we incur a new Americanism, which makes me anxious."[173]

Castorf is not interested in an avant-garde resistance that steps outside the "ponderous apparatus." He is not interested in a scene free and independent of state involvement.[174] He is not interested in a political or artistic underground. He is not interested in abandoning the ensemble or the repertoire. Rather, he is interested in an art of dis/avowal that leans into systems of support as the means by which he undoes—from different sides and in a most ironic fashion—the autocracy of the Party (or parties): "I want to come into the trained, state-theater apparatus with my performances and, together with the performers, change that apparatus from the inside."[175] "I could have never pulled off taking over a smaller theater. But the Volksbühne was so big, so empty, so *kaputt*—it was worth seizing."[176] From deep inside the state apparatus, and crafting productions that, as their signature, made use of every corner of the theater building, Castorf was well positioned to "inspect meticulously" the "German national body,"[177] and to "meddle"[178] in form, in content, in the spaces between and beyond: "I can really work with taboos and must not think about ratings or customers."[179] "Our aim is financial and personal latitude in order to remain mutable."[180] Castorf's argument, however, was not a naive appeal for a more critical stage reality free from Grand Coalition posturing. On the contrary, he insisted sharply that "the structure must be broken apart; new operational units must be created, which . . . are both organizationally and artistically diverse."[181] Castorf understood—and still understands—himself as artist and as producer, and the state-stage, oddly enough, is the aesthetic and infrastructural space in which he feels best poised to launch this project, this critique of a "false [state] obsession with order."[182] "It's not about hindrance," he claims, "but rather about the polarization of chaos in order to be productive."[183] For Castorf, then, it is about battling *for* the institution by battling both with and within it.

◆ ◆ ◆

The pilot lies on her stomach, cheek pressed to the ground, wide-eyed, her (stylized albeit) terrified visage projected large on either side of the tent. Slowly and en masse, the members of the chorus rise from their seats, extending their arms straight ahead as they take small steps toward the pilot, singing in unison, "See how his flesh decays, and his face which / Once we knew, is now strange to us."[184] They have become, in this moment, a "vampire" (or zombie) *Volk*, approaching the pilot slowly, looking straight ahead, reaching for her neck, thirsty, and ready—say the stage directions—to "suck the blood of the living bourgeoisie."[185] As they get closer, the pilot quickly scrambles to flee the tent, but the chorus pursues her unaffected, arms still outstretched, ever so slowly, ever more hungry. At the end of the runway, cornered by the members of the chorus, who are still lurching forward toward her throat, the pilot takes off her shoes and picks up a solitary plastic arm covered with red blood. She begins to caress the arm and then to caress her face with the limb, finally pointing the bloody hand into the choral crowd, greeting them, somehow, with a familiar gesture. This seems to appease them, and at the end of their musical phrase, "Go away from us," the members of the chorus walk, affectless, back to their seats. Without hesitation, the pilot begins her "Dance of Death."[186] Hunched forward, holding the plastic arm straight ahead and then high above her head, she steps, then hops, then gallops to the center of the room, pursuing the chorus and proclaiming, "I cannot die." She crashes to the floor and repeats, "I cannot die," as she raises the bloody arm high into the air, raising her leg, and pausing for a moment in a horizontal *tendu devant*. The chorus members now pick up their chairs and move, in unison, to the center of the room "to get a better view of the performance."[187] Once they are seated with legs crossed, the pilot resumes her dance, rocking the bloody limb back and forth, bending to one side, then to the other. She soon throws the arm away, however, and launches her body across the space, her movements becoming "ever more excessive, existential"[188] kicking, turning, quick, then slow, then quick again, rolling over then tumbling across the space, exhaling, grunting, and traversing again, this time "walking like an Egyptian" à la the Bangles, and then again with a series of off-balance *piqué* turns, after which she falls to the floor, stuffs a paisley pillowcase into her mouth, and transforms, instantly, into a limp ragdoll. Unable to maintain any position for too long now, she rolls on the floor, from one side to another, forward and back, until, finally, she flops down on her back, motionless, still gagged by the pillowcase. The chorus members pick up their chairs and move back, in unison, to their previous positions.

The premiere of *lehrstück* in 1929 caused a major "scandal."[189] The Brecht-Hindemith collaboration had been perhaps the most eagerly anticipated event of the Baden-Baden program; in addition to members of the local and national press and a broad spectrum of government officials and members of high society and the avant-garde, present and future Nobel laureates Gerhardt Hauptmann and André Gide were in attendance.[190] As a critic from

Lehrstück: The Dance of Death. Photograph copyright © Thomas Aurin.

the *Badische Volkszeitung* reported, however, the piece proved to be nothing but a "*Leerstück*," a most "empty" performance that "made a mockery of all the laws of aesthetics and morality."[191] Other members of the press found the evening "distressing" and "tastelessly crass."[192] During the performance, audience members began whistling and shouting, requesting that the show be stopped.[193] And one account, from an actor playing in the performance, reports that it became even more physical than that.[194]

While the most vocal disgust emerged in response to the infamous "Clown Scene," the first harshly negative reactions sprung up in response to an earlier scene, "Look on Death." Here Brecht screened a short film of a dance performance by Valeska Gert, in which she performed a "study of ingeniously horrifying realism," a harrowing Dance of Death. Gert's dance, titled *Death*, was deceptively simple: she stood in place and "died" in silence for about two minutes.[195] Kate Elswit recounts the performance: "The dance was confined to actions of her upper body and face, with the animation negotiated through minute physical shifts. . . . Gert increase[d] and then dissipate[d] tension until her body shook slightly with the effort of supporting itself and then quieted altogether. By the end, 'there stands now no longer a human on stage, no breathing creature, no longer a dancer but death, and not some symbol of death, but the deceased, dead Frau Valeska Gert.'"[196] Although Gert's performance received critical praise in many other contexts—contexts also acknowledged by the critics in Baden-Baden—in this instance, the members of the press found the film to be "simply excruciating."[197] As Krabiel surmises, the haunting intensity of Gert's dance must have seemed an "imposition" on an audience gathered for a "festive and amusing" festival.[198] But Brecht surely expected controversy amid this crowd. And just to drive the point home, he took the stage most provocatively at the end of the performance to demand "'another viewing of the representation of death that was met with aversion,' and the film was repeated."[199]

Castorf in turn makes productive use of this history of audience reactivity—this history of provocation and "scandal." But in place of anything resembling Gert's haunting *Totentanz*, he uses this death scene to explore what he calls a multifaceted "crisis of the audience,"[200] a crisis of communication that both the *Lehrstück* and the Volksbühne are working to confront. Here Castorf has refunctioned the death trope to conduct a more extended meditation, a back-and-forth (across the stage), about possible modes, relations, and failures of communication between pilot and chorus, between individual and collective, between a highly trained opera singer and a group of amateur spectator-performers. Moreover, as is to be expected from Castorf, the scene can be read in at least two ways.

In one reading, the Dance of Death serves as a hyperbolic diagnosis of what Castorf considers to be the routine theatergoing practices of a present-day bourgeoisie in reunified Berlin—very much in line with some of Brecht's critical diagnoses of more traditional forms of unidirectional aesthetic experience at the theater. As they rise from their seats and extend their arms, the chorus members embody a cluster of alienated and undifferentiated "zombie capitalists"[201] in pursuit, most aggressively, of recognition and self-knowledge, by means of a parasitic embrace of the culinary. The pilot, played by the accomplished soprano Ruth Rosenfeld—whose stunning voice stands out prominently amid the chorus of untrained choral performers—is functional-ized, in this moment, for what (most polemically) the culinary opera has to offer: enjoyable, digestible melodies. Castorf explains, "Most audience members are those who always go to the theater, who studied it, and who need the theater as a status symbol, in order to forget their embeddedness in a work-apparatus [*Arbeitsfunktionalität*], in which they are only wheels in a big machine; to forget this and then to refuel a little bit on individualism in the freedom [provided by the theater]. The trend is that the theater becomes important once again as an elitist temple, where you meet others like your-self."[202] Once the chorus of spectators have moved their chairs "to get a better view," they passively consume the pilot's devastating dance. As she throws her-self around the room, she is drained of her beauty and particularity. Ultimately, her voice, like that of the bourgeois theater itself, is purged, rendered inau-dible. Under the affectless gaze of a most consumptive audience and framed by an apparatus designed only for consumption, she is left mute, ineffectual.

This diagnosis underlines the act of provocation—or, as Castorf likes to call it, the act of war—he hopes to wage on the traditional theater audience. As he explains, "I could also say it's like an attack, a war against the archenemy, and the archenemy is the audience. But the general rule still says that a boring evening means good theater. Not with us! We polarize the audience. I often wish a performer would scream to them and say, 'You're a bunch of bums!' And the audience would yell back, 'You're an arrogant, stuttering asshole!' Our society needs this kind of confrontation."[203] Castorf is committed to the "offensive"[204] and, very much in line with the young Bertolt Brecht, to the Volksbühne as "boxing ring."[205] With these principles in mind, from the very start of his tenure as artistic director, he set out to build, and enable, a different kind of audience. He immediately slashed ticket prices to 5 DM for the unemployed, students, and retirees; standard tickets cost only between 12 and 20 DM, dramatically less than for other stages in town. He opened the space to radical political groups both on the Right and the Left. He invited the homeless, the disabled, and other often-marginalized groups inside. He made it a point to reach out to working-class neighborhoods in Berlin and beyond. "The only mandate I feel at the Volksbühne," Castorf explained, "is to bring together people who do not normally meet in the theater."[206] Once they were inside, beer in hand, anything and everything was possible—or so the thinking went. And the interesting irony is that the more provocative, offbeat, or even flat-out offensive the work became, the more people continued to flock: "We have an audience that does not like what we do at all, but they come because of the other climate, as a revolt against total appropriation."[207] Elsewhere: "We at the Volksbühne are fortunate because our standing public does not read reviews. . . . They come to us because they have the feeling that our theater has something to do with their lives."[208] As Lilienthal elaborated, again, most polemically, "We have something against West Berlin dentists. Here, other values apply."[209]

A second possible reading of the *Totentanz*, then, explores the goals and potentials of, and for, this new audience. More than Hindemith's mere democratization of the theater, Castorf was—and remains—interested in exploring the types of tenuous, if not explosive or violent, dynamics (artistic, political, institutional) that emerge in the name of democratization. He is interested in forging an immanent critique of that "discredited notion of community."[210] "You cannot call it communication," he claims. "I want to thematize this inability to communicate with one another anymore."[211] For the first time this evening, the chorus members assume an active role as they finally begin to move through, and occupy, the space—their space. Their purpose is not merely to consume the performance, but—like "vampires"—to participate in, if not enable, a transformation (one that is most certainly violent at certain moments). The chorus here is very much interested in—and not interested in abandoning—its subject, the oh-so-culinary opera; but the chorus is also interested in exploring the pilot's other capacities, interested in taking an active role in the opera's functional transformation. The chorus intends both to make productive use of those culinary capacities *and* to put them to new uses; the chorus even asks, or demands, that the pilot reevaluate her own capacities. This is why the dance that she performs is—as Castorf put it— "existential," and why it is filled with a diverse and overlapping palette of movement forms that extend far beyond the typical operatic repertoire: ballet, modern dance, the MTV music video, a kindergarten gymnastics class, and on and on. In this Dance of Death, the pilot—as an embodiment of the bourgeois apparatus—is refunctioned as a multigenred, and at times violent, mash-up of forms. And by means of this frenetic death-cum-transformation, the previous modes of exchange, of communication between the chorus and the pilot, between the spectator and spectated, have begun to unravel.

For Castorf, then, the Volksbühne was at its best when right-wing skinheads came to a performance and threw rocks at the windows or even came to blows with other audience members.[212] He was doing his job when the arguments in the canteen were just as—or even more—interesting than the works on the stage.[213] The state-stage was most successful when it featured a mix, or jumble, of forms: "Dance, rock music, philosophy, film."[214] And as a work of state infrastructure, it was most resonant—dare one say useful— when it both facilitated and embodied surprise, adventure, chaos, violence, and even its own undoing. Because, as Castorf explains:

> In Berlin, the violence is already there. We're not producing it; we're pointing it out and pointing at it when we show Stalinist trials on the left side and Nazi Theresienstadt films on the right. It's always running on a scale between left-wing autonomous pirate broadcasting on the rooftop and baroque music below. Sometimes we find heroin needles because we don't close at midnight. We let people sit longer and talk. But there's always an excitement. Nowhere do you see more diverse groups of people than here. People speak together. I see that as an opportunity for this society.[215]

✦ ✦ ✦

After an extended "instruction[al]" debate about the pros and cons of "consenting" to becoming "die kleinste Grösse," the least significant element, the yellow light wall is switched off again, and the room takes on the familiar glow of the interrogation chamber. Four stagehands wearing black Volksbühne T-shirts bring a table covered with more bloody mannequin limbs and two large saws to the center of the tent. The two performers who had framed *Lehrstück*'s central question at the start of the evening now promptly prepare to continue the "inquiry": Do men help each other? These performers take off their blue jumpsuit jackets and get to work in their white tank tops. They are two "clowns" now, whose playing style is a mix of "Berlin brat" and "wicked garden gnome."[216] One of the clowns hurries to the end of the runway to fetch a third clown, Herr Schmitt, who has been sitting most patiently with his back to the audience all evening. Herr Schmitt is a life-size puppet replica of Castorf, and Castorf himself is sitting in the next room, out of sight, microphone in hand, waiting to provide Herr Schmitt with a voice. "Lovely evening today, Herr Schmitt," says one of the clowns. "How do you find the evening, Herr Schmitt?" asks the other. Castorf's voice, as Schmitt, fills the room, evoking a sustained giggle from the audience: Herr Schmitt is "not feeling good today." The clowns aggressively fling Herr Schmitt onto the examination table, badly mishandling his body. Yet, without hesitation, they pledge their allegiance: "Then we must try and cheer you up, Herr Schmitt." In the sequence that follows, the clowns attempt to help Herr Schmitt by offering to remove the body parts that ail him. He has pain in his left foot. They violently saw it off—"the sooner, the better." Next they remove the puppet's legs, its ear, its arm. Though Schmitt is initially surprised by the rough treatment—they also beat him with his limbs after removing them—he continues to depend on the other clowns to diagnose and "cure" his ailments, and he is thankful for their attention. But Schmitt is still quite unwell: "Funny, my head's so full of unpleasant thoughts," Castorf whines. One of the clowns tries to cheer him up with a dirty joke about a man who shoves horse shit into the mouth of another. And when that fails to brighten Schmitt's mood, they offer to "saw off the top of [his] head, to let those stupid thoughts out." Schmitt agrees without hesitation, and the clowns proceed, first sawing off all his hair and then, when that is still not sufficient, standing atop the table and shaking him upside-down, smashing his head, again and again, against the tabletop. Finally, they throw Schmitt's mangled body onto the ground and stand on the table looking down at him, laughing loudly: "Now really, Herr Schmitt, you can't have everything."

Though shouts and murmurs began with the screening of Valeska Gert's *Death*, that summer evening in Baden-Baden really heated up with what soon would become known as Brecht's infamous "Clown Scene." One reporter asked, "'How long should Mr. Brecht'—a literary sadist, an 'absolute bungler and bluffer'—'be allowed to spread his artistic revelations among the people, until his artistry is set aside once and for all? . . . Absolute Bolshevism.'"[217] Brecht's "grotesque and bawdy" direction of the scene was read as an outright attack on his mainly bourgeois audience.[218] Herr Schmitt, a massive clown on stilts with oversize papier-mâché head and limbs, was brutally mutilated by the two other clowns "helping" him to confront his ailments "with veritable saws and veritable noises,"[219] and lots and lots of fake blood. The noises were so loud, over Hindemith's haunting march, that a good deal of the public fled the room. And according to Hanns Eisler's account, a well-known music critic actually fainted from the shock of Herr Schmitt's plight.[220]

Schmitt's encounter with the *helpful* clowns is one scene in the *Lehrstücke* collection that has been a focal point—in addition to those of the *Measures Taken*—of highly politicized debate and controversy since 1929. The central worry remains: Is the scene a justification or even a celebration of violence against the individual for the sake of the collective? Later scholars

Lehrstück: The infamous Clown Scene with Castorf as Herr Schmitt. Photograph copyright © Thomas Aurin.

of the *Lehrstücke*, like Reiner Steinweg, have attempted to shift critical focus away from the politically troubling ramifications. Steinweg takes seriously the Benjamin-via-Brecht account of the centrality of *Umfunktionierung*,[221] but to assuage his political worries, he pushes Brecht and Benjamin too far. In turn, Steinweg reduces the *Lehrstücke* to a set of predominantly formal innovations, which merely illustrate Brecht's exploration of the dialectical method onstage. For Steinweg, it was more important, for instance, that contradictions, including the problem of violence, were engaged, even sublated (*aufgehoben*), and not as important to consider just what that engagement might entail.

Steinweg has come under heavy fire over the years for his fragmentary approach to Brecht's writings, his ahistoricism, and most relevant for my purposes, his "harmonizing formalism"[222] and "rationalistic reduction."[223] A number of critics, most notably Hans-Thies Lehmann and Helmut Lethen, jointly criticize Steinweg for ignoring (or worse, subsuming) the subjective, or psychic, content of the *Lehrstücke* in favor of only formal and "rational" criteria.[224] Elizabeth Wright provides a helpful account of their position:

> The strong reaction against the *Lehrstück* suggests a powerful subjective content, something left over, not solved. This something has left traces of violence and terror, the effects of which critics like Steinweg

have disregarded. Even though past critics have misread these effects, they were at least not immune to them, whereas now [in Steinweg] they tend to get tidied away. . . . Lehmann and Lethen argue for a different tragic element, a remainder which cannot be encompassed by rationality, that escapes the dialectic, that testifies to the pain of unresolved contradictions.[225]

According to Lehmann and Lethen, this "second level"[226] of subjective content—their early version of a "psychic remainder"[227]—stands in immanent dialectical relation to, and serves as a necessary check upon, the "first-level" oppositions that are more explicitly, and textually, addressed by the *Lehrstücke*. Lehmann and Lethen's critique of Steinweg should not, however, be read as an unraveling of Benjamin's unraveling of the agitprop critique in "The Author as Producer." While the arguments are very different, and Lehmann and Lethen are operating in an emerging poststructuralist-cum-post-Brechtian idiom, they are also working, much like Benjamin, against attempts to cleave content from form, form from content. While Benjamin undoes the *mere* commitment critique in order to think about the complex imbrications of form and/as content, Lehmann and Lethen undo a *mere* lack-of-commitment position to explore a different side of those same imbrications: content as always and necessarily imbricated in form.[228]

Castorf walks a fine line—and sometimes explodes the line—between these sides. His theoretical sensibilities—with his interest in spontaneity, immediacy, nonidentity, even irrationality—are very much in accord with, if not inspired by, Lehmann and Lethen's critical interventions in "Ein Vorschlag zur Güte." Castorf assumes a world that is "not intact" and insists, at every moment, on a rebellion against "expected schemes" as a form of "spiritual hygiene."[229] "I neither have a destination nor do I want a framework," he insists.[230] At the same time, Castorf makes productive use of Benjamin and Brecht in his explorations of the changing social function of the theater by means of those first-level questions about form and content embedded in *Lehrstück*. His refunctioned "Clown Scene," then, provides a final opportunity to explore how he understands, and simultaneously critiques, his own *modes* of theater making, as always navigating between *and* beyond the technique-al and its potential second-level negation in uncertainty, nonconceptuality, chaos, even violence. Wright could be reviewing Castorf's *Lehrstück* when she writes, "Although Brecht likes to promote the idea that learning is imbued with the pleasure of experiment, in the *Lehrstücke* this pleasure is bound up with the shock of violence. The plays deal with antagonisms which exceed the given oppositions. They reveal the contradictions that any prevailing order wants to suppress, such as that help and violence go together."[231]

Castorf as Schmitt; Schmitt as Castorf. "To this end," wrote Anne Peter of the *Morgenpost*, "Castorf shreds his younger self [or ego] in the form of a life-size doll. Deconstruction of former beliefs—it could hardly be clearer."[232]

Or could it? True, the doll is a fossil from an earlier era—Bronnen's *Rhineland Rebels* from the 1992–93 inaugural season. True, the doll takes quite a beating. But I take Castorf's casting choice here to be an invitation to engage with and stage Castorf himself, as director, as producer, *as* "bungler and bluffer." In other words, he is willing and ready to put his own modes of (theatrical) production on the dissection table. And he is willing to reexamine (and perform) the ways these modes function by engaging with—though not trying to tame or incorporate—the uncertainties, even the violence, inherent in the modes themselves. "Theater for me," he explains, "is the attempt at the synthesis of—strictly stated—the impossible. I begin from the individual, whose life has very strange combinations. . . . In doing so, what matters most for me is the sphere of production, and I try to organize it so that it is a model of free labor."[233]

Castorf's self-staging is thus a way of staging the kinds of productions he hopes he has been making, as well as staging the ways and means by which those productions are themselves made. His self-staging points to a mode of making that is both collaborative and antagonistic. Dependent, vulnerable, generous, but also aggressive and caustic, he does not exempt himself (or his collaborators) from the challenges they wish to impose on their audience. And most important, Castorf's over-the-top, Tarantino-style revenge fantasy points to a mode of theater making that makes sure always to keep one principle in mind: fun.[234] Castorf returns to this point again and again and again:

> Because the basic mystery, as I said, is a very simple one: happy work. . . . The fun that I and a few other people have when we make theater—this was always completely independent of the expectations of this society-apparatus; it was equally anticapitalist and anticommunist; we practiced a freedom that was directed against usurpation and ideological assertions. . . . The conditions of production should be such that the producers do their work willingly, and the product will look accordingly—that was always my impulse to make theater. . . . One should really preserve the carnival spirit and defend it ruthlessly. I'm not afraid of the country fair when it has something to do with the life of the time.[235]

In the rehearsal room and on the stage, then, he suspends (while also most certainly embracing) a certain kind of hierarchy—committed to allow the process and its hiccups to inform the work. He hardly plans. He begins rehearsal, wine spritzer in hand, unsure what will come next . . . until it comes. He screams plenty. And if conflicts with actors or others arise, he works to integrate that into the process and the product. He—notoriously—works with an ensemble of actors that others think are "wrong" for a particular role, or better yet, that others think should not be actors in the first place.[236] He also works with many nonactors—the *Lehrstück* chorus is a case in point. As he elaborates elsewhere:

> I try to create successful productions as a model for free working conditions. Conditions that are generated *internally* and not controlled by the *outside*. This is an old Marxist and also anarchic thought. The images that spring from such work are colored slightly with anarchism and nihilism. They crisscross each other, there are no clear thoughts. Maybe the necessary analytical powers are missing too. These may be accurate criticisms, and people do have problems with productions like these. But they remain indestructible because the secret basic recipe is so simple. It's fun work. And that, in principle, is political.[237]

It is clear, however, that Castorf's is no *mere* anarchic thought. So-called fun is not just about some antianalytical, abstract negation of those limiting structural conditions—of the state-stage or capital more broadly. It is not just about denying the bore, or the oppressive expectations, of that dreadful "outside," and replacing it with some more amusing, unpredictable "inside." Rather, fun—in all its inherent and unpredictable perversities—is itself a kind of infrastructural counterpart to Castorf's refunctionary method of blurring, or even exploding, the bounds between "outside" and "in," between "you" and "us." In other words, fun is an essential element of Castorf's unique art of institutional dis/avowal. To have a good time is, for him, a deeply politicized and dutiful practice of determinate negation, a way of both engaging and undoing—or undoing *by* engaging—the means and relations of production in which he has chosen to inevitably enmesh himself. "I am also the leader of a production institution," Castorf explains:

> I have the opportunity to provide work for two or three hundred people. . . . In times when it is no longer taken for granted in Germany and Europe that everyone can work, it is a privilege to provide work. And it is very strange that this work is not mere wage labor for these people, but that this artistic work joins them together in another way, also politically: joins people together who previously were Left, Right, old, young, ugly, and beautiful.[238]

One must construct and facilitate "conditions of production" that make you "unimpeachable";[239] in doing so, he claims, you "frame a utopia, practicing the future within the existing conditions of the present."[240]

Simultaneously, the "Clown Scene" functions as a second-level check on—or negation of—Castorf's project of perpetual negation. He is all too aware and afraid of the risk of stagnation—a risk that presents itself from all sides. On the one hand, Castorf is most conscious of his status as so-called star director, most aware of the place he has secured in a long tradition of German *Regietheater*. And he is mindful of the danger of resting on these laurels in moments when inspiration is lacking. For this reason, he must imagine himself as "die kleinste Grösse"; he must subject himself to a brutal reminder—with veritable saws—that *all* is in perpetual flux, and that theater making is a process of mutual respect, of interdependence, of "help," even when it hurts. "I must now be careful that I do not feel like too much is lost through routine," he explains. "One has to fight a lot more for these conditions of fun, and not be fixated on the effect of the press, the Theatertreffen and prizes, those things that censor and monitor taste, depriving you of the right to meddle in your own mental state."[241] On the other hand, the prodigious proliferation of alternative or independent infrastructural strategies for devising performance outside of the state-stage poses, for Castorf, an equally pernicious risk. Though the often antiauthoritarian and nonhierarchical mission statements of these free-scene groups can sound very much like his own utopian conditions of production, Castorf asserts, and reasserts, that even with all its radical antiauthoritarian impulses, the Volksbühne will not, *must* not seek to revive an empty or even oppressive *Mitbestimmung* (collective self-management). Just as he worries about a ubiquitous, new American mentality of capitalist efficiency, his experiences in the former East make him equally wary of the ideological affirmation and harmonizing consciousness that can emerge in the attempt to install so-called horizontal structures—even at the theater. No, Castorf also likes to say, most polemically, theater is always a dictatorship.[242] We must always acknowledge what can be gained from "dictatorial thinking," he asserts, "though it must always [also] be called into question by those who practice it"[243]—called into question, again, with veritable saws or even with a veritable, albeit provocative, non sequitur.

◆ ◆ ◆

The pilot, who has returned to the tent dressed in a "decadent" shiny white ball gown, is driven under the piano as the rest of the ensemble sings, over and over again, most celebratorily: "Now is his smallest dimension attained. [Jetzt hat er / Seine kleinste Grösse erreicht.]"[244] The pilot crawls down the aisle on her hands and knees, and when the singing stops, she jumps to her feet and whines, "As a Jew, I have a problem with all of this Bolshevistic monkey business. I love Hindemith."[245] She runs to the piano and grabs a book of sheet music from Stefan, the conductor. He begins to play, and she begins singing, no, *belting* a most dynamic and virtuosic aria—but by Wolfgang Rihm, not Hindemith. As the aria comes to an end, one of the former clowns marches into the center of the space wearing a harness and dragging a military parachute behind her. She confronts the pilot, getting right in her face: "You," she grumbles, "on the tractor or under it?" The two stare at one another for a moment, quite uncomfortably. Finally, Stefan speaks up, breaking the tension: "Ladies, please. Don't fight." Without hesitation the rest of the ensemble smiles and

Lehrstück: "Now is his smallest dimension attained." Photograph copyright
© Thomas Aurin.

shouts, "Too late, Stefan!" With that, he begins to sing, "In the town where I was
born / Lived a man who sailed to sea. . . ." And then, as if nothing had transpired
over the previous seventy-five minutes, the entire ensemble—including the pilot and
the clown—begins to hop up and down, singing along with Stefan. Dreaming of a
sea of green and life beneath the waves, the group hops, claps, and chants its way
out of the tent.

With a final intertext in this highly intertextual evening, it seems that Castorf has stepped away from Brecht and Hindemith and stumbled upon music
critic Peter Doggett. In his book *There's a Riot Going On*, Doggett diagnoses
the famous Beatles track as "culturally empty, . . . a kind of Rorschach test
for radical minds."[246] Doggett quotes Mary Hughes, whose reminiscences
about the anti–Vietnam War protests in Berkeley in the late 1960s seem to
have inspired this final moment of dis/avowal backstage at the Volksbühne:
"The polarisation is much more acute. . . . [F]or the most part we are flipping
the bird to the surrealistic construct in which we live. You know you're going
to get the icepick and soon: so . . . you retaliate with something they don't
understand, you exit en masse singing 'Yellow Submarine.' "[247]

Castorf's art of polarization, of avowal *and* disavowal, however, also
calls polarization itself into question at every turn. In other words, his active
mobilization of the seeming non sequitur serves as a critique of the very
logics that presume to dictate what follows logically and what does not.

Castorf's flip of the bird, his art of retaliation, engages deeply with the varied institutions wielding those dreaded icepicks (and ruling logics) as the means by which he seeks to rethink them. Castorf's Volksbühne, then, was an institution that could accommodate—and must accommodate—both the Rihm aria and the Bolshevist bombast in the same breath. It was one that could and must accommodate both the tractor and what lies beneath it as a means of moving beyond both in order to refunction the state-stage as an essential and ever-evolving public institution—even as a dialectical institution with its mutable and irreconcilable opposites. In every moment of tenuous multigenre mash-up, of miscommunication, of formal and organizational experiment, and lack of consequence, then, Castorf denies us the possibility of any grand sublation, any resolution of conflict between supposed poles in constant tension. And in this particular concluding segment, he flourishes—if only for a brief moment—in the paradoxically *harmonic nonidentity* of John, Paul, George, and Ringo, touting always the immanence of nonreconciliation:

> As we live a life of ease
> Every one of us has all we need
> Sky of blue and sea of green
> In our yellow submarine.[248]

Part 2

✦

Free-Scenes

Chapter 3

✦

Haunted Infrastructures of Public Memory

Performing the Many Facades of the Palast der Republik

Today, founding a building or re-founding something like a city implies a responsibility which has itself to be redefined. What is a responsibility? In what way are we responsible? ... The only law of this re-foundation, if it is the re-foundation of an already existing city bearing the name of Berlin, is the law of Berlin. Berlin is the law. Something named Berlin is the law and we are before the law in that case. This means that being responsible doesn't mean being responsible to something present. We are responsible for "past" Berlin and the many layers, proper names, works, this memory entails. We are responsible to all of them—all of those ghosts—neither living nor simply dead.

—Jacques Derrida, "The Berlin City Forum" (1992)

Airships sway gently
Steel above the canals
The bulging world reflected here
Illuminated by ideas.
Between the facades
We want to discharge
The power of what
We made true together.

—Jan Theiler aka Pastor Leumund, lyrics to the hymn sung in the "Parliament" of the Republic of Facades (2004)

(Infra)structural Memory

On July 4, 2002, members of the German National Parliament, or Bundestag, convened to cast their votes for and against a most controversial proposal.

The infamous Palast der Republik, former East Berlin cultural center and seat of the East German Parliament, would be razed to the ground. In its place, the Prussian Imperial Palace, or Stadtschloss, which had been razed by this same East German government in 1950, would be rebuilt. Sort of.

In November 2000, an International Expert Commission was appointed to provide members of Parliament with a proposal to redesign, refunction, and finance the redevelopment of the "historic center" of Berlin. These so-called city-planning experts envisioned "a novel concept for the twenty-first century," "a concept with cultural-political charisma and strong urban impact."[1] The proposed multipurpose complex, which they called the Humboldt Forum, would function as a "place of dialogue," a place that would "integrate" arts, world cultures, and the sciences. It would include spaces for the Prussian Cultural Heritage Foundation, Humboldt University, the State Library of Berlin, and a large convention center that would present films, theater, music, and dance performances, and house a multitude of restaurants. Finally, it would include an exhibit to "appreciate the historical and architectural significance of the former Schloss and the Palast der Republik and present this information to the public in a vivid manner."[2] The Palast itself could not be preserved, the commission claimed, for reasons of "urban design," but as consolation the "tradition of this people's house would live on in the newly erected building."[3]

By the time the Expert Commission's proposal made its way to the floor of the Parliament, however, the use and function, or *Nutzung*, of the new complex had been sharply sidelined. The Parliament was concerned only with the aesthetic future—the face—of the historic city center and the money that would be used to finance its facades. The proposal on which the politicians would cast their votes read as follows:

> Concerning architectural design, the German Bundestag assents to the recommendation of the [Expert] Commission to rebuild the baroque *facades* of the north, west, and south sides of the former Stadtschloss, in addition to the [Andreas] Schlüter courtyard. The actual architectural design of the building, in particular the relationship between *use* and interior design, will have to be decided upon by a future design competition. This *realization* of history in the historic center of Berlin not only provides a bridge to the architectural styles in the immediate surrounding . . . but is also more likely to allow for the mobilization of private capital.[4]

Just what history was to be realized in the re-creation of three facades and a courtyard? Berlin's historic center is, after all, a burdened landscape haunted by five hundred years of civic history. In the mid-fifteenth century, Friedrich II of Brandenburg erected a fortress on the site from which he would assert the authority of the Hohenzollern family dynasty over the adjacent towns of Berlin and Cölln. Over the next hundred and fifty years, Hohenzollern monarchs reworked the fortress into an ornate Renaissance palace. But it was King Friedrich I of Prussia and his wife, Sophie Charlotte, who financed an enormous and elaborate baroque expansion and completion of the imperial palace between 1698 and 1706. Architect Andreas Schlüter undertook the renovation, which included the landmark ornate yellow facade, new wings, and a new courtyard. As Brian Ladd writes, "[Schlüter's] design has been praised as a masterwork—even *the* masterwork—of northern baroque architecture, effusively sculptural but more restrained than the better-known baroque of southern Europe. Its long and ornate facades, four stories and 100 feet high, established the final scale of the palace and—it has been argued—of all Berlin architecture."[5] Johann Friedrich Eosander von Göthe carried on Schlüter's momentum and style with a second courtyard and extension, bringing the massive rectangular landmark to completion at 192 meters long by 116 meters wide.[6]

Kaiser Wilhelm II was the last monarch to reside in and rule from the Schloss. The November Revolution of 1918 drove him from his throne and into exile in Holland. Around 4:30 P.M. on November 9, Karl Liebknecht appeared on one of Eosander's balconies to inaugurate the short-lived German Free Socialist Republic.[7] The Schloss received little attention during the subsequent rise and fall of the Weimar Republic and National Socialism. And by the end of the Second World War, the once grand facades lay mostly in ruins, bearing witness to the horror and destruction that was Berlin.

The remains of the Schloss became a site of ideological struggle once again in the early days of the German Democratic Republic. In the eyes of Walter Ulbricht and other leaders of the newly established East German government, the structure embodied a troubled history of monarchy, Prussian militarism, capitalist economy, failed revolution, and ultimately Nazi Fascism. At the Third Party Congress in July 1950, Ulbricht announced his plans to demolish what was left of the building: "The centre of our capital . . . must become a large space of demonstration on which our people's will to fight and rebuild can find expression."[8] The Schloss did not fit into the image of the new socialist capital yet to be built, and the remaining ruins were razed.

However, Erich Honecker, who took over leadership of the Socialist Unity Party in 1971, had grand plans for the plot where the Schloss once stood. A very different palace—of the republic—would serve a dual purpose: it would be the official seat of the Volkskammer, the People's Parliament of the GDR, and it would function as the social and cultural center of East Berlin. Construction of Honecker's most ornate Palazzo Prozzo (Ostentatious Palace), as it was later called, took place over a thousand days between 1973 and 1976. Chief architect Heinz Graffunder strove to create a structure that exuded "a bright, effusive elegance,"[9] with a golden orange facade of thermal glass that glistened in the sun by day and glowed (by means of inner illumination) by night. The lavish interior featured an abundance of globular glass chandeliers, seventeen thousand square meters of black-and-white psychedelic-swirling marble, sixteen escalators, sixty-four bathrooms, and five thousand pieces of futuristic, chrome-plated furniture, countered stylistically by banquettes of tufted velvet. There was a five-hundred-seat congress hall for the Volkskammer, which met infrequently and had little public visibility and even less power. The rest of "Erich's Light Shop" was conceived as a multifunctional, state-subsidized community center: a five-thousand-seat auditorium, used for sporting events as well as popular and musical performances; a small albeit innovative theater in the basement; thirteen restaurant options, bars, bowling allies, the best telephone service to the West, and meeting halls well suited for weddings, graduations, and other celebrations.[10] Of course, the choice of location for Honecker's new Palast der Republik was no accident—the leaders of the GDR would also "realize" a particular and partial history that began with Karl Liebknecht in 1918. In August 1990, however, the East German Parliament gathered in the Palast and voted to join the Federal Republic of Germany. A few weeks later, just before this same Parliament—and the whole East German state—ceased to exist, an inspection found large amounts of asbestos in the building, which was immediately closed to the public. It would remain closed until 2004.

So what history was to be "realized"—or not—in the re-creation of three facades and a courtyard on such haunted ground? What kind of memory and strategic forgetting was encouraged by this controversial policy proposal? What is the relation between facade and function, between aesthetic and apparatus, between structure and infrastructure in this attempt to realize or re-create history? And just whose history is at stake? Whose history is realized or re-created by a *public* project that depends expressly on a "mobilization of private capital"? And history, it would seem, doesn't come cheap: the Expert Commission estimated the costs of the entire project at a whopping 670 million euros, only 230 million of which would come from public funds. Another 80 million euros would be raised from private philanthropists to finance the realization of the historical facades, and the remaining 360 million euros would come from private investors promised a profit down the road.[11] A broad swath of 384 members from all political parties (except Die Linke, or The Left) affirmed the proposal.

In an essay published in 2005, Shannon Jackson began to explicate the terms of her "infrastructural politics of performance," which I discussed in the introduction.[12] Already in this work, Jackson illuminates an art of "infrastructural imagination" in which performance "*induce[s]* a reminder of our interdependency with the operations of the public, the economic, and the social." Performance, she continues, induces an "awareness of a shared material relation."[13] Though many of Jackson's questions about the ways aesthetic structures and material structures "engage rather than oppose each other"[14] would carry over into her 2011 book *Social Works*, her orientation in the 2005 essay is somewhat different. As she explains, her "preoccupation [here is] with the way performance and *memory* interact with the apparatus of art-making."[15] To chart this "interaction," Jackson puts forth a term—one in her essay's title, in fact—that dropped out of *Social Works* but around which I want to orient this chapter: the "performance of infrastructural memory." Jackson asks, What is the "conceptual possibility of a tangible story and a material remembering"? How might one use "performance to expose the material and environmental enmeshment of artists and audiences, of remem-berers and listeners, of citizens and civic space"?[16]

In this chapter, I too am interested in the "shared operations"[17] of perfor-mance, of memory, of varied institutional apparatuses and physical structures. I also ask: How can memory be infrastructural? And how might performance *induce* such an infrastructural memory? My purpose here, however, is to shift the focus when asking these questions. Whereas Jackson works predomi-nantly to bring an "infrastructural awareness" to performance and memory, I chart the ways performance and memory animate public institutions. This shift in directionality, I claim, helps us account for the relations among built physical structures, the varied institutional infrastructures invested in and around those structures, and the performance and memory work at play within both structure and infrastructure.

The context for and site of this inquiry is the haunted space of the Palast der Republik—and the ongoing realization of the Schloss. After its closure in 1990, the Palast quickly emerged as one of the most controversial institu-tions of public memory in reunified Berlin. It became a site of heated cultural policy, architectural, and city-planning debates and protests in the early 1990s and continuing into the present, even though the Palast was razed in 2006.[18] These debates set the stage, just after the millennium, for a series of interdisciplinary performance experiments with *and* in the shell of the former Palast, which aimed to critique its planned demolition but also to investigate collectively the possibilities of a new kind of public performance institution in the center of the "new" Berlin. This chapter, then, registers a shift of focus in this book toward different arts of institutional dis/avowal. Here I explore institutional models of performance emerging in Berlin's inde-pendent or "free" theater scene (*freie Szene*) that understand themselves to be working outside of—albeit always in relation to—the stage-stage. Volks-palast was a durational project staged by a collective of free-scene artists amid the ruins of the abandoned Palast in 2004. By examining the project's organizing principles, as well as several performance events staged as part of its three-month run, I argue that Volkspalast enacted a "hauntological" mode of infrastructural reimagining, one that posited an alternative vision—outside the purview of the state-stage—for how a public arts institution might realize history and perform memory: looking both backward for inspi-ration in a history that might not have been *and* forward to one that might still be.

But first, a ghost story.

Whither Marxism?

This was indeed the haunting question of the 1990s. What was to become
of East Berlin, East Germany, the whole of Eastern Europe? What was to
become of its state apparatuses? Of its built structures? Its culture? Its history? In Germany, as in many other parts of the former East, power and
humiliation campaigns were launched to rename (and in some cases destroy)
buildings, landmarks, streets, and so on.[19] Under the moniker of reunification, and amid the catchy rhetoric of amicable partnership (even marriage),
a formerly eastern citizenry watched as many of their systems, customs, and
memories were integrated—some say subsumed—into a more powerful West
that claimed it had won the Cold War. As Francis Fukuyama would soon
proclaim, history had reached its end.[20]

The German reunification treaty dictated that Berlin would once again be
the nation's capital. As might be expected, the historic center of town came
into focus as a site of ideological struggle after so many years of division. To
the question "Whither Marxism?" then, Joachim Fest, a conservative editor
at the *Frankfurter Allgemeine Zeitung*, provided a cutting answer:

> Stronger than any other argument in favor of rebuilding are those
> reasons that led to the demolition of the Schloss in 1950. They
> wanted a Red Square, a site for submissive gestures of devotion pre-
> sented on a large scale and originating in a foreign imaginary that
> was as eastern as it was bygone. The global political debate that is
> now behind us was concerned not least of all with preventing the
> advance of this conception of domination. If the demolition of the
> Schloss was supposed to be a symbol of the victory [of this domina-
> tion], the reconstruction would be the symbol of its failure.[21]

In early 1992, Wilhelm von Boddien, a businessman from Hamburg, answered
Fest's plea by launching the allegedly nonprofit Development Association for
the Berlin Stadtschloss.[22] In line with Fest, Boddien claimed that "the reconstruction of the Schloss, whose detonation and destruction became a symbol
of communist dictatorship" was also "a symbol of both a reclaimed German
unity and the power of democracy to restore and preserve culturally and
historically valuable buildings for posterity."[23] The association immediately
became the most active advocate for (as their website still claims) realizing
or "making history"[24] in the new Berlin: lobbying legislators, appealing to
private companies and wealthy individuals, and staging various events to
gain popular support for the demolition of the Palast and realization of the
Schloss.[25] The association achieved its first success in March 1993, when a
Joint Committee of the Bundestag and Berlin Senate announced its decision
to demolish the Palast "in order to prevent health hazards" from the asbestos
contamination.[26]

In spite of protests—ten thousand strong[27]—against the Joint Committee's decision, the association pressed on in the spring of 1993 with preparations for a most spectacular action-cum-attraction, aimed expressly at influencing public opinion about the new *face* of Berlin's historic center (funded by Mercedes Benz): French artist Catherine Feff was commissioned to stage a life-size, trompe l'oeil re-creation of the Schloss on its original site. Feff's crew hung massive painted canvases on an immense three-sided web of scaffolding. The sunny yellow-ocher canvases were composed with great precision to re-create the windows, moldings, stonework, balconies, and other details of the Schloss's baroque facades. The team also erected a very large mirror that stood flush against the now abandoned Palast der Republik—creating the illusion of a Schloss that extended well beyond its original dimensions and barreled through the Palast's shiny orange exterior. Inside Feff's *Schlossattrappe*, or castle mock-up, Boddien's association hosted an exhibition on the "history" of the Schloss and its function in Berlin, which attracted thousands of visitors every day, at 9 DM per ticket. In Boddien's estimation, "The facade and the exhibitions promoted new reasoning about the architecture of the city center by means of a *creative dispute*. Most important was that the sovereign, the citizens of Berlin, got to have their say as the owners of the space."[28]

The trompe l'oeil project staged—perhaps even induced—a particular kind of infrastructural memory that structured many of the arguments at play, particularly in the pro-Schloss (but even in a segment of the pro-Palast) camp. The mirror itself encouraged the violent act of retribution, of strategic revenge, so crucial to the logic of Fest's plea to reconstruct the Schloss. Ulbricht's attempt to erase German history was mirrored here by the visual albeit illusionary destruction of the Palast. The mirror also permitted, even enabled, a certain re-vision of history, simultaneously nodding to its conscious fabrication. In other words, a glance in the mirror revealed a mocked-up Schloss that extended beyond the dimensions of the original, thus encouraging a subjunctive infrastructural imagining of a history in which the Palast and GDR had never existed—even a history in which the Nazis had never risen to power. Annette Ahme, the head of the Society for Historical Berlin, remarked:

> Everyone, whether left or right, wants a beautiful city, apart from a few intellectuals who say we must continue to suffer from our Nazi-era sins and that these must remain visible. . . . But it makes no sense to overload the city with these pedagogical things that have every building and empty lot proclaim forever, "You evil Germans. You made the war and now you must put up with an ugly city." The city must be beautiful so that people will be happy and they will not repeat these mistakes.[29]

The intricacy, "beauty," and historical accuracy of Feff's facades were also at the heart of a (more academic) "Critical Reconstruction" discourse—championed by the Berlin Senate's building director, Hans Stimmann—which aimed to reconstruct not just a lost identity and a lost Schloss but also the look, the feel, the density, the spatial organization, the land use, and the private ownership structures of the historic center of prewar Berlin. This form of "revanchist urban planning," argues Simone Hain, was "based on a concept of historicity which perceive[d] the post-war history as abnormal, a-historical and destructive."[30]

The pro-Schloss camp brought together a range of unlikely interlocutors: "Conservatives dreaming of reparation of German history with a handsome and somewhat less compromised symbol of unity—businessmen hoping to restore the historical center of Berlin . . .—as well as leading historians, Social-Democrat politicians and liberal journalists."[31] While the nature of the arguments varied in quality and along the political spectrum, the collective calls to reconstruct the Schloss shared what Svetlana Boym calls a "restorative nostalgia" for a history that is itself a kind of facade.[32] According to Boym, "Restoration . . . signifies a return to the original stasis, to the prelapsarian moment. The past . . . is not a duration but a perfect snapshot. Moreover, the past is not supposed to reveal any signs of decay; it has to be freshly painted in its 'original image' and remain eternally young."[33] As restorative nostalgics, pro-Schloss supporters hoped to realize a wobbly scaffold, an uncritical and wishful history, without much interest in its messy interiorities, its apparatuses and infrastructures, its varied perspectives, or its functionality. And they charged an entry fee to boot.

Ironically, many of the arguments from pro-Palast supporters in the early 1990s relied on thought structures similar to those of their opponents. Boym recounts, "In both cases the nostalgia [was] based on a sense of loss that endow[ed] the building[s] with a powerful melancholic aura."[34] While the pro-Palast camp did not seek to "restore" the former GDR regime per se, their brand of nostalgia was also one of selective memory and preservation: the Palast must remain as a visual—but not functional—symbol of a past that must not be overwritten. This particular variant of "Ostalgia"[35]—quite different from a more "reflective" Ostalgia to which I will return later—was driven by a politics of appearance and visibility (via protests, marches, rallies, and so on) and of facades. The facade and structure of the Palast—but not its organizational infrastructure—must be preserved, they argued, as a material trace, a referent for East German collective memory. Karen Till explains:

> People become obsessed with material remnants because the past is a fiction: what remains are memories that are defined by our mourning for that which can no longer be present. We try to preserve memory by creating traces of a past that by definition can never be present. When places are made and understood in this way, their perceived material or emotive presence may seem comforting in the present moment because they are interpreted as giving the past a material form.[36]

And of course, there was an equally healthy dose of politicized finger point-ing that emanated from the pro-Palast camp. Asbestos was a problem that could be solved, they claimed. After all, there had been no talk of razing the International Congress Center in West Berlin, which had been built to the same standards in the 1970s and was found to contain similar levels of asbestos.[37] The Palast had been condemned for a different brand of contami-nation altogether: to rid Berlin, and greater Germany, of the sickness of "real existing socialism," to rid Berlin of the "specters of Marx."[38] For as Foreign Minister Joschka Fischer would later reflect on the priorities of the fledgling Berlin Republic, the *new* Berlin is a city whose "ghosts have been tamed."[39]

The Spectral Turn

On April 22, 1993—just a month after the Joint Committee's decision to raze the Palast—theorists from around the globe gathered at the University of California, Riverside, for an interdisciplinary conference titled "Whither Marxism? Global Crises in International Perspective." Jacques Derrida was invited to deliver the opening plenary address and provide a reflection on the "specters of Marx," "something he had not yet been able to do in a sus-tained and systematic way in print."[40] *Specters of Marx*—the title of Derrida's address and subsequent monograph—took on the school of Fukuyama in an effort to demonstrate the frivolity of a claim that would dare postulate the end of history:

> In the experience of the end, in its insistent, instant, always immi-nently eschatological coming, at the extremity of the extreme today, there would thus be announced the future of what comes. More than ever, for the future-to-come can announce itself as such and in its purity only on the basis of a *past end*: beyond, *if that's possible*, the last extremity. If that's possible, *if there is any* future, but how can one suspend such a question or deprive oneself of such a reserve without *concluding in advance*, without reducing in advance both the future and its chance?[41]

In turn, Derrida posits an alternative, nonteleological, noneschatological mode of historiography, one that refuses strict boundaries between past, pres-ent, and future. Making room for time that is "out of joint"—through a close reading of Hamlet's encounter with the specter of his father—Derrida posits an alternative "*politics* of memory, of inheritance, and of generations."[42] Der-rida's is a theory of ghosts, of "*hauntology*"[43]—a theory of untold stories and forgotten discourses, which refuses authorized events and is necessarily per-spectival. As he explains, "The question is indeed 'whither?' Not only whence comes the ghost but first of all is it going to come back? Is it not already beginning to arrive and where is it going? What of the future? The future can only be for ghosts. And the past."[44] "I'll follow thee," whispers Derrida-via-Hamlet to the ghost, and many others would soon follow suit. As Jeffrey Weinstock argues, Derrida's interest in the ghostly marked the broader "spectral turn"[45] in contemporary theory:

> Because ghosts are unstable interstitial figures that problematize dichotomous thinking, it perhaps should come as no surprise that phantoms have become a privileged poststructuralist academic trope. Neither living nor dead, present nor absent, the ghost functions as the paradigmatic deconstructive gesture, the "shadowy third" or trace of an absence that undermines the fixedness of such binary oppositions. As an entity out of place in time, as something from the past that emerges into the present, the phantom calls into question the linearity of history.[46]

April 1993, however, was not the first opportunity Derrida had to reflect publicly on the "whither" question. In 1991, he was invited to participate in a public conversation about city-planning strategies for the future of Berlin—and on the spectral as well. As the quotation with which I began this chapter makes clear, Derrida blatantly rejects any architectural or planning strategy that would attempt to "tame" the ghosts that roam. Instead, he explains that we share a responsibility to these ghosts; they constitute a law that must guide us. In a most Kafkaesque valence, Derrida proclaims that to build a building or to rebuild a city requires us to stand "before the law," to greet the many ghosts of Berlin.[47]

Alongside Derrida, architect Daniel Libeskind was among the most outspoken critics of the quality of thinking inherent in the planning conversations for reunified Berlin, including those surrounding the Schlossplatz. "The identity of Berlin," Libeskind insists, "cannot be reformed in the ruins of history or in the illusory reconstruction of an arbitrary selected past."[48] He sees the pro-Schloss (and even pro-Palast) arguments as revisionist and abusive of Berlin's complicated—and often violent—history: "That's a haunting thing for those who know something about German history. I don't call it fascist, but I call it very reactionary and very pessimistic."[49] Like Derrida, Libeskind outlines a certain responsibility to honor Berlin's ghosts, to struggle with difficult and conflicted memories, and to articulate the messiness of this difference. "To produce meaningful architecture," he asserts, "is not to erase history but to deal with it."[50] The decision to rebuild the Schloss, he argues further, is a violent attempt on the part of cultural politicians to "suppress and politically legislate against other histories and against the present,"[51] a decision that parodies the memory, the traditions, and the citizenry of East Berlin. In addition to his discursive critique, Libeskind submitted design entries in the competitions held to determine the future of two major (formerly eastern) hubs: Potsdamer Platz and Alexanderplatz. And while his designs were not accepted, they worked to articulate what architectural theorist Mark Wigley terms an "architecture of deconstruction,"[52] one that stands in stark contrast to Stimmann's so-called Critical Reconstruction.

Libeskind proposes what I call a *structural hauntology*, an architectural practice and mode of city planning that stages a different method of doing history. His "deconstructivist architecture"[53] understands the spectral as structural condition and incorporates a Derridean understanding of history and memory into its structural plans. Libeskind insists on a politics and a building practice that value more than appearance and visibility, and that perform an architectural critique of a metaphysics of presence: "The visible is not the only context of the new planning; one has also to deal with the invisible, the annihilated couriers of culture, the true 'spirit of Berlin.' "[54] In place of reconstructed facades, he posits the practice of negative space, the practice of what he calls the *void*. The void is not a pure, abstract negation, Libeskind claims, but rather an interstitial space, an "extraordinary"[55] absence that invites the ghosts of Berlin to roam as they see fit. Libeskind aims to build "spiritual site[s]," which recognize that the "torn pieces of history never preexisted as a whole, neither in the ideal Berlin nor in the real one."[56] Instead, these sites should embody "the precariousness of Berlin's destiny, which [they] should mirror, fracture, and at the same time transgress."[57]

Libeskind's conception of rupture and discontinuity—a "public space for the void"[58]—pervades much of his work and many of his proposed designs for various Berlin sites.[59] With the green-lit construction of the Jewish Museum in 1992, he had an opportunity to erect physically a version of his voids and to explore his structural hauntology concretely.[60] For Andreas Huyssen, Libeskind's Jewish Museum is *the* exemplary building erected in the "new" Berlin: "While all the other major building sites in Berlin today are inevitably haunted by the past," Huyssen writes, "only Libeskind's building attempts to articulate memory and our relationship to it in its very spatial organization."[61] The Jewish Museum is a structure that zigzags across a so-called void-line—"a thin slice of empty space that crosses the path of the zigzag structure at each intersection and that reaches from the bottom of the building to the top."[62] This empty space is not accessible to museum visitors but can be viewed from bridges on every level of the structure. In addition, Libeskind constructed what he called a "voided void,"[63] a concrete tower dedicated specifically to a commemoration—for lack of a better word—of the Holocaust, which is open to visitors. These voids constitute for Libeskind a memory (and performance) of the "permanent presence of absence"[64] of Jews in Berlin. As Huyssen notes, "[The void] points to an absence that can never be overcome, a rupture that cannot be healed, and that can certainly not be filled with museal stuff. Its fundamental epistemological negativity cannot be absorbed into the narratives that will be told by the objects and installations in the showrooms of the museum."[65]

While, for Huyssen, Libeskind's construction epitomizes an "architecture of memory"[66] and enables a structural hauntology, Derrida would not so easily concede. In 1992, Derrida was again invited to Berlin, this time to take part in a public conversation with Libeskind about the Jewish Museum's design and function. On the one hand, Derrida generously complimented Libeskind's project: "How can one respond to such a presentation? It was breathtaking."[67] On the other hand, he was quick to caution Libeskind about making the void synonymous with the spectral. Derrida argued that the void might not perform the function Libeskind hopes, might not constitute an epistemological negativity or a critique of presence. Libeskind's void, even the void as concept, Derrida explained, may also affirm, reify, structure the very thing it hopes to critique. By employing the void as a means of refusing to represent the nonrepresentable—in the case of the Jewish Museum, the insanity of Shoah—Libeskind constructed a space that "is historically determined or circumscribed; and it is not, for example, the indeterminate place in which everything takes place."[68] In place of the void, Derrida proposed a different term, *chora* or *khôra*—"place" in ancient Greek (χώρα)—which he borrows from Plato. The *chora*, he explains, "is a place that is neither divine nor human, neither intelligible nor sensible, a place that precedes history and the inscription of Forms; and it challenges every dialectic between what is and what is not, between what is sensible and what is becoming. Yet this place, which receives all the Forms and which gives place to everything that is inscribed in the Forms, is not a void. Plato insists on that."[69] A void that represents is not really a void, Derrida cautioned. A void that is *built* is not really noneschatological. A void that fills the absence of presence with the presence of absence does not maintain a necessary tension between absence and presence but instead determines that relation. Julia Ng aptly glosses Derrida's critique: "Ultimately, the logic of the *khôra* . . . challenges one to rethink (i.e., philosophize) the way memorial architecture, and we as its spectators, relate to the 'preceding' conditions—the non-being, the non-present, yet nonanthropo-theological conditions—of its own construction."[70] Whether one is ultimately persuaded by the critique—and there are some, like Huyssen, who are not[71]—both Libeskind's void and Derrida's *chora* challenge us to continue investigating just what a structural hauntology might entail in practice. Both *chora* and void constitute a call for structures of public memory quite different from Feff and Boddien's restorative facades and demand that we continue to ask: Can a *built* structure embrace the temporal disjunctions of the spectral? Can a *built* structure enable its own disappearance? Can a *built* structure dis/avow itself?

Derrida's invocation of *chora* also challenges us to read another of his critical discourses into these questions about architecture and the spectral, about structure and hauntology. He invites us to think explicitly about performance. Derrida's conversations with a number of architects, including Libeskind,

Peter Eisenman, and Bernard Tschumi, have since inspired wide-ranging interdisciplinary discussions about a performative turn in architecture,[72] whereby architecture is considered the "event of spacing."[73] These architects are read as writers of space, provocateurs of the event. And this event, Derrida claims, "is subsumed in the very structure of the architectural apparatus: sequence, open series, narrativity, the cinematic, dramaturgy, choreography."[74] *Choreography*, of course—as Derrida points out—has been carried over from *chora*.[75] These performative architects, then, seek the ephemeral in the structural, instability in the material; they seek to write spaces, as Chris Salter explains, "no longer rooted to the earth but revolving, pulsing, swimming, crawling, and flying."[76] And they attempt, Salter continues, to "materialize . . . Derrida's literary techniques within the process of construction, . . . folding and twisting of structure and materials in an effort to achieve what Daniel Libeskind labeled as 'space [that] is not just one space, but a plurality and heterogeneity of spaces.' "[77] In other words, these architects are working to build structures that *induce* and house the comings and goings of the ghosts that haunt us.

And what of the infrastructures, the institutional apparatuses that structure and are structured by these voids, these "chora l works"?[78] How might a performance institution dis/avow itself by embracing the temporal disjunctions of the spectral? In an oft-neglected infrastructural moment in her oft-cited "ghost story"[79] from 1993, Peggy Phelan writes, "Institutions whose only function is to preserve and honor objects—traditional museums, archives, banks and to some degree, universities—are intimately involved in the reproduction of the sterilizing binaries of self/other, possession/dispossession, men/women which are increasingly inadequate formulas for representation. These binaries and their institutional upholders fail to account for that which cannot appear between these tight 'equations' but which nevertheless inform them."[80] Phelan suggests that these institutions, apparatuses, infrastructures—allergic to dialectics, to the ghostly, as they might be—should move beyond economies of preservation, beyond a politics of appearance, beyond a restorative nostalgia, and instead learn to value disappearance. She continues, "These institutions must invent an economy not based on preservation but one which is answerable to the consequences of disappearance."[81] Phelan sees the potential to rethink traditional institutional structures by means of the radically negative; she sees the possibility of shifting the way infrastructures value the visible, the "real," the built, the present. And performance is at the center of this rethinking. For Phelan, it seems, it is performance itself that induces—or at least enables the potential for—institutional disappearance and infrastructural hauntology.[82] In what follows, then, I explore how the ruins of the Palast der Republik served as a performative site both for remembering its conflicted (infra)structural histories *and* simultaneously for reimagining possible futures for a different kind of performance institution in the "new" Berlin.

Zwischennutzung: Volkspalast

Between 1998 and 2002, the Palast der Republik underwent a dramatic decontamination process. Bit by bit, piece by piece—and at great expense to the city—seven hundred tons of asbestos were removed.[83] By the time members of the Bundestag convened in July 2002 to cast their votes on the future of the Schlossplatz, the Palast stood as a bare skeleton of its former self. The giant mass of steel girders, exposed concrete, and signature golden, now tarnished and tagged facade stood in the middle of an open and poorly manicured space surrounded by parked cars and snack carts for passersby. Though the Bundestag decision made clear that the Palast would be razed eventually, it was entirely unclear just when that process would begin. Demolition would be costly, and the approved project hinged upon a great deal of private financing. Almost immediately, the federal minister of culture Julian Nida-Rümelin assembled a working group to attract private partners to fund the demolition and subsequent reconstruction. It became clear rather quickly, however, that this process would be very slow indeed. By October 2003, the working group announced a two-year moratorium. They remained adamant that the Palast should be demolished as soon as possible, but the precise time frame remained unclear.[84]

The Bundestag decision to realize the Humboldt Forum—and the subsequent realization that demolition was a ways off—also catalyzed a good deal of dreaming and coconspiring. A network of interdisciplinary artists and curators, far removed from Nida-Rümelin's working group, formed quickly and began developing alternative proposals for ways the Palast could be *used* while it awaited demolition:

> What uses and activities would be desirable to allow the site and the building to become a public space of the twenty-first century? What new spaces of communication does our society need? . . . How can the ambition for a major public project be implemented despite the lack of willingness to provide public resources? . . . Can a construction site turn into a cultural place? Is it possible to design something other than permanence in a symbolic space? Are public places still about duration, or can they be realized now more in the form of temporary events?[85]

For this group, the abandoned Palast, now reminiscent of a "ruin," held charm and mystery "loaded with myth and meaning."[86] In November 2002, the Urban Catalyst architecture studio hosted an exhibition at the Berlin Technical University to air publicly some of the different ideas for "temporary use," for *Zwischennutzung*, that had rushed to the fore in the previous months. And by early 2003, the group formed a nonprofit association to promote and pursue their proposals; they called themselves Zwischenpalastnutzung, or Temporary-Palast-Use.

As the name indicates, a primary goal of the new association was to shift the nature of the discussions around the Palast. Amelie Deuflhard, artistic director of the Sophiensæle free-scene performance space, who spearheaded the *Zwischennutzung* effort, explained, "The debate on the future of the Schlossplatz is primarily about facades. But I think that one should plan a house from the inside, from its *use*."[87] The initial plans for and debates about the Humboldt Forum were strangely one-dimensional, restorative, and concerned with the *face* of the historic center only: Schloss versus Palast. Temporary-Palast-Use worked to spark new kinds of discussions. Though the group submitted openly—albeit begrudgingly—to the inevitable destruction of the Palast, in the interim, they would explore new uses, and explicitly "temporary uses," of the space. Deuflhard continued, "Temporary use for me does not mean first and foremost to take advantage of ruins. It is more about cultural attitudes and creative input. The engine is a willingness to resist—to stand against the system, against bureaucracy, against creative poverty."[88] Here Deuflhard makes a first (infra)structural citation; she makes clear that Temporary-Palast-Use is attempting to remember and realize an alternative mode of organizing and occupying space that has a rich history in Berlin. Beginning in the late 1970s, amid a dynamic squatters movement, Berlin became a hub for alternative and creative uses of vacant spaces and abandoned buildings. This vibrant counterculture multiplied throughout the 1980s and exploded after the Wall came down, as former East Berliners headed West and many artists moved in.[89] The invocation of "temporary use," then, harks back to and attempts to rethink a countercultural critique of private property and bureaucratic (often hegemonic) institutional structures. Claire Colomb provides a helpful (geographical) précis:

> The key issue at stake in the discourse of the *Zwischennutzung* initiative was therefore the role of culture, arts and public space in a post-socialist inner city dominated by consumption spaces as well as in a capital city centre dominated by representational spaces. It challenges directly the commodification of social and cultural spaces in the inner city and the predominant logic of capitalist urban development in a post-Fordist economy by addressing the following question: "to whom the city, at its most exclusive and meaningful locations, should belong: to all and therefore to nobody in particular or to many different interests and therefore not to the majority any longer."[90]

The new association soon followed up with another exhibition of its ideas at the Council of State building, just one hundred meters from the Palast. The public resonance was immense: several thousand visitors and more than a hundred positive articles in various (international) press outlets.[91] This public excitement put a good deal of pressure on government officials to take the idea of temporary use seriously and simultaneously aroused a great deal of strategic skepticism. The center-right Christian Democratic Union (CDU) party and other staunch pro-Schloss supporters were dead set against a temporary use, as they were worried it would delay—or sidetrack—the already delayed plans for the Humboldt Forum. Günter Nooke, a CDU politician, exclaimed, "In Berlin, there is no shortage of kinky venues, and there is no urgent need for the artistic ventilation of the former seat of the GDR parliament."[92] Deuflhard and company pressed on ambitiously, recruiting the support of Berlin's culture senator Thomas Flierl and Adrienne Goehler, a former culture senator and head of the Hauptstadtkulturfonds Berlin, the Capital City Cultural Fund. Both Flierl and Goehler stepped up as active advocates for temporary use. Architect Benjamin Foerster-Baldenius—one of the temporary-users—recalls that era:

> It was a time when the cultural senator of Berlin was from the Linke Party. . . . Thomas is really—he's a good guy. And he sees crazy shit happening [and says], "Let's do it." And at that time the leader of the Hauptstadtkulturfonds was Adrienne Goehler, from the Green Party, and she is a freak too. . . . And Amelie Deuflhard is just a hardcore freak. She was putting her name on the line behind the craziest ideas.[93]

Before long, Flierl succeeded in arranging a meeting comprising Temporary-Palast-Use, those in the state and federal governments responsible for the Palast, the necessary building inspectors, experts, and artists. The goal of the meeting was to determine the conditions and parameters for a substantial cultural program in the Palast in 2004.

The meeting began with a "bomb":[94] the Palast *would* reopen in the spring of 2004 after a decade of closure. But not for Temporary-Palast-Use. The space had already been leased between March and June to a privately sponsored (and so-called politically neutral) exhibition of the famed terracotta army from the mausoleum of the First Qin Emperor. More challenging news followed: the State Opera had been forced to withdraw its financial support for any project moving forward, as its rigid state-stage budgetary structure would not allow it to assume the substantial monetary risk required to occupy the Palast. The Federal Property Office mandated that a GmbH, a more "flexible" limited-liability company, serve as a partner in the deal, since Temporary-Palast-Use was not capable of taking on the necessary financial responsibility. This constellation of bad news proved no deterrent, however. Instead, it catalyzed Deuflhard and Philipp Oswalt from Urban Catalyst to seek a third partner and coconspirator in dreaming up temporary possibilities for the Palast. Matthias Lilienthal, who had recently left the Volksbühne and become artistic leader of the Hebbel am Ufer theater complex, quickly agreed to join the team to—among other things—fulfill the GmbH requirement. After two years of struggle with political authorities, the wheels were greased: Berlin's two major free-scene performance venues—plus Oswalt's Urban Catalyst—would attempt to realize a new kind of temporary performance institution, a new kind of collective memorial (infra)structure. They called it People's Palace, or Volkspalast.

From August 20 to November 9, 2004, the former Palast der Republik was inaugurated anew: as ballroom, concert hall, conference center, theater, dance, and performance space, club, cinema, sporting arena, exhibition room, marketplace, and labyrinth. This People's Palace was an initial attempt to experiment temporarily with varied concepts of use, to explore the continued relevance of a multifunctional cultural center in the center of Berlin, and to address an audience that extended far beyond the "normal" festival or theater audience.[95]

The name Volkspalast was a strategic choice on the part of the organizers, for it engages a complex set of historical, (infra)structural associations that stretch beyond *Zwischennutzung* itself. The name draws on the ambiguous construction of the Palast der Republik as People's House (*Volkshaus*) and as Palace of Culture (*Kulturpalast*), yet also insists on playing between— and beyond—these concepts. As the Volkspalast program of events made clear to its many thousands of visitors, the idea of the people's house had emerged amid the mass industrialization and urbanization of nineteenth-century Europe. Toynbee Hall in London was the first of these public sites conceived both as a place for the needy and as a cultural, entertainment, and educational center for the working class. These "people's houses" worked to challenge a particular bourgeois understanding of culture and its classical institutional instantiations: museums, concert halls, operas, theaters, and so on. This "cultural emancipation" of the working class came to an end in Germany with the rise of National Socialism; rather, the people's houses became "temples of public activity" to monitor and enforce party allegiance. After the war, the Western nations lost interest (generally speaking) in such consolidated attempts at providing culture for the "whole" of society. The GDR, on the other hand, took the great culture palaces of the Soviet Union as a model and began to build "state-run gifts to the working nation." The Palast der Republik was heralded as the most spectacular "gift" of all: an open, community-oriented, and self-regulating place, independent of state intervention; a people's parliament and people's play space under one roof. The reality, of course, was quite different.[96]

Whereas the GDR had misused—and abused—ideas of the *Volkshaus* and *Kulturpalast*, the initiators of Volkspalast hoped to play productively with this controversial (infra)structural past. In fact, an express agenda of the Volkspalast project was to stage a complicated engagement with both the history and future of the Palast—in other words, to stage a critical engagement with the *whither* question. As the event's initiators explained, "The Palast der Republik is a gift from history, just waiting to be used. Stripped down to its skeleton, it represents a vacuum—an inimitable space. A place that thematizes

Volkspalast, August to November 2004. Photograph copyright © David Baltzer / bildbuehne.de.

Entering the Volkspalast. Photograph copyright © David Baltzer / bildbuehne.de.

the tension between past and future. A transitory space."[97] They hoped to erect a space of both memory and dream, and to shake up the strict bounds between them, for to engage one—so Derrida would claim—is immediately to engage the other. Volkspalast would forge a space of collective memory for a disparate East German citizenry and foreground the Palast as an indispensable part of the cultural life of Berlin. It would also liberate the Palast from its historical burden and provide a thought space, a *Denkraum*, for its future use. Thomas Flier argued, "The project for the cultural temporary use takes the skeleton of the Palast der Republik as something it *could* be: as a shell for a future with a dominantly public use—beyond the ideological confrontation between a retrospective GDR palace and an equally regressive Schloss. The cultural temporary use provides an urban laboratory in the center of the city, a transitory space: not for retrospection, but for prospective exploration."[98] And he continued elsewhere, "The future is not to be sought in the hereafter, let alone in the past, but developed from the fragmentary, uncertain, difficulties of the present."[99]

Volkspalast, then, worked to engage, and stage, a very different kind of (infra)structural memory. It explicitly refused "restorative nostalgia"—and restorative Ostalgia—and instead engaged and staged a version of what Svetlana Boym calls "reflective nostalgia." Reflective nostalgia is no longer concerned with a totalizing and inflexible reconstruction of the past; it is no longer only concerned with scaffolds and facades. Instead, reflective nostalgics "linger on ruins"[100]; they embrace flexibility over stasis, fragments of memory over ossified grand narratives, a critical use of irony (and sometimes humor) over a desperate earnestness and forced gravity. Boym explains:

> Nostalgics of the second [reflective] type are aware of the gap between identity and resemblance; the home is in ruins or, on the contrary, has been just renovated and gentrified beyond recognition. This defamiliarization and sense of distance drives them to tell their story, to narrate the relationship between past, present and future. Through such longing these nostalgics discover that the past is not merely that which doesn't exist anymore, but, to quote Henri Bergson, the past "might act and will act by inserting itself into a present sensation from which it borrows the vitality." The past is not made in the image of the present or seen as foreboding of some present disaster; rather the past opens up a multitude of potentialities, nonteleological possibilities of historic development.[101]

Boym's reflective (n)Ostalgia is compatible, then, with what Peter Thompson calls the quest for an *unheimliche Heimat*, or uncanny homeland, the search for a history of the East that never was but could have been. Thompson's reflective (n)Ostalgia is one that longs for a "future that went missing in the past rather than for a past which never had a future."[102] The past—composed of varying histories, competing memory fragments, a multitude of specters—contains hidden and often unrealized potentials, ripe and waiting to be welcomed inside, gathered together, reassembled anew, realized. Thompson explains:

> The *unheimliche Heimat* . . . is uncanny, unknown and essentially unknowable, because it both is and isn't, was and wasn't the GDR. This is because the GDR itself, as both concept and reality, was not what it claimed to be, indeed was not even, one might argue, what it was. [Slavoj] Žižek maintains that *Ostalgie* is not nostalgia for something which has passed, but for something which never came to pass. It is nostalgia not for the GDR that was, but for the GDR that was not, so that what appears to be a retrospectively imagined community is actually a retrospective imagining of a proleptically imagined community.[103]

How, then, might one build a different, albeit unknown future with tools from a past that both was and never was? This was the project of the Volkspalast: "a *deconstruction* of the ideology of the Palast as a socialist building"[104] and the subsequent creation of a temporary urban laboratory that "experiments with the possibilities of the place and the time."[105] The goal was to create a multipurpose performance space whose doors were open to the many (infra)structural ghosts of Berlin and beyond.

Volkspalast's reflective engagement with the *Volkshaus* and *Kulturpalast* can be read as an attempt both to appreciate the complex histories of these institutions and to explore how they might still be useful (and rethought) for the present and future. Of primary importance to the organizers of Volkspalast was rethinking what it would mean to reintroduce the notion of *das Volk*, "the People"—with a capital "P"—into contemporary discourse (and usage). Who are today's *Volk*, today's People? How must a current notion of *Volk* be expanded beyond traditional notions of the working class? What public is addressed when one speaks of a "public" building, of a "People's" building for the twenty-first century? How might Volkspalast facilitate "open communication"[106] for all, for young and old, for East German, West German, non-German? And how might a "people's palace" stand in stark opposition to a Stadtschloss, an Imperial Palace?

In many ways, these questions are reminiscent of those that Frank Castorf posed in and through his refunctioned Volksbühne. They are also reminiscent of those that Chris Dercon posed in his short-lived attempt to reorient the Volksbühne. Volkspalast's proposed answer, however, was not a centralized, state-supported and state-run facility. Nor were the Volkspalast organizers interested in a neoliberal "event-shed." Rather, Volkspalast proposed what they called a "democratization" of space; it proposed "not an expansion of the public by flattening, but rather an expansion by differentiation. They would work with the protagonists from high-culture realms to the sub- and club cultural spheres."[107] From the ruins, they would erect a diverse, "non-consumerist space"[108] for artistic and political experimentation. Deuflhard and Oswalt claimed:

> VOLKSPALAST was not institutional, not bureaucratic, not commercial. VOLKSPALAST made inaccessible grounds—"forbidden land"—accessible once again, and it gave a building of great public interest back to the public. VOLKSPALAST as occupation. Legal occupation, endowing substantive and artistic meaning. It engaged the architecture and inscribed a different meaning. The project decoded the building, removed it temporarily from the planned valorization process, and opened new possible attributions.[109]

"Cheery diversity," they explained, would replace monolithic, hierarchical thinking and "high-minded unity."[110] Instead, they would erect a "laboratory for a new kind of polyphony."[111]

The organizing rhetoric of Volkspalast aligns with the principles of an explicitly independent or "free" theater scene, which was becoming increasingly institutionalized in post-Wall Berlin. Matthias Lilienthal had only recently left Castorf's Volksbühne to assume leadership of the Hebbel am Ufer and actively transform it into an anchor for the free-scene. Explicit in Volkspalast's organizing language was a criticism of the kind of bureaucratic systems and hierarchal politics so pervasive in Germany's state-stages. (There was even an implicit criticism of the "dictatorial" strain that Castorf acknowledges as essential to his own work.) As a kind of proto-free-scene institution, Volkspalast would attempt to level this privilege—the privilege of both the state-stage and the commercial venture. All sectors of Berlin would be invited to share the space of the Volkspalast. All participants would be treated equally.[112] All projects would be self-organized. The same budget would be available to each participating artistic group. Young or established, large or small, working conditions would be the same. A base budget would be provided, and then each would be left to acquire additional funding. And the days were numbered.[113] In their welcome message to visitors, Lilienthal, Deuflhard, and Oswalt explained:

> The experiment VOLKSPALAST wants to—with a good deal of improvisation—make a proposal out of the raw and unfinished for a revitalization of the city center beyond [i.e., opposed to] the fairground, sales booths, shopping malls—but also beyond museality and institutionalization. A proposal for a qualified, experimental use, which takes the public citizen seriously: as spectator, but also as actor in our society. No elitist art institution, but a popular contemporary utilization [Bespielung]. The VOLKSPALAST is open for all![114]

Zwischennutzung: Fun Palace

On August 20, 2004, Volkspalast opened its doors with pomp and circumstance. Thousands of visitors were greeted by ironically "traditional" premiere rituals. There was a limousine service to escort *das Volk* to the red carpet. There were group photos and confetti cannons. A number of Berlin's free-scene performance groups set up shop: Rimini Protokoll, Nico & the Navigators, LIGNA, and others. Members of the British-German collective Gob Squad donned tuxedos and served as "society" reporters, Joan Rivers–style: "What are you wearing for Democracy?"[115] "If your body were Berlin, which part would YOU get rid of?"[116] The media coverage was extensive. More than a thousand articles, radio announcements, and television spots ran in Germany and around the world, one more hauntingly fond of a spectral vocabulary than the next: "The skeleton dances." "Resurrected as ruins." "The Palast der Republik comes to life."[117] And the crowds continued to grow. Volkspalast hosted over fifty thousand visitors over the course of its three-month run. And in 2006, Volkspalast won the European Prize for Urban Public Space, an architectural prize usually reserved for building projects, not cultural (or performance) projects.[118]

Though I don't place much analytical emphasis on an award of this kind, it is indicative of the shifting boundaries and complex interrelations between architecture and event, structure and infrastructure, performed by the Volkspalast. On October 16 and 17, 2004, the organizers continued their exploration of temporary use *as* institutionalized disappearance by staging a public symposium to interrogate the continued relevance of Cedric Price and Joan Littlewood's Fun Palace, their infamous bastion of (infra)structural flexibility. The symposium, "Fun Palace Berlin 200x," was curated by Philipp Misselwitz, Hans Ulrich Obrist, and Philipp Oswalt, and brought together an international group of more than forty architects, artists, theater makers, and theorists for a transdisciplinary brainstorming session. The goal of the symposium was not a one-to-one comparison of the Volkspalast with the Fun Palace's "architectural paradigm of choice, ambiguity and indeterminacy."[119] The goal was not to *use* the Fun Palace as a means of legitimating the Volkspalast, nor was it an attempt at saving the Palast der Republik. As Mark Wigley—who was invited to give the keynote address—made clear at the outset, Cedric Price himself was "dead set against conservation,"[120] against preservation for preservation's sake, and would have most certainly recommended the elimination of an unused ruin. Instead, the symposium revisited Price's "radical ideas about time, about the openness and instability of architecture, his humor, his habit of posing hard questions and challenging the seemingly self-evident."[121] Ultimately, the task was to explore—from a different angle—the central questions of Volkspalast: What uses are desirable for Berlin's public spaces as it moves into the next century? Are public spaces, places, (infra)structures still about duration, or can they be realized through something temporary in character? And as Philipp Oswalt asked, inaugurating the discussion, "What does *this* central location mean for our society?"[122]

While the Fun Palace is often attributed to Price, it was actually first conceived by Joan Littlewood, a well-known specter of Marxist theater. Fun Palace was the culmination of more than thirty years of thinking about and making public performance. After a start in the left-wing, agitprop Workers' Theatre Movement, she founded and for many years ran the Theatre Workshop. In 1955, Bertolt Brecht refused the rights to the British premiere of *Mother Courage* unless Littlewood agreed to direct and star in the production. And Brecht most certainly had a large impact on Littlewood's interest in the democratization of performance practice, a broader social basis for the theater, and a fundamental rethinking of audience-spectator relations. According to Wigley, architecture was not necessarily a crucial element in Littlewood's early thinking: "She reportedly asked Cedric the rhetorical question: Do you think that there is any room for architecture in this?"[123] At the time, he did not answer the question. But he was most certainly listening.

Littlewood and Price worked tirelessly, albeit unsuccessfully, for many years to realize their conjunction of architecture and performance. The Fun Palace was a concept that would incorporate temporality and flexibility into built structures and avoid, at all costs, solidification and its accompanying forms of bureaucracy and top-down management. Instead, Price and Littlewood worked—somewhat paradoxically—to institutionalize the unpredictable, the ever-changing, by dreaming up a space of informality, where "anything goes,"[124] where nothing is obligatory but everything is possible. They envisioned an "ephemeral" (132) architecture that exhibited this fundamental impermanence on both the micro and macro scales. Price and Littlewood reported in a 1968 article for *The Drama Review*, "Nothing is to last for more than ten years, some things not even ten days: no concrete stadia, stained and cracking; no legacy of noble contemporary architecture, quickly dating; no municipal geranium-beds or fixed teak benches. With informality goes flexibility" (130). There would be no doors, no roof, "no permanent structures" (130); instead they would experiment with new technologies, foreign to most things built: "Charged static-vapor zones, optical barriers, warm-air curtains and fog-dispersal plants, . . . vertical and horizontal lightweight blinds" (132).

These technologies would enable a space that was infinitely transformable, a space that would accommodate the whims and wishes of thousands of visitors simultaneously. Boundaries would appear and disappear per the requirements of each activity, "occasion," "event" (133). In fact, the entire (infra)structure could be conceived more as complex "toy" or "social machine"[125] than as a building; more—Wigley explained—as a "threshold or a transition space between buildings; . . . a non-building that is not going to survive, a fragment of a building that will cease to operate."[126] In this nonbuilding, the boundaries between art, leisure, and life would blend into one another. There would be no distinction between public space and Palace space, no distinction between public citizen and Palace participant. Littlewood explained, "The visitor can enjoy a sense of identity with the world about him" (131). This would be, after all, a mass "generalization of the technique used in Theatre Workshop for many years" (131), a mass expansion of Littlewood's dream of a theater that would dissolve all divisions between spectators and performers. Users would have unlimited ways to express themselves. Artists young and old would be able to make their own work. Scientists could collaborate on experiments together. Amateurs could work alongside experts, and vice versa. All would share a common space. All would determine what that space could be. All would help "realize the possibilities and delights that a twentieth-century city environment owes us."[127] A 1964 draft of a hypothetical Fun Palace brochure envisioned six zones, which would feature "Observation Decks, Adult Toys, Nurseries, Star Gazing, Music, Science Gadgetry, Theatre Clownery, News Service, Instant Cinema, Tele-communication, Fireworks, Swank Promenades, Recording Sessions, Hide Aways, Kunst Dabbling [sic], Dance Floors, Gala Days & Nights, Drink, Genius Chat, Rallies, Gossip Revues, . . . Laboratories, Concerts, Food, Learning Machines, Ateliers."[128] And on and on—the list was not complete; it would never be complete but always in flux. These proposals for a different kind of institution fell very much in line with a more widespread European "artistic critique" in the wake of 1968 that scorned so-called bureaucratic establishments for their lack of social awareness and called in turn for more innovation, experimentation, and creativity. Price and Littlewood did not predict, however, that their antiauthoritarian gestures toward increased flexibility would later be recuperated and remobilized by a burgeoning neoliberal experience economy.[129]

Ultimately, after years of losing battles with politicians and city planners, Price and Littlewood were forced to give up on the project. It would remain a dream, a subjunctive (infra)structural imagining. Yet one might also ask: Was the Palace's fundamental nonbuildability—its subjunctive status—also one of its greatest strengths? After all, in spite of their very vocal efforts to secure a site, both Price and Littlewood were notoriously reluctant to commit to precise plans for and precise definitions of the Fun Palace. Stanley Mathews notes, "They were both deliberately vague about almost every aspect of this new indeterminate architecture. It is significant that in the first major publication produced by the Fun Palace, the explanatory text was introduced by the question: 'What is it?' Indeed, just what was the Fun Palace?"[130] If it had been realized—to continue with the subjunctive—perhaps it would have lost some of its critical potential, its potential as open laboratory, its potential for disappearance. It would no longer have been able to defy definition. Mathews continues, "The Fun Palace was 'Rorschach' architecture, full of possibility, and open to diverse interpretation by different viewers."[131] If the nonbuilding had become a building, however, the dream of permanent temporariness might have transitioned into a kind of temporary permanence.

Fun Palace Berlin 200x, curated by Philipp Misselwitz, Hans Ulrich Obrist, and Philipp Oswalt, October 2004. Photograph copyright © David Baltzer / bildbuehne.de.

After a series of lectures and discussions about the Fun Palace, the curators attempted to redirect the discussion to reflect "on possible future plans for the Schloss grounds and the Palast der Republik."[132] The curators asked participants to reflect on ways the Fun Palace could be *used* to reflect on the contemporary situation, even to intervene in the Schloss-Palast debates. Architectural theorist Werner Sewing responded to the prompt in this way: "The free-scene wants to take over a small portion of the [historic] center, which can be legitimized by Cedric Price's concept of a 'laboratory.' But is our state prepared to accept culture as an experiment and not as 'High' Culture? Is our state willing to risk handing over this central location to creative fringe groups? This is the political question that should not be underestimated; otherwise this project will surely fail."[133] To this, Mark Wigley responded most sharply:

> It must be said again and again that we will not make progress here with the [notion of] Fun Palace. The project was very deliberately thwarted by politicians. I cannot imagine that there would be state money given to something called a "laboratory." Or that anyone even believes in that idea. By definition you would be an idiot if you, as the powers that be, yielded power to a "laboratory." . . . I see no sign that the political forces in Berlin care at all about us. Even the fact that this conversation is more or less public is a sign of its total political irrelevance.[134]

Wigley's response functions on two levels. First, his objection to any framing of Volkspalast as a Fun Palace–like laboratory (tacitly) urges renewed consideration of Derrida's critique of the void. A laboratory with an express purpose—even an "experimental" purpose—is not really a laboratory after all. A laboratory with political *relevance* no longer honors the ghosts of the ruin. It seems that, for Wigley at least, the very act of comparing the Volkspalast to anything, the very act of designating it *as* laboratory, would load it with too much representational content to continue maintaining and performing its status as void. Second, and relatedly, Wrigley points out that to some extent Sewing had missed the powerful—albeit often frustrating— cultural political paradox inherent in "laboratory" projects like Fun Palace or Volkspalast. Why, he suggests, would a governmental funding body be interested in—or have the courage to consider—funding a project whose main purpose and organizational orientation is to make use of such support to call that very governmental body into question? This critical art of institutional dis/avowal, while perhaps less politically "relevant" from one point of view, is—claims Wigley, again in line with Derrida—precisely that which must not be underestimated. The political irrelevance of the laboratory makes it most relevant. And yet, as Philipp Misselwitz chimed in to conclude the session, one must at the same time be careful not to underestimate the very material costs of institutionalized disappearance. Even the "freest" and most interim (infra)structures are *already*, themselves, supported; one must also attend to these systems of support. Misselwitz explained, "[Volkspalast] was made possible by a combination of public funds, private sponsors, and the commitment of many unpaid people. Can this model also be used as a prototype for a longer-term development? Or is it just a model of self-exploitation and neoliberal principles in the context of subculture?"[135] I take up these questions about labor in the free-scene in chapter 4. For now, however, we turn to another architectural performance, another form of *use* laboratory, that challenges us in different ways to continue the investigation of what an (infra)structural hauntology might entail.

Zwischennutzung: Republic of Facades

Between September 3 and 11, 2004, two young teams of "performative architects,"[136] raumlaborberlin and Peanutz Architekten, joined forces in an attempt to converse with the ghosts of the *present* moment: to engage, debate, mock (up), ironize, explore, and complicate the histories and memories of the Schloss-Palast debates. They collaborated to erect and stage a temporary metropolis, a fungible labyrinth, a topical theme park, a do-it-yourself water-park, an "anarchistic"[137] and improvisational laboratory. This Republic of Facades, or *Fassadenrepublik*, attempted to "refound" something like a city within the walls of the Palast. It attempted to refound an artificial republic, in order to explore—to induce—refracted representations and reimaginings of Berlin's own civic (infra)structures.

In an ironic adoption of the purely pro-Schloss versus pro-Palast positions, the Republic of Facades made simulation, facade, and the (merely) representational its explicit focus. It was a project in which the contentless, *use*-less facade was endowed with content. "For us," explains Benjamin Foerster-Baldenius of raumlabor, "the discussion about these things that were supposed to happen—or maybe not happen—there at Schlossplatz was a discussion about facades and not about content. . . . It was never about what is going to happen here, but what does it look like."[138] The Republic of Facades, then, attempted to realize varied histories (of recent city-planning debates) via the scaffold and the facade. The project would, however, realize these varied histories without illusion, without a flattening of messy interiorities, and with an explicit interest in institutional apparatuses, in varied perspectives, in functionality and use. In the Republic of Facades, (infra)structure was constructed of facade; facade became (infra)structure.

And just whose histories were at stake? Whose histories were realized or re-created by this explicitly public project? In contrast to the proposed Humboldt Forum, the (infra)structural imaginings of the Republic of Facades extended way beyond the purview of those almighty commissions of city-planning experts. "Why should some people decide what kinds of facades we have and others don't?" the organizers asked.[139] Everybody could design a facade, and every facade would be accepted. There would be no jury to adjudicate. The call went out a few weeks prior to the opening of Volkspalast and resulted in a number of public do-it-yourself facade-making workshops. Anyone—everyone—began with a blank canvas of 3 × 3 meters, and the results were most diverse: M. C. Escher–style tessellations, colorful bull's-eyes, children's handprints and finger-painting experiments, steaming houses of shit with doors and windows to peek through, expressionistic pie charts, photorealist pictures, found-object collages, and facades made entirely of toast. The Republic of Facades encouraged this alternative swath of city-planning "experts" to envision "a concept with cultural-political charisma and strong urban impact"[140] that focused on the look, the feel, the density, the spatial organization, the use, and the ownership structures of Berlin's historic center.

Once the facades were complete—more than two hundred in all—raumlabor and Peanutz began construction of a complex lagoon, a web of shallow canals, a city of water, a labyrinth constructed of the facades. The idea was simple yet radical: flood the ground floor of the Palast and invite the public inside to play amid their facades. Elke Knöss-Grillitsch of Peanutz Architekten attributes the origin of the idea to an autonomist group that resorted to direct action on behalf of asylum seekers in Berlin in the late 1990s. The group was called Freies Fluten, or Free Flooding, and they burned down a Kaiser's supermarket in protest against backward, "racist" legislation[141] placing limits on where asylum seekers could buy food. "I don't believe in violence," averred Knöss-Grillitsch, "but I thought this name Freies Fluten, it is such a great name."[142] She brought this perspective to the first brainstorming session between raumlabor and Peanutz: "We [would] use flooding to give people a different access to the building, to take a boat and not walk through the building, because this helps you have a more abstract view of the thing."[143]

Like Feff before them—and citing her, of course—raumlabor and Peanutz also staged a life-size trompe l'oeil. They staged an ongoing process of hanging and erecting painted canvases, a process through which the "sovereign, the citizens of Berlin, got to have their say as the owners of the space."[144] The water served as a mirror—on a vertical, not horizontal, plane—shimmering, sparkling, reflecting, refracting, permitting a re-vision of history, while simultaneously nodding to the conscious fabrication of the republic, a republic constructed purely of facades. And the mock-up extended way beyond the dimensions, possibilities, dreams of the Palast—and of the Schloss—encouraging a subjunctive (infra)structural reimagining. "How could this place be a different place?" asked Foerster-Baldenius, in his own version of the *whither* question. "We thought it was important that we go beyond what people expected, that we flood the building, to make clear that this building has a potential beyond what people up to that point thought it could be."[145] Indeed, the Republic of Facades invoked the Schloss-Palast debates in order actively to remember *and* simultaneously move beyond them; it took up Susan Buck-Morss's critique of Feff's mock-up and refunctioned it anew: "What couldn't be resolved politically was resolved aesthetically: a pseudo-Schloss to provide a pseudo-nation with a pseudo-past. It reduces national identity to a tourist attraction and stages the German nation as a theme park."[146]

Thousands of visitors queued each day to enter the republic. Once inside, small groups of visitor-citizens took off their shoes and toured around in rubber dinghies, Venice-style. Gondolier-tour guides in rubber boots pulled the boats from island to island through a series of "attractions," installations, elements essential to any republic: university, post office, television station, café, restaurant, forum, parliament, ancestry bureau, and of course, red-light district. Ironizing the mission statement of the proposed Humboldt Forum, the Republic of Facades functioned as a "place of dialogue," a place that could "integrate" arts, world cultures, and the sciences. It included spaces for heritage and education. It presented theater, music, and dance performances, and housed a multitude of restaurants. Each island, each theme-park attraction, was devised by a different, independent performance ensemble that had been invited to participate. Peanutz and raumlabor maintained no strict control over texts, routines, or dramaturgy. Each performance group was self-regulating. Each boatload of visitor-citizens was self-regulating. The (infra)structure was completely improvisational, interactive, anarchic even. It was a space of informality, where nothing was obligatory but much was possible.

Visitors explore the lagoons of *Fassadenrepublik*, created by raumlaborberlin and Peanutz Architekten, September 2004. Photograph copyright © David Baltzer / bildbuehne.de.

Facades become (infra)structure in *Fassadenrepublik*. Photograph copyright © David Baltzer / bildbuehne.de.

The attractions varied in size and scope, but all worked to explore—and blur—the boundaries between art, leisure, and life. You could fish for sushi snacks. You could make fresh pizzas. You could watch a burlesque show. You could gamble in the casino. You could join a group massage circle. You could train as a gondolier and stay longer than the other guests. You could attend lectures at the academy where new "professors"—architects, artists, and theorists—were invited each day to give interactive lectures on facades. You could even—quite literally—greet, honor, and struggle with the difficult and conflicted memories of the many ghosts of Berlin. Club Real, a Berlin-based free-scene performance group, erected an *Ahnenamt*, an ancestry bureau, as their contribution to the republic. Prior to Volkspalast, members of Club Real had assembled vast archives of ancestor files—photos of unidentified persons collected from flea markets and the trash. Visitor-citizens who felt they had the capacity to care for an additional ancestor were given the opportunity to "adopt" one.[147] The bureau also produced commemorative plaques to honor deceased men and women with close connections to the Palast der Republik: Honecker, Liebknecht, even the kaiser himself. These plaques were fixed to facades throughout the republic, forging a space for the spectral and inviting all to stand (or float) before the ghosts that roam.

Eventually, every citizen-visitor had the opportunity to partake in the republic's Parliament, the largest of the installations. Each boatload could join one of two "political" parties standing on opposing islands. A "president"—often played by Knöss-Grillitsch—facilitated the Parliament from a freestanding podium between the two parties; she donned a stylish dunce cap to indicate her position as mediator of "creative disputes." The Parliament was charged with determining the look and feel of the republic. The parties discussed new facades, debated existing ones, and decided which ones should be moved or removed. "The reason why people should go there," Foerster-Baldenius claims, "should not just be that they can row in rubber dinghies through the palace, but that they are also part of this discourse about what does the city look like and who has a right to decide that."[148] The Parliament, then, was an effort to mock (up) but also perform a so-called democratic process of city building. It was an effort, albeit an ironic one, to examine existing policy and planning practices—the kind of policy and planning practices that could permit and ratify a (real) republic of facades in the "new" Berlin. After each debate and subsequent decision, members of both parties would join in a Kumbaya rendition of the Hymn of the Republic. "Between the facades," "above the canals," and always in harmonic unison, citizen-visitors would question existing "power" structures, "illuminate" a different future through a refracted present *and* past, and "try to answer the question: What would you do instead?"[149]

Ultimately, the republic—and the Volkspalast at large—did not affect whether the Palast would be demolished. This was not its intent. "But it has triggered," Amelie Deuflhard emphasized later, "another sensibility for

The Parliament of the *Fassadenrepublik*. Photograph copyright © David Baltzer /
bildbuehne.de.

political questions in the whole art scene, and, I believe, more confidence
that we can pull something off, even if the government is against it."[150] The
republic—and the Volkspalast—did indeed spur a different kind of public
discussion: a discussion of temporary use via facade, of future via present
and past, of public architecture and public policy, of institutional dis/avowal.
It also provoked a new kind of discussion about the role of the free-scene
within Berlin's broader performance landscape. "We can't leave events just
for the city marketing profession,"[151] Foerster-Baldenius stressed in his own
implicit nod to Derrida. "Maybe we need a holy place," he exclaimed with a
smile. "Maybe we should open up a *Church of Eventology*."[152]

Chapter 4

✦

Occupying the Immaterial Institution; or, Performing Policy Postdramatically

andcompany&Co.'s *(Coming) Insurrection*

The tradition of all dead generations weighs like a nightmare on the brains of the living. And just as they seem to be occupied with revolutionizing themselves and things, creating something that did not exist before, precisely in such epochs of revolutionary crisis they anxiously conjure up the spirits of the past to their service, borrowing from them names, battle slogans, and costumes in order to present this new scene in world history in time-honored disguise and borrowed language.

—Karl Marx, *The Eighteenth Brumaire of Louis Bonaparte* (1852)

The bodies on the street redeploy the space of appearance in order to contest and negate the existing forms of political legitimacy. . . . These are subjugated and empowered actors who seek to wrest legitimacy from an existing state apparatus that depends upon the regulation of the public space of appearance for its theatrical self-constitution. In wresting that power, a new space is created, a new "between" of bodies, as it were, that lays claim to existing space through the action of a new alliance, and those bodies are seized and animated by those existing spaces in the very acts by which they reclaim and resignify their meanings.

—Judith Butler, *Notes toward a Performative Theory of Assembly* (2015)

An audience gathers in the stalls and beholds a sparse proscenium stage littered with a few musical instruments and other handmade props. A rack brimming over with costumes sits upstage left. The signature Erector Set–like light board and sound controls of andcompany&Co. are downstage right and left, respectively. At the back of the stage, an immense freestanding structure looms, wrapped completely in aluminum foil.[1] Nine performers enter hauling large white eggs over their shoulders and looking out into the house. Each wears an oversize gray-felt "beggar's" cape covered in signage, logos, and secret insignias constructed of combinations of red, white, black, and yellow gaffer tape, and each dons an obscenely oversize, aristocratic white paper ruff around his neck. The "committee" of nine places their eggs on the ground and sits gracefully on them, forming a semicircle facing the audience. Joachim Robbrecht rises slowly and assumes a position center stage, turns his back to the house, bows to the others, and begins to speak to the committee, which, without hesitation, repeats each of his clauses in steady unison. Joachim (switching between German, Dutch, and English): "Have no fear." Committee: "Have no fear." Joachim: "We are only actors." Committee: "We are only actors." Joachim: "And this is a rehearsal." Committee: "And this is a rehearsal." The human microphone continues in call and response: "We are rehearsing the insurrection, the Insurrection of the Netherlands that began 444 years ago in Brussels, when citizens—quite normal citizens like yourselves—disguised themselves as beggars, as *Geuzen*, to fight for their freedom and their privileges." Each member of the committee extends both hands, points both index fingers upward, and begins to wiggle—or "twinkle"— them in silent applause at what has been said. Joachim then takes his seat, and without pause, Ward Weemhoff prances—as gracefully as one can prance in wooden clogs—to center stage, still facing the committee: "We will not perform with our backs to the audience." He turns around very slowly and smiles wryly: "This is the rehearsal of an occupation, a *Besetzungsprobe*." Silence from the committee. Ward repeats himself, now gesturing expectantly into the audience: "This . . . is the rehearsal . . . of an occupation. . . ." Just a few audience members get the gist and respond in turn. Ward continues slowly: "We have occupied the stage. . . ." The whole theater repeats now—we've got it. "We have occupied the stage, and the roles as well, and you, the auditorium. And we have brought you a silver gift, which we will unwrap with you tonight."

As is andcompany&Co.'s way, tonight's performance consists of a brilliantly frenetic and kaleidoscopically erudite array of literary, dramatic, historical, and found texts, new writing, art historical allusions, philosophical discourses, pop-cultural reenactments, music, melodrama, comedy, and shock, all held together somehow with a healthy dose of what Hans-Thies Lehmann calls productive *Unfug*—"nonsense," "shenanigans," or "horseplay."[2] In these opening moments alone, the overlapping references are exceedingly thick: Friedrich Schiller's poetic historical tract *Secession of the Netherlands*, and his *Don Carlos*, both of which center around the Dutch uprising against Philip II's Spanish Empire and Inquisition, marking the start of the Eighty Years' War (1568–1648) and the formation of the first modern European capitalist republic; *The Coming Insurrection*, a radical-left political pamphlet from the Invisible Committee, first published in French in 2007, standing in for a contemporary history of global protests, demonstrations, and occupationist movements—both in theory and practice—that rippled

The committee of nine rehearses an occupation in *The (Coming) Insurrection according to Friedrich Schiller* (created by andcompany&Co.) at the Oldenburgisches Staatstheater, which premiered on February 23, 2012. Photograph copyright © Hans Jörg Michel.

through Tunis, Cairo, New York, Oakland, and beyond in recent years; and Ward's insistence on playing *to* us, the audience, explicitly cites the Dutch prime minister Mark Rutte's infamous statement that "the arts have their backs to audiences but their wallets open to the state,"[3] a populist claim that was used to justify the right-wing government's "new vision of cultural policy"[4] and unprecedented austerity cuts for the arts in the Netherlands, and which also inspired recent "culture attacks"[5] in Germany.

In this turn toward the audience, this proposal that we all share the human microphone, andcompany&Co. also invites us to join in their occupation. Together, we rehearse chants, slogans, a protest song, and an elaborate choreography (with musical accompaniment) of hand signals—communicating enthusiasm, skepticism, disagreement, impatience, lack of understanding, despair, and small, religious, or even existential questions—that one might recognize from the general assemblies in Madrid, London, Berkeley, even Oldenburg, where this performance premiered. As we stand and briefly review this embodied aesthetics of occupation, it becomes clear that andcompany&Co. is intentionally playing with multiple-entendre, metaphor, pun, and the ever-fluid mutability of concepts and ideas across time periods and languages. When Ward explains, for instance, that we are here to rehearse an occupation, that this is a *Besetzungsprobe*, he indicates the multiple valences of the term *Besetzung* or "occupation": it could mean to occupy, or to squat, a space; it could mean, as it often does in theater contexts, to take on a role; it could mean to occupy ourselves with some job or activity, an occupation; it could mean to be occupied by something else entirely, by mass media, by capital, by discourse; it could even mean, with the slightest of infelicitous inclinations, a military occupation, or *Besatzung*. Next, when Ward explains, "I occupy [*besetzen*] the role of Rodrigo, the Marquis de Posa," and slides across the stage into a spotlight to utter, with a grin, the immortal "Give us the freedom to think,"[6] he invokes a number of different freedoms, a number of complementary *and* competing autonomies simultaneously: spiritual and academic freedom for Posa; freedom for the Netherlands from the imperial rule of the Spanish Empire, a freedom that coincided with and furthered the development of the global "free" marketplace; freedom from authoritarian governments writ large, like those in the Middle East, North Africa, and beyond; freedom from precarity, austerity, and the free market itself; and freedom (via the free market) from the greatest of all societal leeches—those beggars, those *Geuzen*, those "subsidy slurpers,"[7] those dreaded artists.

In these opening moments, andcompany&Co.'s performance seems expressly interested in the complicated relationships between occupation and freedom—always multiply defined. And to complicate the issue further, Ward soon takes center stage again and poses a question, a "mystery," which he would like us all to "unravel" together: "How do you squat [also *besetzen*] an imaginary space within an imaginary context?"[8] A very long silence ensues, followed by bewildered looks and accompanying hand signals from both the audience and the committee: "Can you repeat the question?" In this moment of pause, we are asked to consider the possibilities: How might we occupy a space that exists only in our imaginations, though not yet in the world as such? Or: How might we, in this very moment, occupy a space dedicated explicitly to our individual and collective imaginations—like a theater space? Are we setting out to occupy an imaginary context, a situation or set of conditions best left explored only by our imaginations, only in theory, and not intended for actualization? Or: Are we, in this very moment, occupying a context of and for the imagination, crafting just the right real-world conditions for our imaginations to function freely? Is the occupation to be prefigured? Has it already arrived, here, now, at the theater? Or, quite paradoxically, is it somehow both *and* neither/nor? In other words, is the coming insurrection always also in parentheses—always "(coming)"?

We do not yet have the answers. But it is clear from Ward's formulation in these opening moments that unraveling the relations between occupation and imagination requires that we also consider the infrastructural conditions of possibility, the spaces and contexts, for both. For these infrastructural conditions, these spaces and contexts of appearance, constitute the silver gift to be "unwrapped," the riddle to be rehearsed or, quite literally, deconstructed on the "stage of theatrical self-constitution"—to borrow Judith Butler's thoughts on occupation and organization.

On February 27, 2013, the Hebbel am Ufer (HAU) performance complex hosted the second in an ongoing series of public interdisciplinary discussions under the title "Phantasm and Politics." The purpose of the gathering on this particular winter evening was to bring artists and scholars together to discuss andcompany&Co.'s *The (Coming) Insurrection according to Friedrich Schiller—Der (kommende) Aufstand nach Friedrich Schiller*—which had had its sold-out Berlin premiere on the very same stage just the previous evening. As HAU advertised on its website, the evening would begin with a "concrete" discussion of the performance in order also to pose broader questions about "whether and to what degree art not only can depict and represent current social movements such as Occupy in the theater but also must be able to abandon the aesthetic distance to empirical reality in order to react appropriately to a social reality perceived as in crisis."[9] And as art theorist Helmut Draxler, the curator of these conversations, clarified in his opening remarks, the overall goal of the "Phantasm" series was to address what he deems to be a "current boom in documentary and interventionist projects"[10]—a "longing" for the so-called real in the interarts context—and more generally, to "look into the claims that the spheres of art and of politics make on one another, and to work out perspectives on whether and how we can get beyond the traditional antagonism between autonomy and engagement."[11] Invited to reflect on these pressing questions in the context of andcompany&Co.'s performance were Hans-Thies Lehmann, German theater theorist and progenitor of the "postdramatic"; Geert Lovink, acclaimed "tactical" media theorist and internet activist from the Netherlands; and sitting between them, Alexander Karschnia, cofounder-codirector of andcompany&Co. and performer in the previous evening's *(Coming) Insurrection*. The final player in the room was, indeed, the room itself: the main stage and full house of HAU 1, the largest of the three-stage HAU complex—an international performing arts center and an epicenter of Berlin's independent theater milieu, or free-scene (*freie Szene*), under the new leadership of Annemie Vanackere, a curator and producer from Flanders.

Since its inception in 2003—when the Hebbel Theater, Theater am Halleschen Ufer, and Theater am Ufer were consolidated as HAU 1, 2, and 3, respectively, under Matthias Lilienthal—HAU has emerged as Berlin's premiere site of international performance and one of the most respected institutions of its kind in Europe. Its three spaces have served as the Berlin home to international performance artists and ensembles: Forced Entertainment, Lone Twin, The Wooster Group, Nature Theater of Oklahoma, Romeo Castellucci, Jerome Bel, Richard Maxwell, Young Jean Lee, Xavier Leroy, and many other stalwarts of the broad postdramatic "panorama."[12] Since its inauguration, HAU has also worked to situate itself as a central venue and support structure for artists and ensembles in Berlin's free-scene: Rimini Protokoll, She She Pop, Gob Squad, andcompany&Co., Showcase Beat Le Mot, and many more.[13] As one of the institutional hubs for this free-scene,

HAU sits at the center of a recent series of heated policy debates and protests regarding the future and sustainability of Germany's independent theater and performance landscape.

Over the past few decades, a *new spirit* of aesthetic and infrastructural tendencies has emerged, which, in denomination at least, set themselves outside of the long-standing state-stage system. This free-scene is made up of a loose and highly heterogeneous grouping of "independently producing artists, ensembles, and independently operated institutions from the fields of architecture, visual art, dance, drama, performance, new media, . . . music, music theater, children's and youth theater, literature, and other multidisciplinary and transdisciplinary forms."[14] As a realm of both artistic labor and administration, Berlin's free-scene occupies a tenuous position. On the one hand, more and more of the artists and ensembles that self-identify as members of this scene play central roles in Berlin's rich and diverse web of artistic activity. At the same time, the free-scene in many ways exemplifies the precarious tendencies of the performing arts within globalized, post-Fordist economies of disavowal, tending more and more often toward immaterial, insecure, highly flexible, freelance, project-based work.

In the months leading up to that cold week in February and continuing to the present moment, a growing number of artists, ensembles, ad-hoc groups, and institution heads banded together and became increasingly vocal about the need for drastic cultural policy reforms to address the crises, contradictions, value discrepancies, and funding inadequacies that structure, so they claim, the contemporary interarts landscape in Berlin. According to this Independent Art Coalition (Koalition der freien Szene), and invoking a familiar "occupationist" rhetorical strategy, 95 percent of the city's cultural budget goes to fund the major state institutions even though free-scene artists represent 95 percent of all artistic production in Berlin.[15] Amid these debates about policy reform and mobilizations for increased support of the free-scene, however, a number of pressing questions have emerged: Just what kinds of performance work(s) and organizational structures actually constitute the free-scene? How do these works of performance, onstage and off, set themselves apart (or not) from the other aesthetic and organizational state-stage configurations? Does the free-scene—in its quest for "freedom" and "autonomy"—also enmesh itself in the very practices and structures from which it is trying to acquire distance? What would it mean, then—and is it indeed possible or politically desirable—to speak of institutions *of* the free-scene or of a cultural policy *for* the free-scene? And finally, what are the relationships between the kinds of performances made, the conditions of work necessary to generate those performances, and the modes of organization—or lack thereof—that structure those aesthetic and labor practices?

In light of these questions, the "phantasmic" discussions on the HAU stage—about the real and representational, the interdependent claims of art and politics, autonomy and engagement—are imbued with a local urgency. Has the HAU, for instance, managed to freeze the "free" in free-scene? Or does it facilitate a different mode of organization best suited to nurture, or represent, a (postdramatic *and/or* precarious) performance aesthetic increasingly resistant to institutionalization itself? In this chapter, I explore the ways in which andcompany&Co.'s *(Coming) Insurrection* helps us track the infrastructural politics of Berlin's free-scene through an immanent critique of recent activist initiatives on its behalf. To do so, I argue further that the performance indexes concurrent, overlapping conversations about performance and precarity in a neoliberal economy; the conjunctions of politics and postdramatic theater; and the commensurability (or lack thereof) of aesthetic practices with ultraleft discourses about alternative modes of social organization—the so-called *communization current*—which arose (or perhaps returned) in the wake of worldwide protest after 2008. In making this claim, I suggest that Alexander Karschnia's place on the HAU stage between Lehmann and Lovink is not a happy coincidence but instead provides a heuristic for thinking about the complex relations between postdramatic theater and new infrastructural modes of (network) organization interested in staging their own undoing. Finally, I posit that the performance highlights the productive moments of negativity in these interrelated conversations, mediating always between the immaterial and the material, the imaginary and the actual, the open question and the direct action, by refusing one or the other and insisting instead on a perpetual state of dis/avowal. To borrow Judith Butler's words again: *The (Coming) Insurrection* creates (or rehearses) a new space and context, a "new 'between' of bodies,"[16] that lays claim to the existing space of the HAU (and its many contradictions), at the same time being animated and supported by the preexisting space of the HAU in the very acts by which it reclaims and resignifies its meanings. To put it differently: andcompany&Co.'s performance explores the ways HAU both perpetuates the precarity of a mobile, project-based performance economy—and the Independent Art Coalition's calls for more state support—while providing a valuable (im)material bastion for artistic laborers to imagine spaces and contexts beyond the "state of exception."[17]

✦ ✦ ✦

A gong sounds. The stage empties. Darkness. A haunting soundscape of thunder, distorted cello, digging, clanking metal, and high-pitched, high-reverb noise fills the room, followed by a deep, omniscient growl: "I am the silver mountain." With each word, a bright white backlight pokes through the spaces between the sheets of aluminum foil covering the massive structure at the back of the stage. "I am the silver mountain of Potosí"—a locus of European wealth and debt, colonization and globalization, greed and death. The flickering lights become more erratic and even brighter now, almost blinding. Behind the aluminum curtain, we sense the specters, the "good spirits" of Bolivian miners hard at work: "I am the perfect cone. I am the silver ocean. On my back, ships travel to Antwerp, their bellies full of silver. . . . I am the flood of silver that breaks through your banks! Let the silver come to you. Guzzle me down like water! I am your fear! I am your bank! Too big to fail! Too big to fail!" Slowly, very slowly, papier-mâché pickaxes and cardboard shovels begin to pierce through the silver facade, through the totality of capital and its relations, releasing increasingly more light into the room. "I am the silver platter in the king's palace in Madrid. . . . I am the blazing funeral pyre on which the financial heretics will burn. . . . I am the national theater, into which the silver-haired audiences cram. I am classical! I am great! I am strong! I am perfect!" With tedious precision, the committee, dressed now as half-naked miners in *lucha libre* wrestling masks, tears down the rest of the silver foil, slowly unwrapping their new play/work space: a life-size, hand-painted comic book. The voice thunders even louder; it is everywhere, and it taunts us: "When is this insurrection of yours going to happen? What could it be? What does it look like? Who is the insurrection? Who is rising up?" The room is now fully illuminated by Potosí's glow. The miners strike a pose—both playful and threatening at the same time. Through a door behind them, Vincent van der Valk emerges dressed as Friedrich Schiller: long, wispy hair, blue peacoat, eccentric white ascot, and frilly cuffs. He observes the scene for a moment, calmly rubbing his hands together, thinking. There is an extended silence. With a very somber face, he centers himself in the doorway and bellows, making sure to overenunciate each word: "What is and to what end does one study universal history, *Universalgeschichte*? . . . Because what do we learn from universal history if not the lesson of vi-o-lence? Naked violence. Brute force. Cruelty. Fanaticism. Persecution."

Grasping some of the dynamics and contradictions at stake in andcompany&Co.'s *(Coming) Insurrection* requires an associational and historical detour through the Netherlands. As Alexander Karschnia explains, one of the goals of the performance is to forge a "connection" between the 2008 financial crisis and the ongoing crises in the arts in the Netherlands and Germany, situating them in their "historical perspectives."[18] Or, as suggested in the program accompanying the performance (also written by Karschnia&Co.), "*Insurrection* breathes the spirit of the Dutch Revolt, in which the name 'beggar' [*Geuzennaam*] was worn with pride, and responds to a societal situation in which the term 'artist' has become a dirty word."[19] To rehearse this Dutch Revolt, then, is to reinhabit versions of its history in the present moment as a means of imagining an "insurrection" in the making, one that is indeed occupied with the dreams (or nightmares, for Marx), the names, the slogans, and especially the costumes of what has come before. For Karschnia and his andcompany&Co. comrades, the infrastructural likenesses to what has come before yield pressing questions: Are the (coming) revolutionaries also always already the agents of capital? And is this enmeshment in capital and its relations a critical cause for concern or the very factor that provides their (coming) revolt with the necessary traction?

The (Coming) Insurrection: Schiller and the silver miners deconstruct the mountain of Potosí. Photograph copyright © Hans Jörg Michel.

The (Coming) Insurrection: King Philip II is force-fed the riches he has plundered as the Grand Inquisitor looks on. Photograph copyright © Hans Jörg Michel.

Amid a frenetic costume change just preceding the looming darkness, Sascha Sulimma, one of the cofounders of andcompany&Co., rapidly sputters into a microphone, explaining that Spanish explorers discovered large deposits of silver in the mountain of Potosí in 1545, the same year Don Carlos was born. Sascha continues: Carlos died (as his father Philip's prisoner, suspected of treason) in 1568, the year in which Counts Egmont and Hoorn were executed and William of Orange returned with an army to face off against the Duke of Alba; this year is considered by many to mark the start of the Eighty Years' War.[20] Then comes the darkness, and these few, quick keywords—Potosí, Philip, Carlos, Alba, Orange, Egmont, and Hoorn—are meant to stand in as the briefest bit of expository orientation in need perhaps of a few additional details. After his father Charles V's abdication, Philip II ascended the throne as Holy Roman Emperor in 1555. In an effort to create stability within an already volatile set of seventeen Dutch provinces under Hapsburg rule, Philip sent his half-sister Margaret to serve as his regent in 1559, working in consort with a small coterie of Dutch nobles. By the time Philip assumed the throne, these nobles—led by the Count of Egmont, the Count of Hoorn, and William of Orange—had grown quite accustomed to a certain level of legal and financial independence, since Charles had relied on them for major financial support during his more than sixty years of war with the French. Very quickly, however, these magnates grew concerned about their shrinking political freedoms under Philip and about the Spanish government's heavy taxation and increasingly harsh response to the rapid proliferation of Protestantism in the region. They respectfully petitioned Philip for a greater degree of religious freedom since, as they argued, "persecution interfered with established laws and procedures; and they saw no reason why differences of belief should be treated so harshly."[21] Philip quickly made his position clear, however: there would be no amelioration of the heresy laws and no more autonomous control for the Dutch high nobility.

In response to Philip's brisk answer and to the ever-mounting violence of the Inquisition, a group of four hundred or so "lesser nobles" formed the League of Compromise in 1565, and in April 1566, about two hundred and fifty of them marched through Brussels to present the regent Margaret with their own petition of demands for antiheresy reforms—which had also been approved by Orange and others. At first, Margaret was alarmed by the sight of such a large group of protesters inside her palace, at which point one of her councilors, likely the seigneur of Berlaymont, famously remarked, "N'ayez pas peur, madame, ce ne sont que des gueux"[22]—Have no fear, Madame, these are only beggars. Little did Margaret or the seigneur know that in the years to come, this noble opposition movement of beggars, of *gueux* or *Geuzen*, would garner widespread popularity throughout the Dutch provinces. In fact, what began as a pejorative aside was reappropriated, across class lines, in all ensuing conflicts with the Spanish.[23] Schiller himself reported, "In a few days the town of Brussels swarmed with ash-gray garments such as were usually worn by mendicant friars and penitents. Every confederate put his whole family and domestics in this dress. . . . Hence the origin of the name 'Gueux,' which was subsequently borne in the Netherlands by all who seceded from popery and took up arms against the king."[24]

Philip reacted most harshly to these first signs of protest—even though they were respectful at first and even affirmed Philip's rightful place as sovereign—and in 1567, he sent the Duke of Alba to Brussels at the head of an army of ten thousand men. Almost immediately, Alba had Egmont and Hoorn (both of whom were actually Roman Catholics) arrested on charges of religious heresy. They were sentenced to death and beheaded in 1568, in the midst of over a thousand executions meted out by Alba's "Blood Court." Later in 1568, William of Orange, who had fled into exile just after Alba's arrival, emerged as the leader of the opposition and returned to Brussels to force out the "Iron Duke"—still claiming, though, to be acting on the king's behalf against an illegitimate despot. William's army was no match for Alba, however. After briskly defeating William's military campaign, the duke pushed forward in his tyrannical repression of the Protestants and upped his financial pressure on the region by imposing harsh new taxes, quickly creating "universal loathing"[25] and laying the groundwork for many years of revolt to come.

But what of Mount Potosí? Why are we sitting in the dark listening to the booming proclamations of the great *Silberberg* itself? Interestingly, it is Hartmut Schories, the performer who also plays the role of Philip II in a number of subsequent scenes, who gives voice to Potosí here. This casting choice seems intentional, as it is indicative of the provocative imbrications of free markets and "free" states, and of debt and revolution, that andcompany&Co. wants to examine. In the same breath, literally, Potosí represents both the source of Spanish wealth and colonial might, as well as Spain's (financial) demise due to the expansion of a global capitalist marketplace it could not colonize—one that was augmented by Potosí's riches—and which indeed flourished thanks in large part to the rapidly expanding Dutch economy. The program notes to *The (Coming) Insurrection* explain:

> Between 1550 and 1650, the Spanish Empire had to declare bankruptcy six times—despite the tons of gold and silver they imported from the New World. Even more paradoxical was this (as Schiller writes): "Even during the war, Philip could not stop the Dutch Republic from trading with his own subjects, and he would not even have wanted this. He himself paid the costs of the rebels' defense: for it was precisely the war that was intended to wear them down that also increased sales of their goods." While Philip II dreamed of an empire, of a universal monarchy, he was ruined by the emerging world market.[26]

Ironically, the Habsburg monarchs themselves installed the fiscal reforms that provided the Dutch with financial advantages over their sovereign—for the Dutch were slowly becoming far superior capitalists. Graham Darby explains, "Under the constant fiscal pressure to raise revenue for Charles V's wars, the States of Holland had managed to achieve increased control of the fiscal machinery of the province. The States thereby gained considerable experience floating loans on the credit of the province and collecting taxes to support them."[27] James Tracy elaborates further that each of the infrastructural arrangements originally introduced to fund Charles's wars involved a "transfer of authority from the central [Habsburg] government to parliamentary assemblies, and each was to prove of vital importance for the new rebel government."[28] Tracy continues, "As revenues came to be controlled by the provincial or General States, bankers on the Antwerp exchange drew the obvious conclusion; neglecting their erstwhile [Spanish] clients, the treasury officials of the hard-pressed central government, they went to the source of funds, demanding, as surety for their loans, the promissory notes of parliamentary assemblies."[29]

Over time, the provinces and their new republican parliaments were thus able to establish credit of their own and, ironically, become the creditors, at least in part, of the Spanish regime they were fighting. To make matters worse for the Spanish, the Dutch accrued additional wealth from the increasing trade their port cities brought in, and with the formation in 1602 of the Dutch East India Company, the world's first multinational corporation, they were well on their way to dominating all global trade. Karschnia remarks, "All the wars [Philip] waged against the Dutch made them even richer and him poorer."[30] Locked into a world in which they could no longer compete, the Spanish were unable to pay their debts or their armies, and they declared bankruptcy for the third time in 1575. "And that was the major shift," according to Karschnia. "That the Netherlands managed to defeat Spain was also a victory of the forces of modernity, especially the market: capital became the driving motor that could not be controlled anymore."[31]

As the committee of beggars dressed as miners slowly deconstruct Potosí from the inside out, unearthing their new play space within the walls of silver ore, we begin to understand the paradoxical structural position occupied by the *Geuzen*. Many of the people Philip used to fund his wars and expand his empire also brought about his undoing from within. This point is made explicit just a few minutes later, when act 1, scene 6 and act 3, scene 2 of Schiller's *Don Carlos* are rewritten and restaged in the new play space as Philip's worst "nightmare."[32] Sitting on his throne, the king is force-fed the liquefied gold and silver he has plundered from Potosí, administered by the miners-cum-*Geuzen* he has conquered. Joachim, dressed now as the Grand Inquisitor, presides over the torture as Philip chokes and groans. The Inquisitor proclaims, "And so the heretics convert the faithful into creditors of a debt to which you have also committed yourself, my king, through the loan the heretics accord the king so that he can go to war with them, and this, this is how they will defeat him."[33] Of course, for Schiller, "the good German Protestant"[34]—who also watches over Philip's persecution here—the Dutch Revolt was indeed a revolution to be celebrated, for it yielded the first modern, republican nation-state in Europe. But as Karschnia notes, "These *Geuzen* were not just rebels and little Robin Hoods but also the mercenaries of capital, fighting so that the market forces would not be stopped by some bigot king or the authority of the church."[35] Egmont, Hoorn, and Orange collaborated with the Spanish for a long time. They were the region's wealthiest and most powerful aristocrats and fully integrated "citizens of empire."[36] Many of their initial demands and petitions merely sought to return old rights to the Dutch aristocracy. And so, Karschnia exclaims, the ongoing debate throughout the production of *(Coming) Insurrection* and beyond was indeed, "Were they revolutionaries or not?"[37]

The associational, historical detour through the Netherlands continues into the present day, for it is in the face of severe austerity measures that took effect in the Netherlands in 2013 that the performance seeks to examine whether artists, particularly performance artists, have become the new beggars or if they are still working as agents of capital dressed up in beggars' clothes. As the program note narrates, echoing Potosí's gravelly voice, "The sovereigns are gone, but now the ocean [of silver] is bursting through the banks: global capitalism, whose course was set by Dutch merchants, is shipwrecked in the storm that it unleashed. Banking crises and state bankruptcies are both the beginning and the end of this story."[38] Even more ironic (or typical), Karschnia claims, is that some of the most aggressive neoliberal measures in response to the financial crisis happened in the Netherlands, still one of the richest countries in Europe. So, when Hartmut-as-Potosí instructs the *Geuzen*-miners to "guzzle" down the resources he has on offer—resources mobilized by and for those ever-reliable "silver-haired" audiences and that are indeed "too big to fail"—he seems also to be serving as a mouthpiece for the "new" cultural policy instituted by the current "conservative-liberal" Dutch administration under Mark Rutte.[39]

On June 10, 2011, the state secretary for culture Halbe Zijlstra unleashed a "tsunami"[40] with his proposal "More Than Quality: A New Vision of Cultural Policy," which announced the new Dutch government's intention of cutting the federal arts budget by 265 million euros—25 percent of its then-current expenditure. Paying no heed to the national Culture Council's recommendations, and even admitting that he "lacks any understanding of art and culture,"[41] Zijlstra argued that the austerity measures and accompanying set of "demand-driven"[42] funding instruments would create an "independent, strong and flexible cultural sector"[43] in the Netherlands by requiring arts institutions to justify their activities economically and compete for limited funds. Zijlstra's proposal criticized the arts writ large for being "too [detached] from reality" and continually displaying "a mismatch of supply and demand with audiences."[44] To support his claims further, Zijlstra mobilized a wide-reaching albeit mean-spirited rhetoric, "paint[ing] artists as elitist, parasitic, sophisticated beggars, living off state subsidies," explains Ann Demeester, director of De Appel art center in Amsterdam.[45]

Of course, in comparison to the American National Endowment for the Arts' 150 million annual dollars, a budget reduction to 600 million from 800 million euros still seems more than lush. However, since the early 1970s, artists and cultural organizations in the Netherlands have been supported almost exclusively by the state, and there is practically no culture of private or corporate philanthropy. Speculation and panic therefore ran deep in the Dutch arts community, especially since Zijlstra's proposal would institute these drastic new measures without providing any leeway for artists or institutions to adjust. As of January 2013, the budgets of half the nation's contemporary visual arts institutes, including Witte de With, De Appel, BAK, and Marres, would be slashed. Budgets for cultural foundations such as SKOR (Foundation for Art in the Public Domain) and NiMK (Netherlands Media Art Institute) would be slashed. Public funds for postgraduate and postacademic educational institutions like the Rijksakademie and Jan van Eyck Akademie would be slashed. Magazines and literary journal budgets would be slashed due to their "limited public outreach."[46] Hit hardest of all, however, would be the performing arts. Of the 118 performing arts organizations in the Netherlands, approximately 70 would receive no more public financing at all.[47] Interestingly, the budgets of the big, historic institutions, those that Zijlstra considered to be "world-class,"[48] such as De Nederlandse Opera and Het Nationale Ballet, would be spared entirely from the cuts, and the larger repertory theater companies, like Toneelgroep Amsterdam, would face only minor budget adjustments. But this strong bias toward "top institutions" meant that the incredibly expansive, and unique, field—or scene—of smaller, independent ensembles, "free" organizations, and festivals in the Netherlands would be decimated.[49]

It is in the realm of this expansive "free" scene that the Dutch and German situations begin to coincide—at least, again, associationally. The German military occupation (*Besatzung*) during the Second World War inspired the establishment of those "top institutions" in the Netherlands. Convinced that artists could help distribute the Nazi message, federal subsidies to theater artists increased sixtyfold during the war. The Germans also planned a centralized arts council and state-stages in the major Dutch cities, which would be realized only after the war and the occupation had ended.[50] Then, on the stage of the Stadsschouwburg, the municipal theater in Amsterdam, a few tomatoes changed the course of Dutch theater history. On October 9, 1969, two disgruntled theater students, Lien Heyting and Ernst Katz, threw tomatoes at performers during the premiere of the Nederlandse Comedie's production of *The Tempest*. This "tomato action," or *Aktie Tomaat*, provoked discussions and sustained structural debates across the country about the "conservative" nature of the Dutch theater, the outdated repertoire, the lack of political relevance, and the drastic need for new artistic forms and accompanying funding instruments outside the state-stage. The tomato controversy lasted for months, with a few added stink bombs to boot, and ultimately provoked a massive and radical restructuring of the entire Dutch theater infrastructure, spearheaded by Marga Klompé, the head of the Ministry of Culture at the time.[51] The number of subsidized theaters, both big and small, increased almost fivefold between 1969 and 1985.[52] But more important, Klompé's initiative allocated a substantial budget *directly* to artists for "experimental and innovative work."[53] This new funding instrument facilitated an unprecedented boom of activity and the emergence of "independent"—and ultimately quite influential—smaller ensembles and individual artists, who have come to constitute the unique and heterogeneous scene placed under siege by the neoliberal reforms of Rutte, Zijlstra, and others. Karschnia explains:

> During the following four decades, a completely distinct cultural landscape evolved, with independent ensembles, free production houses, new university courses, and an institutional infrastructure that had given rise to the "miracle of Dutch theatre" (Hans-Thies Lehmann). Thanks to this campaign, Dutch theatre came to be the model for all "iconoclasts" of the stage . . .—a structural reform Germany is still waiting for! As every independent theatre maker knows: the municipal theatre of a small provincial town has a larger budget than the so-called "independent scene" in Germany.[54]

We return, finally, to the situation in Berlin, by means of this associational tour. For as Karschnia continues, "This is an irony of history, too: while the German system of municipal theatres is struggling for reforms inspired by the Dutch model, the Dutch system is being restructured according to the German model."[55] It was just months before Zijlstra's reforms went into effect that Annemie Vanackere left the Schouwburg in Rotterdam and signed on as the new artistic director of the HAU in Berlin—only to find herself at the center of strikingly familiar debates.

While there was no distinctive tomato-based catalyst that launched the development of the free-scene in Berlin (and greater Germany), its origins can also be traced back to those long, antiauthoritarian marches through the institutions—including the theaters[56]—in the wake of 1968. In the 1960s and '70s, more and more collectives of young theater artists defined themselves as "free groups" as a means of differentiation from and protest against the "dictatorial" regime of auteurial *Regietheater* and its accompanying state-stage subsidy structures that had become, and in many ways still are, the norm in postwar German theater.[57] Many of these groups borrowed both aesthetic and organizational inspiration from those hallowed "off" institutions of the

American and European (post-)avant-gardes: The Living Theatre, La MaMa E.T.C., Performing Garage, Odin Teatret, and so on. The burgeoning scene garnered additional momentum in the 1980s on a variety of fronts. In West Berlin, an expanding alternative scene of squats and other temporary use (*Zwischennutzung*) projects provided a laboratory for an independent, do-it-yourself ethos, which included clowning and other children's theater forms, street and site-specific performance, wandering spectacles, and other interdisciplinary experiments.[58] In 1982, Andrzej Wirth and Hans-Thies Lehmann founded the Institut für Angewandte Theaterwissenschaft (Institute for Applied Theater Studies) in Giessen, a pedagogical environment that fostered experimentation for a new generation of often postdramatic performance practitioners, many of whom were expressly interested in working outside of the German state-stages. This model of laboratory-based pedagogy has since been taken up at the University of Hildesheim as well.[59] There was also a move toward centralization (or further "scenification") with the establishment of the first self-designating "free" institutions to receive different forms, and amounts, of government funding: the new Theater am Turm (1980) and Künstlerhaus Mousonturm (1988) in Frankfurt, Kampnagel in Hamburg (1982), Theater im Pumpenhaus in Münster (1985), Theater am Halleschen Ufer (1992), and Sophiensæle (1996) in Berlin, as well as the first semiannual "free" festivals, like Impulse Theater Biennale in 1990.[60] In 1999, the Federal and Berlin city governments also voted to establish a new funding instrument, the Hauptstadtkulturfonds (Capital City Cultural Fund) to support innovative individual projects and events, which has, since its inception, become one of the central means of support for "free" projects in Berlin (like the Volkspalast, for example).[61]

As a result of this piecemeal and heterogeneous coming of age, it is difficult to determine just what kinds of performance work constitute the so-called free-scene. In fact, advocates for and practitioners in the scene tend to emphasize the "countless different institutions and organizational forms," which "cannot be reduced to one idea."[62] The result is a broad swath of multi- and interdisciplinary artists, ensembles, and institutions that consider themselves part of the same field of activity: both the expat street performer, for example, and the internationally acclaimed, postdramatic performance ensemble performing on the HAU stage as part of an international tour might—and often do—call themselves free-scene artists. What unites these artists, at least discursively, is that they understand themselves to be "work[ing] beyond predetermined structures."[63] They see themselves as acting outside of and differently from the so-called top institutions, those repertoire- and ensemble-based state-stages that are, for the most part, still considered to be *the* theater in Germany. Annemarie Matzke, a professor at Hildesheim and one of the founding members of She She Pop, suggests, "The conditions of production are conceptualized by the artists themselves—as much as is possible within economic constraints."[64]

In Berlin, however, these "economic constraints" have become more and more constraining. Again, an American reader might guffaw when hearing that the Berlin Senate recently approved a cultural budget of 625 million euros for 2018 and 603 million euros for 2019—an increase of nearly 20 percent, or 120 million euros, from the previous budget.[65] But only 6.5 million euros of that increased culture allocation was dedicated to the free-scene.[66] A major portion of this money was to be used to cover the rising salaries of those artists already employed by state-stage institutions as well as renovations of the buildings that house those institutions.[67] As of 2013, approximately nineteen hundred performance-based artists—actors, dancers, musicians, and opera singers—were employed permanently by Berlin's state-stages;[68] those numbers have only increased marginally in the ensuing years. The rest of Berlin's performing artists—at least twenty times that number—work consistently as freelancers without any long-term job security.[69] Many of these artists, when they can score a job on publicly funded projects (which has become an increasingly difficult proposition in the face of enormous competition), work for far less than the minimum wage. A good number of them work on projects for free.[70] The average annual income for freelance performing artists across Germany is 16,000 euros[71]—and in Berlin that number is even lower.[72]

The wide array of free-scene institutions now operating in Berlin are no better off, as their budgets are, oddly enough, not available to be used for artistic purposes. Since commercial rents have risen so much in the past fifteen years thanks to gentrification and Berlin's ever-increasing star status, many institutions must use up to 75 percent of their funding for rent.[73] Ballhaus Ost, for example, receives 157,000 euros per year from the Berlin Senate and pays 120,000 euros back to the city in rent, leaving hardly any money for programming, let alone fair wages.[74] Even a well-supported institution like the Neuköllner Oper, which receives 1.1 million per annum, can pay its performers only 100 euros per show and 1,200 euros for eight weeks of full-time rehearsal. Many groups pay nothing for rehearsal time and can afford only 30–60 euros per evening.[75] Many artists are therefore forced either to live on unemployment or to work multiple jobs to make ends meet.[76] And in the midst of extensive austerity measures across Europe, coproduction partners and money for touring (to the Netherlands, for instance) have increasingly waned in recent years.

Free-scene artists are united, therefore, to some extent by the very real "economic constraints" of precarity. And indeed, precarity provides another vocabulary for narrating—albeit more critically—the state of things in Berlin (as well as the Netherlands). For as Nicholas Ridout and Rebecca Schneider remind us, "Analyzing the production of feelings and the various practices or structures through which affect circulates is essential to understanding the neoliberal condition."[77] In their coedited special issue for *TDR: The Drama Review* in 2012, Ridout and Schneider curated a number of essays that tracked the complicated imbrications of performance and precarity in order to ask, "Does the place of the arts in global capitalism, and the particular relations implied by 'affective labor,' mean that, in some ways, theatrical labor has a particular purchase on the contemporary scene in which such life and work appears?"[78] In the preceding pages about Berlin's contemporary scene, then, I could have also told a story about the ways in which the antiauthoritarian "artistic critiques" of the post-1968 free-sceners were not breaks with, or even marches through, the institutions, but rather how these "critiques" have been neatly recuperated by the "new spirit" of neoliberal capital. I could have told a story about the ways flexibility, innovation, experimentation, and creativity have become the cages that mark performance-based art's complicity with post-Fordism. This story is one that asks us to inquire, if we didn't already: How *free* is the free-scene after all?[79]

The link between this alternative narration and andcompany&Co.'s *(Coming) Insurrection* becomes clearer when we examine a recent set of debates and mobilizations "for a new cultural policy"[80] in Berlin. On August 23, 2013, the Independent Art Coalition launched an extended advocacy campaign with "precarity" as its rallying cry. Over the next month—and continuing sporadically into the present—the coalition coordinated a series of radio and television appearances, feature articles, social media blasts, petitions, marches, demonstrations, public conversations, letters to and discussions with politicians, sit-ins during the Berlin Senate Cultural Committee's budget deliberations, a custom-designed splash page for all free-scene institution websites, and a converted "informational" fire truck roaming the city with flyers, posters, and stickers.[81] As Christophe Knoch, the longtime public face of the coalition, made clear in each of his appearances, "All artists initiatives working in the field of the independent arts in Berlin, no matter what genre or format, collaborate for a strengthening and higher financial support for independent art production."[82]

The coalition's campaign and accompanying arguments for a new perspective on cultural policy proceeded in three stages. The first step was to increase knowledge about and visibility for the free-scene. The coalition began with many of the statistics I laid out above, confirming that the desired flexibility of the free-scene has ultimately resulted in widespread infrastructural insecurity. "It cannot be the case," Knoch exclaimed, "that publicly financed and selected artistic projects are possible only through self-exploitation and that people who make this rich cultural scene possible with their work have an income below the subsistence minimum."[83] One of the reasons for this lack of support, he continued, is that Berlin's political decision makers are mostly unaware of the free-scene's extensive activities and accompanying financial uncertainty. On this point, the coalition is not far off: even the former state secretary for culture André Schmitz expressed his bewilderment: "Working conditions for young artists in Berlin cannot be so catastrophic; otherwise they would hardly come to live in the city."[84] "All politicians have said basically the same thing," Knoch responded. "'What would a bus tour of the free-scene look like?' They do not know what the free-scene is! . . . Make them aware of what you are doing!"[85]

Second, in 2012 the coalition laid out its broad-sweeping ten-point plan, one that, as they claimed with an ironic twist, would make Berlin's funding infrastructures "more *flexible* in order to adapt to the needs of changing artistic practice."[86] This standard "flexicurity"[87] platform called for the following reforms:

1. an overall increase by 20 million euros of public spending for the free-scene—which should come from the newly instituted "city tax" on tourism;
2. new "flexible" funding instruments for the free-scene, which "enables a timely response and flow of funds";
3. an increase of financial support for free-scene institutions, to "facilitate continuity in the development process and in long-term planning";
4. a strategic reallocation from existing funding instruments for the free-scene, and not for state-stages, which already have a steady subsidy;
5. a minimum wage (of 2,000 euros per month) for artists working on federal- or state-supported projects;
6. a new grant infrastructure to support visual arts and music projects;
7. a moratorium on the sale of state property to private developers, to curb gentrification and real-estate inflation;
8. increased support to fund individual projects in each of Berlin's neighborhoods;
9. increased support and solidarity between the established "top institutions" and the free-scene; and finally,
10. greater transparency in budget negotiations and allocations and fair representation for the free-scene on granting juries.[88]

The third and final prong of the coalition's argument was the most sticky but also the most productive in the context of this discussion, for it brings us back directly to that question I have raised in different guises throughout this section: Are the (new) beggars-cum-revolutionaries always already agents of capital? In fact, that is precisely the claim the Independent Art Coalition makes, supplementing their call for a politics of visibility and flexicurity with arguments about their immaterial use-value. All the promotional materials distributed via Web and print during the month of action and beyond began with this catchphrase: "Creative spirit is even more ephemeral than capital—hold on to it!"[89] Knoch and other representatives of the coalition then followed up on this motto, this unmediated mash-up of commerce and counterculture, with statements justifying the free-scene as a post-Fordist poster child: "Artists and cultural workers create the intellectual value of the city of Berlin."[90] Or: "The city's independent cultural scene therefore plays a key role in the future prospects of Berlin."[91] Or: "The arts in all their variety and interplay constitute the attractiveness of Berlin and are a crucial factor for both tourism and the economy."[92] And finally: "Art's creative impulses are increasingly a motor for the city's economic development processes. The boom in Berlin's creative economy would not have taken place without the free art scene."[93] In another prescient diagnosis, also from that special *TDR* issue, Bojana Cvejić and Ana Vujanović sum up the situation as if they had been writing specifically about Berlin's free-scene (and perhaps they were in part):

> The recent implementation of post-Fordism in the performing arts has occurred largely without critical appraisal. Performance workers in Europe have looked at current forms of freelance work, as well as lifestyles, conditioned by the neoliberal market, and mistaken them for innovative and creative formats: production of artistic research in residencies, laboratories, and other temporary working situations; festivalization and the coproduction of projects that atomize and multiply work without end or limit; the proliferation of small-scale projects that rejuvenate the labor force under cheap labor contracts, etc. As undying individualism prevents performance workers from reflecting their conditions in terms of political economy, the post-Fordist condition is seen by many as a positive attribute of an avantgarde with which they overidentify. This paradoxically leads not only to increased economic self-precarization, . . . but also to political complicity with neoliberal capitalism, for which performance practices today supply a training ground.[94]

It is precisely these overlapping ideas of complicity and critique, of art as occupation and occupation as art,[95] that andcompany&Co.'s *(Coming) Insurrection* continues to probe throughout the rest of its associational tour.[96] Some minutes after Joachim-as-Inquisitor subjects King Philip to his own private inquisition-by-silver, for example, the entire committee—all dressed as inquisitors now, with long red robes and not a small degree of Mel Brooks and Monty Python irony—demands that we all "confess, confess, confess" amid torturously high-pitched, screeching notes bowed on a homemade *erhu* and flickering lights. Finally, unable to stand the torture any longer, Joachim is forced to his knees, stripping off his Grand Inquisitor costume and undershirt, and he confesses bare-chested, screaming:

> I confess. I confess that this body tries to create money from nothing too. I confess that this body has a house with a huge mortgage. I confess that this body is an artist's body that leases a cute little red car that he can't afford. I confess that this body produces a child that an artist cannot afford either. I confess that this body has a credit card on which I buy books on Amazon to steal the ideas of other authors.[97]

On the one hand, as Karschnia reflected later on the coalition's activist efforts, "I was highly critical of people saying, 'We as artists—thanks to us, real estate prices are rising, and we should have a share of it.' I totally reject that. . . . I would not allow my company's name on any leaflet that would say we are value producers."[98] "The 'free groups,'" he continues elsewhere, "need to be aware that they are not freely acting in some romantic, premodern outside, but that they are part of the market, which has subsumed the entire society."[99] On the other hand, however, and only a few sentences later, Karschnia speaks of the "great opportunity," even the "political potential" of a free-scene.[100] He and the rest of the andcompany&Co. ensemble attended a number of the coalition's activist events; Karschnia even spoke on behalf of the free-scene at the largest of their demonstrations in front of the Schlossplatz on September 28, 2013, and has since made claims like these: "I want to constructively support this effort. I think the coalition is important, and what they demand is sound. They do good work, and it is important to also have cultural politicians who are really able to come up with an agenda that politicians can understand."[101] Or, even farther-reaching: "This is why I am . . . for maintaining this term 'free-scene'—*because* of the inevitable discussions about what should be 'free' in our scene now. Surprisingly, the attempt to answer this question leads quickly to the heart not only of what constitutes the political in political theater but in our time as well."[102] How then are we to reconcile these two kinds of statements? How does andcompany&Co.'s occupational aesthetics of rehearsal critique and/or make use of the aesthetics of protest employed by the Independent Art Coalition in support of Berlin's free-scene?

✦ ✦ ✦

Hartmut rises from his egg-seat and moves center stage to confront the committee with his frustration, reprising, in a different tone, his earlier skepticism: "Where is it? Where is this insurrection of yours?" With increasing aggravation, he starts moving frenetically around the stage as the others try to calm him down. He kneels and knocks loudly: "Is it in this egg? Hallo! Hallo! No, it's not. Is it in Vincent's guitar?" He runs across the stage and accosts Vincent—who is still dressed as Schiller. He then moves into the house and starts running up and down the stairs, stepping over audience members along the way and shouting, "Is it in the audience? Hallo! Hallo! No, not there either! Where is it then?" With even more aggression now, he runs up the stairs and into the former-Potosí play space: "Is it in the royal palace? Is it under the king's desk? No. Nothing. Is it behind the wallpaper [*Tapete*]? Oh!" He stops short after pulling a piece of wallpaper off the back wall, only to reveal another painted backdrop. "Behind the wallpaper . . . [*pause*] . . . is simply more wallpaper," he screams, as he runs around the set pulling other large pieces of paper off the walls. "Shit. Wallpaper. Wallpaper everywhere. Wallpaper. A wallpaper insurrection." He charges at Joachim and repeats, "When is it going to happen? Where could it be?" Joachim quiets Hartmut down by slowly explaining, first to him and then to the rest of us, that the content of a particular occupation is not as important as "what happens between the bodies, between us and you." This remark inspires Vincent to take up his guitar again and play a few chords on repeat as he explains that he recently wrote a cover version of the Bots' 1979 hit song, titled coincidentally enough, "Opstaan," "Aufstehen," "Stand Up." Vincent begins to sing, most melodically and with cello accompaniment: "All those who want a better life should stand up!" The song builds slowly in intensity and volume as he continues singing about "fucking capitalism," the "reign of the selfish," about "oil," and "big brands," and those who "drink piña coladas while walking over the corpses of the 99 percent." Slowly, with each new verse, members of the committee begin to stand up, followed by members of the audience. And by the time Vincent returns to that opening refrain, everyone in the house begins clapping, singing, chanting, even shouting together on repeat, "All those who want a better life should stand up!" While Rüdiger Hauffe blares his saxophone and Vincent continues the jam, other members of the committee run stage right and left to don their red Inquisition attire. Surrounded then by eight members of an Inquisition committee, there is a very, very pregnant pause, in which Vincent sits silently, stuttering a little bit, biting his cuticle, as if "he doesn't know how to go on."[103] Finally, he asks the audience meekly, "So, what do you think is gonna happen to the economy?" The Inquisition microphone echoes, "What do you think is gonna happen to the economy?" With a jolt, Vincent snaps to, answering immediately without hesitation, without stopping for a breath, and harnessing—verbatim—the spirit of the controversial day trader Alessio Rastani, of BBC fame: "It's gonna crash, and it's gonna fall pretty hard, because markets are ruled right now by fear. Investors and the big money, the smart money—I'm talking about the big funds, the hedge funds, the institutions—they don't buy this rescue plan. They basically know the market is toast. They know the stock market is finished. The euro, as far as they are concerned, they don't really care. They are moving their money away to safer assets, like treasury bonds and the US dollar. So, it's not gonna work. Look, I'm only playing a trader here! If I see an opportunity to make money, I go with that. We don't really care how they're gonna fix the economy, how they're gonna fix the whole situation. Our job is to make money from it. And I have a confession to make: personally, I've been dreaming of this recession for years."

At the "Phantasm and Politics" conversation that took place on the HAU stage just one night after *(Coming) Insurrection*'s Berlin premiere, the question on the table was "whether and to what degree art can not only depict and represent current social movements such as Occupy in the theater but also must be able to abandon the aesthetic distance to empirical reality in order to react appropriately to a social reality perceived as in crisis."[104] This opening provocation proceeds by means of a number of traditional assumptions about the relationships between supposed binaries: reality and representation, heteronomy and autonomy, and so on. It understands aesthetic representation (*Darstellung*) as a kind of distance from social or political reality, and it

The (Coming) Insurrection: The Inquisition. Photograph copyright © Hans Jörg Michel.

assumes that art's reaction to or engagement with said reality requires in turn a retreat from representation. Hans-Thies Lehmann was invited to begin the evening at HAU with prepared remarks, a condensed version of a lecture he gave in Berlin in 2012 about the borders and potential "border crossings [*Grenzgänge*] between art and politics."[105] By means of his meditations on the differences between what he terms an "aesthetics of insurrection" (*Ästhetik des Aufstands*) and an "aesthetics of resistance" (*Ästhetik des Widerstands*), Lehmann worked here to reprise some of his long-standing arguments about what I have elsewhere called postdramatic theater's *paradoxically parallaxical* relationship to the political.[106] By means of this terminological distinction between *Aufstand* and *Widerstand*, insurrection and resistance, Lehmann also argues, albeit implicitly, for a dialectical reworking of the text used to frame the HAU event: How might postdramatic theater—and on this evening, how might *The (Coming) Insurrection*—represent current social movements in the theater *and* also abandon aesthetic distance to a social reality in crisis?

Ironically, and in spite of andcompany&Co.'s title, Lehmann is not particularly interested in the dynamics of an aesthetics of insurrection. As he explained early on in his remarks, "The aesthetic is never an unproblematic companion on the route to political praxis."[107] He questions any artistic practices (in the theater or beyond) that cling to a preconceived ideology or political message, or practices that consciously attempt to participate in a particular political movement (or moment). In Lehmann's polemical reading, so-called insurrectionist practitioners—who range, he explains, from the *piqueteros*, Zapatistas, and Occupiers to Hans Haacke, Rimini Protokoll, Reverend Billy, and the Yes Men—understand and institute, maybe even to the detriment of their own work, "aesthetic action *as* direct political action,"[108] as unmediated intervention, predictable in its effects. Lehmann is far less interested in an aesthetics of insurrection, he claims, because it constitutes a category of practices that reify the binarizing logics that have structured so much of the historical discourse on art and politics.

Lehmann is much more interested in practices that work to overcome these kinds of static divisions, and his dialectical imagination commits him to an ongoing series of ever-tenuous mediations. An aesthetics of resistance, then, is for Lehmann a complicated notion that requires extensive reflection on the (unintended) possibilities of politics at the theater—the kind of politics that Lehmann wants ultimately to attribute to the postdramatic. "Resistance" is not the polar opposite, the so-called autonomous counterpoint, of an insurrectionary aesthetic of heteronomous demands. Rather, for Lehmann, resistance challenges our "understanding of what politics in theatre can be,"[109] challenges us to move "beyond the traditional antagonism between autonomy and engagement."[110] Harking back—both on the HAU stage and in earlier writings—to Theodor Adorno's more messianic leanings, Lehmann's resistance recasts theater's (negative) political potential as more indirect, more unpredictable. An aesthetics of resistance is an "aesthetics in the subjunctive,"[111] one that highlights potential doubts, possible failures, and unanswered questions, and reflects on the "memory of a possible future of the past."[112] Resistance refuses binarization, but it also moves beyond a mere *blurring* of lines or *dissolution* of dichotomies, beyond a more idealist *Aufhebung*, or sublation. Lehmann contends that the postdramatic both embraces *and* challenges—or, as he says over and over again, "interrupts"— the fundamental differences (even contradictions) between art and politics, between representation and reality, between autonomy and heteronomy. To do so, it both incorporates elements of the insurrectionary *and* moves beyond a direct politics, thus producing situations that "separat[e] the new theater" from what he calls more traditional political forms.[113]

It is no coincidence that Lehmann was invited to talk about *The (Coming) Insurrection* and resistance on the HAU stage. Karschnia had studied with Lehmann in Frankfurt, and the two remain friends and consistent interlocutors. As Karschnia explains, "We've had many discussions with him [Lehmann], because we have always wanted to achieve political efficacy and still make theater. I myself am always torn between theater and activism."[114] This "tear," this "between"—again, despite andcompany&Co.'s chosen title—must not be read as an insurrectionary taking of sides, as a neat and tidy, one-sided rendering. Instead, andcompany&Co.'s performance seems to situate itself consciously within the negatively dialectical contours of Lehmann's thinking about resistance. On the one hand, as Karschnia makes clear, the group thought concretely about their "staging of occupation" as a move *beyond* mere fantasy and a means of *real* intervention in both the Dutch and German situations.[115] "I was pushing not just to perform it, represent it, but to really see it as a rehearsal for an occupation—[to] take it seriously," he explains. "And that was the tricky stuff—because we wanted to reduce the acting part as much as possible." Karschnia continues:

> We talked about occupations and theater spaces. And the Dutch situation was interesting because a lot of those theaters that were threatened by the cuts used to be squats and were turned into theaters only after squatting saved them. But that history is forgotten. So, in a way, we wanted to activate that history and say, "Okay, this used to be a squat; maybe it will be a squat." Look at Teatro Valle in Rome and the Embros Theater in Athens; they keep theaters by squatting them. . . . It was, in a way, a situation that was not just fiction. We said, "Maybe this is really a rehearsal for a squat, a *Besetzungsprobe*." . . . And maybe that will become the situation. Enter a theater space and then keep it.[116]

On the other hand, Karschnia explains that the performance insists most emphatically on an *Abstand*, a "distance" from real political practice: "There is also something playful, the politics of art require a moment of nonseriousness. We don't just practice cultural policy and make realistic proposals, which are necessary, of course, but also boring, like: We want a portion of the city tax."[117] For Karschnia, this insistence on play—with all its Schillerian connotations—is "indispensable [*unverzichtbar*] for aesthetic praxis" as a social practice charged with "exceeding" (*überschreiten*) the dichotomy between earnestness and irony, and dichotomous thinking more broadly.[118]

This insistence on perpetual flux—between reality and representation, earnestness and irony, and so on—is certainly evident in the associational and historical tours described in the preceding pages. Relentless "play" also provides a cipher for reading the "clash between anarchist violence and Schillerian aestheticism,"[119] staged as a series of tenuous mash-ups of *Don Carlos* and the Invisible Committee's *Coming Insurrection* sprinkled throughout the performance. For instance, act 1, scene 2 of *Don Carlos*, in which Carlos admits to the marquis that he loves his mother and needs Posa to repay an old debt, has here been newly written as a melodramatic and highly stylized metareflection about the nature of friendship, affinity, and encounter in times of persecution.[120] Act 1, scene 5, in which Carlos's mother instructs him to preserve his love for her for his future kingdom, has also been rewritten—with a bit of flamenco dancing to boot—as a metareflection on the possibilities, or lack thereof, of love under capital, and the nefarious role of the (heterosexual) couple, the family, and other traditional modes of organization, including the theater.[121] Even the famous act 3, scene 10, in which Posa tells the king that he cannot and will not work as a royal servant and instead demands "freedom of thought"—*Gedankenfreiheit*—has been revamped as a metareflection-cum-madrigal (featuring a giant Pac-Man puppet) about the impossibility of contemporary *Gedankenfreiheit*: "Freedom is no longer a name scrawled on walls, for today it is always followed, as if by its shadow, with the word 'security.'"[122]

Perhaps the most explicit example of andcompany&Co.'s attempts to stage the tenuous both *and* neither/nor of Lehmann's paradoxically resistant postdramatic aesthetics can be found in the scenic movement across the pregnant pause described at the start of this section: the movement (or clash) between Vincent's insurrectionary protest song and his invocation of Alessio Rastani's controversial appearance on the BBC. Vincent's song—and the audience's response—facilitate, on the one hand, a moment in *The (Coming) Insurrection* that feels improvisational, open, yet also openly committed to its cause. The entire group sits around, hangs out, plays music, sings, and even cuddles together with their oversize eggs. In the immediacy of the moment—and especially once Vincent starts to sing—we really do begin to experience the materiality of the protest, the vulnerability of the squat, the spirit of the picket. The boundaries between audience and performer begin to dissolve. Direct address yields entirely to call and response. We all stand together, sing together, chant and clap together, united in the present and in the quest for a "better life." As the song progresses toward its conclusion, even melody yields to an intensity of feeling "between the bodies," in which absolutely nothing feels rehearsed, and the genuine expression of frustration, wants, needs, rage, and hope feels possible. In Erika Fischer-Lichte's rather romantic vocabulary, one might say that the song facilitates a few "moments of enchantment"[123] where the boundaries between artist and spectator blur, and the focus turns instead toward contingency, participation, and "bodily co-presence"[124]—a 99 percent come alive, come together in that moment, all *committed* to "fucking capitalism." In Lehmann's more cautious vocabulary—hesitant ever to commit to such an easy insurrectionary aesthetic—we might say that the song forges, or at least gestures at, an insurrectionary moment that becomes "more presence than representation, more shared than communicated experience, more process than product, more manifestation than signification, more energetic impulse than information."[125] And just a few minutes later, Sascha takes center stage and invokes a different insurrectionary vocabulary to expound on the power of the music: "Revolutionary movements do not spread by contamination but by *resonance*. . . . An insurrection is not like a plague or a forest fire—a linear process which spreads from place to place after an initial spark. It rather takes the shape of a music, whose focal points, though dispersed in time and space, succeed in imposing the rhythm of their own vibrations, always taking on more density."[126] We are then overtaken by long, uncomfortable, nervous silence.

On the other side of this most productive non sequitur, Vincent stages a verbatim reenactment of Alessio Rastani's rambling tirade—a performance that itself staged a fierce face-off between seriousness and satire. Rastani, a self-proclaimed stock and foreign exchange trader, appeared on the BBC in September 2011, proclaiming that Goldman Sachs rules the world and prophesizing the inevitable collapse of the euro, saying that the "savings of millions of people are going to vanish."[127] He announced without a flinch—and to the astonishment of his BBC interviewer—that he had been dreaming of the ongoing recession for years because, "when the market crashes, if you know what to do, if you have the right plan set up, you can make a lot of money."[128] Rastani's appearance caused waves in the blogosphere and beyond, and the video went viral, making him, as David Frost announced the following week, "an internet sensation." But, as Frost queried the camera, "was he an honest but brutal money man or a devious hoaxer?"[129] No one could be sure. In the days following Rastani's appearance, speculation ran deep that the whole episode might be another in a long string of "tactical performance"[130] hoaxes from those mischievous Yes Men. However, a few days later, the Yes Men published an article in the London *Guardian* emphatically dismissing the rumors that Rastani's confession was a prank: "We Yes Men heard about it right away, because soon after the broadcast, people started emailing from all over the world to congratulate us on another prank well done. They couldn't imagine that a real trader could possibly speak so candidly about the market, so they assumed Rastani was one of our posturings. He wasn't."[131]

Of course, it is possible that this op-ed was just another strategic piece of the multimedia performance puzzle, but there has been no subsequent evidence to substantiate claims one way or the other. Vincent's re-presentation of Rastani's remarks, then, serves as a re-presentation of—and a simultaneous opportunity to reflect upon—a kind of performance that remains wholly unpredictable, that thrives on its dissonance, its unintended consequences, one that issues no guarantee (for better or worse) that its desired effect will be achieved or even understood. In other words, a performance that—to invoke the seemingly Adornian voice of Joe Kelleher—is both effective and affective thanks to "'its seeming fragility and tendency to *un*truth' rather than from the strength of its representations and the justice of its political 'messages.'"[132] Or, in the case of Rastani the inadvertent Yes Man, the ever unpredictable (in)justice of his (a)political message.

For Lehmann, it is of vital importance that *The (Coming) Insurrection* consciously includes both of these scenes, as well as the uncomfortable transition between them. It is essential that the performance *both* carves out—or occupies—a physical space dedicated most explicitly to our collective imaginations *and* also reserves—or occupies—an imaginary space, a space that exists only in and for our imaginations. Like Adorno, and always also citing

Rancière, Lehmann reads this instance of both *and* neither/nor as a resistant reconfiguration of the "landscape of the possible,"[133] a fleeting glance toward a different future. And as Lehmann explained during the HAU discussion, andcompany&Co. performs this kind of resistant glance in their persistent albeit tenuous movement across the existential chasm, their insistence on scenic juxtapositions that produce "absolute *Unfug*, absolute Dada" and facilitate "a kind of stop, a kind of self-interruption."[134]

We too must stop here for a quick moment, however, and in line with the performance, ask whether Lehmann has fallen prey—against his will—to a different kind of *easy* politics, a different kind of aesthetic romanticism, or even political complicity. Has Lehmann indeed fallen prey to the lure of a "wallpaper insurrection," to the lure of that pure aesthetic experience so conveniently oblivious to desired effects? Moreover, is postdramatic theater—and especially postdramatic theater in Berlin's free-scene—a mere apologia for the neoliberal state of things? The most adamant proponent of this critical position in the context of the recent free-scene debates has been Thomas Ostermeier, artistic director of the Schaubühne Berlin. In a special fiftieth anniversary edition of *Text+Kritik*, in which Ostermeier was invited to reflect on "the future of [German] theater," he comes down harshly on the pervasive discourse of the postdramatic as precisely an "affirmative aesthetic of capitalist realism."[135] Ostermeier sardonically glosses Lehmann's thinking:

> There are just as many subjective truths in the auditorium as there are spectators, but no valid objectifiable truth behind all that happens on the stage; our experience of reality is completely fragmented, and this experience of reality is looking for an expression onstage. A complex world, multifaceted experiences that are expressed through the use of many media: body, dance, image, video, music, projection, documentary, autobiography, spoken word. This sampling of fragments proves to me that my experience of reality is correct, namely that the complexity of the world is impenetrable, and therefore the question of political responsibility, and even more important, of guilt, cannot be answered. . . . In a world of neoliberal doctrine, nothing could be better for the profiteers than the belief that there would no longer be anyone to blame—everything is so complex and convoluted, no one can be held responsible for anything.[136]

Ostermeier then goes on to make a case for reinstituting an insurrectionary version of what Lehmann calls a "theatre of sense and synthesis," a theater in which the "possibility of synthesizing interpretation"[137] remains intact, in order to critique the "devastating sociopolitical developments of the past twenty years"[138]—flexible work hours, digitalization of the everyday, consistently flexible labor contracts that mandate consistent debt insecurity, and so on. Ostermeier is emphatic that his theater at the Schaubühne can confront the pervasive neoliberal condition: "We *can* talk about these things on the stage; quite competently, if we nourish our imaginations with all that is taking place around us."[139]

Karschnia is most critical of Ostermeier's brand of a mere *aestheticization* critique. In a direct, albeit coded, response to Ostermeier, he writes, "Anyone today who still only wants to talk about content instead of form wants to remain silent about the institutions. But the political in the theater begins with the conditions of production."[140] In the next section, I return to the larger implications of Karschnia's claim as it pertains specifically to the different modes of artistic organization and production on Berlin's state-stages and in the free-scene. But before we can make that turn, we must also notice that Karschnia redeploys another, lesser-known side of Lehmann's thinking against Ostermeier's mode of argument here. In fact, he cites Lehmann almost verbatim—though without reference—when he writes, "The old formula remains true: it is not about making political theater, but rather about making theater politically."[141] Lehmann has long been adamant that "questions of aesthetic form *are* political questions."[142] And included in his idea of "form"—à la Brecht and Benjamin—is an explicit idea of the functional transformation, the *Umfunktionierung*, of the theater as a social institution. As Lehmann explained in Berlin, "There can be no interesting theater about political issues that does not also call its own modes of production into question."[143] He makes the point even more eloquently in a passage omitted from the English translation of *Postdramatic Theater*, in which he calls—by means of a large qualification—for conceptualizing the relations between the resistant relevance of the postdramatic and the ways its modes of organization and apparatuses of production induce a potential politics:

> Nowadays, theater does not—or only rarely—become political by directly thematizing the political, but by the implicit content of its modes of representation [*Darstellungsweise*]. (These modes involve, by the way, not only certain [aesthetic] forms but also particular modes of labor. This study has hardly mentioned such labor forms, but they merit their own analysis: how theater is made, and how the political content of theater can be grounded in the way it is made.) Theater represents—not in theory, but in praxis—an example of a conjunction of the heterogeneous, which symbolizes the utopias of "another life." In the theater, mental, artistic, and physical labor, individual and collective praxis, are mediated. It can claim to be a resistant form of praxis already by dissolving the reification of actions and works into products, objects, and information. By pushing its event-character, theater manifests the soul of the dead product, the living artistic labor, for which everything remains unpredictable and to be invented tomorrow.[144]

Lehmann's Adornian language abounds in this enunciation, in which the postdramatic resists the active forgetting of reification (*Verdinglichung*) by forgoing outright insurrectionary commitment—the kind Ostermeier embraces—and forging different modes, or arts, of labor, organization, collaboration, and institutionality. And though Lehmann admits that he has not allotted ample time to the analysis of these new "forms and instruments of production,"[145] it is, it seems, in this negative praxis of formal "heterogene[ity]" that he understands the postdramatic also as a *"promesse du bonheur."*[146]

❖ ❖ ❖

In preparation for the performance's final few scenes, the committee moves frantically under the cover of flashing strobe lights and threatening electronic noise-music. They work in tandem and with great speed to transform the former-Potosí play space again, this time into a squat-cum-comic-book-graveyard that overflows with stacked "wallpaper" coffins, skeletons, hazmat skulls, signs, posters, graffiti, and a banner stretching across the entire space: "All milieus are counterrevolutionary because they are only concerned with the preservation of their sad comfort."[147] Just as the crescendo becomes unbearably loud, Vincent interrupts by switching off the soundboard and explains that he would like briefly to discuss the current situation in Holland. As the stage clears, he pulls a letter out of his breast pocket and explains further that andcompany&Co. would like to provide an "important" and most concrete "example of how artists in Holland are being treated." Ward crawls forth, shirtless now and wearing a blond wig (with wonderful bangs), and takes the letter. Vincent explains that Ward will perform the contents of the letter in Dutch, while he translates—more like paraphrases—the text into German so that we can all understand. Ward begins, still on his knees, head hanging, most dejected: "This letter explains our rejection of your proposal. We don't know why you are doing this performance. Your project has too much in the way of politics and too little in the way of imagination. . . . We don't want to give money to a political demonstration. Your project would be better if you did more of Schiller's *Don Carlos*." Ward's performance mounts in intensity and absurdity, as he bellows, rolls around, smashes his face into the floor, while continuing to read. Vincent calmly continues his translation: "The historical relationship between Germany and the Netherlands goes back a very long way. It was the German 'Occupy Movement' that founded a German theater in The Hague in 1940 and continues to function very well. We are very happy with this subsidy system. We are happy that the Maoist years of the 1960s are over. That the Dutch population once again has a good theater that will host top companies." Tears flow. The sweat is profuse. Ward beats his chest and begins humping one of the large eggs. He continues—stuttering—in hysterical falsetto, almost incomprehensible now: "The production houses have become collecting tanks of anti-artists [and] nest-foulers. The proliferating boil that is this asocial social stratum is to be combatted and exterminated as a matter of urgency." Ward collapses and is dragged off the stage by two committee members, at which point Vincent jumps right in without hesitation and with a sly smile—he is a natural

The (Coming) Insurrection: A squat-cum-comic-book-graveyard. Photograph copyright © Hans Jörg Michel.

networker: "There is not a lot of work in Holland, and I wanted to say that I find German theater to be much better than Dutch theater, and I would prefer to work in Germany." He seamlessly leads us through the highlights of his CV, pitching his services as a virtuosic performer: "So when you watch me and think, 'Now there's a great actor, maybe I want to work with him,' you can talk to me in the lobby after the show. I speak German, French, English. I play music, and I think I'm the most likable in the group. So talk to me after the performa—" Sudden darkness, and Vincent too is dragged off the stage squirming and screaming, "I hate Holland!"[148]

Thomas Ostermeier's critique of the free-scene as mere aestheticizing (and anesthetizing) affirmation of neoliberal debt insecurity relies on a version of an argument—positing the state-stage as the superior infrastructural model—that we have seen in various iterations throughout this book. Echoing Frank Castorf to some degree, Ostermeier praises a subsidy system that enables relative economic and political autonomy for the state-stages. Ostermeier sees the state-stage—though it must also be said that the Schaubühne is structured differently than Castorf's more "anarchistic" Volksbühne—as a last bastion of artistic freedom, an "elite island of resistance"[149] against a kind of "capitalist efficiency."[150] He writes:

> This neoliberal dream of flexibility, however, means projects that receive support must be successful in the short term. Long-term

artistic developments, which are so important in the theater, become impossible. Jobs that are financed by project-based funds are more precarious than permanent positions. Contributions to social security are rarely paid; the status of health insurance is unclear. The artistic work suffers because you must often take on a second job. . . . Many artists simply do not see the opportunity of institutionalized theater infrastructures financed by the public sector over generations. They offer us work opportunities and the means of production necessary to convey our different rendition of society. It would be fatal for artists to give up on these places, which will become even more vulnerable in the economic crises that lie ahead of us.[151]

One must ask, however: Are the state-stages really such protected, even autonomous spaces, free from market forces and economic constraints? Certainly not, if the State-Stage Complex has anything to say about it. And is the free-scene really suggesting that we abandon all sense of organization and infrastructure? Also, no. Or, are these "top companies," these dominant bastions of "critical" Culture—with a capital "C"—in some way threatened by the different kinds of work opportunities and alternative modes of production encouraged, at least potentially, by a free-scene of "nest foulers"? It has been widely acknowledged for many years that the state-stages are astonishingly hierarchical, bureaucratic, and infamously attached to their "sad comforts." In Karschnia's polemical account, they continue to insist on a division of labor reminiscent of factory work: "Their working methods are Fordist, with an assembly line of premiere outputs, and their internal structures are pre-Fordist (or even feudal)."[152] Ensemble actors are "doubly unfree," Karschnia explains, "almost serfs"[153] bound by their permanent contracts and always at the mercy of the almighty directors' whims. "When we worked at the state-theater," he continues, "one of the actors said to us, 'My mother is dying. Can I please go and visit her? And we said, 'Yes, sure, of course.' And he responded, 'But I need you to sign this paper, otherwise I cannot leave.' They are kept captive. They cannot go more than thirty kilometers without permission if they are performing the next day."[154] It was in this moment, Karschnia claims, that he came to appreciate the real "structural limitations"[155] imposed by the state-stage system. Artists are not seen as collaborators. They are not permitted to make self-determined choices about how they want to work, what they want to create, and with whom. They are not—and here Karschnia's language takes on an insistent tone—"*autonomous* as producers of their work."[156] He writes elsewhere: "For independent theater makers, it is high time to talk about the 'autonomy of theater work.' . . . Here, we propose a perspective that . . . looks for initiative on the side of the artists who seek to liberate themselves from the disciplining of authoritarian operations."[157] And again:

> I think this is one of the most important steps for the free-scene. It's
> not just about money and financing, and not just the form-content
> debates; it's really about autonomy. . . . Because if it is not about that,
> I don't know what it is about. Then it is just about a bunch of people
> who didn't make it into the institutions knocking at the door—who
> want state money. And that is how they see us. And maybe that is
> even true for a few people. But the rest of us should be aware that this
> is what our struggle is about.[158]

How does Karschnia's strategic retort to Ostermeier look toward modes
of artistic and institutional organization that might also serve as a means of
rethinking the free-scene? With this emphatic invocation of "autonomy," his
argument becomes more slippery and also more interesting. Over and over
again, in his meditations on the possibilities of what he wittily calls a "*free*
free-scene,"[159] Karschnia redeploys this word loaded with so much historical
and theoretical baggage, which, in this particular context, has been the rallying cry of two positions he hopes to critique: both the state-stage as bastion of
artistic autonomy (read: bureaucratic sausage factory) *and* the free-scene as
bastion of artistic autonomy (read: precarious captain of creative industry).
Why, then, does Karschnia bother? In what follows, I look to *The (Coming)
Insurrection*'s explicit invocation of a body of theory and practice working quite explicitly—albeit in a different context—to explore new modes of
relating and organizing socially against modes and relations of capitalist production, both Fordist and post-Fordist. By means of this explicit invocation,
the performance registers its interest in a shift in tactics—from protest to
occupation, from insurrection to resistance. In contrast to the predominantly
visibility- and media-based activism of previous generations (also employed
by both Ostermeier's insurrectionary aesthetics and the coalition's "month of
action"), this slew of resolutely autonomous occupationist struggles—which
also arose in response to austerity, unemployment, privatization, financializa-
tion, and other global instantiations of neoliberal disavowal—calls attention
to the exhaustion of these preexisting forms of protest and focuses explicitly
on the direct and immediate redeployment of space and the remobilization
of resources. This Occupy movement—referred to in some circles as the
communization current—is inspired by and also inspiring a growing body
of Italian, French, and more recently, Anglo-American ultraleft theory that
analyzes capitalist social relations and the despotic value-form, as well as
suggesting that autonomy or freedom from capitalism will not happen after
some revolutionary break (by an imagined proletariat or precariat), but rather
through the direct, immediate, and ongoing process of instituting communist
relations—now. For these occupationists, there is no need for a separation
between means and ends. There is no need for mediation by a leader or a unified message, by organized labor or a Communist Party.[160] There need be no

"demands," since a reduction to that which is demandable would be a denial of the central premise that capital cannot be fought piecemeal, one issue at a time. And perhaps most radically, there is no need for a transitional period that looks toward an already conceptualized communist future. For these writer-occupiers, "communization" is the activity of doing communism itself in the present moment. Tautologically stated, "Communization is only the *communist production of communism*."[161]

This final premise about the form of transition has inspired fiery and productive tensions in the various communization camps. Certain contingents understand the immediate production of communism as an activity that should and must begin in the present as a mode of organization and occupation within—and by means of refunctioning—the very infrastructures (of capital) that are to be overcome through communization itself. Other contingents are committed to an exclusive (and fundamental) practice of negation that is loath to posit any kind of positive prescriptions for organization beyond occupation itself, which should thus remain wholly unpredictable and nonconceptualizable. In his edited volume, which works to track some of the contours of these debates, Benjamin Noys provides a helpful orientation:

> What does it mean to say that communization is or should be immediate? It suggests there is no transition to communism, no stage of socialism required before we can achieve the stage of communism, and so no need to "build" communism. This, however, has a very different meaning in different hands. For Tiqqun and others influenced by anarchist prefigurative politics this immediacy means that we must begin enacting communism *now*, within capitalism. . . . On the other hand, TC [Théorie Communiste] and Endnotes give this "immediacy" a rather different sense, by arguing that communization implies the immediacy of communism in the process of revolution. In fact, they are deeply suspicious of a prefigurative or alternative politics, regarding such forms of struggle as mired in capitalism and often moralistic. Instead, if anything, contemporary struggles can only be *negatively* prefigurative, indicating the limits of our forms of struggle and indicating only possible new lines of attack.[162]

In a 2013 lecture titled "The Aesthetics of Communization," Noys tried to tease out the "implications" these quite palpable and animating differences have for contemporary art practice: "This figural context, in which prefiguration lies unstably on either side, both here-and-now and in the process of revolution, seems to me the tension communization bequeaths to contemporary practice, and contemporary artistic practice."[163] At the risk of further aestheticization (and anesthetization), I want to follow Noys's lead and suggest that these tensions at the heart of the communization discourse parallel, and also help fill out productively, the dialectics of resistance animating andcompany&Co.'s performance. In fact, it seems that we have returned to those original animating questions: Is the occupation to be prefigured? Is it already arriving here, now, at the theater, at *this* HAU theater? Or, paradoxically, is it somehow both *and* neither/nor.

In the remainder of this final section, I explore how andcompany&Co. and *The (Coming) Insurrection* work, quite explicitly, to institute a different mode of social and/as artistic production by means of an occupational aesthetics of rehearsal. For andcompany&Co., the figure and practice of rehearsal is one in which these different modes of occupation (as autonomy) are both performed and set in contradiction with one another: insisting on immediacy, indeterminacy, demandlessness, even the accidental, while never relinquishing an insistence on the importance of infrastructures—both historical and contemporary—to be reimagined along the way as the spaces in which that indeterminate between the bodies of occupation unfolds. For andcompany&Co., the space and context of rehearsal mediates between the prefiguration of a final version (of a performance) that has not yet arrived *and* the thing (the performance) itself in its current state of becoming. It is a doing, a concrete making, that is itself something but not yet *the* thing. The rehearsal both anticipates and structures the thing to come, though decidedly not waiting for its arrival, and also brings about its arrival—in a form that is influenced by the ways the rehearsal makes concrete use of what has come before (in previous rehearsals) to move beyond it, a forging together of the old and the new.

On the one hand, then, andcompany&Co. describes its desired modes of organization and production in primarily negative terms. Its founding manifesto, from 2003, includes statements like "&Co. is . . . no concept of art or capital, no part of the musical-industrial complex, no commercial adventure."[164] Or: "&Co. is an ANTIDOT.COM, a free association of autonomous producers drifting through the system in conflict with the ruling production- & communication-regime, searching for collaborative ways of working & collective structures."[165] Or: "&Co. is not a party, not a progressive political project that projects the coming commune"; or "&Co. is the no-name of an open context, it's a merry militant practice."[166] In these "no" articulations, andcompany&Co. echoes the sentiments described by Endnotes and others when they claim that communization has very little positive advice to impart. Instead, they understand performance as a denial or undoing of the kinds of constitutive social relations and forms of mediation so central to capital's reproduction. The insistent &Co. appellation—which appears next to almost every proper name listed in the program notes—serves as an interruption of predetermined roles, categories, and specializations. The ensemble understands itself as in perpetual flux, always involving a varied group of interarts "friends," and always also inviting them onto the stage: participatory game designers, radio-play fanatics, media theorists, photographers, musicians, and political activists—none of them actors (at least in their earlier projects).[167]

As Karschnia claims, returning to the idea of autonomy as instability, spontaneity, always receding from view: "Theater . . . must be free or it will not be; that means that it must try to create a suitable time-space and to detonate the homogeneity of (capitalist) duration: an anti-state-stage that works not to stabilize identity but to liquefy it."[168]

In rehearsal too, andcompany&Co. facilitates a perpetually open and ever-evolving process—in which even production remains *in* rehearsal. Karschnia is adamant: "There are no rules. . . . We never nominated an ultimate decision maker. . . . The secret is that it is not really fixed. It is always fluid. And if you do a project with us, you think maybe this is the first project we do together, because you have the feeling that we invent the wheel again."[169] In his description of the rehearsal process, Karschnia explains that the ensemble tries (albeit always admittedly failing) to achieve totally "neutral" ways of being together, ways of "finding a presence onstage that is not yet occupied [*besetzt*]."[170] Once you achieve this "point zero," once you "burn the layers of bullshit," Karschnia claims, "things fall into place just because we have a feeling for what is working."[171] In certain moments, Karschnia seems to demonstrate a radical optimism for the spontaneous, collective forms of organization articulated by another communization theorist, Léon de Mattis: "An adequate form of organisation of this revolution will only be provided by the multiplicity of communising measures, taken anywhere by any kind of people, which . . . will generalise of their own accord, without anybody knowing who conceived them and who transmitted them."[172] In Karschnia's words, something like a spontaneous "group think" starts to unfold in rehearsal: "I do think that collective thinking processes are possible. Maybe an idea jumps like an electric charge into someone's head—who never expected to have an idea—maybe it is alien to the person articulating it. I believe in that a little bit. If you create this kind of field, and there is a creative flow going, then it is more or less a coincidence sometimes out of whose mouth it pops."[173] At the same time, and just as crucial, this kind of collective action and organization only emerges in the midst of often intense antagonism and even aggressive struggle.[174] There is little time for or emphasis on compromise; andcompany&Co. is, in the end, no harmonious or homogeneous community, no "clichéd collective."[175] Karschnia explains, "Very seldom you say, 'I have an idea,' and everybody goes, 'Wow, that is the solution to the problem, let's do it.' . . . Often, you have to fight with the resistances. It's not working in this idealized collective. . . . It's a lot about fighting. We fight a lot. And after ten years, you're sometimes even tired of it. You say, 'Okay, it means a lot of fighting basically.' "[176]

On the other hand, andcompany&Co.'s desired modes of organization and production also incorporate and explore critiques of a primarily negative articulation of autonomy as *purely* spontaneous, horizontal, indeterminate, immediate, and so on. There are, after all, certainly more than a number of debates to be waged—and they have been waged by communization theorists and those critical of Occupy more broadly[177]—about the implications of a position that insists exclusively on negative prefiguration. Does this version of communization advocate for mere insurrectionism without any anticipated outcome? Is the abandonment (or even destruction) of *all* social forms implicated in the reproduction of the capitalist class relation really the best way forward? Is it even possible to move beyond all forms of mediation? Might there be some benefit to considering a more positive prefigurative conception of communism, however imperfect or embryonic its articulations?[178] In other words, might there also be some benefit to thinking concretely about "organization" itself, about what it might mean to "institute" different modalities of social relations? Alberto Toscano makes a compelling two-pronged case for thinking positively about transition and taking forms of strategy seriously:

> The first is the hopeful conviction, already alluded to in regard to the problem of strategy, that such determinations will simply arise in the collective processes of abolishing the value-form. I can see no reason to have such confidence, especially in light of the formidable organizational and logistical difficulties that face any attempt to undo the ubiquitous identification of social existence and capitalist mediation—not to mention the often catastrophic challenges previously confronted by really-existing communisms. The second factor is the entirely untenable notion that communism involves "direct social relations." As authors from Fourier to Harvey have suggested, it makes much more sense to conceive a non-capitalist future as one that will involve infinitely more varied and more complex forms of social mediation, forms for which the refunctioning of many (though definitely not all) of the devices which permit the reproduction of capital will be necessary. If the world we inhabit is one that has been thoroughly shaped by the history of capital (and of class struggle), it stands to reason that simple negation—with its tendency to facile fantasies of communism rising like a phoenix from the ashes of anomie and the thorough collapse of social reproduction—is no proposal at all. In a world where no object or relation is untouched by capital, the logistical, strategic and political question is in many ways what will require abolishing, and what converting, or, in a more dialectical vein, what is to be negated without remainder and what sublated.[179]

These are precisely the kinds of strategic questions that Karschnia brings to bear on the state of things in Berlin. He insists that we "proceed dialectically, thinking not only one position (free-scene) against the other (state-stage), but also thinking about their relationship." Karschnia is quite clear, however: he is not interested in a lazy dialectic that yields a kind of "trivial 'we need both as they are'" approach.[180] Certain iterations of the Independent Art Coalition's position tend in this direction.[181] Nor is Karschnia interested in what he calls a highly "unlikely" and pure sublation, or *Aufhebung*, in which either the free-scene simply vanishes along with neoliberalism, postmodernity, and finance capital, or the state-stages simply dissolve into free-floating production teams. Instead, he advocates for what he calls a "crisp" or critical dialectic, one that avoids both weak pluralism and the hostile takeover of one side by another, and instead explores a negative set of mediations in which, echoing Toscano, "both somehow vanish and are somehow preserved"[182]—a both and neither/nor. This *free* free-scene" would understand itself, therefore, to be "work[ing] beyond predetermined structures"[183] by means of a process of dis/avowal, of engagement with and differentiation from the very things to be superseded—*both* the state-stage *and* the free-scene, in all their immanent contradictions. In other words, this free free-scene would take up the challenge of imagining and performing sustainable modes of infrastructural organization that also, simultaneously, privilege multiplicity, fragility, immediacy, and perhaps even their own undoing.

In very (almost overly) concrete terms, some of these critical or contradictory forms of engagement and differentiation are evident in the ways *The (Coming) Insurrection* was organized. The performance was billed as a coproduction of andcompany&Co., the Oldenburgisches Staatstheater, and Frascati, a midsize free-scene producing and presenting house in Amsterdam. Coproduction funds were provided by Forum Freies Theater in Düsseldorf and Theater im Pumpenhaus in Münster—two of the major German free-scene institutions—and a number of other project-based funding instruments (and presenting houses, like the HAU) throughout Germany and the Netherlands.[184] Both Frascati and the Oldenburg State-Stage provided space and resources over the course of the rehearsal and devising process; in addition, andcompany&Co. were the official artists-in-residence at HAU between 2007 and 2012, until the performance was in its final stages. Oldenburg also "provided" two performers from their ensemble—Rüdiger and Hartmut—with the hope that they would acquire "new kinds of experiences."[185] Other than Sascha Sulimma and Alexander Karschnia, two of the cofounders of andcompany&Co., the other five performers—Vincent van der Valk, Ward Weemhoff, Joachim Robbrecht, Reinier van Houdt, and Simon Lenski—are free-scene performers from across the Netherlands and Flanders, with interdisciplinary CVs similar to Vincent's. As Karschnia explains, it was important to the group not just that free-scene artists had the "opportunity" to join state-stage performers but also that those performers (with their very particular and rigid German acting school backgrounds) work outside the walls of the state theaters—other than when they were shooting a film. These alternative modes of organization are much more commonplace in the Netherlands, Karschnia says. "There, this sliding between structures has been familiar for decades. Players often work in collectives, as soloists, sometimes as directors and authors, who are also—as in our case—on the stage as well."[186] "What is at stake," he continues, "is that the state-stages must stop understanding themselves as 'the' theater and instead allow a perspective that includes many different forms of theater production and ways of working."[187]

To flesh out this image of the different, often contradictory, even autonomous forms of artistic labor and production that are also, somehow, to be organized, structured, and even institutionalized, Karschnia returns, quite strategically, to the language of immateriality and precarity: "This gives rise to the new task of the theater, which can no longer remain just a public place, but would, in short, have to become a common, a communal place: a place where the egalitarian structures of immaterial, intellectual, and affective labor materialize. To put it bluntly: the theater of the 21st century faces the challenge of becoming an institution that incorporates the internet."[188]

At this moment, we understand *finally* why Geert Lovink was also invited to join the "Phantasm" discussion on the HAU stage. And though Lovink sat quietly for most of the night, it becomes clear now just how indebted Karschnia is to his work. Lovink, after all, has been central, alongside Ned Rossiter and Brett Neilson, in developing an ambitious line of thinking about "new modalities of organization" and "new institutional forms" seeking to "reinvent a politics of autonomy in the time of networks."[189] This theory of "organized networks,"[190] as they are called, emphasizes "horizontal, mobile, distributed, and decentralized modes of relation,"[191] while simultaneously trying to give "political form to this multiplicity—to determine the indeterminate."[192] In other words, Lovink, Rossiter, and Neilson work to imagine concrete modes of "'organization without ends' or 'organizing the unorganizable,'" which are not simply elegant paradoxes but rather "signal the real challenges faced by political creativity in an institutional environment still dominated by the market and state."[193] Neilson and Rossiter write:

> The question then becomes how to create new institutions, new political spaces and concepts, rather than simply defending the old institutions or, as some would have it, defending politics. Such institutions would need to arise in the social forms that networks and other forms of cooperation develop as part of their daily life. But, in so doing, they should never entertain the fantasy . . . of the stabilisation of precariousness through the imposition of rigid structure. Rather, . . . they would have to remain open to the brute precariousness of human potentiality while simultaneously recognising that this potentiality is necessarily installed in the world. It is in this immanence that we need to become attuned to the intersections of experience and movement, as well as the ways in which they are constrained or enabled by modern institutions.[194]

Here, Neilson and Rossiter explicitly remobilize and expand upon a version of what might be called the dis/avowal of precarity itself—where precarity supplies the preconditions for new forms of creative, even communist, organization by exploiting flexible modes of relating socially.[195] The goal is not, however, to flee institutions in search of short-term, horizontal, also often precarious collaboration (a version of the coalition's argument). Nor is the goal to celebrate a return to bureaucratic structure once again (a version of Ostermeier's argument). Rather, the goal is, echoing Paolo Virno, to force the "'state of nature,'"[196] in all its precariousness, into the heart of the institution itself.[197] Or slightly differently, the goal is to find an infrastructural coming to terms with the "continual, if not interminable" negative dialectical motion that structures the constant and productive flow between "partiality and multiplicity, determination and indetermination,"[198] between stability and flexibility, strategies and tactics.

In light of this infrastructural redeployment, or refunctioning, of precarity as organized network, we have a better sense of just what Karschnia envisions when he talks about artistic autonomy as always toeing the finest of lines "between self-determination and self-exploitation."[199] We also have a better sense of the significance of a "fictional" letter representing a "real" precarious situation, devised spontaneously in rehearsal and performed by two "real" free-scene Dutch performers who foreground—even advertise—their own "real" precarity in order to provoke mediated reflection (across two and sometimes three languages) on the relationships between "top" institutions and "free" ensembles, between Dutch and German performance infrastructures, between culture and policy at the theater. We understand, too, what andcompany&Co.'s founding manifesto is getting at when it says that the ensemble is "an island of social cooperation in productive networks."[200] Or that andcompany&Co. is a "new class of immaterial & intellectual workers, the copy-code FOR ALL! . . . DOT DOT DOT COMMUNISM."[201] Or, elsewhere: "To make theater politically, then, would mean to allow for the unfolding of the communicative and cognitive skills that are simultaneously promoted and suppressed in today's production processes, and thus to bring into consciousness the social cooperation without which all wheels would stand still—not from outside by means of a (Leninist) Party, but within the work itself, within the (artistic) process."[202]

In this artistic process, *The (Coming) Insurrection* inaugurates a different kind of imagining *as* infrastructural organization on the HAU stage. That is, andcompany&Co. sets its fundamentally "vulnerable"[203] process to work within the HAU as a means of both shoring up *and* destabilizing it. To invoke Judith Butler's thoughts on occupation one more time, we see how andcompany&Co.'s performance is one that "opens up time and space outside and against the established architecture and temporality of the regime, one that lays claim to materiality, leans into its supports, and draws from its material and technical dimensions to rework their functions."[204] *The (Coming) Insurrection*'s occupational aesthetics of rehearsal explores what it means to be both immediate and prefigurative, to be both against the performerism of precarity and prone to engaging it as the material of—and the modes of organizing—the new, inherently immaterial, even precarious institutions of an uncertain, always (coming), future. By means of an occupationist aesthetics of rehearsal, andcompany&Co.'s *(Coming) Insurrection* explores just what it might mean to perform policy postdramatically.

Epilogue

✦

Dis/avowing Dis/avowal?

Dercon Debacle Redux

Let's begin this epilogue with a prologue, actually the first of two prologues (following the dedication) to Goethe's *Faust, Part I*. This backstage conversation between a theater manager, a poet, and a performer is Goethe's famous metatheatrical gesture toward the broader social formations that shape a theater performance. Indeed, "Prelude on Stage" explores how working artists must negotiate the inevitably conflicting agendas of theatrical production, including the actor's desire for recognition, the poet's longing for so-called truths, the manager's commitment to the finances of the house, and of course the whims of an always fickle audience. Goethe does not suggest that one set of interests wins out onstage or behind the scenes. Rather, "Prelude" stages a rhetorical compromise, a set of infrastructural interdependencies, between the aesthetic and the institutional, among authors, performers, producers (and other managers), and their publics.

Frank Castorf is rarely interested in compromise. He prefers the intensity of contradiction. Castorf's *Faust*, his final production at the Volksbühne before his directorship ended in summer 2017, was no exception. In this seven-hour epic performance, Castorf probed the horrors of European Enlightenment, in which Faust emerges as a player (and destroyer) on the global stage and on a global scale. According to dramaturgs Sebastian Kaiser and Carl Hegemann, Castorf's Faust is the "prototype of a totalitarian economic world ruler and colonizer"—a forbearer of the "Me-First-Above-Anything-and-Anyone-Else Scientological attitude"—who continues to spread havoc, violence, and terror in order to "escape the anonymity and contingency of [his] existence."[1] Moving from the "human creation" scenes in act 2 of *Faust, Part 2*, to Zola's Paris of the Second Empire, to the colonial reality of the Algerian War, Castorf and company—onstage first at Rosa-Luxemburg-Platz and later at the 2018 Theatertreffen—built a blazing inferno in which the "wretched of the earth" writhe in a colonial nightmare, all the while fighting (with the help of Franz Fanon and a large cast of literary and theoretical intertexts) for decolonial horizons of possibility.

It should come as no surprise, then, that Castorf's take on Goethe's "Prelude" eschews harmony among varying perspectives and instead luxuriates in the potential for conflict inherent in the scene—with a healthy dose of screaming, slapstick, and spilled beer. "Prelude" is also the only moment in Castorf's *Faust* when the director cites the sprawling infrastructural antagonisms that animated the Volksbühne while this performance was in production. Thirty or so minutes into the show,[2] Aleksandar Denić's massive stage design begins to rotate as actor Alexander Sheer tap-dances toward the front of the stage, followed by Martin Wuttke (Faust here playing the Prelude's poet with a voice resembling—as the stage directions indicate—legendary actor Bernhard Minetti).[3] With his tan suit, matching hat, thin black tie, and charming smile, Sheer is a pure showman, a seasoned hoofer. As he begins to recite the first lines of Goethe's "Prelude" with a thick and highly exaggerated Belgian accent, the spoof becomes clear. With a slick swagger and a hand in one pocket, Sheer's Chris Dercon–like manager proclaims, "I'd rather like the crowd to enjoy it / Since they live and let live, truly / . . . How can we make it all seem fresh and new, / Weighty, but entertaining too?" Or later: "Make sure, above all, plenty's happening there! / They come to look, and then they want to stare."[4] And after Wuttke dumps a half liter of beer over his head, Sheer-as-Dercon says with a slump and a shrug—amid a loud cackle from the audience: "That is not nice. I haven't even started yet. I don't deserve this. I really don't deserve this."[5]

There is little ambiguity here. Castorf stages a manager at permanent and irreconcilable odds with his ensemble and the other supporting structures that make his institution viable. And as it turned out, this skeptical prognosis for Dercon's "event-shed" did not prove too far off base. On April 12, 2018, Klaus Lederer, Berlin's new culture senator, fired Chris Dercon after just seven months as *Intendant* of the Volksbühne. Three days earlier, Dercon had been invited to Lederer's office to discuss the economic and artistic state of the theater—which was a shambles. Between January 2015 and December 2016, Dercon's vision for the new Volksbühne brand unraveled. Many of the Volksbühne's star directors and performers—including René Pollesch, Herbert Fritsch, Christoph Marthaler, Sophie Rois, Kathrin Angerer, Fabian Hinrichs, and Martin Wuttke—refused to work under the new administration. Dercon and his team would therefore have no access to the old repertoire and would have to start from scratch. However, the budget was already maxed out due to mismanagement. As Gabriele Gornowicz, the managing director under Castorf, reported, "At the end of 2015, I met with Marietta Piekenbrock [Dercon's second in command] for a conversation. I was ready to help her, to explain how a state-stage functions economically. She could have asked me; after all, she had never run a state-stage. Scarier than her ignorance was her utter lack of interest in understanding how this apparatus works."[6] And as the new managing director, Klaus Dörr, explained, the budget was completely exhausted by the excessive costs of guest productions on top of the fixed operating costs of the state-stage. The theater would only manage to stay in the black if it moved two planned shows from 2018 to 2019. However, this meant they did not have enough performances to establish a sustainable repertoire. Under Dercon's tenure, the 824-seat theater was dark more than 50 percent of the time and often reported less than 25 percent attendance. To make matters worse, as a result of all the bad press, many of the private partners Dercon hoped to attract pulled out, making the massive new space at Tempelhof impossible in the long term.[7]

In his recent analysis of the "crisis of leadership" at the Volksbühne, Christopher Balme stages a different version of Goethe's always contingent compromise:

> A theater institution consists not only of its management, technical staff, and performers, but also, as neo-institutional theory argues, of a wider environment . . . , which also includes the "supporting public" . . . and the political consensus across parties that this system is necessary. When however, one key part of this institutional environment, the management, radically questions another part, the political decision-makers, and when yet another part, the supporting public, . . . feels deprived of its entitlement, then the whole configuration may become destabilised.[8]

For Balme, the crisis at the Volksbühne—both onstage and behind the scenes—demands a new "theory and methodology" to analyze the various configurations of interdependent elements that constitute what he calls an "institutional aesthetics."[9] "Moments of succession, the instantiation of new leaders," Balme writes, "can be seen as critical junctures when well-trodden paths are deviated from and new institutional trajectories defined."[10] Throughout this book, I have worked to elaborate just how a more robust theory and practice of "institutional aesthetics" might look at and for the theater. In the preceding chapters, I examined cases in which policies of neoliberal disavowal in Berlin provided opportunities for new trajectories of institutional dis/avowal. I have focused on moments since the fall of the Wall in which artists performed policy in different ways as their means of rethinking, reorienting, and reorganizing the institutions—both state-stages and free-scenes—in which they were deeply enmeshed.

In this most recent instance in which policy found its way onstage, however, we do not find Castorf interested in the messy logics of *Umfunktionierung*. With his "Prelude" (though not necessarily his *Faust* as a whole), Castorf exchanges the productive uncertainty, polemic, chaos even—so essential to his Volksbühne project—for a more static diagnosis of the Dercon debates. With his soft-shoe, his commercial ideas, and his "cosmopolitan" brogue, the Dercon-like manager reifies a set of unmediated and unproductive binaries that structured one version of the recent controversy: *Intendant* versus curator, state-stage versus presenting house, local versus global, public versus private, antagonism versus conviviality, German-language theater versus interdisciplinary dance and visual art. With "Prelude," then, Castorf overlooks an opportunity to once again radically interrogate his own modes of theatrical production. By staging his anxiety (and perhaps rage) about the "abolition"[11] of the Volksbühne at the hands of party politicians and their backroom power brokering, Castorf (via Dercon) reperforms what Evelyn Annuss calls the "testosterone-fueled fantasy of masterminding 'the transition from one overman to another.'"[12] Castorf seems much less interested in how the Dercon debacle might inspire new opportunities to refunction the state-stage system in a moment of crisis by rethinking the position of the *Intendant* itself. Instead, in this most recent instance, Castorf and his ensemble resort to a mode of staging policy questions that have taken on different monikers throughout this book: naive and sentimental protest, restorative (in place of reflective) nostalgia, an aesthetics of insurrection (in place of an aesthetics of resistance), disavowal in lieu of dis/avowal. Dercon versus Castorf: all that was left to do was pick a side. But, as Annuss continues, "Given the grandiose failure of these macho visions, a "philosopher-king" empowered to make "wise staffing decisions" is about the last thing Berlin needs now. These are pipe dreams that say less about how work in the theater is actually done than about how the laws of the media attention economy compel a personalization of substantive issues, the contemporary variant of what used to be called charisma."[13]

With his charismatic take on "Prelude," Castorf also passes on an opportunity to think through some of the broader implications of Dercon's appointment. The protests against Dercon not only mourned the destruction of a beloved theater institution but, as Annuss also suggests, "registered people's objections to the increasing devaluation of creative and intellectual labor in a neoliberal society and the ongoing displacement of less affluent residents from the inner cities."[14] On one level, then, these various protests— including the occupation of the Volksbühne between September 22 and 28, 2017—serve as yet another opportunity, and a highly visible one, to continue posing the questions of precarious institutionality that animated the second part of this book. How, in other words, might alternative modes of social and aesthetic organization—be it *Zwischennutzung* or an occupational aesthetics of rehearsal—spark new arts of imagination in and for the future of Berlin's public performance institutions?

On another level, and as Annuss intimates in her critique of the "testosterone-fueled" fantasies of directors and cultural politicians, the controversies over the Volksbühne gave voice to other forms and arts of institutional reorientation. These conflicts, in other words, were not only attempts to dis/avow neoliberal disavowal; they also provide an opportunity to rethink dis/avowal itself by bringing additional—and markedly absent—vocabularies and constituencies to bear on the discussions of precarious labor raised by members of the free-scene. Though the free-scene debates I examine work on a variety of levels to question the hierarchical constitution of the state-stage and the infrastructural makeup of the theater economy writ large, at times they invoke "precarity" without accounting thoroughly for its increasing use as a universalizing catchall. In his introductory essay to the 2013 special issue of *Women & Performance* on performance and precarity, Tavia Nyong'o registers his worry that although precarity "may accurately limn one aspect of neoliberal governmentality," it also risks assuming homogeneity along lines of race, gender, and sex. "If 'precarious life' is to offer a means towards new solidarities based on shared vulnerabilities," Nyong'o continues, "then those who proceed under its sign must remain scrupulously attentive to the constitutive and uneven distribution of that vulnerability, and must not simply fall back upon a well-meaning but empty humanism."[15] We see this kind of critical omission, for instance, in the well-meaning *lucha libre* scene of andcompany&Co.'s *(Coming) Insurrection*, in which the company seems to conflate the *Geuzen* with the silver miners. While this moment in the performance does illuminate the paradoxical ways in which the *Geuzen* were both targets and profiteers in Philip II's war, it also flattens the differences between these emerging capitalist profiteers and the working subjects (Bolivian, Dutch, and Spanish) who suffered under monarchy and global capital alike, profiting from neither. Indeed, the many avowals and disavowals analyzed throughout this book have been made from exclusively white and, most often, male subject positions—a striking feature of Berlin's theatrical establishment.

The occupation of the Volksbühne was an explicit call to attend more closely to questions of difference in Berlin's precarious performance landscape. However, the action also reveals the real challenges of bringing, as Nyong'o writes, "the twin operations of collectivity and differentiation into our analyses of what precarity is or does."[16] In their published materials, the occupiers refused to separate questions of urban policy and capitalist exploitation from questions of identity and (political) representation: "The Volksbühne Collective is feminist, antiracist, and queer, and will promptly develop appropriate tools to prevent age-based discrimination and to guarantee accessibility." And in the very next sentence: "The Volksbühne is the new center of antigentrification."[17] While the occupiers hoped to reactivate the theater as a space of possibility to negotiate new forms of "social experimentation,"[18] their seamlessly effortless negotiation of class politics and identity politics proved to be a rather naive and sentimental salve for deeper points of controversy, polarization, and unmediated antagonism.

As the debates around the Volksbühne heated up in the spring of 2017, cultural critic Diedrich Diederichsen published a perceptive polemic profiling the various political camps within Berlin's so-called Left that were reflected in and activated by the controversy. Diederichsen sketches two fronts, which resemble what he considers a bizarre "refinement . . . of a split in the postreunification Left." On the one side, there is a "primarily gentrification-critical, at times anti-imperial, local Left, which does not want to break entirely with traditions of working-class Marxism and is annoyed by tourists."[19] This contingent worries that the "political correctness" of identity politics is dangerously compatible with neoliberal globalization (and curators like Dercon) and produces a "self-indulgence" that is to blame for the rise of the Far Right. On the other side, Diederichsen sketches a "primarily antiracist, anti-anti-Semitic, feminist, and postcolonial"[20] camp that supports Dercon's commitment to working with more women and artists of color. For many in this contingent, the critique of Dercon's cosmopolitan brand by the "rather un-feminist, East-socialist, anti-American Brecht-and-Müller heirs"[21] risks assuming a pseudo-"nationalist" or even "colonial" tone—hell-bent on defending a theater system based on primarily German-language productions helmed predominantly by white German men. Diederichsen cites Hito Steyerl, among other artists and curators of color, who exclaimed on an *e-flux* online forum:

> Has anyone even noticed that Volksbühne has been using a Reichsparteitags-Gothic letter font on neon for past decades to shove their kind of white-German-guys-yelling-hysterically indigenist tantrum theater down people [*sic*] throats? . . . [T]he campaign against Chris Dercon has since long taken on the indigenist undertones seen in populist campaigns around Europe, just this time from the local cultural representatives of the indigenous middle class, who feel their cultural hegemony threatened.[22]

To compound the complications, as Steyerl suggests, these conflicts came to a head just as the far-right Alternative for Germany (Alternative für Deutschland; AfD) party gained national traction and earned seats in the Bundestag as Germany's third-largest party—on the same weekend as the Volksbühne occupation. A number of other critics, including Peter Boenisch, worried publicly that the "hostility and sabotage of [Dercon's] tenure showed frightening resonances with both the rhetoric [and] the irate agitation . . . of the new nationalist right."[23] Alternatively, the AfD published a high-profile condemnation of the occupation, voicing support for the "regular operations" of Dercon's program.[24] Diederichsen finds himself lost in the "cognitive dissonance" of this scrambled political matrix that opposes white, male Marxists to neoliberal feminists and in which both share curious (if unintended) alliances with the far right. "While politically and theoretically," he writes, "I rather situate myself with . . . those interested in Critical Whiteness and Queer Studies, aesthetically and culture-politically I rather see myself on the side of the old Volksbühne."[25]

Diederichsen's staging of these polarized and seemingly irreconcilable camps is indicative of widespread anxieties about what now constitutes a radical position on the Left. His analysis of the situation in Berlin models a set of international debates—also in the mainstream media—that flourished in the wake of the Brexit vote and the election of Donald Trump in 2016. As Steve Bannon proclaimed just a few months into Trump's first term, "The longer they talk about identity politics, I got 'em. I want them to talk about racism every day. If the left is focused on race and identity, and we go with economic nationalism, we can crush the Democrats."[26] In a 2018 special issue of the journal *Historical Materialism* titled "Identity Politics," the editors argue that this kind of irreconcilable bifurcation between the struggles of raced, gendered, and sexual marginalities and the struggles of the economically dispossessed is "untenable for any serious, comprehensive Left project."[27] They claim instead that this opposition is "itself a constructed, naturalised, and—crucially—effective innovation of the Right's many incarnations," which creates an "organisational culture of individualised, positionality politics that preclude[s] the possibility of broad-based co-operation."[28] The special issue as a whole works to historicize and therefore untangle the ways identity has come to be seen solely as a performance of self-fashioning, and how a dematerialized identity-based politics is conceivable (even welcomed) within the logics of neoliberalism. The editors hope that this historicization of "identity as it figures in contemporary conditions" will help undo static divisions and generate new "organisational strategies."[29]

How should these organizational strategies, then, inform both the institutional and aesthetic orientations of Berlin's theater landscape moving forward? As I write this epilogue, Matt Cornish and David Savran are coediting a special issue of *TDR: The Drama Review* that explores how this question is currently mobilizing a new generation of performance practice in Berlin's free-scene. This is also the pressing question confronting the Volksbühne—as state-stage—in the wake of Dercon's dismissal. How, in other words, might a *new* "new" Volksbühne attend to pressing questions of internationality, as well as to race and gender politics, while refusing to genuflect fully to the demands—the normalizations and regulations—of city marketing? How might a *new* "new" Volksbühne work both to confront urgent problems of institutional racism and sexism and to establish alternative spaces for collective existence within the hegemonic structures of the German theater?

For some, the Maxim Gorki Theater under the leadership of Shermin Langhoff is another state-stage in Berlin that could—or should—serve as a model.[30] Together with co-*Intendant* Jens Hillje and an ensemble that is the youngest and most diverse in Germany, since 2013 Langhoff has radically rethought the Gorki as a vibrant space for "postmigrant theater."[31] This emergent theater form often employs mimetic—or what Lizzie Stewart calls "semi-documentary"—modes of representation to thematize the history of migration in Germany and redress the lack of these perspectives on the German stage.[32] As Langhoff explains, "Postmigrant means that we critically question the production and reception of stories about migration and about migrants which have been available up to now and that we view and produce these stories anew, inviting a new reception."[33] Though postmigrant theater initially focused on narratives of Turkish-German culture, it has become a capacious label to describe performances by and about a broad spectrum of artists of color living and working in Germany, including black Germans and refugees from around the globe.[34] In a series of essays as well as her forthcoming book on contemporary Berlin, *Theatre of Anger*, Olivia Landry argues that, through a "disavowal of the divisive history and politics of migration and citizenship in Germany," Langhoff and her team have made theater history.[35] The Gorki is the first state-stage explicitly to cultivate "a repertoire of plays and performances that pursued a vast transnational scope"[36] and, in so doing, foreground the theater as both a medium and vital social institution instrumental for galvanizing discussions about the ongoing "refugee crisis," about intersectional histories of immigration, discrimination, and human rights, about Germany's colonial legacy, and about the dearth of a robust racial vocabulary and accompanying critical race theory in the German context.[37] As a state-stage, as Landry suggests elsewhere, the Gorki "not only offers a representational agora for transcultural reflection but also a tangible forum for political activism, mobilization, and transformation."[38] It seems, then, that culture senator Klaus Lederer initially had something like the Gorki in mind as he suggested over and over again that the new "new" Volksbühne must be "more diverse, more female, younger."[39]

On June 12, 2019, however, Lederer announced that René Pollesch would be the next *Intendant* of the Volksbühne. The responses to the appointment have been decisively mixed. For some, Pollesch, a white man pushing sixty, hardly fits Lederer's search criteria.[40] For others, he represents the best possible ties to the Castorf era: he led the Prater, the Volksbühne's experimental studio theater, to great acclaim from 2001 to 2007 before becoming a mainstay on the main stage at Rosa-Luxemburg-Platz. According to Sarah Waterfeld, he was also highly supportive of the Volksbühne occupation.[41] While Pollesch is known for his staunch anticapitalist, antiracist, queer, and feminist politics, his approach to questions of representation onstage looks much different than the postmigrant paradigm at the Gorki. Indeed, Pollesch's aesthetic and institutional tendencies question many of the assumptions upon which the postmigrant approach often depends. Katrin Sieg voices one version of the concern: "I wonder whether that particular dramatic form, organized around the autobiographical, humanist self, fully endowed with the capacity to reason among equals and persuade without recourse to violence, as cosmopolitan thinkers in the Enlightenment tradition have envisioned it, is actually able to register conditions of living under the contemporary structures of absolute sovereignty and bare life described by [Giorgio] Agamben."[42]

Pollesch's distinctly postdramatic praxis specifically questions the conditions of possibility for thinking about authenticity and identity in our current socioeconomic moment. Instead, as Shane Boyle argues, referencing Joshua

Clover's work, Pollesch's theater "gives tangible form to the 'subjective lifeworld of labor' under post-Fordism, specifically the new experiences of alienation it engenders in which individuals find themselves estranged from their emotional and creative" selves.[43] The affective qualities of this alienation are the key formal properties of Pollesch's theater: no dissolving into character, no explicit "roles" with which an audience member can identify, enormous blocks of highly dense text performed so rapidly that a prompter follows the performers around the stage with script in hand to give them cues when they lose their place. Bettina Brandl-Risi elaborates:

> Pollesch's style jumps from manifesto passages or quotes from movies and songs, as well as theoretical jargon, to platitudes or a montage of clichés and bon mots, linked only by puns or associations and characterized by exaggeration, redundancy, parody, and incongruence. Pollesch offers nothing akin to realism onstage. . . . [H]is characters speak with the awareness that everything has already been said before. . . . Each piece produces and perpetuates . . . a mixture of sociological and feminist discourse, economic theory and criticism (especially dealing with post-Fordist work life or globalized cities), transferred to first-person utterances.[44]

Pollesch's response, then, to the experience of neoliberal disavowal is not to confront the situation as something we can step beyond. Instead, he critiques power's relations and its inherent structures by making our experience of them perceptible from within. And he does it always with more than a heavy dose of the ironic and the productively nonsensical.

Although he works in a highly collaborative mode with predominantly female artists, when asked about the role of theater to intervene directly in ongoing political discussions—of diverse representation on the German stage, for instance—Pollesch is adamantly indirect. "The problem," he explains, "is that political theater is still being produced as a theater of representation, in which criticism is based upon agreement but does not have a critical attitude within the process of production. . . . We are willing to exploit ourselves totally and to fulfill the maximum requirements. Furthermore, we sell our subjectivity as a product in theater. The question is: Where are the practices of resistance?"[45] Here Pollesch reveals the enduring influence and importance of Hans-Thies Lehmann's thinking for his own positions. (He was Lehmann's student in Giessen from 1983 to 1989.) Pollesch's aesthetics of resistance seeks new forms and instruments of production as its means of engaging social and political questions. His work articulates (and performs) the need for new kinds of theatrical space in which we might communicate and exist with one another differently.

In the press conference held at the Volksbühne to announce his directorship from 2021 to 2026, Pollesch made clear that his broader vision for the theater is based on an expansion of his desire to "make theater politically" (as opposed to making political theater), as well as the critique of representation essential to his own practice.[46] Pollesch is not interested in being the theater's charismatic manager. He is not interested in developing yet another brand or corporate identity. Rather, he hopes to facilitate a context for different kinds and structures of collaborative work based always in openness, uncertainty, and unpredictability. And while I surmise that the theater to come will also look much "more diverse, more female, younger," the rest of the details are still in the works. What is clear, however, is that from deep within the heart of this state-stage in ruins, Pollesch hopes to discover yet another art of institutional imagination. In this public call to radically reevaluate once again the Volksbühne's public mission, he opens a door, clears a space, sets a stage for new forms, new constituencies, and new modes of performing policy. I look forward to seeing how it goes.

ABBREVIATIONS

AdK: Archives of the Akademie der Künste, Berlin, including the following:

    AVM: Sammlung audiovisueller Medien

    Schriften-DK: Schriftensammlung Darstellende Kunst

    TiW: Sammlung Theater in der Wende

    VB: Archiv der Volksbühne Berlin

GBFA: Bertolt Brecht, *Werke: Grosse Kommentierte Berliner und Frankfurter Ausgabe*, 30 vols., ed. Werner Hecht et al. (Berlin: Aufbau-Verlag and Frankfurt: Suhrkamp Verlag, 1988–2000)

SFB: Sender Freies Berlin (Radio Free Berlin)

Unless otherwise indicated, all translations from German are mine.

Introduction

EPIGRAPHS: Theodor W. Adorno, "Culture and Administration," trans. Wes Blomster, in *The Culture Industry: Selected Essays on Mass Culture*, ed. J. M. Bernstein (New York: Routledge Classics, 2001), 107; Evelyn Annuss, "On the Future of the Volksbühne—Failure Is an Option," *Texte zur Kunst* 110 (June 2018): 92.

1. John Goetz and Peter Laudenbach, "Chronologie eines Desasters: Die 255 Tage von Chris Dercon," *Süddeutsche Zeitung*, April 20, 2018, https://projekte.sueddeutsche.de/artikel/kultur/intendant-der-volksbuehne-chris-dercons-scheitern-e608226, archived at https://perma.cc/85A6-LVK5.

2. Chris Dercon, interview by Peter Boenisch, "Systemic Crisis in European Theatre" conference, Goethe Institute, London, April 27, 2018, https://www.youtube.com/watch?v=k-bkWQfKYJE; Sarah Waterfeld, interview by author, Berlin, May 11, 2018.

3. Waterfeld, interview by author.

4. "The Battle over the Volksbühne Director Is a Battle for the Future of Berlin," *e-flux conversations*, May 2017, https://conversations.e-flux.com/t/the-battle-over-the-volksbuhne-director-is-a-battle-for-the-future-of-berlin/6641, archived at https://perma.cc/XV7W-75JF.

5. Peter Boenisch, "(Re)thinking the Meaning of the European Theatre Institution: Some Lessons from the Recent Crisis at Volksbühne Berlin, Kammerspiele Munich and Elsewhere" (paper presented at the "Decentering the Vision(s) of Europe: The Emergence of New Forms" conference, European Association for the Study of Theater and Performance, Théâtre de la Cité, Paris, October 25–27, 2018).

6. According to published statistics from the Deutscher Bühnenverein, theater subsidy for the whole of Germany in 2017–18 was just over 2.6 billion euros. See Deutscher Bühnenverein, *Theaterstatistik 2017/2018: Die wichtigsten Wirtschaftsdaten der Theater, Orchester und Festspiele, 53. Auflage* (Cologne: Deutscher Bühnenverein, Bundesverband dt. Theater, 2019).

7. For an annotated review of the discussion in the German press, see Christian Rakow, "Warum hört der Streit nicht auf?," *Nachtkritik*, September 19, 2017, https://www.nachtkritik.de/index.php?option=com_content&view=article&id=14413:debatte-um-die-berliner-volksbuehne&catid=101&Itemid=84, archived at https://perma.cc/HLM9-CBZE.

8. Dercon, interview by Boenisch.

9. Goetz and Laudenbach, "Chronologie eines Desasters."

10. Goetz and Laudenbach, "Chronologie eines Desasters."

11. Goetz and Laudenbach, "Chronologie eines Desasters."

12. Claus Peymann, open letter to Michael Müller, April 1, 2015, https://www.nachtkritik.de/images/stories/pdf/Offener_Brief_Claus_Peymann_Michael_Muller.pdf, archived at https://perma.cc/C5VT-LCLU.

13. Their open letter of June 20, 2016 was published in English as "Volksbühne Staff on Chris Dercon: We Fear Job Cuts and Liquidation," *e-flux conversations*, June 2016, https://conversations.e-flux.com/t/volksbuhne-staff-on-chris-dercon-we-fear-job-cuts-and-liquidation/3911, archived at https://perma.cc/2FGK-2J96.

14. The petition, "Re-negotiating the Future of the Berlin Volksbühne," initiated by Evelyn Annuss, can be found in English at https://www.change.org/p/re-negotiating-the-future-of-the-berlin-volksbühne, archived at https://perma.cc/5R5S-ELPG (accessed May 1, 2020).

15. Gero Schliess, "New Berlin Theater Director Chris Dercon Responds to Poo Protests with Dance," *Deutsche Welle*, September 11, 2017, https://p.dw.com/p/2ji1A.

16. The open invitation in German can be found at https://cryptpad.fr/pad/#/1/view/tCFG8CCUnhtpyQtAKaYCVg/dYZWdWZTWKcAxlodMl-JK6b7ksGxYEQ8V70jwHCS2W8.

17. David Farley, "A Guide to the Weird and Wacky in Berlin," *New York Times*, April 24, 2018.

18. Peter Gumbel, "Hip Berlin: Europe's Capital of Cool," *Time Magazine*, November 16, 2009.

19. As Ingo Bader and Albert Scharenberg write, this "lively and politically rebellious subculture" was "based on new social movements (squatters, community organizations), the gay scene and student milieu, and culturally located between Punk, Industrial and *Neue Deutsche Welle* (the German counterpart of new wave and the first pop music in the German language to dominate the national charts for some years)." Ingo Bader and Albert Scharenberg, "The Sound of Berlin: Subculture and the Global Music Industry," *International Journal of Urban and Regional Research* 34, no. 1 (2010): 82.

20. According to Johannes Novy, the "development of tourism in Berlin since German reunification reads like a singular success story. . . . While there were 7 million overnight stays in 1993, in 2012 there were already almost 25 million. The number of actual overnight stays is believed to be at least double the number officially registered by the city's accommodation industry. . . . Furthermore, the 'gray market' accommodations have also grown considerably in the recent past. According to a study by the tenants association *Berliner Mietergemeinschaft*, in 2011 . . . there were already around 12,000 vacation apartments in Berlin with 50,000 beds—and the number is rising." Johannes Novy, "'Berlin Does Not Love You': Notes on Berlin's 'Tourism Controversy' and Its Discontents," in *The Berlin Reader: A Compendium on Urban Change and Activism*, ed. Matthias Bernt, Britta Grell, and Andrej Holm (Bielefeld: Transcript Verlag, 2013), 224.

21. Novy explains that "the lines between tourism and other forms of (temporary) migration are also becoming increasingly blurred. The growing number of highly mobile academics, artist, and 'creative' workers and entrepreneurs that can be encountered in Berlin is a case in point. . . . [T]hese temporary 'city users' cannot be unambiguously classified as either tourists or residents," and they

constitute an "increasingly mobile 'cosmopolitan consuming class.'" "'Berlin Does Not Love You,'" 229.

22. Luc Boltanski and Eve Chiapello, *The New Spirit of Capitalism*, trans. Gregory Elliott (New York: Verso, 2005).

23. See Peter Boenisch's introductory remarks in Dercon, interview by Boenisch.

24. According to Andrej Holm, "As a result of the high renovation quota (around 80 percent of the buildings) scarcely 25 percent of the original resident bases still live in the renewal areas. . . . Sociological investigations have demonstrated that the average income level for Prenzlauer Berg has increased from 75 percent of the citywide level in 1993 to 140 percent of it in 2007." Andrej Holm, "Berlin's Gentrification Mainstream," in *Berlin Reader*, ed. Bernt, Grell, and Holm, 177–78. For more on the history of gentrification in Berlin's Mitte neighborhood—specifically through the lens of alternative cultural and artistic projects—see Daniela Sandler, *Counterpreservation: Architectural Decay in Berlin since 1989* (Ithaca, NY: Cornell University Press, 2016): 90–131 (chap. 3).

25. Klaus Biesenbach quoted in Ted Loos, "In Berlin, Artists Find a Home," *New York Times*, April 24, 2018.

26. Chris Dercon, "'Ich habe mich noch nie so unfrei gefühlt wie in Berlin,'" interview by Thomas E. Schmidt and Adam Soboczynski, *Zeit Online*, May 17, 2017, https://www.zeit.de/2017/21/chris-dercon-berlin-volksbuehne-intendant.

27. Volksbühne Berlin, "About," https://www.volksbuehne.berlin/en/haus/529 /about (accessed December 20, 2017).

28. Sven Lütticken, "Art as Immoral Institution," *Texte zur Kunst*, October 3, 2017, https://www.textezurkunst.de/articles/sven-lutticken-volksbuhne -occupation/?highlight=art%20as%20immoral%20institution, archived at https://perma.cc/E9ZJ-2S67.

29. A text posted by the occupiers in the Volksbühne, quoted in Lütticken, "Art as Immoral Institution."

30. Sarah Waterfeld, "B6112—Art after All: The Alleged Occupation of the Volksbühne am Rosa-Luxemburg-Platz," *Theatre Survey* 59, no. 2 (2018): 278.

31. I have slightly modified Peter Boenisch's translation, which he cited in the introductory remarks to his interview with Dercon. The original citation can be found in "Chris Dercon über seine Ziele an der Volksbühne und im kosmopolitischen Berlin," *Süddeutsche Zeitung*, April 25, 2015.

32. Traute Schölling, "On with the Show? The Transition to Post-Socialist Theatre in Eastern Germany," trans. Marc Silberman, *Theatre Journal* 45, no. 1 (1993): 21. David Ashley Hughes provides a longer historical overview: "The peculiar character of German theater structures owes in large measure to the privileged role of culture in German history. As Alan Steinweiss comments in his article on the Nazi Theatre Chamber, 'The very term *Kultur* has connoted a merging of national identity with an appreciation of artistic achievement, and artists, generally speaking, have traditionally been highly respected members of German society.' In fact, German identity has been predicated on culture ever since the *Sturm und Drang* playwrights of the 1770s sought to change German dependence on French theatrical models, which pandered to the court of Louis XIV: 'From Lessing and the *Sturm und Drang* playwrights to Goethe and Schiller, from Büchner to Hauptmann, to Brecht and Müller, the German theater has always attracted or generated writers who regard the stage as a place of national discourse and a tool of historical

change.' . . . Because the theater has always been integral to national identity in Germany, it has, historically, received abnormally high state subsidies that make no sense whatsoever based on free-market logic." David Ashley Hughes, "Notes on the German Theatre Crisis," *TDR: The Drama Review* 51, no. 4 (2007): 134–35.

33. Hughes, "Notes on the German Theatre Crisis," 134. According to the Deutscher Bühnenverein, theater subsidy for the whole of West Germany in the 1989 fiscal year was just over 2 billion DM. See Deutscher Bühnenverein, *Theaterstatistik 1989/90, 25. Heft* (Cologne: Deutscher Bühnenverein, Bundesverband Deutscher Theater, 1990). In West Berlin, during the 1988–89 season, the theater received approximately 170 million DM in subsidy. See Ivan Nagel, "Zur Zukunft der Berliner Theater: Gutachten an den Senat von Berlin," in *Streitschriften: Politik, Kulturpolitik, Theaterpolitik 1957–2001* (Berlin: Siedler, 2001), 128. Germany officially switched to the euro on January 1, 2002, at a rate of exchange of 1.96 DM per euro.

34. Total theater subsidy in East Germany in 1988 amounted to 514.8 Million GDR-Mark. See Staatliche Zentralverwaltung für Statistik, *Statistisches Jahrbuch der Deutschen Demokratischen Republik 1989, 34. Jahrgang* (Berlin: Rudolf Haufe Verlag, 1990), 272–73. During the 1988–89 season, theater subsidy in East Berlin was approximately 130 million GDR-Mark. See Nagel, "Zukunft der Berliner Theater," 128.

35. Stephen Brockmann traces the origins of a related term, *Kulturnation*, back to the work of historian Friedrich Meinecke, who formulated the concept in the early twentieth century. As Brockmann explains, "The concept of the *Kulturnation* implies that because of its political division Germany was, for centuries after the political solidification of its chief European rivals France and England, a fragmented, indeed non-existent political entity in the middle of Europe, and that because of this fragmentation Germans could experience national identity and unity only in and through culture. What brought Bavarians, Prussians, Swabians, and Saxons together in the first half of the nineteenth century was not a common political home but rather the sense of a German culture that existed prior to and independent of any political nation-building." Brockmann suggests further that the concept is "useful as a way of understanding not just the German division of the early nineteenth century but also the divided Germany of the postwar years." Stephen Brockmann, *Literature and German Reunification* (Cambridge: Cambridge University Press, 1999), 6, 10. Matt Cornish's *Performing Unification: History and Nation in German Theater after 1989* (Ann Arbor: University of Michigan Press, 2017) impressively extends Brockmann's discussion to the arena of theater and drama.

36. This English translation is quoted in Schölling, "On with the Show?," 21–22.

37. As Chris Salter explains, "The idea of the *[K]ulturstaat* was already established in the post-war *[G]rundgesetz* (constitution), dictating that art and culture is a legal obligation to be met by the individual states or *[L]änder*. Within German constitutional law, culture has the equivalent place in the social hierarchy as education, social security and health care. In other words, the generous cultural subsidies which enabled artists as wide ranging as Wim Wenders, Pina Bausch, William Forsythe and Peter Stein to make their work over the past thirty years emerged from the state and local (i.e., city) level." Chris Salter, "The Kulturstaat in the Time of Empire: Notes on Germany Thirteen Years After," *Performing Arts Journal* 26, no. 2 (2004): 3.

38. Matthias Bernt, Britta Grell, and Andrej Holm, "Introduction," in *Berlin Reader*, ed. Bernt, Grell, and Holm, 11–21.

39. Godfrey Carr and Georgina Paul, "Unification and Its Aftermath: The Challenge of History," in *German Cultural Studies: An Introduction*, ed. Rob Burns (New York: Oxford University Press, 1995), 325–48.

40. See, for example, Erika Fischer-Lichte, "Zur Einleitung," in *Transformationen: Theater der neunziger Jahre*, ed. Erika Fischer-Lichte, Doris Kolesch, and Christel Weiler (Berlin: Theater der Zeit, 1999), 7–11; Hughes, "Notes on the German Theatre Crisis"; Sabine Zolchow, "The Island of Berlin," in *Theatre in the Berlin Republic: German Drama since Reunification*, ed. Denise Varney (Berlin: Peter Lang, 2008), 55–80. For other detailed narratives about the German theater landscape after the fall of the Wall, see Carl Weber, "German Theatre: Between the Past and the Future," *Performing Arts Journal* 13, no. 1 (1991): 43–59; Schölling, "On with the Show?"; Carl Weber, "Crossing the Footbridge Again; or, A Semi-Sentimental Journey," *Theatre Journal* 45, no. 1 (1993): 75–89; Carl Weber, "Periods of Precarious Adjustment: Some Notes on the Theater's Situation at the Beginning and after the End of the Socialist German State," *Contemporary Theatre Review* 4, no. 2 (1995): 23–36; Chris Salter, "Forgetting, Erasure, and the Cry of the Billy Goat: Berlin Theatre Five Years After," *Performing Arts Journal* 18, no. 1 (1996): 18–28; Cornish, *Performing Unification*.

41. Amid a growing scholarly interest in the work of a number of contemporary performance artists and ensembles who have made Berlin their home, *Institutional Theatrics* situates these artists within the shifting infrastructural landscapes that also constitute their "work." And although over the past twenty-five years there have been a few articles and book chapters that described some of the infrastructural adjustments I consider, this book traces—through sustained ethnographic and archival excavation—the performative intersections of the policy debates, institutional transformations, and performance practices that constituted the ongoing series of "theater crises" in Berlin.

42. Peter M. Boenisch, "Encountering a 'Theatre of (Inter-)Singularity': Transformations and Rejections of Shifting Institutional Dramaturgies in Contemporary German Theatre," in *Shifting Dramaturgies: Composing Experiences of Interweaving Performance Cultures*, ed. Erika Fischer-Lichte, Christel Weiler, and Torsten Jost (Abingdon: Routledge, forthcoming).

43. Boenisch, "(Re)thinking the Meaning of the European Theatre Institution." As Balme elaborates, "Whereas art history has successfully integrated questions of patronage, and latterly museum studies, into research paradigms, this has been less pronounced in the performing arts, although the institutional focus would seem to be particularly relevant for the latter because of their traditional reliance on labour-intensive organisations and usually expensive, purpose-built buildings for reception." Christopher Balme, "Institutional Aesthetics and the Crisis of Leadership," in *The Routledge Companion to Theatre and Politics*, ed. Peter Eckersall and Helena Grehan (New York: Routledge, 2019), 169. Just as this book went to press, Christopher Balme and Tony Fisher published a coedited collection examining the ongoing crises of European theater institutions, including an essay by Peter Boenisch that tracks some of the complicated "fault lines that came to a head" in the Dercon debacle. See Christopher Balme and Tony Fischer, eds., *Theatre Institutions in Crisis: European Perspectives* (London: Routledge, 2020).

44. Some prominent examples of books that develop an infrastructural imaginary as central to their critical methodologies include Michael McKinnie's *City Stages: Theatre and Urban Space in a Global City* (Toronto: University of Toronto Press, 2007); Shannon Jackson's *Social Works: Performing Art, Supporting Publics* (New York: Routledge, 2011); Jen Harvie's *Fair Play: Art, Performance and Neoliberalism* (Houndmills, Basingstoke, UK: Palgrave Macmillan, 2013); Paul Bonin-Rodriguez's *Performing Policy: How Contemporary Politics and Cultural Programs Redefined U.S. Artists for the Twenty-First Century* (Houndmills, Basingstoke, UK: Palgrave Macmillan, 2015); Hillary Miller's *Drop Dead: Performance in Crisis, 1970s New York* (Evanston, IL: Northwestern University Press, 2016); Ric Knowles's *Performing the Intercultural City* (Ann Arbor: University of Michigan Press, 2017); and Patricia Ybarra's *Latinx Theater in the Times of Neoliberalism* (Evanston, IL: Northwestern University Press, 2018). Bonin-Rodriguez's book is the only one in this collection of titles to attend predominantly to the intersections of policy and performance—though his book has a very different geographical focus, in that it charts the development of US policy discourse over the past two decades. While Bonin-Rodriguez and I do share an interest in examining how performing artists might reimagine their own capacities for collaboratively performing policy on the local and national levels, his focus on the ways policy has "redefined" how artists might forge sustainable futures in their communities seems almost sympathetic (or resigned) to avowing a policy platform that understands artists as entrepreneurial value producers. Alternatively, my own project explores artists' abundant capacity for more critical engagement, or dis/avowal, as the very means by which they might perform policy in and for the twenty-first century.

45. For an overview of these "debates," see Stuart Cunningham, *Framing Culture: Criticism and Policy in Australia* (Sydney: Allen & Unwin, 1992); Tom O'Regan, "(Mis)Taking Policy: Notes on the Cultural Policy Debate," in *Australian Cultural Studies: A Reader*, ed. John Frow and Meaghan Morris (Chicago: University of Illinois Press, 1993), 192–206; Toby Miller, "Leavis to Beaver: Culture with Power, Culture as Policy," in *Technologies of Truth: Cultural Citizenship and the Popular Media* (Minneapolis: University of Minnesota Press, 1998), 64–98; Justin Lewis and Toby Miller, eds., *Critical Cultural Policy Studies: A Reader* (Oxford: Wiley-Blackwell, 2003); Oliver Bennett, "Review Essay: The Torn Halves of Cultural Policy Research," *International Journal of Cultural Policy* 10, no. 2 (2004): 237–48; Jim McGuigan, *Rethinking Cultural Policy* (Maidenhead, UK: Open University Press, 2004).

46. Tony Bennett, "Putting Policy into Cultural Studies," in *Cultural Studies*, ed. Lawrence Grossberg, Cary Nelson, and Paula Treichler (New York: Routledge, 1992), 29, 25.

47. Bennett, "Putting Policy into Cultural Studies," 32.

48. Miller, "Leavis to Beaver," 69.

49. Tony Bennett, *Culture: A Reformer's Science* (Thousand Oaks, CA: SAGE Publications, 1998), 10.

50. Tony Bennett provides an extensive explication of this "instrumental" notion of culture in his historical study on the museum: *The Birth of the Museum: History, Theory, Politics* (New York: Routledge, 1995). In a later work, Bennett admits that his positions stem from "a particular approach to, and adaptation of, Foucault's writings." He continues: "I may well be putting words in Foucault's

mouth here, as the subject of culture was not one Foucault himself wrote about directly. My account, then, is an extrapolation of how culture might be theorised given a particular set of theoretical axioms, rather than a summary of what Foucault said—or might have said had he got round to it." Bennett, *Culture: A Reformer's Science*, 5, 10.

51. Bennett, *Culture: A Reformer's Science*, 4.

52. Bennett, "Putting Policy into Cultural Studies," 29.

53. Bennett, "Putting Policy into Cultural Studies," 33.

54. Fredric Jameson, "On 'Cultural Studies,'" *Social Text*, no. 34 (1993): 29–30.

55. Bennett, *Culture: A Reformer's Science*, 34.

56. Bennett, *Culture: A Reformer's Science*, 5.

57. Bennett, *Culture: A Reformer's Science*, 194.

58. O. Bennett, "Review Essay," 237.

59. Adorno, "Culture and Administration," 129, 128.

60. Adorno, "Culture and Administration," 129. For a helpful analysis of Benjamin's own reflections on the "task of the critic," see Uwe Steiner, *Walter Benjamin: An Introduction to His Work and Thought*, trans. Michael Winkler (Chicago: University of Chicago Press, 2010), chap. 4.

61. Adorno, "Culture and Administration," 130.

62. Bennett, *Culture: A Reformer's Science*, 198–99.

63. Bennett, *Culture: A Reformer's Science*, 200.

64. Theodor W. Adorno, "Theses upon Art and Religion Today," *Kenyon Review* 7, no. 4 (1945): 678.

65. Adorno, "Culture and Administration," 128.

66. Bennett, "Putting Policy into Cultural Studies," 32.

67. Adorno, "Culture and Administration," 119.

68. Bennett, *Culture: A Reformer's Science*, 199.

69. Adorno, "Culture and Administration," 108.

70. Adorno, "Culture and Administration," 127.

71. Adorno, "Culture and Administration," 128.

72. Toby Miller and George Yúdice, *Cultural Policy* (Thousand Oaks, CA: SAGE Publications, 2002), 3.

73. Angela McRobbie, "All the World's a Stage, Screen or Magazine: When Culture Is the Logic of Late Capitalism," *Media, Culture & Society* 18 (1996): 335.

74. Miller and Yúdice, *Cultural Policy*, 3.

75. George Yúdice, *The Expediency of Culture: Uses of Culture in the Global Era* (Durham, NC: Duke University Press, 2003), 25.

76. Yúdice, *The Expediency of Culture*, 25.

77. Yúdice, *The Expediency of Culture*, 44.

78. Miller and Yúdice, *Cultural Policy*, 12.

79. Miller and Yúdice, *Cultural Policy*, 14.

80. Miller and Yúdice, *Cultural Policy*, 14–15.

81. Yúdice, *Expediency of Culture*, 58–59.

82. Yúdice, *Expediency of Culture*, 59.

83. Yúdice, *Expediency of Culture*, 77–78.

84. Yúdice, *Expediency of Culture*, 317.

85. Yúdice, *Expediency of Culture*, 319–20.

86. Yúdice, *Expediency of Culture*, 337; emphasis in original.

87. Peter Osborne, "'Whoever Speaks of Culture Speaks of Administration as Well,'" *Cultural Studies* 20, no. 1 (2006): 43.

88. Miller and Yúdice, *Cultural Policy*, 1.

89. Miller and Yúdice, *Cultural Policy*, 2.

90. Miller and Yúdice, *Cultural Policy*, 2.

91. Judith Butler, *Notes toward a Performative Theory of Assembly* (Cambridge, MA: Harvard University Press, 2015), 29; emphasis in original. Subsequent citations are given parenthetically in the text.

92. Jackson, *Social Works*, 21.

93. Jackson, *Social Works*, 25, 24; emphasis in original.

94. Judith Butler and Shannon Jackson, "Keynote Address" (lecture-performance presented at the "How Are We Performing Today?" symposium at the Museum of Modern Art, New York, November 16, 2012).

95. Butler and Jackson, "Keynote Address."

96. Shannon Jackson, "Working Publics," *Performance Research* 16, no. 2 (2011): 10–11.

Chapter 1

EPIGRAPHS: Friedrich Schiller, *On the Aesthetic Education of Man: In a Series of Letters*, ed. and trans. Elizabeth M. Wilkinson and L. A. Willoughby (Oxford: Clarendon Press, 1982), 7, 300. The latter passage was included in a footnote in the 1795 edition, and, according to Wilkinson and Willoughby, was excluded from later versions.

1. Stefan Berg, "Der Senator spielt mit," *Deutsches Allgemeines Sonntagsblatt*, June 25, 1993.

2. Ulrich Roloff-Momin, *Zuletzt: Kultur* (Berlin: Aufbau-Verlag, 1997), 98.

3. "Der Senat kürzt die Kunst," *Die Tageszeitung*, June 22, 1993.

4. Hildburg Bruns, "Geheim! Senats-Sparliste: Uni dicht, Theater weg, Steuer rauf," *Bild*, June 21, 1993.

5. Volker Oesterreich, "Harald Juhnke fordert das Publikum zum Protest auf," *Berliner Morgenpost*, July 4, 1993.

6. Video clip of Roloff-Momin in Hans-Christoph Knebusch, "Schillers Tod: Ein bürgerliches Trauerspiel?" (3sat, September 4, 1993), AdK, TiW 1034, AVM 33.8254.

7. Roloff-Momin in Knebusch, "Schillers Tod."

8. Eberhard Diepgen, "'Berlin zuliebe darf es kein Schwanken und Wanken geben,'" *Berliner Morgenpost*, July 18, 1993.

9. Staatliche Schauspielbühnen Berlin, "Einnahmen und Ausgaben der Staatlichen Schauspielbühnen Berlin 1992–1994," Vorabdruck zur Beratung im Abgeordnetenhaus, September 1993, AdK, TiW 1260.

10. Ulrich Roloff-Momin, "Der Ort, an dem sich Geister scheiden," *Der Tagesspiegel*, June 26, 1993.

11. Diepgen, "'Berlin zuliebe darf es kein Schwanken und Wanken geben.'"

12. Diepgen, "'Berlin zuliebe darf es kein Schwanken und Wanken geben.'"

13. Der Senat von Berlin, "Senatsbeschluss Nr. 3528/93" (Berlin, June 22, 1993).

14. Julie Wedow, "Sturm und Drang at the Schiller," *Checkpoint*, August 1993.

15. Berg, "Der Senator spielt mit."

16. "'Ein Attentat,'" *Der Tagesspiegel*, June 23, 1993.

17. Carola Pompetzki and Ute Wegner, "Es tut mir in der Seele weh," *B.Z.*, June 23, 1993.

18. Personalrat der Staatlichen Schauspielbühnen Berlin, "Anschlag auf die Deutsche Kulturlandschaft—Heute wir, morgen Ihr!," public call (Aufruf des Personalrats an alle Personal- und Betriebsräte der deutschen Theater), June 23, 1993, AdK, TiW 1227.

19. Ulrich Roloff-Momin, letter to Volkmar Clauß, June 22, 1993, AdK, TiW 1190.

20. Jürgen Flimm quoted in "Die Stadt schlägt sich selbst ins Gesicht," *Der Tagesspiegel*, June 24, 1993.

21. Claus Peymann quoted in "Die Stadt schlägt sich selbst ins Gesicht."

22. August Everding quoted in "Die Stadt schlägt sich selbst ins Gesicht."

23. Clauß quoted in Joachim Werner Preuss, "Die Staatlichen Schauspielbühnen sollen geschlossen werden," *Theaterredaktion*, SFB, June 27, 1993, unpublished transcript, AdK, TiW 1003.

24. Boris Wendt quoted in Wedow, "Sturm und Drang at the Schiller."

25. Tyler Marshall, "Schiller Closure Looms Despite German Protests," *Los Angeles Times*, July 21, 1993.

26. Friedrich Schiller, *"Don Carlos" and "Mary Stuart,"* trans. Hilary Collier Sy-Quia and Peter Oswald (Oxford: Oxford University Press, 1999), 116.

27. Knebusch, "Schillers Tod."

28. Julia Schön, "Aus für Schiller Theater," *Berliner Zeitung*, June 23, 1993.

29. Roloff-Momin quoted in Pompetzki and Wegner, "Es tut mir in der Seele weh."

30. Roloff-Momin quoted in Ute Wegner, "Berlin darf nicht Las Vegas werden," *B.Z.*, June 24, 1993.

31. Wilfried Mommert, "Roloff-Momin Gerät auf dem Sparkurs ins Schlingern," *Berliner Morgenpost*, June 26, 1993.

32. Nadja Klinger, "Die Berge kreissen," *Junge Welt*, September 11, 1993.

33. Clauß quoted in Wegner, "Berlin darf nicht Las Vegas werden."

34. Roloff-Momin, "Der Ort, an dem sich Geister scheiden."

35. Roloff-Momin quoted in Klaudia Brunst, "Das Paket ist geschnürt," *Die Tageszeitung*, June 26, 1993.

36. Günther Rühle, "Über das Staatstheater," *Der Tagesspiegel*, July 14, 1993.

37. Die Mitarbeiter der Staatlichen Schauspielbühnen Berlin, "Wir spielen weiter—Wir werden dieses Theater nicht verlassen," resolution, June 23, 1993, AdK, TiW 1227.

38. Personalrat der Staatlichen Schauspielbühnen Berlin, "Anschlag auf die Deutsche Kulturlandschaft—Heute wir, morgen Ihr!"

39. Theaterleitung, Ensemble, und Belegschaft der Staatlichen Schauspielbühnen Berlin, open invitation to the "Protestveranstaltung," June 23, 1993, AdK, TiW 1227.

40. "Die Berliner Kulturszene brodelt: Protest-Aktionen halten an; Sparpläne des Senats im Kreuzfeuer der Kritik," *Berliner Morgenpost*, June 26, 1993.

41. "Pina-Bausch-Gastspiel ist abgesagt," *B.Z.*, June 28, 1993.

42. Cay Dobberke, "Intendanten drohen mit Boykott," *Die Welt*, June 28, 1993.

43. Harald Martenstein, "Im schwersten Sturm wird der Tanker flott," *Der Tagesspiegel*, June 28, 1993.

44. "Die Kassiererin im Schiller-Theater kann noch 'Ausverkauft' sagen," *Der Tagesspiegel*, June 28, 1993.

45. "Die Kassiererin im Schiller-Theater kann noch 'Ausverkauft' sagen."

46. "Die Kassiererin im Schiller-Theater kann noch 'Ausverkauft' sagen."

47. Gisela Sonnenburg, "Die Theaterfamilie macht mobil," *Neues Deutschland*, June 28, 1993. The relevant passage from the original English translation of "Surabaya-Johnny" (Broadway, 1977) is this: "You said a lot, Johnny. It was all lies. / You sure had me fooled, right from the start. / I hate you when you laugh at me like that. / Take that pipe out of your mouth, Johnny." Bertolt Brecht, Kurt Weill, and Dorothy Lane [pseud. Elisabeth Hauptmann], *Happy End: A Melodrama with Songs*, trans. Michael Feingold (London: Methuen, 1982).

48. Video clip of Brecht citation in "Weiterspielen im Schiller trotz Schliessungsbeschluss," *Abendschau*, SFB, July 2, 1993), AdK, TiW 1028, AVM 33.8243.

49. Edward Albee quoted (in German) in Sonnenburg, "Die Theaterfamilie macht mobil."

50. Staatliche Schauspielbühnen Berlin, petition (Vorlage für Unterschriftenliste), June 23, 1993, AdK, TiW 122.

51. Clauß quoted in "Pina-Bausche-Gastspiel ist abgesagt."

52. Sonnenburg, "Die Theaterfamilie macht mobil."

53. Martenstein, "Im schwersten Sturm wird der Tanker flott."

54. Roloff-Momin quoted in "Fastenzeit," *Frankfurter Allgemeine Zeitung*, June 30, 1993.

55. Gerhard Stadelmaier, "Adieu, Dinosaurier," *Frankfurter Allgemeine Zeitung*, June 24, 1993.

56. Susanne Böwe quoted in Bernd Lubowski, "Politiker sind doch keine Theater-Kenner: Interview mit Susanne Böwe über die Situation junger Schauspieler," *Berliner Morgenpost*, July 26, 1993.

57. Volkmar Clauß, "Zu dem Beitrag von Ulrich Roloff-Momin zur Situation des Schillertheaters," fax to the Tagesspiegel Feuilletonredaktion, June 26, 1993, AdK, TiW 1167.

58. Ulrich Roloff-Momin, "'An die Pfründe gehen,'" *Kölner Stadt-Anzeiger*, July 1, 1993.

59. Roloff-Momin quoted in Martin Lutz, "Kultursenator Roloff-Momin: 'Ich trete zurück, wenn . . . ,'" *Berliner Kurier*, July 4, 1993.

60. Roloff-Momin, "Der Ort, an dem sich Geister scheiden."

61. Roloff-Momin, "Der Ort, an dem sich Geister scheiden."

62. Roloff-Momin, "Der Ort, an dem sich Geister scheiden."

63. Claire Colomb, *Staging the New Berlin: Place Marketing and the Politics of Urban Reinvention Post-1989* (New York: Routledge, 2012), 72.

64. Elizabeth A. Strom, *Building the New Berlin: The Politics of Urban Development in Germany's Capital City* (Lanham, MD: Lexington Books, 2001), 87.

65. Colomb, *Staging the New Berlin*, 89. As Sabine Zolchow explains, "Chancellor Konrad Adenauer's slogan from the fifties—No Experiments!—became the desire of the majority of [former] GDR citizens, this time under different

circumstances. Conservative was also the predominant choice in the first elections for a House of Representatives that represented all of Berlin. Berlin residents hoped for security and economic strength." Zolchow, "The Island of Berlin," 65.

66. Colomb, *Staging the New Berlin*, 90.

67. Stefan Krätke, "City of Talents? Berlin's Regional Economy, Socio-Spatial Fabric and 'Worst Practice' Urban Governance," *International Journal of Urban and Regional Research* 28, no. 3 (2004): 523.

68. Krätke, "City of Talents?," 524.

69. Colomb, *Staging the New Berlin*, 223.

70. Krätke, "City of Talents?," 525.

71. Colomb, *Staging the New Berlin*, 224. As Chris Salter explains further, "The Bankgesellschaft Berlin's additional weight on the city's budget has had an extreme and potentially damaging effect on cultural support, particularly on the city's numerous small and innovative cultural institutions. Already in the early quarter of 2002, directors of cultural institutions were speaking of a '[S]treichlist[e]' (literally, a list of cuts) that would painfully slice through the city's cultural budget." Salter, "The *Kulturstaat* in the Time of Empire," 7–8.

72. Eberhard Diepgen, "Halbjahresbilanz des Berliner Senats," press conference, June 28, 1993, AdK, TiW 1043.

73. Diepgen, "Halbjahresbilanz des Berliner Senats."

74. Diepgen, "Halbjahresbilanz des Berliner Senats."

75. Diepgen, "Halbjahresbilanz des Berliner Senats."

76. "Veni, Vidi, Vici? Eberhard Diepgen zur Berliner Theaterpolitik," *Der Tagesspiegel*, July 9, 1991.

77. Eberhard Diepgen, "Halbjahresbilanz des Berliner Senats."

78. For the text of the bid, see Berlin Olympia GmbH, ed., *Berlin 2000: Die Stadt für Olympia* (Berlin: Berlin 2000 Olympia GmbH, 1992).

79. Colomb, *Staging the New Berlin*, 96; emphasis in original.

80. Colomb, *Staging the New Berlin*, 104.

81. Jennings quoted in Colomb, *Staging the New Berlin*, 104–5. See also Andrew Jennings, *The New Lords of the Rings: Olympic Corruption and How to Buy Gold Medals* (London: Pocket Books, 1996).

82. Horst Knietzsche, "'Wo Kultur wegbricht, wird Platz frei für Gewalt,'" *Neues Deutschland*, June 29, 1993.

83. Klaus Pierwoß, "Solidarität ja, aber . . ." *Der Freitag*, July 2, 1993.

84. Pierwoß, "Solidarität ja, aber . . ."

85. Martin Linzer, "Entree," *Theater der Zeit* (August–September 1993): 1.

86. This and the following Everding quotations are all from August Everding, "Nein, So geht das nicht!" (lecture presented at "Grossveranstaltung—Solidarität der deutschen Theater mit den Staatlichen Schauspielbühnen," Schiller Theater, Berlin, June 27, 1993), AdK, TiW 1230.

87. Weber, "Periods of Precarious Adjustment," 24.

88. Everding, "Nein, So geht das nicht!"

89. Clauß quoted in "Schiller-Theater: Anhaltende Proteste," *Der Tagesspiegel*, June 30, 1993.

90. Die Mitarbeiter der Staatlichen Schauspielbühnen Berlin, "Wir spielen weiter."

91. Michael Merschmeier, open letter to Ulrich Roloff-Momin and Eberhard Diepgen, June 25, 1993, AdK, TiW 1123.

92. Hartmut Krug, "Kunst oder Bürokratie," *Der Freitag*, July 9, 1993.

93. Hartmut Krug, "Armes Theater?" *Der Freitag*, July 2, 1993.

94. Krug, "Armes Theater?"; emphasis added.

95. Benjamin Henrichs, "Schiller—Tod in Berlin," *Die Zeit*, July 2, 1993.

96. Henrichs, "Schiller—Tod in Berlin."

97. Henrichs, "Schiller—Tod in Berlin."

98. Henrichs, "Schiller—Tod in Berlin."

99. Krug, "Armes Theater?"

100. Christopher Balme, "Stadt-Theater: Eine Deutsche Heterotopie zwischen Provinz und Metropole," in *Großstadt: Motor der Künste in der Moderne*, ed. Burcu Dogramaci (Berlin: Gebr. Mann Verlag, 2010), 63.

101. Article 35 of the reunification treaty quoted in Schölling, "On with the Show?," 21.

102. Balme, "Stadt-Theater," 64. Subsequent citations are given parenthetically in the text.

103. As Balme explains, the "Court Theaters were a well-funded and much envied exception. Their employees were civil servants and eligible, at least partially, to receive pensions—which is still the desire of, and ideal position for, every theater artist." "Stadt-Theater," 64.

104. Diepgen, "Halbjahresbilanz des Berliner Senats."

105. Arno Paul and Martha Humphreys, "The West German Theatre Miracle: A Structural Analysis," *TDR: The Drama Review* 24, no. 1 (1980): 4–6.

106. Salter, "*Kulturstaat* in the Time of Empire," 9.

107. Paul and Humphreys, "West German Theatre Miracle," 13.

108. Paul and Humphreys, "West German Theatre Miracle," 24.

109. Ernst Schumacher, "Aufbau und Schleifung einer Bastion," *Berliner Zeitung*, June 25, 1993.

110. Völker Klaus, ed., *Beckett in Berlin: Zum 80. Geburtstag* (Berlin: Edition Hentrich, Frölich & Kaufmann, 1986).

111. Die Mitarbeiter der Staatlichen Schauspielbühnen Berlin, "Wir spielen weiter."

112. Merschmeier quoted in Zolchow, "Island of Berlin," 69.

113. Staatliche Schauspielbühnen Berlin, "Einnahmen und Ausgaben."

114. Lothar Schirmer, "Das Ende kommt immer plötzlich: Theater zwischen Kultur und Event," in *"Damit die Zeit nicht stehenbleibt": Theater in Berlin nach 1945—Teil 4: Nach der Wende*, ed. Stiftung Stadtmuseum Berlin (Berlin: Henschel, 2003), 17.

115. Zadek quoted in Schirmer, "Das Ende kommt immer plötzlich."

116. Robin Detje, "Drachentöter, Denkmalpfleger," *Die Zeit*, July 9, 1993.

117. A report on the survey was published the next day as "Umfrage zur Kultur in Berlin: Mehrheit will keine Änderung," *Der Tagesspiegel*, July 5, 1993.

118. "Schiller-Theater: Andrang wie beim SSV," *Berliner Kurier*, July 5, 1993.

119. "Besuchergemeinden: Kritik an Struktur und Schliessung," *Berliner Morgenpost*, July 5, 1993.

120. Sibylle Wirsing, "Die Nacht der offenen Türen," *Der Tagesspiegel*, July 6, 1993; Bernd Lubowski, "Schiller-Theater wurde zum Tempel bunter Kreativität und heisser Debatten," *Berliner Morgenpost*, July 6, 1993.

121. Detlef Friedrich, "Rotkäppchen und der Einheitswolf," *Berliner Zeitung*, July 7, 1993.

122. August Everding, "Es liegt am System," *Die Welt*, July 14, 1993.

123. Detlef Friedrich, "Die belebende Wirkung des Geldes," *Berliner Zeitung*, August 2, 1993. There was, however, most certainly cause for concern. A large percentage of the Schiller Theater ensemble departed Berlin for their regularly scheduled vacations. After Minetti's performance, press coverage began to dwindle dramatically. Some papers printed occasional coverage of the protest program. But much of the vigor from previous days had faded, in the pages of the press at least.

124. Roloff-Momin, "'An die Pfründe gehen.'"

125. Clauß quoted in "Abwicklung verschlingt zwei volle Jahresetats," *Berliner Zeitung*, July 23, 1993.

126. Everding, "Es liegt am System."

127. Roloff-Momin, *Zuletzt: Kultur*, 108.

128. Raue quoted in "Letzte Chance auf Kompromiss im Schiller-Streit vertan," *B.Z.*, July 28, 1993.

129. Raue quoted in "Schiller-Urteil erst am Donnerstag," *Der Tagesspiegel*, July 28, 1993.

130. Diepgen quoted in "Diepgens Halbzeitbilanz: Wir sind im Zeitplan—Theater-Schliessung bleibt," *Berliner Morgenpost*, June 29, 1993.

131. Finkelnburg quoted in Detlef Friedrich, "Zunächst die heiligen Kühe schlachten? Schiller Theater: Verfassungsgerichtsentscheidung hat die Schliessung aufgeschoben, nicht aufgehoben," *Berliner Zeitung*, July 30, 1993.

132. Friedrich, "Zunächst die heiligen Kühe schlachten?"

133. "Schiller Theater: Noch alles offen," *Berliner Zeitung*, July 28, 1993.

134. Finkelnburg quoted in Hans-Rüdiger Karutz, "'Die Grenzen beachten': Interview mit Verfassungsgerichts-Präsident Finkelnburg," *Die Welt*, July 30, 1993.

135. Clauß quoted in "'Die Chance zum kämpfen,'" *Der Spiegel*, August 2, 1993.

136. Staatliche Schauspielbühnen Berlin, "Positionen—Theaterkultur und Theatermodelle: Eine Strukturdebatte am Schiller Theater," Programmzettel zur Veranstaltungsreihe im Foyer des Schiller-Theaters, program sheet, August 19–September 2, 1993, AdK, TiW 1197.

137. Clauß quoted in "'Die Chance zum kämpfen.'"

138. Staatliche Schauspielbühnen Berlin, "Positionen—Theaterkultur und Theatermodelle."

139. Gerhard Ahrens quoted in Iris Roebling, "Auf dass wir nicht noch blöder werden, als wir schon sind: Im Gespräch mit Gerhard Ahrens," *Neues Deutschland*, August 17, 1993.

140. Peter Wapnewski, "Vom Vermögen der Kultur: Auszüge aus dem Vortrag von Peter Wapnewski im Schiller-Theater," *Der Tagesspiegel*, August 25, 1993.

141. Sven Krügel, "Hochhuths Plädoyer für sein Theater der Autoren," *Berliner Morgenpost*, September 3, 1993.

142. Ivan Nagel et al., "Überlegungen zur Situation der Berliner Theater" (Berlin: April 6, 1991), AdK, TiW 1755. Selections from these "Considerations" can

be found in Ivan Nagel, "Zur Zukunft der Berliner Theater: Gutachten an den Senat von Berlin," in *Streitschriften*, 127–36.

143. Nagel quoted in Ausschuss für Kulturelle Angelegenheiten— Abgeordnetenhaus von Berlin, "Wort-Protokoll," 6th Sitzung (Berlin, May 27, 1991), 45.

144. Nagel et al., "Überlegungen zur Situation der Berliner Theater," 4.

145. Martin Risel, "Verschon' mein Haus, Zünd' andre an," *Berliner Morgenpost*, August 22, 1993.

146. Ivan Nagel, "Gibt es eine Alternative? Zur Schließung des Schiller-Theaters," in *Streitschriften*, 155.

147. Nagel, "Gibt es eine Alternative?," 165.

148. Albert Hetterle quoted in "Gorki-Intendant gegen Nagels Pläne," *Berliner Kurier*, August 23, 1993.

149. Facets of the East-West conflict implicit in the Schiller debates are addressed in a different context in chapter 2. The sour reaction to Nagel's suggestion is indicative of the many tensions still aflame in 1993. Nagel could not resist biting back in an open letter to the formerly eastern *Berliner Zeitung*: "Berlin cultural policy, after reunification, is careful with the high theater culture of the GDR, almost awestruck." See "Realität gegen Ressentiment: Ein offener Brief von Ivan Nagel an die Berliner Zeitung," *Berliner Zeitung*, August 25, 1993.

150. Klaus Pfützner, "Bilde. Künstler! Rede nicht!—Oder Doch?," *Neues Deutschland*, August 27, 1993.

151. Dietmar Göllner, "Foyer Gespräch: Weshalb kleine Teams effizienter arbeiten," *Berliner Morgenpost*, August 23, 1993.

152. Flimm spoke again later with Michael Merschmeier about the financial benefits of the GmbH, drawing on his experience in Hamburg. See Michael Merschmeier, "Jetzt wird es ernst. Das kann ja heiter werden: Ein Theater heute-Gespräch," *Theater Heute Jahrbuch* (1993): 53–54.

153. "Ideen für das Theater der Zukunft," *Die Welt*, August 26, 1993; emphasis added.

154. Flimm quoted in Sibylle Wirsing, "Wir bleiben Hier und spielen weiter: Der Hamburger Intendant Jürgen Flimm redet Tacheles mit Berlin," *Der Tagesspiegel*, August 27, 1993.

155. Flimm quoted in Wirsing, "Wir bleiben Hier und spielen weiter."

156. Everding quoted in "Luxus, der dem Leben Sinn gibt: August Everding zur aktuellen Diskussion," *Neue Zeit*, August 21, 1993.

157. In chapter 4, I return in much greater detail to the question of free-scene organizational models—especially in relation to the state-stage.

158. Clauß quoted in "Abwicklung verschlingt zwei volle Jahresetats."

159. Volkmar Clauß, letter to all the Abgeordneten [members of Parliament] and Senatoren in Berlin, August 23, 1993, AdK, TiW 1195.

160. Clauß, letter to all the Abgeordneten and Senatoren in Berlin.

161. "Presseerklärung der Staatlichen Schauspielbühnen Berlin: Senatsvorlage zur Schliessung des Schiller Theaters," press release, September 1, 1993, AdK, TiW 1167.

162. Staatliche Schauspielbühnen Berlin, "Entwurf zur strukturellen Veränderung," proposal, August 23, 1993, AdK, TiW 1195.

163. Staatliche Schauspielbühnen Berlin, "Entwurf zur strukturellen Veränderung."

164. Staatliche Schauspielbühnen Berlin, "Entwurf zur strukturellen Veränderung."

165. Staatliche Schauspielbühnen Berlin, "Entwurf zur strukturellen Veränderung."

166. "Jedes Haus evaluiert sich selbst: Gespräch mit Klaus Siebenhaar über die Berliner Situation," *Neue Zeit*, August 28, 1993.

167. Klaus Pierwoß, "Gegenrede: Der Retter als Totengräber," *Berliner Zeitung*, August 27, 1993.

168. Pierwoß, "Gegenrede."

169. Klein quoted in Abgeordnetenhaus von Berlin, "Plenarprotokoll 12/51," 12th Wahlperiode, 51st Sitzung (Berlin, September 2, 1993), 4342.

170. von Braun quoted in Abgeordnetenhaus von Berlin, "Plenarprotokoll 12/51," 4344.

171. Lehmann-Brauns quoted in Abgeordnetenhaus von Berlin, "Plenarprotokoll 12/51," 4342.

172. Bernd Lubowski, "Schiller-Theater: Zur Eröffnung gibt's eine Sommernachts-Party," *Berliner Morgenpost*, September 1, 1993.

173. "CDU/SPD-Mehrheit brachte Schiller-Aus," *Neues Deutschland*, September 17, 1993.

174. "Schiller Theater: Politiker bespuckt," *B.Z.*, September 17, 1993.

175. Laurien quoted in Abgeordnetenhaus von Berlin, "Plenarprotokoll 12/52," 12th Wahlperiode, 52nd Sitzung (Berlin, September 16, 1993), 4381.

176. Eckert quoted in Abgeordnetenhaus von Berlin, "Plenarprotokoll 12/52," 4438.

177. Abgeordnetenhaus von Berlin, "Plenarprotokoll 12/52," 4453.

178. Brigitte Fehrle, "Lehrstück Schiller," *Berliner Zeitung*, September 17, 1993.

179. In mid-October, it was announced that the State-Stage Complex would be put up for rent as a theater space or music venue in the New Year; the Senate planned to run ads in regional German papers, the *London Times*, and the *New York Times*. See "Schiller-Theater zu vermieten," *Der Tagesspiegel*, October 17, 1993.

180. "Schiller-Theater zu vermieten."

Chapter 2

EPIGRAPHS: Bertolt Brecht, "Die dialektische Dramatik," in *GBFA* 21.439. This translation is mine; for a translation of the entire essay, see "Dialectical Dramatic Writing," in *Brecht on Theatre*, 3rd ed., ed. Marc Silberman, Steve Giles, and Tom Kuhn (London: Bloomsbury, 2014), 57; Bertolt Brecht, "Dialektische Planung," in *GBFA* 23.223.

1. These interspersed close readings come from my recollections of having seen the performance live on October 8, 2012, supplemented by repeated viewings of a DVD of the performance, generously supplied by the Volksbühne am Rosa-Luxemburg-Platz.

2. Bertolt Brecht, *The Baden-Baden Lesson* [i.e., *Lehrstück*] *on Consent*, trans. Geoffrey Skelton, in *Collected Plays: Three*, ed. John Willett (London: Bloomsbury Methuen Drama, 1997), 23.

3. John Willett, "Editorial Notes," in Brecht, *Collected Plays: Three*, 330.

4. The score recommends that this phrase be played/sung *sehr breit*—or *larghissimo* in Italian—to emphasize its importance. For a very thorough and thoughtful analysis of Hindemith's score, see Andreas Lehmann, "Hindemiths *Lehrstück*," *Hindemith Jahrbuch / Annales Hindemith* 11 (1982): 36–76.

5. This is the version printed in the *GBFA*.

6. Stephen Hinton, *Weill's Musical Theater: Stages of Reform* (Berkeley: University of California Press, 2012), 183. According to Richard Taruskin, Hinton has a predetermined agenda "to expunge the taint of 'ideology' from the 'content of art.'" See Richard Taruskin, *The Danger of Music and Other Anti-Utopian Essays* (Berkeley: University of California Press, 2009), 385.

7. John J. White, *Bertolt Brecht's Dramatic Theory* (Rochester, NY: Camden House, 2004), 25.

8. White, *Bertolt Brecht's Dramatic Theory*, 25. These questions form part of a larger debate—mostly in the German context—about the "coherence" of Brecht's *Lehrstücktheorie*. Reiner Steinweg more or less launched the critical discussion in his 1972 book, which attempted to postulate the *Lehrstück* as a brand new "type" of dramaturgy—quite distinct from the epic theater. Steinweg has since come under intense criticism, most extensively from Klaus-Dieter Krabiel, who discusses the problematic methodology employed in Steinweg's book, in addition to criticizing the "harmonizing formalism" of the work, its disregard for the content of the plays, even its shallow understanding of the complex dialectics at play within the works themselves. For a small selection of the many voices involved in these debates, see Reiner Steinweg, *Das Lehrstück: Brechts Theorie einer politisch-ästhetischen Erziehung* (Stuttgart: J. B. Metzler, 1972); Hans-Thies Lehmann and Helmut Lethen, "Ein Vorschlag zur Güte. Zu doppelten Polarität der Lehrstücke," in *Auf Anregung Bertolt Brechts: Lehrstücke mit Schülern, Arbeitern, Theaterleuten*, ed. Reiner Steinweg (Frankfurt: Suhrkamp, 1978), 302–18; Roswitha Mueller, *Bertolt Brecht and the Theory of Media* (Lincoln: University of Nebraska Press, 1989); Elizabeth Wright, *Postmodern Brecht: A Re-Presentation* (New York: Routledge, 1989); Klaus-Dieter Krabiel, *Brechts Lehrstücke: Entstehung und Entwicklung eines Spieltyps* (Stuttgart: J. B. Metzler, 1993); Reiner Steinweg, "Re-Konstruktion, Irrtum, Entwicklung oder Denken fürs Museum: Eine Antwort auf Klaus Krabiel," *Brecht Yearbook* 20 (1995): 217–37; Klaus-Dieter Krabiel, "Spieltypus Lehrstück: Zum aktuellen Stand der Diskussion," in *Bertolt Brecht I*, ed. Heinz Ludwig Arnold and Jan Knopf (Munich: Text+Kritik, 2006), 41–52; Michael D. Richardson, *Revolutionary Theater and the Classical Heritage: Inheritance and Appropriation from Weimar to the GDR* (Oxford: P. Lang, 2007).

9. Dirk Nümann, "Feuerwasser," *Der Freitag*, January 19, 1996.

10. Laura Bradley, *Brecht and Political Theatre: "The Mother" on Stage* (Oxford: Oxford University Press, 2006), 14.

11. Nümann, "Feuerwasser."

12. Castorf quoted in Peter von Becker and Michael Merschmeier, "'Ich möchte nicht in den Untergrund!': *Theater heute*-Gespräch mit dem Ostberliner Regisseur Frank Castorf," *Theater heute* 12 (1989): 21.

13. Hans-Dieter Schütt and Frank Castorf, *Die Erotik des Verrats: Gespräche mit Frank Castorf* (Berlin: Dietz, 1996), 150.

14. "Mit Frank Castorf sprach Frank Raddatz," *Theater der Zeit* (August–September 1993): 21–22.

15. Castorf quoted in Joachim Lux, "Wie dem Menschen die Haare wachsen: Ein Gespräch mit Frank Castorf," in program for *Hamlet* by William Shakespeare (Schauspiel Köln, March 1989), 12; emphasis added.

16. For more on the problems of breaking down Brecht's oeuvre by "phase," see Wright, *Postmodern Brecht*.

17. Frank Castorf, "Klassiker: Frank Castorf in São Paulo am Tag der Wahl des Deutschen Bundestags," in *Prärie: Ein Benutzerhandbuch* (program for *Im Dickicht der Städte* by Bertolt Brecht), ed. Jutta Wangemann (Volksbühne am Rosa-Luxemburg-Platz, Berlin, February 2006), 20.

18. Benjamin Henrichs, "Murx den Brecht!" *Die Zeit*, January 19, 1996.

19. Castorf quoted in Dirk Nümann, "Stahlgewitter in der Volksbühne," *Junge Welt*, December 30, 1994.

20. Castorf quoted in "Ich hasse Verstellungskünstler," *Die Zeit*, July 12, 2001.

21. Castorf quoted in "Mit Frank Castorf sprach Frank Raddatz," 19.

22. As a guest director at the Residenztheater in Munich in 2015, Castorf's controversial production of *Baal* provoked legal proceedings with the Brecht estate that eventually resulted in the production being shut down. He also staged a production of *Life of Galileo* at the Berliner Ensemble as part of the 2019–20 season.

23. Marvin Carlson, "Frank Castorf and the Volksbühne: Berlin's Theatre of Deconstruction," in *Contemporary European Theatre Directors*, ed. Maria M. Delgado and Dan Rebellato (London: Routledge, 2010), 119.

24. Goethe-Institut, "Frank Castorf," www.goethe.de/kue/the/reg/reg/ag/cas/enindex.htm, (accessed 20 December 2017 [defunct]), archived at https://perma.cc/3EFP-A2BV.

25. Goethe-Institut, "Frank Castorf."

26. Goethe-Institut, "Frank Castorf."

27. Rüdiger Schaper, "Beschreibung eines Krampfs," *Der Tagesspiegel*, February 25, 2006.

28. Schaper, "Beschreibung eines Krampfs."

29. Peter Laudenbach, "Pathos-Parodien," *Süddeutsche Zeitung*, March 22, 2008.

30. Simon Strauss, "Castorf und Kennedy in Berlin: Zwei Zwiespaltspiele," *Frankfurter Allgemeine Zeitung*, December 4, 2017.

31. Bertolt Brecht, journal entry: March 4, 1953, in *GBFA* 27.346.

32. Martin Esslin, *Brecht, a Choice of Evils: A Critical Study of the Man, His Work, and His Opinions*, 4th rev. ed. (London: Methuen, 1984), 144–45.

33. Esslin, *Brecht, a Choice of Evils*, 84.

34. Brecht, *Baden-Baden Lesson on Consent*, 24.

35. Brecht, *Baden-Baden Lesson on Consent*, 24.

36. Brecht, *Baden-Baden Lesson on Consent*, 25.

37. Brecht, *Baden-Baden Lesson on Consent*, 25.

38. John Willett, "Introduction," in Brecht, *Collected Plays: Three*, xiii.

39. John Willett, "Introduction," in Brecht, *Collected Plays: Three*, xiv.

40. Bertolt Brecht, "Anmerkung zu den Lehrstücken," in *GBFA* 23.418.

41. Steinweg, *Das Lehrstück*, 62.

42. Castorf quoted in "Dann gibt es Krieg: Der Regisseur und Intendant Frank Castorf über Die Berliner Theater-Krise," *Der Spiegel*, June 28, 1993.

43. Castorf quoted in "Dann gibt es Krieg."

44. Castorf quoted in "Dann gibt es Krieg."

45. Salter, "Forgetting, Erasure, and the Cry of the Billy Goat," 22.

46. For instance, see Salter, "Forgetting, Erasure, and the Cry of the Billy Goat," 22; Gitta Honegger, "Gossip, Ghosts, and Memory: *Mother Courage* and the Forging of the Berliner Ensemble," *TDR: The Drama Review* 52, no. 4 (2008): 98–117; and David Barnett, *A History of the Berliner Ensemble* (Cambridge: Cambridge University Press, 2015).

47. There has been surprisingly little sustained engagement with Castorf and his Volksbühne project written in English, with a few notable exceptions: Katya Bargna, "Der Weg ist nicht zu Ende, wenn das Ziel explodiert: Frank Castorf and the Survival of Political Theatre in the Postmodern Age" (PhD diss., University of Sheffield, Arts and Humanities, 2000); Bettina Brandl-Risi, "The New Virtuosity: Outperforming and Imperfection on the German Stage," *Theater* 37, no. 1 (2007): 9–37; Marvin Carlson, *Theatre Is More Beautiful than War: German Stage Directing in the Late Twentieth Century* (Iowa City: University of Iowa Press, 2009); and Cornish, *Performing Unification*.

48. Honegger, "Gossip, Ghosts, and Memory," 104.

49. The literature on Brecht's life, work, and political orientations in the GDR is extensive. In English, see James K. Lyon, "Brecht in Postwar Germany: Dissident Conformist, Cultural Icon, Literary Dictator," in *Brecht Unbound*, ed. James K. Lyon and Hans-Peter Breuer (London: Associated University Presses, 1995): 76–88; Meg Mumford, "Brecht Studies Stanislavski: Just a Tactical Move?," *New Theatre Quarterly* 11, no. 43 (1995): 241–58; Matthew Philpotts, *The Margins of Dictatorship: Assent and Dissent in the Work of Günter Eich and Bertolt Brecht* (Oxford: Lang, 2003); Bradley, *Brecht and Political Theatre*; Laura Bradley and Karen Leeder, eds., *Brecht and the GDR: Politics, Culture, Posterity* (Rochester, NY: Camden House, 2011).

50. Wekwerth quoted in Ute Scharfenberg, "Überlegungen und Fragestellungen zur Fortsetzung der künstlerischen Arbeit des Berliner Ensemble nach der politischen Wende" (lecture presented at "Why Theater? Choices for a New Century: An International Conference and Theatre Festival," University of Toronto, November 1–4, 1995), 3, AdK, TiW 612.

51. Lyon, "Brecht in Postwar Germany," 82.

52. Klaus Völker, "Brecht Today: Classic or Challenge," *Theatre Journal* 39, no. 4 (1987): 432. Indeed, Wekwerth was president of the (East German) Academy of Arts from 1982 to 1990, a member of the Central Committee, and an informant for the Stasi. For a thorough account of the impact of his political involvements in the GDR on his work at the Berliner Ensemble, see Barnett, *History of the Berliner Ensemble*.

53. Salter, "Forgetting, Erasure, and the Cry of the Billy Goat," 22.

54. Martin Linzer, "Thoughts on a Walking Corpse: The Berliner Ensemble Five Years after the 'Wende,'" *Brecht Yearbook* 21 (1996): 292.

55. Matthias Langhoff quoted in Linzer, "Thoughts on a Walking Corpse," 293.

56. G.St., "Mann im Kalk," *Frankfurter Allgemeine Zeitung*, July 24, 1991.

57. For more on Wekwerth's program, see Linzer, "Thoughts on a Walking Corpse."

58. Roloff-Momin quoted in Linzer, "Thoughts on a Walking Corpse," 293.

59. Roloff-Momin quoted in Linzer, "Thoughts on a Walking Corpse," 293.

60. Linzer, "Thoughts on a Walking Corpse," 293.

61. "BE gegen Privatisierung," *Berliner Zeitung*, March 10, 1992.

62. "Berliner Ensemble mbH," *Frankfurter Allgemeine Zeitung*, October 6, 1992.

63. Günther Rühle, "Ein Bann und seine Lösung," *Der Tagesspiegel*, September 13, 1991.

64. Linzer, "Thoughts on a Walking Corpse," 293.

65. Ivan Nagel quoted in "Berliner Ensemble: Entscheidung vertagt," *Berliner Morgenpost*, February 11, 1992.

66. Salter, "Forgetting, Erasure, and the Cry of the Billy Goat," 23.

67. "Statt des Löwen fünf Fünftelintendanten," *Neue Zeit*, September 10, 1991.

68. Linzer, "Thoughts on a Walking Corpse," 295.

69. Honegger, "Gossip, Ghosts, and Memory," 111.

70. Zadek quoted in Linzer, "Thoughts on a Walking Corpse," 297.

71. Stephen Kinzer, "Dueling Playwrights at Bertolt Brecht's Berliner Ensemble," *New York Times*, June 25, 1995.

72. Linzer, "Thoughts on a Walking Corpse," 297.

73. Salter, "Forgetting, Erasure, and the Cry of the Billy Goat," 23–24.

74. Volker Oesterreich, "Heiner Müller hat jetzt das Sagen," *Berliner Morgenpost*, March 16, 1995.

75. Scharfenberg, "Überlegungen und Fragestellungen," 9.

76. Scharfenberg, "Überlegungen und Fragestellungen," 6–7.

77. Kinzer, "Dueling Playwrights at Bertolt Brecht's Berliner Ensemble."

78. Swiss-born Besson left the Volksbühne after his proposed program for the 1977–78 season was rejected by the East Berlin city government three times. He took a number of prominent actors and directors with him.

79. Ivan Nagel cited in Carlson, "Frank Castorf and the Volksbühne," 108.

80. Carlson, "Frank Castorf and the Volksbühne," 108.

81. The Freie Volksbühne closed in 1991 and the Stage-Stage Complex in 1993; regarding the latter see chapter 1.

82. Ivan Nagel, "Zur Zukunft der Berliner Theater: Gutachten an den Senat von Berlin," in *Streitschriften*, 135; emphasis in original.

83. Castorf had developed quite a reputation as a political nuisance in the GDR, where his early productions attracted the ire (and sometimes censorship) of party officials. After the fall of the Wall, Castorf became even better known as a freelance director, working more and more often in Berlin. His 1990 production of Schiller's *The Robbers* at the Volksbühne was considered an important "prototype of the new German theatre of provocation" in the wake of reunification (Gert Reifarth, "Fostering Cultural Schizophrenia: East German Theatres Re-create the GDR," in *Theatre in the Berlin Republic: German Drama since Reunification*, ed. Denise Varney [Berlin: Peter Lang, 2008], 239). In 1990–91, Castorf was invited to work as in-house director at Berlin's Deutsches Theater, where his production of Ibsen's *John Gabriel Borkman* received an invitation to the Theatertreffen festival.

84. Hans-Dieter Schütt and Kirsten Hehmeyer, *Castorfs Volksbühne: Schöne Bilder vom hässlichen Leben,* with Andreas Kämper (Berlin: Schwarzkopf & Schwarzkopf, 1999), 30.

85. Georg Diez, "Eine Liebesgeschichte: Frank Castorf, Berlin, Deutschland— Eine Frage der Ära," *Frankfurter Allgemeine Zeitung,* June 16, 2002.

86. Diez, "Eine Liebesgeschichte."

87. Schütt and Hehmeyer, *Castorfs Volksbühne,* 30.

88. Siegfried Wilzopolski, "Famous or Dead? The Volksbühne Theater under Frank Castorf" ["Berühmt oder tot? Die Volksbühne unter Frank Castorf"] (lecture presented at "Why Theater? Choices for a New Century"), AdK, Schriften-DK 152.

89. Katya Bargna, "'Die Sache Castorf': All Quiet on the Eastern Front" (MA thesis, University of Liverpool, 1995), 21, AdK, Schriften-DK 152.

90. Schütt and Hehmeyer, *Castorfs Volksbühne,* 28.

91. Schütt and Hehmeyer, *Castorfs Volksbühne,* 28.

92. Schütt and Castorf, *Die Erotik des Verrats,* 10.

93. Schütt and Hehmeyer, *Castorfs Volksbühne,* 29.

94. Schütt and Hehmeyer, *Castorfs Volksbühne,* 11.

95. Schütt and Hehmeyer, *Castorfs Volksbühne,* 29.

96. Thomas Irmer, "Leitbild, Glauben, Depression und Erniedrigung: Frank Castorfs Volksbühnenarbeit ab Mitte der neunziger Jahre," in *Zehn Jahre Volksbühne: Intendanz Frank Castorf,* ed. Thomas Irmer and Harald Müller (Berlin: Theater der Zeit, 2003), 47.

97. Matthias Lilienthal, "Die Chance des Scheiterns der Betonarbeiterbrigade," in Schütt and Hehmeyer, *Castorfs Volksbühne,* 37.

98. For more on nostalgia in the former East—or so-called *Ostalgie*—see chapter 3.

99. Castorf quoted in Schütt and Castorf, *Die Erotik des Verrats,* 26.

100. Castorf quoted in Rolf Michaelis, "Oberlehrer überall," *Die Zeit,* January 13, 1995.

101. Castorf quoted in Katja Burghardt, "'Dann kommt der Amazonas': Wie macht man aus einem Fahrrad in der Fahrt ein Flugzeug?," *Szene Hamburg,* June 1994, 32.

102. Castorf quoted in "Mit Frank Castorf sprach Frank Raddatz," 20.

103. Castorf quoted in "Mit Frank Castorf sprach Frank Raddatz," 20.

104. Castorf quoted in "Mit Frank Castorf sprach Frank Raddatz," 20.

105. Castorf, "Klassiker," 18–19.

106. Castorf quoted in Burghardt, "'Dann kommt der Amazonas,'" 32; emphasis added.

107. Castorf quoted in Schütt and Castorf, *Die Erotik des Verrats,* 19.

108. Colomb, *Staging the New Berlin.*

109. Castorf quoted in Michaelis, "Oberlehrer überall."

110. Schütt and Hehmeyer, *Castorfs Volksbühne,* 11.

111. Matthias Lilienthal, "Die Chance des Scheiterns," 36.

112. Schütt and Hehmeyer, *Castorfs Volksbühne,* 31.

113. Schütt and Castorf, *Die Erotik des Verrats,* 10.

114. The wheel was designed by Bert Neumann for the production of Schiller's *The Robbers* that Castorf directed at the Volksbühne in 1990. It was meant

to evoke a secret language of tricksters and thieves, and Castorf and his team immediately adopted the wheel as the Volksbühne's official insignia when they assumed leadership in 1992. The large iron sculpture was created by Rainer Haussmann and installed in 1994.

115. Brecht, *Baden-Baden Lesson on Consent*, 26.

116. Brecht, *Baden-Baden Lesson on Consent*, 26.

117. Bertolt Brecht, Paul Hindemith, and Frank Castorf, *Lehrstück* (Regiebuch—Fassung Hinterbühne), Volksbühne am Rosa-Luxemburg-Platz, Berlin, premiered October 5, 2010, 9. This unpublished director's script was generously supplied by the Volksbühne am Rosa-Luxemburg-Platz.

118. Brecht, Hindemith, and Castorf, *Lehrstück*, 9.

119. Brecht, "Note to the Text Printed in *Versuche 2*," in *Collected Plays: Three*, 329.

120. Brecht, Hindemith, and Castorf, *Lehrstück*, 10.

121. Brecht, *Baden-Baden Lesson on Consent*, 26–27.

122. Krabiel, *Brechts Lehrstücke*, 122.

123. For more on the concept of *Gebrauchsmusik*, see Stephen Hinton, "Didactic Theater (*Lehrstück*)," in *Weill's Musical Theater*, 176–98; and Hinton, *The Idea of Gebrauchsmusik: A Study of Musical Aesthetics in the Weimar Republic (1919–1933) with Particular Reference to the Works of Paul Hindemith* (New York: Garland, 1989). See also Hindemith's own 1922 essay "Gemeinschaft für Musik," in Paul Hindemith, *Aufsätze, Vorträge, Reden*, ed. Giselher Schubert (Zürich: Atlantis-Musikbuch-Verlag, 1994), 8.

124. Hindemith, "Introduction to Hindemith's Piano Score," in Brecht, *Collected Plays: Three*, 326.

125. Hindemith, "Introduction to Hindemith's Piano Score," 327; emphasis added.

126. Brecht quoted in Hinton, *Weill's Musical Theater*, 182. For a more extended treatment of this "misunderstanding," see Krabiel, *Brechts Lehrstücke*, 122.

127. Brecht quoted in Hinton, *Weill's Musical Theater*, 182; ellipsis in Hinton.

128. Brecht, "Note," in *Collected Plays: Three*, 328; emphasis added.

129. Hinton, *Weill's Musical Theater*, 193.

130. Krabiel, *Brechts Lehrstücke*, 51.

131. From 1930 onward, things heated up politically for Brecht amid the downfall of the Weimar Republic: the shock and bloodshed of May 1929 (*Blutmai*, or Bloody May); the deepening economic crisis; and the beginning of his collaboration with the more "radical" Hanns Eisler and Slatan Dudow.

132. Bertolt Brecht, "Schwerfällige Apparate," in *GBFA* 21.126. Per my searching, this coinage from 1926 is Brecht's first use of "apparatus," a word that would become very important for him.

133. For a comprehensive account of Brecht and Benjamin's dynamic friendship, see Erdmut Wizisla, *Walter Benjamin and Bertolt Brecht: The Story of a Friendship*, trans. Christine Shuttleworth (New Haven, CT: Yale University Press, 2009).

134. Theodor W. Adorno and Walter Benjamin, *The Complete Correspondence, 1928–1940*, ed. Henri Lonitz, trans. Nicholas Walker (Cambridge, MA: Harvard University Press, 1999), 132.

135. Maria Gough, "Paris, Capital of the Soviet Avant-Garde," *October* 101 (2002): 53. Gough's essay is a long overdue contribution that makes very compelling claims about the importance of Benjamin's "The Author as Producer." On page 61, she writes: "Such attention is necessary, I think, given that the essay, although very often cited, has been comparatively little read in recent years. This has partially to do with its having been so often coupled with, and, as a result, overwhelmingly overshadowed by the famous 'Work of Art' essay of 1936. In fact, with the exception of the explosive significance of its materialist concerns for the New Left in the wake of its very first publication by Rolf Tiedemann in 1966, 'The Author as Producer' has rather suffered at the hands of caricature, or simply fallen altogether through the cracks of the great expansion of the House of Benjamin that has occurred over the last several decades."

136. Walter Benjamin, "The Author as Producer," in *The Work of Art in the Age of Its Technological Reproducibility, and Other Writings on Media*, ed. Michael William Jennings, Brigid Doherty, and Thomas Y. Levin (Cambridge, MA: Belknap Press, 2008), 89.

137. Benjamin, "The Author as Producer," 84.

138. Theodor W. Adorno, "Commitment," in *Aesthetics and Politics*, ed. Ronald Taylor (New York: Verso, 1977), 177–95.

139. Benjamin, "The Author as Producer," 85–86.

140. Brecht, "Notes on the Opera *Rise and Fall of the City of Mahagonny*," in *Brecht on Theatre*, 62.

141. Mueller, *Bertolt Brecht and the Theory of Media*, 15.

142. Benjamin, "The Author as Producer," 81; emphasis in original.

143. Benjamin, "The Author as Producer," 81.

144. Walter Benjamin, "The Work of Art in the Age of Its Technological Reproducibility: Second Version," in *The Work of Art in the Age of Its Technological Reproducibility*, 42. According to Jennings et al., the second version of the "Work of Art" essay was penned between December 1935 and February 1936.

145. Benjamin, "The Author as Producer," 85.

146. Benjamin, "The Author as Producer," 89.

147. Benjamin, "The Author as Producer," 85; emphasis added.

148. Wright, *Postmodern Brecht*, 75.

149. Benjamin, "Author as Producer," 85.

150. Mueller, *Bertolt Brecht and the Theory of Media*, 25. For a full translation of the *Threepenny* essay, see Bertolt Brecht, "The *Threepenny* Lawsuit," in *Brecht on Film and Radio*, ed. and trans. Marc Silberman (London: Methuen, 2000), 147–99. Steve Giles's book-length treatment of the essay is also very useful: Steve Giles, *Bertolt Brecht and Critical Theory: Marxism, Modernity and the "Threepenny" Lawsuit* (Bern: P. Lang, 1997).

151. Brecht, "Die dialektische Dramatik," 439.

152. Bertolt Brecht, "The Radio as a Communications Apparatus," in *Brecht on Film and Radio*, 45. For a more thorough interrogation of Brecht's thoughts on "innovation," see Michael Shane Boyle, "Brecht's Gale: Innovation and Postdramatic Theatre," *Performance Research* 21, no. 3 (2016): 16–26.

153. Bertolt Brecht, "Teils der Gewohnheit meinesgleichen folgend, teils dem Auftrag," in *GBFA* 14.100.

154. Bertolt Brecht, "Explanatory Notes," in *Collected Plays: Three*, 319.

155. Brecht, "*Threepenny* Lawsuit," 163; emphasis added.

156. Mueller, *Bertolt Brecht and the Theory of Media*, 21. I return to another version of this discussion in chapter 4.

157. Gough, "Paris, Capital of the Soviet Avant-Garde," 66.

158. Gough, "Paris, Capital of the Soviet Avant-Garde," 67. Gough continues: "While elsewhere in Benjamin's writings, particularly of the later 1930s, we find evidence of his interest in a nondeterminist reading of Marx's theory of history . . . a determinist reading of that theory nevertheless provides the theoretical armature for the producer essay's assertion of the functional interdependence of tendency and technique" (67).

159. Shannon Jackson's explication of a post-Brechtianism and post-Marxism is very helpful here: "While it could never be said that Brecht bought into a fixed vision of society's supporting apparatus, it can be said that his theater labored under a determining vision of labor. . . . But if a post-Marxist vision is, in part, about antagonizing the values and reality effects given to certain 'underlying principles,' then a post-Brechtian theater might also ask what it means to imagine material necessity—not as given, foundational, or determining 'in the last instance' but as a 'partial limitation on the field of contingency.' A twenty-first century post-Brechtianism would also be skeptical of any theater that imagined itself outside or uncorrupted by the social structures it tried to question. . . . At the same time, a post-Brechtian theater that takes seriously post-Marxist revisions will have to be careful of giving such material registers—whether imagined in bodies, in economies, in necessities, or in 'territorial moments'—a structurally determining place. Such reflection is an important check on my own tendencies to give the material operations of support a certain kind of determining value." *Social Works*, 148.

160. See, for example: *GBFA* 21(1).176, *GBFA* 24.49, or *GBFA* 24.99. Nikolaus Müller-Schöll also argues that these infrastructural questions are already dialectically bound up with the questions about help and death within the play: "In [l]ehrstück, death is (still) largely an individual problem. But this individual problem—the pilot who asks for help because she does not want to die—is at the same time comparable, following the construction of the play itself, to that of the theater that relies on the intervention of the public for its refunctioning." See Nikolaus Müller-Schöll, "Brechts 'Sterbelehre,'" in *Ende, Grenze, Schluss? Brecht und der Tod*, ed. Stephen Brockmann, Mathias Mayer, and Jürgen Hillesheim (Würzburg: Königshausen & Neumann, 2008), 25.

161. Brecht, "Radio as a Communications Apparatus," 45.

162. Mueller, *Bertolt Brecht and the Theory of Media*, 42–43.

163. Brecht, "Radio as a Communications Apparatus," 42.

164. Brecht, "Radio as a Communications Apparatus," 42.

165. Brecht, "Radio as a Communications Apparatus," 43; emphasis in original.

166. Castorf quoted in "Ach, zu sehr möchte ich mich nicht ändern," *Der Freitag*, August 2, 1991.

167. Castorf quoted in "Feudale Krawallbude," *Theater-Rundschau*, October 1993, 5.

168. Frank Castorf, "Theater ist eine alte Widerstandsinsel," *Berliner Zeitung*, July 16, 1993.

169. Castorf quoted in "Mit Frank Castorf sprach Frank Raddatz," 22–23.

170. Castorf quoted in "Feudale Krawallbude," 5.

171. Castorf quoted in Schütt and Castorf, *Die Erotik des Verrats*, 36.

172. Castorf, "Klassiker," 31; emphasis added.

173. Castorf quoted in "Feudale Krawallbude," 5.

174. For a sustained analysis of the relations (and ongoing debates) between state-stage and free-scene institutions in Berlin, see chapter 4.

175. Castorf quoted in Becker and Merschmeier, "'Ich möchte nicht in den Untergrund!,'" 23.

176. Castorf quoted in Jürgen Balitzki, *Castorf, der Eisenhändler: Theater zwischen Kartoffelsalat und Stahlgewitter* (Berlin: Christoph Links Verlag, 1995), 78.

177. Frank Castorf, "Ich komme aus dem Fussball, dem Rock 'n' Roll, dem rausgebrüllten Unmut, aus der Neurose," *Theater Heute Jahrbuch* (1993): 98.

178. Wilzopolski, "Famous or Dead?"

179. Castorf quoted in "Mit Frank Castorf sprach Frank Raddatz," 22–3.

180. Castorf quoted in "Die Polarisierung von Chaos," *Berliner Zeitung*, February 10, 1992.

181. Castorf quoted in "Die Polarisierung von Chaos."

182. Castorf quoted in "Zadek und Ich haben uns nichts zu Sagen," *Berliner Zeitung*, June 15–16, 1996.

183. Castorf quoted in "Die Polarisierung von Chaos."

184. Brecht, *Baden-Baden Lesson on Consent*, 41.

185. Brecht, Hindemith, and Castorf, *Lehrstück*, 12.

186. Brecht, Hindemith, and Castorf, *Lehrstück*, 13.

187. Brecht, Hindemith, and Castorf, *Lehrstück*, 13.

188. Brecht, Hindemith, and Castorf, *Lehrstück*, 13.

189. Valeska Gert uses this word in her autobiography to describe the premiere. See Valeska Gert, *Ich bin eine Hexe: Kaleidoskop meines Lebens* (Munich: Schneekluth, 1968), 48. See also Krabiel, *Brechts Lehrstücke*, 64–65.

190. Krabiel, *Brechts Lehrstücke*, 51.

191. Elsa Bauer quoted in Monika Wyss, *Brecht in der Kritik: Rezensionen aller Brecht-Uraufführungen sowie ausgewählter Deutsch- und fremdsprachiger Premieren: Eine Dokumentation* (Munich: Kindler Verlag, 1977), 97. Krabiel (*Brechts Lehrstücke*, 339n1) claims that Wyss incorrectly attributes these citations to Elsa Bauer, saying they should be correctly cited as follows: Inge Karsten, "Deutsche Kammermusik 1929: *Lehrstuck*," *Badische Volkszeitung*, July 30, 1929, 4.

192. Bauer quoted in Wyss, *Brecht in der Kritik*, 97 (but see note 191).

193. Krabiel, *Brechts Lehrstücke*, 65.

194. Actor Theo Lingen cited in Joel Schechter, "Brecht's Clowns: *Man Is Man* and After," in *The Cambridge Companion to Brecht*, ed. Peter Thomson and Glendyr Sacks (Cambridge: Cambridge University Press, 1994), 76.

195. Video footage of an earlier rendition of the dance (from 1925) is available on the DVD accompanying Susanne Foellmer's book *Valeska Gert: Fragmente einer Avantgardistin in Tanz und Schauspiel der 1920er Jahre* (Bielefeld: Transcript Verlag, 2006). According to other sources, including Gert's own autobiography,

the film that premiered in Baden-Baden in 1929 was made by Karl Koch. See Ulrich Scheinhammer-Schmid, "'Schmeiss die Beine vom Arsch': Bertolt Brecht und der Totentanz," in *Ende, Grenze, Schluss?*, 115.

196. Kate Elswit, "Berlin . . . Your Dance Partner Is Death," *TDR: The Drama Review* 53, no. 1 (2009): 84.

197. Bauer quoted in Wyss, *Brecht in der Kritik*, 97 (but see note 191).

198. Krabiel, *Brechts Lehrstücke*, 65.

199. Bertolt Brecht, "Zur Theorie des Lehrstucks," in *GBFA* 22(1).352.

200. Castorf quoted in "Mit Frank Castorf sprach Frank Raddatz," 23.

201. Rebecca Schneider, "It Seems as If . . . I Am Dead: Zombie Capitalism and Theatrical Labor," *TDR: The Drama Review* 56, no. 4 (2012): 152.

202. Castorf quoted in "Mit Frank Castorf sprach Frank Raddatz," 23.

203. Castorf quoted in Wilzopolski, "Famous or Dead?"

204. Castorf quoted in "Wir sind Asozial," *Der Spiegel*, December 27, 1993, 152.

205. Castorf quoted in "Paar Sicherungen können da schon durchknallen," *Neues Deutschland*, March 19–20, 1994.

206. Castorf quoted in "Die Volksbühne als unmoralische Anstalt," *Neue Zürcher Zeitung*, December 9, 1997.

207. Castorf quoted in "Mit Frank Castorf sprach Frank Raddatz," 20.

208. Castorf quoted in "Wir sind Asozial," 153.

209. Lilienthal quoted in Bargna, "'Die Sache Castorf,'" 25.

210. Castorf, "Klassiker," 32. See also Miranda Joseph, *Against the Romance of Community* (Minneapolis: University of Minnesota Press, 2002).

211. Castorf quoted in "Die Volksbühne als unmoralische Anstalt."

212. Castorf quoted in "Mit Frank Castorf sprach Frank Raddatz," 23.

213. Castorf quoted in "Mit Frank Castorf sprach Frank Raddatz," 23.

214. Castorf, "Theater ist eine alte Widerstandsinsel."

215. Castorf quoted in Wilzopolski, "Famous or Dead?"

216. Brecht, Hindemith, and Castorf, *Lehrstück*, 20. All lines quoted here from the "Clown Scene" derive from the Regiebuch.

217. Inge Karsten quoted in Krabiel, *Brechts Lehrstücke*, 67.

218. Krabiel, *Brechts Lehrstücke*, 66.

219. Max Marschalk quoted in Krabiel, *Brechts Lehrstücke*, 66.

220. Hanns Eisler, "Bertolt Brecht and Music," in *Brecht, As They Knew Him*, ed. Hubert Witt, trans. John Peet (New York: International Publishers, 1974), 93. For the most comprehensive recounting of these critical reactions, see Wyss, *Brecht in der Kritik*; Krabiel, *Brechts Lehrstücke*.

221. Steinweg, *Das Lehrstück*, 122.

222. Wright, *Postmodern Brecht*, 14.

223. Lehmann and Lethen, "Ein Vorschlag zur Güte," 304.

224. In addition to Lehmann and Lethen, see Rainer Nägele, "Brecht's Theater of Cruelty," in *Reading after Freud: Essays on Goethe, Hölderlin, Habermas, Nietzsche, Brecht, Celan, and Freud* (New York: Columbia University Press, 1987), 111–34.

225. Wright, *Postmodern Brecht*, 17.

226. Lehmann and Lethen, "Ein Vorschlag zur Güte," 309.

227. Judith Butler, *The Psychic Life of Power: Theories in Subjection* (Stanford, CA: Stanford University Press, 1997), 88.

228. In chapter 4, I engage in more detail with Lehmann's subsequent thinking on the politics of (postdramatic) performance. See also my explication of Lehmann on Brecht and Benjamin: Brandon Woolf, "Towards a Paradoxically Parallaxical Postdramatic Politics?," in *Postdramatic Theatre and the Political: International Perspectives on Contemporary Performance*, ed. Karen Jürs-Munby, Jerome Carroll, and Steve Giles (London: Bloomsbury Methuen, 2013), 31–46.

229. Castorf quoted in "Von Kohl lernen heisst Sigen lernen," *Der Tagesspiegel*, January 8, 1993.

230. Castorf quoted in "Maschinengewehr-Theater," *Focus*, January 1995.

231. Wright, *Postmodern Brecht*, 18.

232. Anne Peter, "Brüllen bis der Kopf platzt," *Berliner Morgenpost*, October 7, 2010.

233. Castorf quoted in Becker and Merschmeier, "'Ich möchte nicht in den Untergrund!,'" 21.

234. Interestingly, this is also reminiscent of a young Brecht thinking about the potential of a Volksbühne in Berlin. Brecht writes: "The Volksbühne never began. And it should. It has only dragged the old, outdated theater system in another direction and now is nothing more than a worthless shithole of tickets for its members. . . . If the Volksbühne wanted to start something new today, it could, for instance, establish a theater laboratory, where actors, writers, and directors enjoy the work they do, without a special intention. Anyone who wishes to can behold the laboratory and performances of this experimental theater. . . . But they do not dare; they have no courage." Brecht, "Die Volksbühnenbewegung und die junge Generation," in *GBFA* 21.138.

235. Castorf quoted in Schütt and Castorf, *Die Erotik des Verrats*, 110–11.

236. Castorf quoted in Becker and Merschmeier, "'Ich möchte nicht in den Untergrund!,'" 21.

237. Castorf quoted in Wilzopolski, "Famous or Dead?"; emphasis added. For more on Castorf's work with actors, see Holger Schott Syme, "A Theatre without Actors," *Theatre Survey* 59, no. 2 (2018): 265–75.

238. Castorf, "Klassiker," 31.

239. Castorf quoted in "Ich hasse Verstellungskünstler."

240. Castorf quoted in Becker and Merschmeier, "'Ich möchte nicht in den Untergrund!,'" 20.

241. Castorf quoted in "Mit Frank Castorf sprach Frank Raddatz," 23.

242. Castorf paraphrased in Robin Detje, *Castorf: Provokation aus Prinzip* (Berlin: Henschel, 2002), 188.

243. Castorf quoted in "Berühmt oder tot," *Manager Magazin*, October 1992.

244. Brecht, *Baden-Baden Lesson on Consent*, 38.

245. Brecht, Hindemith, and Castorf, *Lehrstück*, 37.

246. Peter Doggett, *There's a Riot Going On: Revolutionaries, Rock Stars and the Rise and Fall of '60s Counter-Culture* (Edinburgh: Canongate, 2009), 82.

247. Hughes quoted in Doggett, *There's a Riot Going On*, 82.

248. John Lennon and Paul McCartney, "Yellow Submarine," copyright Sony/ATV Tunes LLC dba ATV on behalf of ATV (Northern Songs Catalog).

Chapter 3

EPIGRAPHS: Jacques Derrida, Kurt Forster, and Wim Wenders, "The Berlin City Forum," *Architectural Design* 62, nos. 11–12 (1992): xix–xx; Jan Theiler aka Pastor Leumund, lyrics to the hymn sung in the "Parliament" of the Republic of Facades (2004). The original German lyrics are "Luftschiffe schaukeln sanft / Stahl über den Kanälen / Prall spiegelt sich Die Welt, / die sich in Ideen erhellt / Zwischen Fassaden / wollen wir die Kraft / des miteinander Wahrgemachten / entladen."

1. Ellen Mickley, Annalie Schoen, and Lutz Jürgens, eds., *Internationale Expertenkommission—Historische Mitte Berlin: Abschlussbericht* (Berlin: Bundesministerium für Verkehr, Bau- und Wohnungswesen—Senatsverwaltung für Stadtentwicklung, 2002), 18.

2. Mickley, Schoen, and Jürgens, *Internationale Expertenkommission*, 18.

3. Mickley, Schoen, and Jürgens, *Internationale Expertenkommission*, 18.

4. Deutscher Bundestag, "Beschlussempfehlung und Bericht des Ausschusses für Kultur und Medien," Drucksache 14/9660 (Berlin, July 2, 2002), 4; emphasis added. Italian architect Franco Stella's proposal for the Humboldt Forum won the international design competition in 2008, and his (re)construction began in June 2013.

5. Brian Ladd, *The Ghosts of Berlin: Confronting German History in the Urban Landscape* (Chicago: University of Chicago Press, 1997), 52; emphasis in original.

6. For more comprehensive histories of the Schloss and its reconstruction as the Humboldt Forum, see Förderverein Berliner Schloss, *Das Schloss? Eine Ausstellung über die Mitte Berlins*, ed. Kristin Feireiss and Wilhelm von Boddien, trans. Annette Wiethüchter (Berlin: Ernst & Sohn, 1993); Ladd, *Ghosts of Berlin*; Rudy Koshar, *From Monuments to Traces: Artifacts of German Memory, 1870–1990* (Berkeley: University of California Press, 2000); Svetlana Boym, *The Future of Nostalgia* (New York: Basic Books, 2001); Hartmut Ellrich, *Das Berliner Schloss Geschichte und Wiederaufbau* (Petersberg: Imhof, 2008); Thomas Flierl and Hermann Parzinger, eds., *Humboldt-Forum Berlin—Das Projekt / The Project* (Berlin: Theater der Zeit, 2009); Rainer Haubrich, ed., *Das Neue Berliner Schloss: Von der Hohenzollernresidenz zum Humboldt-Forum* (Berlin: Nicolai, 2012); Friedrich Dieckmann, *Vom Schloss der Könige zum Forum der Republik: Zum Problem der architektonischen Wiederaufführung* (Berlin: Theater der Zeit, 2015); and Horst Bredekamp and Peter-Klaus Schuster, eds., *Das Humboldt-Forum: Die Wiedergewinnung der Idee* (Berlin: Wagenbach, 2016).

7. Förderverein Berliner Schloss, *Das Schloss?*, 67.

8. Ulbricht quoted in William J. V. Neill, "Changing Representational Landscapes: 'Reading' Stormont in Belfast and the Palast der Republik in Berlin," in *Palast der Republik: Politischer Diskurs und private Erinnerung*, ed. Alexander Schug (Berlin: Berliner Wissenschafts-Verlag, 2007), 156.

9. Graffunder quoted in Michael Z. Wise, *Capital Dilemma: Germany's Search for a New Architecture of Democracy* (New York: Princeton Architectural Press, 1998), 51.

10. For more on the ins and outs of the Palast der Republik, see Ladd, *Ghosts of Berlin*; Wise, *Capital Dilemma*; Thomas Beutelschmidt and Julia M. Novak, eds., *Ein Palast und seine Republik: Ort–Architektur–Programm* (Berlin: Bauwesen, 2001); Boym, *Future of Nostalgia*; Andreas Ulrich, *Palast der Republik: Ein*

Rückblick / A Retrospective (Munich: Prestel, 2006); Conrad Tenner, *Der Palast der Republik: Bilder und Geschichten* (Berlin: Das Neue Berlin, 2009); and Thorsten Klapsch, *Palast der Republik* (Mannheim: Ed. Panorama, 2010).

11. Mickley, Schoen, and Jürgens, *Internationale Expertenkommission*, 19. As of spring 2020, the breakdown of costs looks somewhat different in that the project has secured a good deal more public funding. The total cost is now estimated at 644 million euros, of which 532 million euros are to come from the federal government and 32 million euros from the city-state of Berlin, with the 80 million euros in private donations still required for the reconstruction of the facades. See Humboldt Forum, "FAQ," https://www.humboldtforum.org/en/faq (accessed May 6, 2020).

12. Jackson, *Social Works*, 21.

13. Shannon Jackson, "*Touchable Stories* and the Performance of Infrastructural Memory," in *Remembering: Oral History Performance*, ed. Della Pollock (New York: Palgrave Macmillan, 2005), 46–47; emphasis added.

14. Jackson, "*Touchable Stories*," 47.

15. Jackson, "*Touchable Stories*," 46; emphasis added.

16. Jackson, "*Touchable Stories*," 47.

17. Jackson, "*Touchable Stories*," 46.

18. In May 2015, it was announced that the Humboldt Forum would be led by a team of three founding directors: Neil MacGregor (former director of the British Museum), Horst Bredekamp (professor of art history at Humboldt University of Berlin), and Hermann Parzinger (president of the Prussian Cultural Heritage Foundation). As Parzinger explained—not uncontroversially: "The Humboldt Forum . . . is the most important cultural policy project in Germany at the beginning of the 21st century. With a trend-setting use-concept, which at the same time draws on the history of the place, it will bring non-European cultures into the center of Berlin and present Germany as a cosmopolitan country. . . . The Humboldt Forum will become a place of arts and cultures of Africa, America, Australia, Oceania and Asia, an extension of the Museum Island with its cultural treasures from Europe and the Middle East. Together [the Humboldt Forum and Museum Island] form a newly emerging place of world cultures in which every continent has its place." Hermann Parzinger, "Vorwart," in *Das Neue Berliner Schloss*, ed. Haubrich, 6. Though not the focus of this chapter, the most recent debates about the Humboldt Forum center not on the facades but on the broader colonialist implications of the project. The Forum's leaders have been harshly criticized for their planned display of an extensive array of objects obtained by colonial plunder (the Benin Bronzes, for example) as well as their lackluster response to widespread calls for the restitution of these objects. "No Humboldt 21!" is an international campaign demanding "that the work on the Humboldt Forum in the Berlin Palace be ceased and that a public debate is held: the current concept violates the dignity and property rights of communities in all parts of the world, it is Eurocentric and restorative. The establishment of the Humboldt Forum is a direct contradiction to the aim promoting equality in a migration society." No Humboldt 21!, "Stop the Planned Construction of the Humboldt Forum in the Berlin Palace!," http://www.no-humboldt21.de/resolution/english, archived at https://perma.cc/C3FR-5TGB. See also Mareike Heller, ed., *No Humboldt 21! Dekoloniale Einwände gegen das Humboldt-Forum* (Berlin: AfricAvenir International, 2017).

19. Sonja Kuftinec, "[Walking through a] Ghost Town: Cultural Hauntologie in Mostar, Bosnia-Herzegovina or Mostar—a Performance Review," *Text and Performance Quarterly* 18, no. 2 (1998): 81–95.

20. Francis Fukuyama, *The End of History and the Last Man* (New York: Free Press, 1992).

21. Fest quoted in Anna-Inés Hennet, *Die Berliner Schlossplatzdebatte im Spiegel der Presse* (Berlin: Braun, 2005), 40–41.

22. Benjamin Foerster-Baldenius, of raumlaborberlin (to whom I return later in this chapter), had very strong words about the legitimacy of Boddien's project: "[He was] such a slick asshole kind of guy, that you wouldn't buy a package of Pampers from him." Benjamin Foerster-Baldenius, interview by author, Berlin, February 16, 2012.

23. Articles of Incorporation of the Förderverein Berliner Schloss quoted in Hennet, *Die Berliner Schlossplatzdebatte im Spiegel der Presse*, 60.

24. "Förderverein wirbt für Schloss-Spenden," https://berliner-schloss.de/blog/pressespiegel/fourderverein-wirbt-fuer-schlossspenden, archived at https://perma.cc/99HT-24YL.

25. Claire Colomb, "Requiem for a Lost *Palast*: 'Revanchist Urban Planning' and 'Burdened Landscapes' of the German Democratic Republic in the New Berlin," *Planning Perspectives* 22, no. 3 (2007): 292.

26. Joint Committee decision quoted in Anke Kuhrmann, *Der Palast der Republik: Geschichte und Bedeutung des Ost-Berliner Parlaments- und Kulturhauses* (Petersberg: Imhof, 2006), 70. This decision was delayed, questioned, and debated further in subsequent years. The final decision to raze the Palast would not come until 2003.

27. Beutelschmidt and Novak, *Ein Palast und seine Republik*, 238.

28. Boddien quoted in Hennet, *Die Berliner Schlossplatzdebatte im Spiegel der Presse*, 67–68; emphasis added.

29. Ahme quoted in Wise, *Capital Dilemma*, 114–15.

30. Hain quoted in Colomb, "Requiem for a Lost *Palast*," 302.

31. Boym, *Future of Nostalgia*, 183.

32. Boym, *Future of Nostalgia*, 41–48. Also citing Boym on "restorative nostalgia," Claire Colomb suggests—from the perspective of urban planning—that the "task, for planners and architects, is thus to 'suture the city together' with a 'unifying aesthetics' borrowed from that idealized past." Colomb, "Requiem for a Lost *Palast*," 300.

33. Boym, *Future of Nostalgia*, 49.

34. Boym, *Future of Nostalgia*, 189.

35. The discourse on *Ostalgie* (*Ost* [East] + *Nostalgie*) is expansive. For a start, see Charity Scribner, *Requiem for Communism* (Cambridge, MA: MIT Press, 2003); and Karen Leeder, ed., "From Stasiland to Ostalgie: The GDR Twenty Years After," special issue, *Oxford German Studies* 38, no. 3 (2009).

36. Karen E. Till, *The New Berlin: Memory, Politics, Place* (Minneapolis: University of Minnesota Press, 2005), 14.

37. Strom, *Building the New Berlin*, 40.

38. Jacques Derrida, *Specters of Marx: The State of the Debt, the Work of Mourning, and the New International*, trans. Peggy Kamuf (New York: Routledge, 1994).

39. Fischer quoted in Roger Cohen, "Berlin in Search of Itself," *New York Times*, November 21, 1999.

40. Bernd Magnus and Stephen Cullenberg, "Editors' Introduction," in Derrida, *Specters of Marx*, ix–x.

41. Derrida, *Specters of Marx*, 37; emphasis in original.

42. Derrida, *Specters of Marx*, xix; emphasis in original.

43. Derrida, *Specters of Marx*, 10; emphasis in original.

44. Derrida, *Specters of Marx*, 37.

45. Jeffrey Andrew Weinstock, "Introduction: The Spectral Turn," in *Spectral America: Phantoms and the National Imagination*, ed. Jeffrey Andrew Weinstock (Madison: University of Wisconsin Press, 2004), 3–17.

46. Weinstock, "Introduction," 4.

47. Derrida, Forster, and Wenders, "Berlin City Forum," 48. Derrida's call to stand "before the law" (cf. his 1985 *Préjugés: Devant la loi*) was subsequently echoed by a number of other critics working specifically to make sense of the complex intersections of memory, history, and placemaking in post-Wall Berlin. See, for example: Ladd, *Ghosts of Berlin*; Eric Jarosinski, "Architectural Symbolism and the Rhetoric of Transparency: A Berlin Ghost Story," *Journal of Urban History* 29, no. 1 (2002): 62–77; Andreas Huyssen, *Present Pasts: Urban Palimpsests and the Politics of Memory* (Stanford, CA: Stanford University Press, 2003); Till, *New Berlin*; and Andrew J. Webber, *Berlin in the Twentieth Century: A Cultural Topography* (Cambridge: Cambridge University Press, 2008).

48. Libeskind quoted in Boym, *Future of Nostalgia*, 191.

49. Libeskind quoted in Rick Atkinson, "Building a Better Berlin? Critics See Too Much of Its Past in Its Future," *Washington Post*, January 8, 1995.

50. Daniel Libeskind, "Deconstructing the Call to Order," in *Berlin*, ed. Alan Balfour (London: Academy Editions, 1995), 36.

51. Libeskind, "Deconstructing the Call to Order," 36.

52. Mark Wigley, *The Architecture of Deconstruction: Derrida's Haunt* (Cambridge, MA: MIT Press, 1993).

53. Philip Johnson and Mark Wigley, *Deconstructivist Architecture*, exh. cat. (New York: Museum of Modern Art, 1988); Libeskind is profiled on 34–45.

54. Daniel Libeskind, "Trauma," in *Image and Remembrance: Representation and the Holocaust*, ed. Shelley Hornstein and Florence Jacobowitz (Bloomington: Indiana University Press, 2003), 47.

55. Libeskind, "Trauma," 46.

56. Daniel Libeskind, "Between the Lines: The Jewish Museum, Berlin," *Research in Phenomenology* 22 (1992): 85, 86–87.

57. Libeskind, "Between the Lines," 85.

58. Libeskind, "Trauma," 47.

59. The void was also a central component in Libeskind's redesign of the World Trade Center in New York City.

60. Libeskind won the bid to design Berlin's new Jewish Museum in 1989, but construction was put on hold until 1992 due to financial restraints.

61. Huyssen, *Present Pasts*, 66.

62. Huyssen, *Present Pasts*, 68.

63. Libeskind, "Between the Lines," 86.

64. Libeskind quoted in Gerard Delanty and Paul R. Jones, "European Identity and Architecture," *European Journal of Social Theory* 5, no. 4 (2002): 459.

65. Huyssen, *Present Pasts*, 69.

66. Huyssen, *Present Pasts*, 66.

67. Jacques Derrida, "Response to Daniel Libeskind," *Research in Phenomenology* 22 (1992): 88.

68. Derrida, "Response to Daniel Libeskind," 92.

69. Derrida, "Response to Daniel Libeskind," 92.

70. Julia Ng, "The Museum, the Street, and the Virtual Landscape of Berlin," in *Urban Space and Cityscapes: Perspectives from Modern and Contemporary Culture*, ed. Christoph Lindner (New York: Routledge, 2006), 141.

71. See Huyssen, *Present Pasts*, 168n13.

72. For starters, see Branko Kolarevic and Ali M. Malkawi, *Performative Architecture: Beyond Instrumentality* (New York: Spon Press, 2005).

73. Jacques Derrida, "Point de folie—maintenant l'architecture," trans. Kate Linker, in *Rethinking Architecture: A Reader in Cultural Theory*, ed. Neil Leach (New York: Routledge, 1997), 335.

74. Derrida, "Point de folie," 325.

75. Jacques Derrida, "Why Peter Eisenman Writes Such Good Books," in *Rethinking Architecture*, ed. Leach, 339. For more on choreography and architecture, see Carol Brown, "Making Space, Speaking Spaces," in *The Routledge Dance Studies Reader*, 2nd ed., ed. Alexandra Carter and Janet O'Shea (New York: Routledge, 2010), 58–72.

76. Chris Salter, *Entangled: Technology and the Transformation of Performance* (Cambridge, MA: MIT Press, 2010), 82.

77. Salter, *Entangled*, 77.

78. This is the title of the book documenting the collaboration between Jacques Derrida and Peter Eisenman, *Chora L Works: Jacques Derrida and Peter Eisenman*, ed. Jeffrey Kipnis and Thomas Leeser (New York: Monacelli Press, 1997).

79. Peggy Phelan, *Unmarked: The Politics of Performance* (New York: Routledge, 1993), 6.

80. Phelan, *Unmarked*, 165.

81. Phelan, *Unmarked*, 165. In this passage, it seems that Phelan anticipates and already begins to accommodate the arguments Rebecca Schneider would make about the "remains" of performance years later. See Rebecca Schneider, "Archives: Performance Remains," *Performance Research* 6, no. 2 (2001): 100–108; and Rebecca Schneider, *Performing Remains: Art and War in Times of Theatrical Reenactment* (New York: Routledge, 2011).

82. For more varied treatments of the ghostly and spectral within theater and performance studies see, for example: Herbert Blau, *Take Up the Bodies: Theater at the Vanishing Point* (Urbana: University of Illinois Press, 1982); Diana Taylor, "Dancing with Diana: A Study in Hauntology," *TDR: The Drama Review* 43, no. 1 (1999): 59–78; Marvin Carlson, *The Haunted Stage: The Theatre as Memory Machine* (Ann Arbor: University of Michigan Press, 2002); and Alice Rayner, *Ghosts: Death's Double and the Phenomena of Theatre* (Minneapolis: University of Minnesota Press, 2006).

83. Hennet, *Die Berliner Schlossplatzdebatte im Spiegel der Presse*, 108.

84. Kuhrmann, *Der Palast der Republik*, 82.

85. Philipp Misselwitz and Philipp Oswalt, "Einführung," in Misselwitz, Obrist, and Oswalt, *Fun Palace 200x—Der Berliner Schlossplatz*, 36–37.

86. Simon Ward, "Material, Image, Sign: On the Value of Memory Traces in Public Space," in *Memory Traces: 1989 and the Question of German Cultural Identity*, ed. Silke Arnold-de Simine (Oxford: P. Lang, 2005), 302.

87. Deuflhard quoted in Moritz Holfelder, *Palast der Republik: Aufstieg und Fall eines symbolischen Gebäudes* (Berlin: Christoph Links Verlag, 2008), 98; emphasis added.

88. Deuflhard quoted in Holfelder, *Palast der Republik*, 161.

89. As Elke Knöss-Grillitsch, of Peanutz Architekten (to whom I return in what follows), explains: "After the Wall came down, there were so many spaces, and people just sort of appropriated space and did some *Zwischennutzung* without asking anyone. . . . So this was a method of using space without asking anyone. This happened in the 1990s. And then later, of course, everything was regulated and former owners of buildings came back or whatever. But after the Wall came down, there were lots of buildings; no one knew who they belonged to. And so no one took care; people just occupied them and used them for clubs or galleries or whatever." Elke Knöss-Grillitsch, interview by author, Berlin, February 24, 2012. For more on the history of squatting and *Zwischennutzung* in Berlin, see Klaus Overmeyer, *Urban Pioneers: Temporary Use and Urban Development in Berlin* (Berlin: Jovis, 2007); Philipp Oswalt, Klaus Overmeyer, and Philipp Misselwitz, eds., *Urban Catalyst: The Power of Temporary Use* (Berlin: DOM Publishers, 2014); Andrej Holm and Armin Kuhn, "Squatting and Urban Renewal: The Interaction of Squatter Movements and Strategies of Urban Restructuring in Berlin," *International Journal of Urban and Regional Research* 35, no. 3 (2011): 644–58; Hanna Katharina Göbel, *The Re-Use of Urban Ruins: Atmospheric Inquiries of the City* (New York: Routledge, 2015); and Sandler, *Counterpreservation*.

90. Colomb, "Requiem for a Lost *Palast*," 310.

91. Amelie Deuflhard and Philipp Oswalt, "The Making of Volkspalast," in *Volkspalast: Zwischen Aktivismus und Kunst*, ed. Amelie Deuflhard and Sophie Krempl-Klieeisen (Berlin: Theater der Zeit, 2006), 43.

92. Nooke quoted in Sindy Duong, "Zwischennutzung im Palast der Republik. Ein Kreativfeld ohne ideologische Interessen?" in *Palast der Republik*, ed. Schug, 128.

93. Foerster-Baldenius, interview by author.

94. Deuflhard and Oswalt, "Making of Volkspalast," in *Volkspalast*, ed. Deuflhard and Krempl-Klieeisen, 45.

95. The complete Volkspalast schedule, with descriptions of each of the performances that took place between August and November 2004, can be found online in German at Volkspalast, "Programm," http://www.zwischenpalastnutzung.de/sites/vp2004_reworked/programm.html.

96. Amelie Deuflhard, Matthias Lilienthal, and Philipp Oswalt, "Vorwort," in Volkspalast, untitled program, ed. Sophie Krempl-Klieeisen (August–September 2004).

97. Zwischenpalastnutzung, "1000 Tage," in *Volkspalast*, ed. Deuflhard and Krempl-Klieeisen, 31.

98. Thomas Flierl quoted in Kuhrmann, *Der Palast der Republik*, 82; emphasis added.

99. Thomas Flierl, "Grußwort," in Volkspalast, untitled program, ed. Krempl-Klieeisen.

100. Boym, *Future of Nostalgia*, 41.

101. Boym, *Future of Nostalgia*, 50.

102. Peter Thompson, "'Die Unheimliche Heimat': The GDR and the Dialectics of Home," *Oxford German Studies* 38, no. 3 (2009): 278.

103. Thompson, "'Die Unheimliche Heimat,'" 284.

104. Duong, "Zwischennutzung im Palast der Republik," in *Palast der Republik*, ed. Schug, 129; emphasis added.

105. Zwischenpalastnutzung, "1000 Tage," in *Volkspalast*, ed. Deuflhard and Krempl-Klieeisen, 31.

106. Deuflhard and Oswalt, "Making of Volkspalast," in *Volkspalast*, ed. Deuflhard and Krempl-Klieeisen, 50.

107. Deuflhard and Oswalt, "Making of Volkspalast," in *Volkspalast*, ed. Deuflhard and Krempl-Klieeisen, 46–47.

108. Colomb, "Requiem for a Lost *Palast*," 309.

109. Deuflhard and Oswalt, "Making of Volkspalast," in *Volkspalast*, ed. Deuflhard and Krempl-Klieeisen, 47.

110. Sophie Krempl-Klieeisen, "Volkspalast. Was Tragen Sie Zur Demokratie?," in *Volkspalast*, ed. Deuflhard and Krempl-Klieeisen, 55.

111. Zwischenpalastnutzung, "1000 Tage," in *Volkspalast*, ed. Deuflhard and Krempl-Klieeisen, 32.

112. Although the organizers of Volkspalast were committed, in a certain sense, to diversifying and democratizing Berlin's independent cultural scene—in repudiation of the homogenizing tendencies of many state-stage institutions—their (infra)structural investigations were not particularly attuned to the raced and gendered exclusions that often reified the homogeneity they were working to critique. I address some of these critical oversights in the book's epilogue.

113. Zwischenpalastnutzung, "1000 Tage," in *Volkspalast*, ed. Deuflhard and Krempl-Klieeisen, 33.

114. Deuflhard, Lilienthal, and Oswalt, "Vorwort," in Volkspalast, untitled program, ed. Krempl-Klieeisen.

115. Deuflhard, Lilienthal, and Oswalt, "Vorwort," in Volkspalast, untitled program, ed. Krempl-Klieeisen.

116. Jane Paulick, "East German Architecture's Second Chance," *Deutsche Welle*, November 14, 2004, http://www.dw.de/east-german-architectures-second -chance/a-1326277, archived at https://p.dw.com/p/5Z1Z.

117. Tim Birkholz, *"Schloss mit der Debatte!"?: Die Zwischennutzungen im Palast der Republik im Kontext der Schlossplatzdebatte* (Berlin: Technische Universität Berlin, Inst. für Stadt- und Regionalplanung, 2008), 35.

118. Holfelder, *Palast der Republik*, 162.

119. Stanley Mathews, *From Agit-Prop to Free Space: The Architecture of Cedric Price* (London: Black Dog Publishing, 2007), 13.

120. Mark Wigley quoted in Hans Ulrich Obrist, Juan Herreros, Jean-Philippe Vassal, and Mark Wigley, "Diskussion," in Misselwitz, Obrist, and Oswalt, *Fun Palace 200x—Der Berliner Schlossplatz*, 77.

121. Misselwitz and Oswalt, "Einführung," in Misselwitz, Obrist, and Oswalt, *Fun Palace 200x—Der Berliner Schlossplatz*, 36.

122. Philipp Oswalt quoted in Nikolaus Bernau et al., "Diskussion," in Misselwitz, Obrist, and Oswalt, *Fun Palace 200x—Der Berliner Schlossplatz*, 131; emphasis added.

123. Mark Wigley, "Cedric Price's Fun Palace," opening lecture at *Fun Palace Berlin 200X*, October 16, 2004. Thank you to Philipp Oswalt for sharing the original English text. A German translation, "Der Fun Palace," is published in Misselwitz, Obrist, and Oswalt, *Fun Palace 200x—Der Berliner Schlossplatz*, 89–103.

124. Cedric Price and Joan Littlewood, "The Fun Palace," *TDR: The Drama Review* 12, no. 3 (1968): 130. Subsequent citations are given parenthetically in the text.

125. Salter, *Entangled*, 310.

126. Wigley, "Cedric Price's Fun Palace."

127. Price quoted in Mathews, *From Agit-Prop to Free Space*, 136.

128. Brochure quoted in Mathews, *From Agit-Prop to Free Space*, 135.

129. As Claire Bishop notes in her critique of New York's Shed, Price and Littlewood have been falsely rebranded by contemporary art-world elites as "proto-neoliberal" progenitors of "prosumerism." Claire Bishop, "Palace in Plunderland," *ArtForum*, September 2018, https://www.artforum.com/print/201807/palace-in-plunderland-76327, archived at https://perma.cc/34BJ-WUHV.

130. Mathews, *From Agit-Prop to Free Space*, 173.

131. Mathews, *From Agit-Prop to Free Space*, 173.

132. Philipp Oswalt quoted in Bernau et al., "Diskussion," in Misselwitz, Obrist, and Oswalt, *Fun Palace 200x—Der Berliner Schlossplatz*, 131.

133. Sewing quoted in Bernau et al., "Diskussion," in Misselwitz, Obrist, and Oswalt, *Fun Palace 200x—Der Berliner Schlossplatz*, 136.

134. Wigley quoted in Bernau et al., "Diskussion," in Misselwitz, Obrist, and Oswalt, *Fun Palace 200x—Der Berliner Schlossplatz*, 142.

135. Misselwitz quoted in Bernau et al., "Diskussion," in Misselwitz, Obrist, and Oswalt, *Fun Palace 200x—Der Berliner Schlossplatz*, 132.

136. Both raum*labor* and Pea*nutz* refer to themselves as "performative architects," or "darstellende Architekten." See Foerster-Baldenius, interview by author; Knöss-Grillitsch, interview by author. Note also the importance of "laboratory" (*Labor* in German) and "use" (*Nutzen* in German) in the names of these two architecture teams. Raumlabor's website elaborates: "Architecture is an experimental laboratory for a moment related to the participatory work practice in urban areas. Architecture is understood not as an object, but rather as history, a layer of the history of the place. . . . Architecture is a tool, in the search for a city of possibilities, the city of tomorrow!" "Statement," https://raumlabor.net/statement, archived at https://perma.cc/6MQB-8TUN.

137. Foerster-Baldenius, interview by author.

138. Foerster-Baldenius, interview by author. Elke Knöss-Grillitsch elaborated on Foerster-Baldenius's point: "It is only about facades in a way. It is just the facade of the Schloss, of the Palace, they are going to build. Inside it will be a modern building. There is nothing left: just some stones and figures." Knöss-Grillitsch, interview by author.

139. Foerster-Baldenius, interview by author.

140. Mickley, Schoen, and Jürgens, *Internationale Expertenkommission*, 18.

141. "Kommando Ketchup," *Der Spiegel* 42 (October 13, 1997): 50.

142. Knöss-Grillitsch, interview by author.

143. Knöss-Grillitsch, interview by author. Interestingly, Freies Fluten also invokes—though I am not sure raumlabor or Peanutz was aware of the reference, as it did not come up in our discussions—another pertinent (infra)structural citation. In 1448, in a revolt known as the Berliner Unwille, or Berlin Indignation, a group flooded the excavated building site of the future Stadtschloss in protest against its erection and against Friedrich II's legitimacy as ruler of the territory.

144. Boddien quoted in Hennet, *Die Berliner Schlossplatzdebatte im Spiegel der Presse*, 67–68; emphasis added.

145. Foerster-Baldenius, interview by author.

146. Susan Buck-Morss quoted in Boym, *Future of Nostalgia*, 192.

147. Club Real, "Das Ahnenamt," https://clubrealblog.com/2016/12/12 /ahnenamt-ministry-for-ancestors, archived at https://perma.cc/XEF7-WBUR.

148. Foerster-Baldenius, interview by author.

149. Foerster-Baldenius, interview by author.

150. Amelie Deuflhard, interviewed by Andrea Rottmann, in Schug, *Palast der Republik*, 237.

151. Foerster-Baldenius, interview by author.

152. Foerster-Baldenius, interview by author.

Chapter 4

EPIGRAPHS: Karl Marx, *The Eighteenth Brumaire of Louis Bonaparte* (Marx/ Engels Internet Archive, 1999), https://www.marxists.org/archive/marx/works /1852/18th-brumaire/ch01.htm, archived at https://perma.cc/6GPS-XL8U, emphasis added; Judith Butler, *Notes toward a Performative Theory of Assembly* (Cambridge, MA: Harvard University Press, 2015), 85.

1. These interspersed close readings come from my recollections of having seen the performance live at HAU on February 26, 2013, supplemented by repeated viewings of a DVD of the performance, generously supplied by andcompany&Co.

2. Helmut Draxler et al., "Phantasma und Politik #1," Hebbel am Ufer, Berlin, February 27, 2013. An audio recording of this discussion had been available at http://english.hebbel-am-ufer.de/programme/archive/p/phantasma-und-politik-1 (accessed October 24, 2013 [defunct]), the site itself is archived at https://perma .cc/6D89-UYTY.

3. Mark Rutte quoted in Simon van den Berg, "Mit dem Rücken zum Pub- likum?," *Nachtkritik*, June 23, 2011, http://nachtkritik.de/index.php?option =com_content&view=article&id=5815%3Adie-subventionskuerzungen-im -niederlaendischen-kunstbereich, archived at https://perma.cc/KZ4T-DGYQ.

4. The full Dutch text of Halbe Zijlstra's memorandum "More Than Quality: A New Vision of Cultural Policy" (*Meer dan kwaliteit; een nieuwe visie op cul- tuurbeleid*) can be downloaded at https://www.tweedekamer.nl/kamerstukken /brieven_regering/detail?id=2011Z12464&did=2011D30836 (accessed May 12, 2020).

5. Dieter Haselbach et al., *Der Kulturinfarkt: Von Allem zu viel und überall das Gleiche* (Munich: Albrecht Knaus Verlag, 2012).

6. Schiller, *"Don Carlos" and "Mary Stuart,"* 116.

7. andcompany&Co., *Der (kommende) Aufstand nach Friedrich Schiller* (Textfassung), GO WEST Festival, Oldenburgisches Staatstheater, premiered February 23, 2012. GO WEST is a festival for Dutch and Flemish theater hosted by the state-stage in Oldenburg.

8. andcompany&Co., *Der (kommende) Aufstand nach Friedrich Schiller* (Textfassung).

9. Draxler et al., "Phantasma und Politik #1," archived at https://perma.cc /6D89-UYTY.

10. Draxler in Draxler et al., "Phantasma und Politik #1."

11. As the HAU website elaborates: "Current editions of cultural events such as the 'Berlin Biennale,' the 'Berlinale' or 'documenta' are symptomatic of this longing for the real, as is the sustained interest on the part of theatre in documentary techniques, in 're-enactments' of significant historical events, and investigations of urban space, but also in the return of the protest song. It seems as if artists, curators, and cultural managers are downright obsessed with finding the right formula to diagnose our times and to deal with the crisis, and thus to represent the truly political." See Hebbel am Ufer, "Phantasm and Politics: A Series of Events on Real Longings and Desire for Relevance in Theatre, Art and Music," https://english.hebbel-am-ufer.de/programme/festivals-projects/2014-2015/phantasm-and-politics (accessed July 4, 2018 [defunct]), archived at https:// perma.cc/N58E-ZQ5S.

12. Hans-Thies Lehmann, *Postdramatic Theatre*, trans. Karen Jürs-Munby (New York: Routledge, 2006), 23.

13. A selection of performances (archived as texts) from some of these Berlin-based free-scene groups are collected in Matt Cornish, ed., *"Everything" and Other Performance Texts from Germany* (London: Seagull Books, 2019).

14. Koalition der freien Szene, "Über die Koalition der freien Szene aller Künste," August 21, 2017, http://www.koalition-der-freien-szene-berlin.de/2017/08 /21/ueber-die-koalition-der-freien-szene-aller-kuenste, archived at https://perma .cc/2H4K-KG5R.

15. Koalition der freien Szene, "Das erste Jahr Rot-Rot-Grün—eine ernüchternde Bilanz für die Freie Szene," December 21, 2017, http://www.koalition-der-freien -szene-berlin.de/2017/12/21/das-erste-jahr-rot-rot-gruen-eine-ernuechternde- bilanz-fuer-die-freie-szene, archived at https://perma.cc/XDS3-7CW9. See also Patrick Wildermann, "Das 40-Millionen-Spiel," *Der Tagesspiegel*, November 16, 2012. Interestingly, funding allocations for the free-scene have not changed very much in the past thirty years in spite of the massive proliferation of independent groups. As Arno Paul and Martha Humphreys reported in 1980: "The sector of the West German theatre system funded by public monies, which includes approximately two-thirds of the theatregoing public, receives 96 percent of the subsidies. The other 4 percent must be divided among the resident and touring private companies and the Free Groups, which together attract an audience of approximately nine to 10 million annually." "The West German Theatre Miracle," 16.

16. Butler, *Notes toward a Performative Theory of Assembly*, 85.

17. andcompany&Co., *Der (kommende) Aufstand nach Friedrich Schiller* (Textfassung).

18. Alexander Karschnia, interview by author, Berlin, October 11, 2013.

19. Alexander Karschnia, Nicola Nord, and Joachim Robbrecht&Co., "Occupy History," in program for *Der (kommende) Aufstand nach Friedrich Schiller*, Hebbel am Ufer, February 2013. Note that andcompany&Co. routinely appends "&Co." to artists' names to stress the collaborative nature of their work.

20. There is a lack of consensus about the starting dates of the "Revolt" because it actually consists, as Graham Darby explains, of "a highly complex series of events, or even episodes, some of which are self-contained." Graham Darby, introduction to Graham Darby, ed., *The Origins and Development of the Dutch Revolt* (New York: Routledge, 2001), 1.

21. Graham Darby, "Narrative of Events," in Darby, *Origins and Development of the Dutch Revolt*, 16–17.

22. Karschnia, Nord, and Robbrecht&Co., "Occupy History."

23. In Dutch, *geuzennaam* refers to a pejorative word that has been reclaimed with pride (as, for example, "punk" or "pirate"). For a fuller account and analysis of the "beggars" as symbolic inversion, see Henk van Nierop, "A Beggars' Banquet: The Compromise of the Nobility and the Politics of Inversion," *European History Quarterly* 21, no. 4 (1991): 419–43.

24. Friedrich Schiller, *History of the Revolt of the United Netherlands*, trans. E. B. Eastwick and A. J. W. Morrison (New York: Anthological Society, 1901). The entire text is available at http://www.gutenberg.org/files/6780/6780-h/6780-h.htm.

25. Darby, "Narrative of Events," in Darby, *Origins and Development of the Dutch Revolt*, 18.

26. Karschnia, Nord, and Robbrecht&Co., "Occupy History." James Tracy's research further substantiates this claim: "Spain's seasoned troops had a clear edge in land warfare (if not at sea), but the spectacular economic growth of the rebel provinces . . . proved more than a match for the stream of silver that flowed into Spain from the mines of Spanish America." James D. Tracy, "Keeping the Wheels of War Turning: Revenues of the Province of Holland, 1572–1619," in Darby, *Origins and Development of the Dutch Revolt*, 133.

27. Darby, introduction to Darby, *Origins and Development of the Dutch Revolt*, 5.

28. James D. Tracy, *The Founding of the Dutch Republic: War, Finance, and Politics in Holland, 1572–1588* (Oxford: Oxford University Press, 2008), 39.

29. Tracy, *The Founding of the Dutch Republic*, 39.

30. Karschnia, interview by author.

31. Karschnia, interview by author.

32. andcompany&Co., *Der (kommende) Aufstand nach Friedrich Schiller* (Textfassung).

33. andcompany&Co., *Der (kommende) Aufstand nach Friedrich Schiller* (Textfassung). The point is further stressed in the very next bit of spoken text. Alexander, still in a *lucha libre* mask, returns to the human mic, as the king, Carlos, Schiller, and the Grand Inquisitor follow suit: "The king may not be able to bear the sight of the riches. He must first have the treasure melted down in order to turn the gold into money, into a means of exchange, that allows him to turn things into goods, which thanks to money can turn themselves into each other, from goods into other goods. And this power of transformation, of

metamorphosis, the goods owe it to the money, and the money owes it to the gold and the silver, to the precious metals that living men claw out of the Potosí mountain, treasure chamber of the world, king of the mountains, the envy of kings."

34. Karschnia, interview by author.

35. Karschnia, interview by author.

36. andcompany&Co., *Der (kommende) Aufstand nach Friedrich Schiller* (Textfassung).

37. Karschnia, interview by author.

38. Karschnia, Nord, and Robbrecht&Co., "Occupy History."

39. andcompany&Co., *Der (kommende) Aufstand nach Friedrich Schiller* (Textfassung).

40. Sophie Lambo (managing director of Internationaal Danstheater in Amsterdam) quoted in Larry Rohter, "In Europe, Where Art Is Life, Ax Falls on Public Financing," *New York Times*, March 24, 2012.

41. Bruce Sterling, "The Dark Age Netherlands," *Wired*, June 28, 2011, http://www.wired.com/2011/06/the-dark-age-netherlands, archived at https://perma.cc/P7PN-BHH2.

42. Zijlstra quoted in Isabel Löfgren, "Collateral Damage: Cultural Politics in the Age of Cultural Depression," *Paletten Art Journal* 284–85 (September 2011): n.p.

43. Sigrid Merx, "The Argument for Autonomy: The Missing Link in the Discursive Arena," *Teorija koja hoda (Walking Theory)* 20 (2012): 26.

44. Zijlstra quoted in Löfgren, "Collateral Damage."

45. Nina Siegal, "Dutch Arts Scene Is under Siege," *New York Times*, January 29, 2013.

46. Löfgren, "Collateral Damage."

47. Siobhán Dowling, "European Arts Cuts: Dutch Dance Loses out as Netherlands Slashes Funding," *The Guardian*, August 2, 2012.

48. Zijlstra quoted in Sterling, "Dark Age Netherlands."

49. Berg, "Mit dem Rücken zum Publikum?"

50. Don Rubin, Péter Nagy, and Philippe Rouyer, *The World Encyclopedia of Contemporary Theatre: Volume 1* (New York: Routledge, 1994), 596. In Karschnia's more sarcastic words: "Later the Dutch rejected Greater Germany's generous offer to [turn back] those 400 years of error which had caused both countries to grow apart from each other, when they decided not to gratefully integrate into the 'Thousand-Year Reich' as blonde blood brothers. They merely examined and took over the fully finalized funding plans for theaters, which Germans had left on the desks of their office of culture and propaganda." Alexander Karschnia, "Cultural Counterrevolution Gaining Ground," November 2011, http://www.nettime.org/Lists-Archives/nettime-l-1111/msg00125.html, archived at https://perma.cc/7LAB-D5BU.

51. For more on the resonance of *Aktie Tomaat*, see Anthony Keller, "The Tomato Revolution," *Journal of Arts Management and Law* 13, no. 1 (1983): 170–76; S. E. Wilmer, "Decentralisation and Cultural Democracy," in *Theatre Worlds in Motion: Structures, Politics and Developments in the Countries of Western Europe*, ed. H. van Maanen and S. E. Wilmer (Amsterdam: Rodopi, 1998), 17–36; and Merx, "Argument for Autonomy," 23.

52. Wilmer, "Decentralisation and Cultural Democracy," 28.

53. Merx, "Argument for Autonomy," 24.

54. Karschnia, "Cultural Counterrevolution Gaining Ground."

55. Karschnia, "Cultural Counterrevolution Gaining Ground."

56. For more on the "Long March through the Theaters" in the context of 1960s Germany, see Michael Shane Boyle, "The Ambivalence of Resistance: West German Antiauthoritarian Performance after the Age of Affluence" (Ph.D. diss., Performance Studies, University of California, Berkeley, 2012), 169–94.

57. For an analysis of the histories and theoretical stakes of *Regietheater*, see Peter M. Boenisch, *Directing Scenes and Senses: The Thinking of Regie* (Manchester: Manchester University Press, 2015).

58. See chapter 3 for more on the free-scene's *Zwischennutzung* in Berlin's Palast der Republik.

59. For more on the wider influence of Giessen's Applied Theater Studies model, see Annemarie Matzke, Christel Weiler, and Isa Wortelkamp, eds., *Das Buch von der angewandten Theaterwissenschaft* (Berlin: Alexander Verlag, 2012).

60. The list in Berlin has expanded significantly in the past fifteen years to include Ballhaus Naunynstraße, theaterdiscounter, Ballhaus Ost, Neuköllner Oper, Theater unterm Dach, Tanzbüro, Radialsystem, Heimathafen Neukölln, Literaturwerkstatt, DOCK 11, English Theater Berlin, Initiative Neue Musik Berlin, Theaterkapelle, and many more.

61. For helpful narratives on the genealogy of the free-scene in Germany (in English), see Jonas Tinius, "Between Professional Precariousness and Creative Self-Organization: The Free Performing Arts Scene in Germany," in *Mobile Autonomy: Exercises in Artists' Self-Organisation*, ed. Nico Dockx and Pascal Gielen (Amsterdam: Valiz, 2015): 171–93; and Henning Fülle, "A Theatre for Postmodernity in Western European Theatrescapes," in *Independent Theatre in Contemporary Europe: Structures—Aesthetics—Cultural Policy*, ed. Manfred Brauneck and ITI Germany (Bielefeld: Transcript Verlag, 2017): 275–320. For more comprehensive accounts in German, see: Henning Fülle, "Freies Theater—Worüber reden wir eigentlich?," *Kulturpolitische Mitteilungen* 147, no. 4 (2014): 27–30, available at https://www.kupoge.de/kumi/pdf/kumi147/kumi147_27-30 .pdf; and Henning Fülle, *Freies Theater: Die Modernisierung der deutschen Theaterlandschaft (1960–2010)* (Berlin: Theater der Zeit, 2016).

62. Annemarie Matzke, "Jenseits des freien Theaters," *Nachtkritik*, November 21, 2012, http://nachtkritik.de/index.php?view=article&id=7472 %3Ahildesheimer-thesen-v-n, archived at https://perma.cc/4R66-VY2N.

63. Matzke, "Jenseits des freien Theaters."

64. Matzke, "Jenseits des freien Theaters."

65. Gabriela Walde, "An diesen Stellen investiert der Senat in Berlins Kultur," *Berliner Morgenpost*, December 22, 2017, https://www.morgenpost.de/kultur /article212920039/Millionenspritze-fuer-Berlins-Kultur.html.

66. "Doppelhaushalt 2018/19: Fast 120 Millionen mehr für Kultur," *Süddeutsche Zeitung*, September 4, 2017, https://www.sueddeutsche.de/politik /kulturpolitik-berlin-doppelhaushalt-2018-19-fast-120-millionen-mehr-fuer -kultur-dpa.urn-newsml-dpa-com-20090101-170904-99-905038.

67. Walde, "An diesen Stellen investiert der Senat in Berlins Kultur."

68. Birgit Walter, "Künstler hoffen auf Bettensteuer," *Berliner Zeitung*, June 26, 2013.

69. Elena Philipp, "Berliner Künstler wollen mehr Geld vom Staat," *Berliner Morgenpost*, September 7, 2013.

70. Peter Laudenbach, "Die freie Szene in Berlin ist ein Wirtschaftsfaktor," *tip Berlin*, August 14, 2013.

71. Ulrike Baureithel, "Arte Povera," *der Freitag*, June 27, 2018, https://www.freitag.de/autoren/ulrike-baureithel/arte-povera.

72. Ingo Arend, "Das Parlament der Kunst," *Die Tageszeitung*, November 19, 2012.

73. Izabela Dabrowska-Diemert, "Verspielt Berlin sein kulturelles Kapital?," *Neues Deutschland*, September 11, 2013.

74. Philipp, "Berliner Künstler wollen mehr Geld vom Staat."

75. Peter Laudenbach, "Die freie Szene Berlins will endlich bessere Finanzierung," *tip Berlin*, August 29, 2013.

76. Laudenbach, "Die freie Szene Berlins will endlich bessere Finanzierung."

77. Nicholas Ridout and Rebecca Schneider, "Precarity and Performance: An Introduction," *TDR: The Drama Review* 56, no. 4 (2012): 8.

78. Ridout and Schneider, "Precarity and Performance," 6.

79. It seems that Shannon Jackson's contribution to the special "Precarity and Performance" *TDR* issue could just as well be describing—or diagnosing—the emergence of Berlin's free-scene when she writes: "Flexibility seemed, after all, to be the key to social agency. . . . Laborers are now 'free' to juggle many jobs, to construct nimbler lives, and to avoid situations that offer the dubious protections of regulation, social welfare, or employment security. . . . [W]hat we now, in 2012, call 'precarity' is the other side of a coin that used to be celebrated as 'flexibility.' . . . Indeed, in the rush to avoid becoming Marcuse's 'one-dimensional man' (1964), the conformist image of the un-nimble, salaried worker was something that creative laborers sought to avoid. . . . Workers are now encouraged to find happiness in many jobs, and to be thankful not to be weighed down by regular salaries, health insurance, or the possibility of pensions. The emergence of today's precarity was thus helped along by the fact that so many of us cathected to flexibility's marketing campaign." "Just-in-Time: Performance and the Aesthetics of Precarity," *TDR: The Drama Review* 56, no. 4 (2012): 22.

80. Koalition der Freien Szene, "Welcome to the Independent Art Coalition," May 1, 2013, http://www.koalition-der-freien-szene-berlin.de/2013/05/01/independent-art-coalition, archived at https://perma.cc/M5X3-DWED.

81. This protest-program was most certainly reminiscent of the more "naive" tactics employed, rather unsuccessfully, by supporters of the State-Stage Complex, which I profile extensively in chapter 1.

82. Koalition der Freien Szene, "Welcome to the Independent Art Coalition."

83. Knoch quoted in Laudenbach, "Die freie Szene in Berlin ist ein Wirtschaftsfaktor."

84. Schmitz quoted in Laudenbach, "Die freie Szene Berlins will endlich bessere Finanzierung."

85. Koalition der Freien Szene, "Arbeitstitel: 'Bye Bye Berlin?,' " https://www.koalition-der-freien-szene-berlin.de/2013/05/25/arbeitstitel-bye-bye-berlin, archived at https://perma.cc/E76H-9X4F.

86. Koalition der Freien Szene, "Welcome to the Independent Art Coalition"; emphasis added.

87. Brett Neilson and Ned Rossiter provide a sustained critique of this kind of "flexicurity" (a portmanteau of *flexi[ble]* and *[se]curity*), which they categorize as a form of dependence on the state that thereby "reinforces the dominant rhetoric of security in a period of global war." They continue: "For while precarity provides a platform for struggle against the degradation of labour conditions and a means of imagining more flexible circumstances of work and life, it also risks dovetailing with the dominant rhetoric of security that emanates from the established political classes of the wealthy world. This is particularly the case for those versions of precarity politics that place their faith in state intervention as a means of improving or attenuating the worsening conditions of labour." "From Precarity to Precariousness and Back Again: Labour, Life and Unstable Networks," *Fibreculture Journal* 5 (2005), http://five.fibreculturejournal.org/fcj -022-from-precarity-to-precariousness-and-back-again-labour-life-and-unstable -networks, archived at https://perma.cc/BJM8-3KHM.

88. The coalition's original ten-point plan from November 2012 can be found here: http://www.bbk-berlin.de/con/bbk/front_content.php?idart=2085&refId= 199 (accessed July 1, 2018 [defunct]), archived at https://perma.cc/S7LV-8LP7. Since the publication of the original ten points, the coalition has continued to update and revise the program based on the "needs of the scene." The most up-to-date eleven-point plan, from May 1, 2018, can be found here: http://www .koalition-der-freien-szene-berlin.de/2018/05/01/11-punkte, archived at https:// perma.cc/YFZ6-XBPV.

89. Koalition der Freien Szene, "Freie Szene stärken! Geist ist noch flüchtiger als Kapital—haltet ihn fest," August 19, 2013, http://www.koalition-der-freien -szene-berlin.de/2013/08/19/freie-szene-staerken-geist-ist-noch-fluechtiger-als -kapital-haltet-ihn-fest, archived at https://perma.cc/VUB2-PSVQ.

90. Koalition der Freien Szene, "Freie Szene stärken!"

91. Koalition der Freien Szene, "Freie Szene stärken!"

92. Koalition der freien Szene, "Über die Koalition der freien Szene aller Künste."

93. Koalition der Freien Szene, "Hintergrund zum Berliner Kulturhaushalt," May 27, 2013, http://www.koalition-der-freien-szene-berlin.de/2013/05/27 /berliner-kulturhaushalt, archived at https://perma.cc/53GM-ZQU5.

94. "Precarity Talk: A Virtual Roundtable with Lauren Berlant, Judith Butler, Bojana Cvejić, Isabell Lorey, Jasbir Puar, and Ana Vujanović," *TDR: The Drama Review* 56, no. 4 (2012): 167.

95. Artist Hito Steyerl terms the implementation of post-Fordism in the (performing) arts, most polemically, "artistic occupation." "Art as Occupation: Claims for an Autonomy of Life," *e-flux* 30 (December 2011), https://www.e-flux.com /journal/30/68140/art-as-occupation-claims-for-an-autonomy-of-life, archived at https://perma.cc/ARF4-CG5A.

96. Ridout and Schneider raise a similar point in a their own series of questions: "Might a similar technique regarding precarity be emerging in performance-based art, in which a body producing affective engagement simultaneously critiques deployments of affective engagement in the neoliberal affect factory? Can affect critique affect? Can complicity critique complicity? If not only 'creatives' but also 'artistic critique' has been coopted by neoliberalism's management modes of 'flexibility,' 'disalienation,' and 'freedom,' as Holmes has argued, what kinds of

art activity promote non-capitalist modes of exchange?" Ridout and Schneider, "Precarity and Performance," 8–9.

97. andcompany&Co., *Der (kommende) Aufstand nach Friedrich Schiller* (Textfassung).

98. Karschnia, interview by author.

99. Alexander Karschnia, "(Post-)Performerism as a Way of Life oder das Theater der Produktion des Lebens," in *Politisch Theater machen: Neue Artikulationsformen des Politischen in den darstellenden Künsten*, ed. Jan Deck and Angelika Sieburg (Bielefeld: Transcript Verlag, 2011): 94.

100. Karschnia, "(Post-)Performerism as a Way of Life," 94

101. Karschnia, interview by author.

102. Alexander Karschnia, "Für ein freies und d.h. freies freies Theater!," October 30, 2013, http://www.andco.de/media/fuer-ein-freies-und-d-h-freies-freies-theater, archived at https://perma.cc/CV46-DNFK; emphasis added.

103. andcompany&Co., *Der (kommende) Aufstand nach Friedrich Schiller* (Textfassung).

104. Draxler et al., "Phantasma und Politik #1."

105. Hans-Thies Lehmann, "Ästhetik des Aufstands? Grenzgänge zwischen Politik und Kunst in den neuen sozialen Bewegungen" (lecture presented at Foreign Affairs Festival, Berliner Festspiele, Berlin, Germany, October 16, 2012). A video recording of this lecture and the Q&A session that followed can be found at https://www.youtube.com/watch?v=X2KeX-Jp0Ug.

106. Woolf, "Towards a Paradoxically Parallaxical Postdramatic Politics?"

107. Lehmann in Draxler et al., "Phantasma und Politik #1."

108. Lehmann in Draxler et al., "Phantasma und Politik #1."

109. Lehmann, *Postdramatic Theatre*, 105.

110. Hebbel am Ufer, "Phantasm and Politics."

111. Lehmann in Draxler et al., "Phantasma und Politik #1."

112. Lehmann, "Ästhetik des Aufstands?"

113. Lehmann, *Postdramatic Theatre*, 105.

114. Karschnia quoted in Patrick Wildermann, "Interview zu Der(kommende) Aufstand im HAU," *tip Berlin*, February 26, 2013.

115. Karschnia in Draxler et al., "Phantasma und Politik #1."

116. Karschnia, interview by author.

117. Karschnia quoted in Wildermann, "Interview zu Der (kommende) Aufstand im HAU."

118. Karschnia in Draxler et al., "Phantasma und Politik #1."

119. Karschnia, interview by author.

120. The Invisible Committee, *The Coming Insurrection* (Los Angeles: Semiotext(e), 2009), 98.

121. The Invisible Committee, *The Coming Insurrection*, 41.

122. The Invisible Committee, *The Coming Insurrection*, 85.

123. Erika Fischer-Lichte, *The Transformative Power of Performance: A New Aesthetics*, trans. Saskya Iris Jain (New York: Routledge, 2008), 9. In many ways, Fischer-Lichte's theorization shares much in common with the equally romantic concept of "relationality" developed by Nicolas Bourriaud in the field of contemporary visual art. *Relational Aesthetics*, trans. Simon Pleasance and Fronza Woods (Dijon: Les Presses du réel, 2002).

124. Fischer-Lichte, *Transformative Power of Performance*, 32.

125. Lehmann, *Postdramatic Theatre*, 85.

126. The Invisible Committee, *The Coming Insurrection*, 13.

127. Alessio Rastani, interviewed by Martine Croxall on BBC News, September 26, 2011, http://www.youtube.com/watch?v=aC19fEqR5bA (accessed January 29, 2014 [defunct]); now at https://www.bbc.com/news/av/business-15059135/anyone-can-make-money-from-a-crash-says-market-trader .

128. Rastani, interviewed by Martine Croxall.

129. David Frost, lead-in to interview of Alessio Rastani, Frost over the World, Al Jazeera English, October 10, 2011, http://www.youtube.com/watch?annotation_id=annotation_936910&feature=iv&src_vid=aC19fEqR5bA&v=9sdHTYS9Uic.

130. L. M. Bogad, *Tactical Performance: The Theory and Practice of Serious Play* (New York: Routledge, 2016).

131. The Yes Men, "Sorry, but This Trader's Banking Confession Was No Prank," *The Guardian*, September 29, 2011.

132. Joe Kelleher, *Theatre and Politics* (New York: Palgrave Macmillan, 2009), 43; emphasis in original.

133. Jacques Rancière, *The Emancipated Spectator*, trans. Gregory Elliott (London: Verso, 2009), 103.

134. Lehmann in Draxler et al., "Phantasma und Politik #1."

135. Thomas Ostermeier, "Ein paar Narren im Dienst der Gesellschaft," *Nachtkritik*, July 1, 2013, https://www.nachtkritik.de/index.php?view=article&id=8327:thomas-ostermeier-ueber-die-zukunft-des-theaters&option=com_content&Itemid=84.

136. Thomas Ostermeier, "Die Zukunft des Theaters," in "Zukunft der Literature," special issue, *Text+Kritik 5*, no. 13 (2013): 42–50. The full text also appears in English as "The Future of Theatre (2013)," trans. Peter M. Boenisch, in Peter M. Boenisch and Thomas Ostermeier, *The Theatre of Thomas Ostermeier* (London: Routledge, 2016), 237–45, with the passage I've translated here corresponding to 242–43.

137. Lehmann, *Postdramatic Theatre*, 25.

138. Ostermeier, "Die Zukunft des Theaters."

139. Ostermeier, "Die Zukunft des Theaters"; emphasis added.

140. Karschnia, "Für ein freies und d.h. freies freies Theater!"

141. Karschnia, "(Post-)Performerism as a Way of Life," 103. Lehmann made the very same claim (to significant applause) during the Q&A session following his lecture "Ästhetik des Aufstands?"

142. Hans-Thies Lehmann, Karen Jürs-Munby, and Elinor Fuchs, "Lost in Translation?" *TDR: The Drama Review* 52, no. 4 (2008): 16; emphasis in original.

143. Lehmann during the Q&A session following his lecture "Ästhetik des Aufstands?"

144. Hans-Thies Lehmann, *Postdramatisches Theater* (Frankfurt am Main: Verlag der Autoren, 1999), 456–57.

145. Benjamin, "The Author as Producer," 85.

146. Theodor W. Adorno, *Aesthetic Theory*, ed. Gretel Adorno and Rolf Tiedemann, trans. and ed. Robert Hullot-Kentor (New York: Bloomsbury Academic,

2013), 15. For a more sustained investigation of form as a site of the intersection of the aesthetic structures and social conditions of postdramatic performance, see Michael Shane Boyle, Matt Cornish, and Brandon Woolf, eds., *Postdramatic Theatre and Form* (London: Bloomsbury Methuen, 2019).

147. The Invisible Committee, *The Coming Insurrection*, 101.

148. andcompany&Co., *Der (kommende) Aufstand nach Friedrich Schiller* (Textfassung).

149. Castorf quoted in "Mit Frank Castorf sprach Frank Raddatz," 22–23.

150. Castorf quoted in "Feudale Krawallbude," 5.

151. Ostermeier, "Die Zukunft des Theaters." For an examination of both the institutional and aesthetic transformations of the Schaubühne under Ostermeier's direction, see Peter Boenisch, ed., *The Schaubühne Berlin under Thomas Ostermeier: Reinventing Realism* (London: Bloomsbury Methuen, 2020).

152. Karschnia, "Für ein freies und d.h. freies freies Theater!"

153. Karschnia, "Für ein freies und d.h. freies freies Theater!"

154. Karschnia, interview by author.

155. Karschnia, interview by author.

156. Karschnia, interview by author; emphasis added.

157. Karschnia, "(Post-)Performerism as a Way of Life," 92.

158. Karschnia, interview by author.

159. Karschnia, "Für ein freies und d.h. freies freies Theater!"

160. Jodi Dean does see Occupy—rather controversially—as an opportunity to rethink the Party. In *The Communist Horizon*, she writes: "I end this book by taking up the question of the communist party. Although actively calling for the reclamation of communism as the name for a revolutionary universal egalitarianism, Badiou insists on a communism disconnected from the 'outmoded' forms of Party and State. Hardt and Negri likewise reject Party and State: 'Being communist means being against the State.' They emphasize instead the constituent power of desire and the affective, creative productivity of the multitude as the communism underpinning and exceeding capitalism. This is not my view. I agree with Bosteels and Žižek that a politics without the organizational form of the party is a politics without politics." *The Communist Horizon* (New York: Verso, 2012), 19.

161. Théorie Communiste, "Communization in the Present Tense," in *Communization and Its Discontents: Contestation, Critique, and Contemporary Struggles*, ed. Benjamin Noys (New York: Autonomedia, 2012), 58; emphasis in original.

162. Benjamin Noys, "The Fabric of Struggles," in *Communization and Its Discontents*, 9.

163. Benjamin Noys, "The Aesthetics of Communization" (lecture presented at Xero, Kline & Coma Gallery, London, England, May 11, 2013), 6. The full text can also be found online at: http://www.academia.edu/3515652/The_Aesthetics _of_Communication.

164. andcompany&Co., "Manifesto," http://www.andco.de/index.php?lang =en (accessed October 1, 2013). The "Manifesto" text has since been revised, and this portion no longer appears on the site. The earlier version, mostly in German but with some English, is available in a Dutch theater program for andcompany&Co.'s 2011 production of *Pandämonium Germanicum: Lenz im Loop* at https://s3.eu-central-1.amazonaws.com

/desingel-media/a1ib000000AIBUTAA5.pdf. See also "All You Need Is Stamps: andcompany&Co.," https://doublestandards.net/work/all-you-need-is-stamps.

165. andcompany&Co., "Manifesto." This portion also no longer appears on the site, but see the program for *Pandämonium Germanicum*. See also "All You Need Is Stamps."

166. andcompany&Co., "Manifesto." These portions also no longer appear on the site, but see the program for *Pandämonium Germanicum*.

167. Karschnia, interview by author.

168. Karschnia, "(Post-)Performerism as a Way of Life," 105.

169. Karschnia, interview by author.

170. Karschnia, interview by author.

171. Karschnia, interview by author.

172. Léon de Mattis, "What Is Communisation?," *SIC—International Journal for Communisation* 1 (2011): 28.

173. Karschnia, interview by author.

174. For de Mattis, the insurrectionary impulse is at the heart of communization: "The overcoming of all existing conditions can only come from a phase of intense and insurrectionist struggle during which the forms of struggle and the forms of future life will take flesh in one and the same process, the latter being nothing else than the former. This phase, and its specific activity, is what we propose to call by the name of communisation. Communisation does not yet exist, but the whole present phase of struggles, as mentioned above, permits us to talk about communisation in the present." "What Is Communisation?," 25.

175. Karschnia, interview by author.

176. Karschnia, interview by author.

177. Critics of Occupy's overall tactics tend to voice a different kind of critique than those trying to articulate and take seriously its implications and internal contradictions. As Jodi Dean explains, "The ideas of autonomy, horizontality, and leaderlessness that most galvanized people at the movement's outset . . . came later to be faulted for conflicts and disillusionment within the movement. Emphases on autonomy encouraged people to pursue multiple, separate, and even conflicting goals rather than work toward common ones. Celebration of horizontality heightened skepticism toward organizing structures like the General Assembly and the Spokes Council, ultimately leading to the dissolution of both. Assertions of leaderlessness as a principle incited a kind of paranoia around leaders who emerged but who could not be acknowledged or held accountable as leaders." *Communist Horizon*, 210.

178. In Karschnia's words, "But of course it doesn't always happen like that. Often it is a waste of time. You try to make your dramaturgical problems very transparent, and the participants are often annoyed. They say, 'Why don't you solve it and come back with a solution and we'll do it?' Of course, often we do that. Especially when you work in the state theater, you have to play the part of the director." Karschnia, interview by author.

179. Alberto Toscano, "Now and Never," in Noys, *Communization and Its Discontents*, 100.

180. Karschnia, "Für ein freies und d.h. freies freies Theater!"

181. For instance: "The response, however, cannot be the redistribution of resources from government-subsidized institutions—like theaters, opera houses, or museums—in favor of the free-scene. The Independent Art Coalition

understands the different structures of artistic production in Berlin as a shared and unique cultural landscape that makes up the city's identity. The mandatory correction of the imbalance in the Berlin cultural subsidy must be achieved by an increase in the total cultural budget in order to benefit structures of free production. The Independent Art Coalition is fighting for the allocation of 50% of the revenue from the City Tax as *one* source of 'fresh money' for culture." Koalition der Freien Szene, "Hintergrund zum Berliner Kulturhaushalt"; emphasis in original. Compare these words from another cultural practitioner: "The coalition doesn't want to lead a debate about redistribution and envy. 'Reform can only be achieved with fresh money,' says Jochen Sandig, a cofounder of Radialsystem." Udo Badelt, "Es geht nur mit frischem Geld," *Der Tagesspiegel*, April 5, 2012.

182. Karschnia, "Für ein freies und d.h. freies freies Theater!"

183. Matzke, "Jenseits des freien Theaters."

184. Karschnia, Nord, and Robbrecht&Co, "Occupy History."

185. Karschnia, interview by author.

186. Karschnia, "Für ein freies und d.h. freies freies Theater!"

187. Karschnia, "Für ein freies und d.h. freies freies Theater!"

188. Karschnia, "(Post-)Performerism as a Way of Life," 100.

189. Geert Lovink and Ned Rossiter, "Urgent Aphorisms: Notes on Organized Networks for the Connected Multitudes," in *Managing Media Work*, ed. Mark Deuze (Thousand Oaks, CA: SAGE, 2011): 282.

190. For a comprehensive account of this theory of organized networks and its development—especially in relation to theorizations of precarity—see Geert Lovink and Ned Rossiter, "Dawn of the Organised Networks," *Fibreculture Journal* 5 (2005), http://journal.fibreculture.org/issue5/lovink_rossiter.html, archived at https://perma.cc/KB43-EAU9; Ned Rossiter, *Organized Networks: Media Theory, Creative Labour, New Institutions* (Amsterdam: Institute of Network Cultures, 2006); and Brett Neilson and Ned Rossiter, "Precarity as a Political Concept, or, Fordism as Exception," *Theory, Culture and Society* 25, nos. 7–8 (2008): 51–72.

191. Lovink and Rossiter, "Urgent Aphorisms," 282.

192. Brett Neilson and Ned Rossiter, "Towards a Political Anthropology of New Institutional Forms," *Ephemera: Theory Politics in Organization* 6, no. 4 (2006): 406.

193. Neilson and Rossiter, "Towards a Political Anthropology," 396.

194. Neilson and Rossiter, "Towards a Political Anthropology," 400.

195. As Neilson and Rossiter rearticulate elsewhere: "It is necessary to acknowledge that the concept of precarity is constitutively doubled-edged. On the one hand, it describes an increasing change of previously guaranteed permanent employment conditions into mainly worse paid, uncertain jobs. In this sense, precarity leads to an interminable lack of certainty, the condition of being unable to predict one's fate or having some degree of stability on which to construct a life. On the other hand, precarity supplies the precondition for new forms of creative organisation that seek to accept and exploit the flexibility inherent in networked modes of sociality and production." Neilson and Rossiter, "From Precarity to Precariousness and Back Again."

196. Neilson and Rossiter, "Towards a Political Anthropology," 404. This invocation of Virno is also reminiscent of Nicholas Ridout's work in *Passionate Amateurs*: "The aim will be to explore what kind of communicative labor might

constitute a mode of political action in the theatre. The crucial word here may be *in*. Just as the logic of Virno's argument might be that we should not be looking for political action outside the workplace, we might hold on to the possibility that the political action of the theatre will take place in the theatre, rather than seeking to extend itself into any other part of the so-called real world. This is to insist, once again, that the theatre does not stand to one side of the 'real' world or offer an alternative to it: the theatre is a real place, where real people go to work, and where their work takes the form of 'conversation.' " Nicholas Ridout, *Passionate Amateurs: Theatre, Communism, and Love* (Ann Arbor: University of Michigan Press, 2013), 124; emphasis in original.

197. Karschnia makes a similar kind of claim: "Following Rancière, we would say that it means the withdrawal from the place that the police has laid out and to return to politics, to the conflict zone which precedes the order of things, the chaos before the differences are defined between this or that. What if the stage is that place? Or better said: should become that place in which this original turmoil takes place?" Karschnia, "Politics in the Sense of Making Things Impossible," October 3, 2010, https://alextext.wordpress.com/2010/10/03/politics-in-the-sense-of, archived at https://perma.cc/G4T6-RCTA.

198. Neilson and Rossiter, "Towards a Political Anthropology," 408.

199. Karschnia, "(Post-)Performerism as a Way of Life," 92.

200. andcompany&Co., "Manifesto." This portion also no longer appears on the site, but is found in "All You Need Is Stamps" and (in German) in the program for *Pandämonium Germanicum*.

201. andcompany&Co., "Manifesto." This portion also no longer appears on the site, but is found in "All You Need Is Stamps."

202. Karschnia, "(Post-) Performerism as a Way of Life," 103.

203. Karschnia, "Für ein freies und d.h. freies freies Theater!" Karschnia's invocation of "vulnerability" echoes Judith Butler's mobilization of vulnerability as a "specific kind of performative politics . . . operating in various ways in recent kinds of mobilizations." "Bodily Vulnerability, Coalitions, and Street Politics," in *Differences in Common: Gender, Vulnerability and Community*, ed. Joana Sabadell-Nieto and Marta Segarra (New York: Rodopi Publishing, 2014): 107. In Butler's contribution to the Ridout and Schneider *TDR* volume, she continues this thinking when she writes: "In this sense, precarity is indissociable from that dimension of politics that addresses the organization and protection of bodily needs. Precarity exposes our sociality, the fragile and necessary dimensions of our interdependency." "Precarity Talk," 170.

204. Butler, *Notes toward a Performative Theory of Assembly*, 75.

Epilogue

1. Sebastian Kaiser and Carl Hegemann, "Faust: The Masculine Must Pass," trans. Bettina Seifried, https://volksbuehne.adk.de/praxis/en/faust/index.html, archived at https://perma.cc/8JPJ-Q4M5.

2. These recollections come from my viewing of the performance live at the Theatertreffen festival in Berlin on May 7, 2018, as well as production photos housed in the archives of the Akademie der Künste; AdK, VB 3589.

3. Johann Wolfgang von Goethe and Frank Castorf, *Faust* (Regiebuch), Volksbühne am Rosa-Luxemburg-Platz, Berlin, premiered March 3, 2017, AdK, VB

3589. In 1982 Minetti had played Faust in a stripped-down, four-character adaptation at the Freie Volksbühne Berlin, directed by Klaus-Michael Grüber. See Gerhard Ahrens, ed., *Bernhard Minetti / Faust* (Berlin: Medusa, 1983).

4. Johann Wolfgang von Goethe, *Faust, Part 1*, trans. A. S. Kline, https://www .poetryintranslation.com/PITBR/German/FaustIProl.php#Prelude_On_Stage, archived at https://perma.cc/P2BG-GWZA.

5. Goethe and Castorf, *Faust* (Regiebuch), 21.

6. Goetz and Laudenbach, "Chronologie eines Desasters."

7. Goetz and Laudenbach, "Chronologie eines Desasters."

8. Balme, "Institutional Aesthetics and the Crisis of Leadership," 171–72.

9. Balme, "Institutional Aesthetics and the Crisis of Leadership," 172.

10. Balme, "Institutional Aesthetics and the Crisis of Leadership," 169.

11. Carl Hegemann quoted in Sigrid Brinkman, "Künstler protestieren gegen Intendantenwechsel," https://www.deutschlandfunkkultur.de/volksbuehne-berlin -kuenstler-protestieren-gegen.1013.de.html?dram:article_id=357814, archived at https://perma.cc/6SZT-M4K5.

12. Annuss, "On the Future of the Volksbühne," 100.

13. Annuss, "On the Future of the Volksbühne," 100.

14. Annuss, "On the Future of the Volksbühne," 94.

15. Tavia Nyong'o, "Situating Precarity between the Body and the Commons," *Women and Performance: A Journal of Feminist Theory* 23, no. 2 (2013): 158.

16. Nyong'o, "Situating Precarity between the Body and the Commons," 158.

17. Waterfeld, "B6112—Art after All," 277.

18. Waterfeld, "B6112—Art after All," 278.

19. Diedrich Diederichsen, "Weder Wohnung Noch Währung," *Texte zur Kunst* 105 (2017): 159.

20. Diederichsen, "Weder Wohnung Noch Währung," 159.

21. Diederichsen, "Weder Wohnung Noch Währung," 162.

22. Hito Steyerl posted this as an online comment to "Volksbühne staff on Chris Dercon: We fear job cuts and liquidation," *e-flux conversations*, June 2018, https://conversations.e-flux.com/t/volksbuhne-staff-on-chris-dercon-we-fear-job -cuts-and-liquidation/3911, archived at https://perma.cc/2FGK-2J96.

23. Peter Boenisch's introductory remarks in Dercon, interview by Boenisch. Sven Lütticken cites a number of German newspapers that worked to delegitimize the occupation without attending to the large outpouring of community support it garnered. For example, he paraphrases an article from the *Süddeutsche Zeitung* that reported on the "suspicious radicals and normal-seeming people harboring a quaint preoccupation with gender issues and radically democratic procedures" and "warned of the occupiers' supposed ties to the Black Bloc and broader *autonome Szene* (autonomy scene)—both readymade bogeymen after the riots at this summer's G20 summit in Hamburg." Lütticken continues: "And so, while of course one cannot speak of the press as a single homogenous voice, it was still curious that some of the most well respected and visible 'liberal' newspapers seemed to go out of their way to present the occupation as the product of a small cabal of professional troublemakers and misguided souls, using imagery that made the occupiers appear to be part ISIS, part genderqueer snowflakes rather than an initiative sprung from a much wider movement." See Lütticken, "Art as Immoral Institution."

24. "Antrag der AfD-Fraktion—Geltendes Recht durchsetzen statt Kumpanei mit Hausbesetzern: Volksbühne umgehend räumen," Abgeordnetenhaus Berlin, Drucksache 18/0557, September 26, 2017, https://www.parlament-berlin.de/ados/18/IIIPlen/vorgang/d18-0557.pdf, archived at https://perma.cc/7GE9-7G2N.

25. Diederichsen, "Weder Wohnung Noch Währung," 160.

26. Steve Bannon quoted in Robert Kuttner, "Steve Bannon, Unrepentant," *American Prospect*, August 16, 2017, https://prospect.org/article/steve-bannon-unrepentant, archived at https://perma.cc/CV86-X6JB.

27. Ashok Kumar, Dalia Gebrial, Adam Elliott-Cooper, and Shruti Iyer, "Marxist Interventions into Contemporary Debates," in "Identity Politics," special issue, *Historical Materialism* 26, no. 2, (2018): 5, http://www.historicalmaterialism.org/articles/marxist-interventions-into-contemporary-debates#_ftn2, archived at https://perma.cc/RG52-CU6R.

28. Kumar et al., "Marxist Interventions into Contemporary Debates," 5.

29. Kumar et al., "Marxist Interventions into Contemporary Debates," 19, 6.

30. The Maxim Gorki Theater was voted "Theater of the Year" in 2014 and 2016 by the magazine *Theater heute*.

31. There has been a surge of new writing in English on postmigrant theater in the German context. See, for example, Olivia Landry, *Theatre of Anger: Radical Transnational Performance in Contemporary Berlin* (Toronto: University of Toronto Press, 2021); Matt Cornish, "Migration: Common and Uncommon Grounds at Berlin's Gorki Theater," in *Postdramatic Theatre and Form*, ed. Boyle, Cornish, and Woolf, 179–95; Azadeh Sharifi, "Multilingualism and Postmigrant Theatre in Germany," *Modern Drama* 61, no. 3 (2018): 328–51; Matt Cornish, "Epilogue: Hybridized History," in *Performing Unification*, 171–90; Katrin Sieg, "Class of 1989: Who Made Good and Who Dropped Out of German History? Postmigrant Documentary Theater in Berlin," in *The German Wall: Fallout in Europe*, ed. Marc Silberman (New York: Palgrave Macmillan, 2011): 165–83; Katrin Sieg, "Black Virgins: Sexuality and the Democratic Body in Europe," *New German Critique* 37, no. 1 (2010): 147–85; and Lizzie Stewart's *Staging New German Realities: Turkish-German Scripts of Postmigration* (Palgrave Macmillan, forthcoming).

32. Lizzie Stewart, "Black Virgins, Close Encounters: Re-Examining the 'Semi-Documentary' in Postmigrant Theatre," in *In der Welt der Proteste und Umwälzungen: Deutschland und die Türkei*, ed. Seyda Ozil, Michael Hofmann, and Yasemin Dayioglu-Yücel (Göttingen: V&R Unipress, 2015), 81–102.

33. Shermin Langhoff quoted in Lizzie Stewart, "Postmigrant Theatre: The Ballhaus Naunynstraße Takes on Sexual Nationalism," *Journal of Aesthetics and Culture* 9, no. 2 (2017): 57.

34. In another gloss on "postmigrant," Olivia Landry explains that the term has "precipitated an exigent cultural and political rethinking about migration and its conceptual misuse. That first-, second-, third-generation Germans and Germans of color are frequently referred to as 'migrants' or 'Menschen mit Migrationshintergrund' [i.e., "people with a migration background"], reduces their status to what Fatima El-Tayeb has referred to as 'a flat, one-dimensional existence in which she or he always has just arrived.' . . . Yet in a more recent publication, El-Tayeb has also expressed misgivings about the label 'postmigrant' for potentially

exonerating the history and persisting racialization of non-ethnic Germans, not dissimilar to the service of the term 'post-racial' in the United states. . . . In any case, the semantic adoption of the prefix 'post' has motivated widespread discussion about the designation of the words 'migrant' and 'migration'—their past, their present, and their future." "Rethinking Migration: The Intervention of Theater," in "Forum: Migration Studies," *The German Quarterly* 90, no. 2 (2017): 223.

35. Olivia Landry, "On the Politics of Love and Trans-Migrant Theater in Germany," *TSQ: Transgender Studies Quarterly* 5, no. 1 (2018): 39.

36. Landry, "On the Politics of Love and Trans-Migrant Theater," 38.

37. For work that explores related questions about performance and shifting discourses around immigration in the French context, see Emine Fişek, *Aesthetic Citizenship: Immigration and Theater in Twenty-First-Century Paris* (Evanston, IL: Northwestern University Press, 2017).

38. Landry, "Rethinking Migration," 224.

39. Christine Dössel, "Was für eine kleinmütige Entscheidung der Berliner Kulturpolitik," *Süddeutsche Zeitung*, June 13, 2019, https://www.sueddeutsche.de/kultur/rene-pollesch-berliner-volksbuehne-klaus-lederer-1.4483583, archived at https://perma.cc/4WM7-AG7A.

40. Dössel, "Was für eine kleinmütige Entscheidung der Berliner Kulturpolitik." Pollesch was born in 1962.

41. Waterfeld, interview by author.

42. Sieg, "Class of 1989," 180.

43. Michael Shane Boyle, "'Love Is Colder than Capital': The Post-Fordist Labor of René Pollesch's Postdramatic Theater" (paper presented at "Away from Drama? Debating Postdramatic Theater," working session, American Society for Theater Research, Dallas, Texas, November 6, 2013), 3.

44. Brandl-Risi, "The New Virtuosity," 19.

45. Pollesch quoted in Brandl-Risi, "The New Virtuosity," 34.

46. Video of the press conference at the Volksbühne on June 12, 2019 can be found at https://www.facebook.com/StaubzuGlitzer/videos/676746606107842 (accessed September 25, 2019).

BIBLIOGRAPHY

Abgeordnetenhaus von Berlin. "Plenarprotokoll 12/51." 12th Wahlperiode, 51st Sitzung. Berlin, September 2, 1993.

———. "Plenarprotokoll 12/52." 12th Wahlperiode, 52nd Sitzung. Berlin, September 16, 1993.

Adorno, Theodor W. *Aesthetic Theory*. Edited by Gretel Adorno and Rolf Tiedemann. Translated and edited by Robert Hullot-Kentor. New York: Bloomsbury Academic, 2013.

———. "Commitment." In *Aesthetics and Politics*, edited by Ronald Taylor, 177–95. New York: Verso, 1977.

———. "Culture and Administration." Translated by Wes Blomster. In *The Culture Industry: Selected Essays on Mass Culture*, edited by J. M. Bernstein, 107–31. New York: Routledge Classics, 2001.

———. "Theses upon Art and Religion Today." *Kenyon Review* 7, no. 4 (1945): 677–82.

Adorno, Theodor W., and Walter Benjamin. *The Complete Correspondence, 1928–1940*. Edited by Henri Lonitz. Translated by Nicholas Walker. Cambridge, MA: Harvard University Press, 1999.

Ahrens, Gerhard, ed. *Bernhard Minetti / Faust*. Berlin: Medusa, 1983.

andcompany&Co. *Der (kommende) Aufstand nach Friedrich Schiller*. Textfassung. GO WEST Festival, Oldenburgisches Staatstheater, premiered February 23, 2012.

Annuss, Evelyn. "On the Future of the Volksbühne—Failure Is an Option." *Texte zur Kunst* 110 (June 2018): 92–105.

———. "Re-negotiating the Future of the Berlin Volksbühne." https://www.change.org/p/re-negotiating-the-future-of-the-berlin-volksbühne. Archived at https://perma.cc/5R5S-ELPG.

Ausschuss für Kulturelle Angelegenheiten—Abgeordnetenhaus von Berlin. "Wort-Protokoll." 6th Sitzung. Berlin, May 27, 1991.

Bader, Ingo, and Albert Scharenberg. "The Sound of Berlin: Subculture and the Global Music Industry." *International Journal of Urban and Regional Research* 34, no. 1 (2010): 76–91.

Balitzki, Jürgen. *Castorf, der Eisenhändler: Theater zwischen Kartoffelsalat und Stahlgewitter*. Berlin: Christoph Links Verlag, 1995.

Balme, Christopher. "Institutional Aesthetics and the Crisis of Leadership." In *The Routledge Companion to Theatre and Politics*, edited by Peter Eckersall and Helena Grehan, 169–72. New York: Routledge, 2019.

———. "Stadt-Theater: Eine Deutsche Heterotopie zwischen Provinz und Metropole." In *Großstadt: Motor der Künste in der Moderne*, edited by Burcu Dogramaci, 61–76. Berlin: Gebr. Mann Verlag, 2010.

Balme, Christopher, and Tony Fisher, eds. *Theatre Institutions in Crisis: European Perspectives*. London: Routledge, 2020.

Bargna, Katya. "Der Weg ist nicht zu Ende, wenn das Ziel explodiert: Frank Castorf and the Survival of Political Theatre in the Postmodern Age." PhD diss., University of Sheffield, Arts and Humanities, 2000.

———. "'Die Sache Castorf': All Quiet on the Eastern Front." MA thesis, University of Liverpool, 1995. AdK, Schriften-DK 152.

Barnett, David. *A History of the Berliner Ensemble*. Cambridge: Cambridge University Press, 2015.

"The Battle over the Volksbühne Director Is a Battle for the Future of Berlin." *e-flux conversations*, May 2017. https://conversations.e-flux.com/t/the-battle-over-the-volksbuhne-director-is-a-battle-for-the-future-of-berlin/6641. Archived at https://perma.cc/XV7W-75JF.

Becker, Peter von, and Michael Merschmeier. "'Ich möchte nicht in den Untergrund!': *Theater heute*-Gespräch mit dem Ostberliner Regisseur Frank Castorf." *Theater heute* 12 (1989): 18–27.

Benjamin, Walter. "The Author as Producer." In *The Work of Art in the Age of Its Technological Reproducibility, and Other Writings on Media*, edited by Michael William Jennings, Brigid Doherty, and Thomas Y. Levin, 79–95. Cambridge, MA: Belknap Press, 2008.

———. "The Work of Art in the Age of Its Technological Reproducibility: Second Version." In *The Work of Art in the Age of Its Technological Reproducibility, and Other Writings on Media*, edited by Michael William Jennings, Brigid Doherty, and Thomas Y. Levin, 19–55. Cambridge, MA: Belknap Press, 2008.

Bennett, Oliver. "Review Essay: The Torn Halves of Cultural Policy Research." *International Journal of Cultural Policy* 10, no. 2 (2004): 237–48.

Bennett, Tony. *The Birth of the Museum: History, Theory, Politics*. New York: Routledge, 1995.

———. *Culture: A Reformer's Science*. Thousand Oaks, CA: SAGE Publications, 1998.

———. "Putting Policy into Cultural Studies." In *Cultural Studies*, edited by Lawrence Grossberg, Cary Nelson, and Paula Treichler, 23–34. New York: Routledge, 1992.

Berg, Simon van den. "Mit dem Rücken zum Publikum?" *Nachtkritik*, June 23, 2011. http://nachtkritik.de/index.php?option=com_content&view=article&id=5815%3Adie-subventionskuerzungen-im-niederlaendischen-kunstbereich. Archived at https://perma.cc/KZ4T-DGYQ.

Berlin Olympia GmbH, ed. *Berlin 2000: Die Stadt für Olympia*. Berlin: Berlin 2000 Olympia GmbH, 1992.

Bernt, Matthias, Britta Grell, and Andrej Holm. "Introduction." In *The Berlin Reader: A Compendium on Urban Change and Activism*, edited by Matthias Bernt, Britta Grell, and Andrej Holm, 11–21. Bielefeld: Transcript Verlag, 2013.

Beutelschmidt, Thomas, and Julia M. Novak, eds. *Ein Palast und seine Republik: Ort–Architektur–Programm*. Berlin: Bauwesen, 2001.

Birkholz, Tim. *"Schloss mit der Debatte!"?: Die Zwischennutzungen im Palast der Republik im Kontext der Schlossplatzdebatte*. Berlin: Technische Universität Berlin, Inst. für Stadt- und Regionalplanung, 2008.

Bishop, Claire. "Palace in Plunderland." *ArtForum*. September 2018. https://www.artforum.com/print/201807/palace-in-plunderland-76327. Archived at https://perma.cc/34BJ-WUHV.

Blau, Herbert. *Take Up the Bodies: Theater at the Vanishing Point*. Urbana: University of Illinois Press, 1982.

Boenisch, Peter M. *Directing Scenes and Senses: The Thinking of Regie*. Manchester: Manchester University Press, 2015.

———. "Encountering a 'Theatre of (Inter-)Singularity': Transformations and Rejections of Shifting Institutional Dramaturgies in Contemporary German Theatre." In *Shifting Dramaturgies: Composing Experiences of Interweaving Performance Cultures*, edited by Erika Fischer-Lichte, Christel Weiler, and Torsten Jost. Abingdon: Routledge, forthcoming.

———. "(Re)thinking the Meaning of the European Theatre Institution: Some Lessons from the Recent Crisis at Volksbühne Berlin, Kammerspiele Munich and Elsewhere." Paper presented at the "Decentering the Vision(s) of Europe: The Emergence of New Forms" conference, European Association for the Study of Theater and Performance, Théâtre de la Cité, Paris, October 25–27, 2018.

———, ed., *The Schaubühne Berlin under Thomas Ostermeier: Reinventing Realism*. London: Bloomsbury Methuen, 2020.

Boenisch, Peter M., and Thomas Ostermeier. *The Theatre of Thomas Ostermeier*. London: Routledge, 2016.

Bogad, L. M. *Tactical Performance: The Theory and Practice of Serious Play*. New York: Routledge, 2016.

Boltanski, Luc, and Eve Chiapello. *The New Spirit of Capitalism*. Translated by Gregory Elliott. New York: Verso, 2005.

Bonin-Rodriguez, Paul. *Performing Policy: How Contemporary Politics and Cultural Programs Redefined U.S. Artists for the Twenty-First Century*. Houndmills, Basingstoke, UK: Palgrave Macmillan, 2015.

Bourriaud, Nicolas. *Relational Aesthetics*. Translated by Simon Pleasance and Fronza Woods. Dijon: Les Presses du réel, 2002.

Boyle, Michael Shane. "The Ambivalence of Resistance: West German Antiauthoritarian Performance after the Age of Affluence." PhD diss., Performance Studies, University of California, Berkeley, 2012.

———. "Brecht's Gale: Innovation and Postdramatic Theatre." *Performance Research* 21, no. 3 (2016): 16–26.

———. "'Love Is Colder than Capital': The Post-Fordist Labor of René Pollesch's Postdramatic Theater." Paper presented at "Away from Drama? Debating Postdramatic Theater," working session, American Society for Theater Research, Dallas, Texas, November 6, 2013.

Boyle, Michael Shane, Matt Cornish, and Brandon Woolf, eds., *Postdramatic Theatre and Form*. London: Bloomsbury Methuen, 2019.

Boym, Svetlana. *The Future of Nostalgia*. New York: Basic Books, 2001.

Bradley, Laura. *Brecht and Political Theatre: "The Mother" on Stage*. Oxford: Oxford University Press, 2006.

Bradley, Laura, and Karen Leeder, eds. *Brecht and the GDR: Politics, Culture, Posterity*. Rochester, NY: Camden House, 2011.

Brandl-Risi, Bettina. "The New Virtuosity: Outperforming and Imperfection on the German Stage." *Theater* 37, no. 1 (2007): 9–37.

Brecht, Bertolt. *The Baden-Baden Lesson on Consent.* Translated by Geoffrey Skelton. In *Collected Plays: Three*, edited by John Willett, 21–43. London: Bloomsbury Methuen Drama, 1997.

———. "Dialectical Dramatic Writing." In *Brecht on Theatre*, 3rd ed., edited by Marc Silberman, Steve Giles, and Tom Kuhn, 51–60. London: Bloomsbury, 2014.

———. "Notes on the Opera *Rise and Fall of the City of Mahagonny*." In *Brecht on Theatre*, 3rd ed., edited by Marc Silberman, Steve Giles, and Tom Kuhn, 61–71. London: Bloomsbury, 2014.

———. "The Radio as a Communications Apparatus." In *Brecht on Film and Radio*, edited and translated by Marc Silberman, 41–48. London: Methuen, 2000.

———. "The *Threepenny* Lawsuit." In *Brecht on Film and Radio*, edited and translated by Marc Silberman, 147–99. London: Methuen, 2000.

———. *Werke: Grosse Kommentierte Berliner und Frankfurter Ausgabe.* 30 vols. Edited by Werner Hecht, Jan Knopf, Werner Mittenzwei, and Klaus-Detlef Müller. Berlin: Aufbau-Verlag and Frankfurt: Suhrkamp Verlag, 1988–2000.

Brecht, Bertolt, Paul Hindemith, and Frank Castorf. *Lehrstück.* Regiebuch—Fassung Hinterbühne. Volksbühne am Rosa-Luxemburg-Platz, Berlin, premiered October 5, 2010.

Brecht, Bertolt, Kurt Weill, and Dorothy Lane [pseud. Elisabeth Hauptmann]. *Happy End: A Melodrama with Songs.* Translated by Michael Feingold. London: Methuen, 1982.

Bredekamp, Horst, and Peter-Klaus Schuster, eds. *Das Humboldt-Forum: Die Wiedergewinnung der Idee.* Berlin: Wagenbach, 2016.

Brockmann, Stephen. *Literature and German Reunification.* Cambridge: Cambridge University Press, 1999.

Brown, Carol. "Making Space, Speaking Spaces." In *The Routledge Dance Studies Reader*, edited by Alexandra Carter and Janet O'Shea, 58–72. 2nd ed. New York: Routledge, 2010.

Butler, Judith. "Bodily Vulnerability, Coalitions, and Street Politics." In *Differences in Common: Gender, Vulnerability and Community*, edited by Joana Sabadell-Nieto and Marta Segarra, 99–119. New York: Rodopi Publishing, 2014.

———. *Notes toward a Performative Theory of Assembly.* Cambridge, MA: Harvard University Press, 2015.

———. *The Psychic Life of Power: Theories in Subjection.* Stanford, CA: Stanford University Press, 1997.

Butler, Judith, and Shannon Jackson, "Keynote Address." Lecture-performance presented at the "How Are We Performing Today?" symposium at the Museum of Modern Art, New York, November 16, 2012.

Carlson, Marvin. "Frank Castorf and the Volksbühne: Berlin's Theatre of Deconstruction." In *Contemporary European Theatre Directors*, edited by Maria M. Delgado and Dan Rebellato, 103–23. London: Routledge, 2010.

———. *The Haunted Stage: The Theatre as Memory Machine.* Ann Arbor: University of Michigan Press, 2002.

———. *Theatre Is More Beautiful Than War: German Stage Directing in the Late Twentieth Century.* Iowa City: University of Iowa Press, 2009.

Carr, Godfrey, and Georgina Paul. "Unification and Its Aftermath: The Challenge of History." In *German Cultural Studies: An Introduction*, edited by Rob Burns, 325–48. New York: Oxford University Press, 1995.

Castorf, Frank. "Ich komme aus dem Fussball, dem Rock 'n' Roll, dem rausgebrüllten Unmut, aus der Neurose." *Theater Heute Jahrbuch* (1993): 97–98.

———. "Klassiker: Frank Castorf in São Paulo am Tag der Wahl des Deutschen Bundestags." In *Prärie: Ein Benutzerhandbuch* (program for *Im Dickicht der Städte* by Bertolt Brecht), edited by Jutta Wangemann, 12–39. Volksbühne am Rosa-Luxemburg-Platz, Berlin, February 2006.

Colomb, Claire. "Requiem for a Lost *Palast*: 'Revanchist Urban Planning' and 'Burdened Landscapes' of the German Democratic Republic in the New Berlin." *Planning Perspectives* 22, no. 3 (2007): 283–323.

———. *Staging the New Berlin: Place Marketing and the Politics of Urban Reinvention Post-1989*. New York: Routledge, 2012.

Cornish, Matt, ed. *"Everything" and Other Performance Texts from Germany*. London: Seagull Books, 2019.

———. *Performing Unification: History and Nation in German Theater after 1989*. Ann Arbor: University of Michigan Press, 2017.

Cunningham, Stuart. *Framing Culture: Criticism and Policy in Australia*. Sydney: Allen & Unwin, 1992.

"Dann gibt es Krieg: Der Regisseur und Intendant Frank Castorf über Die Berliner Theater-Krise." *Der Spiegel*, June 28, 1993.

Darby, Graham, ed. *The Origins and Development of the Dutch Revolt*. New York: Routledge, 2001.

Dean, Jodi. *The Communist Horizon*. New York: Verso, 2012.

Delanty, Gerard, and Paul R. Jones. "European Identity and Architecture." *European Journal of Social Theory* 5, no. 4 (2002): 453–66.

Dercon, Chris. Interview by Peter Boenisch. "Systemic Crisis in European Theatre" conference, Goethe Institute, London, April 27, 2018. https://www.youtube.com/watch?v=k-bkWQfKYJE.

Derrida, Jacques. "Point de folie—maintenant l'architecture." Translated by Kate Linker. In *Rethinking Architecture: A Reader in Cultural Theory*, edited by Neil Leach, 324–36. New York: Routledge, 1997.

———. "Response to Daniel Libeskind." *Research in Phenomenology* 22 (1992): 88–94.

———. *Specters of Marx: The State of the Debt, the Work of Mourning, and the New International*. Translated by Peggy Kamuf. New York: Routledge, 1994.

———. "Why Peter Eisenman Writes Such Good Books." In *Rethinking Architecture: A Reader in Cultural Theory*, edited by Neil Leach, 336–47. New York: Routledge, 1997.

Derrida, Jacques, and Peter Eisenman. *Chora L Works: Jacques Derrida and Peter Eisenman*. Edited by Jeffrey Kipnis and Thomas Leeser. New York: Monacelli Press, 1997.

Derrida, Jacques, Kurt Forster, and Wim Wenders. "The Berlin City Forum." *Architectural Design* 62, nos. 11–12 (1992): 46–53.

Detje, Robin. *Castorf: Provokation aus Prinzip*. Berlin: Henschel, 2002.

Deuflhard, Amelie, and Sophie Krempl-Klieeisen, eds. *Volkspalast: Zwischen Aktivismus und Kunst*. Berlin: Theater der Zeit, 2006.

Deutscher Bühnenverein, *Theaterstatistik 1989/90, 25. Heft.* Cologne: Deutscher Bühnenverein Bundesverband Deutscher Theater, 1990.

———. *Theaterstatistik 2017/2018: Die wichtigsten Wirtschaftsdaten der Theater, Orchester und Festspiele, 53. Auflage.* Cologne: Deutscher Bühnenverein Bundesverband dt. Theater, 2019.

Deutscher Bundestag. "Beschlussempfehlung und Bericht des Ausschusses für Kultur und Medien." Drucksache 14/9660. Berlin, July 2, 2002.

Dieckmann, Friedrich. *Vom Schloss der Könige zum Forum der Republik: Zum Problem der architektonischen Wiederaufführung.* Berlin: Theater der Zeit, 2015.

Diederichsen, Diedrich. "Weder Wohnung Noch Währung." *Texte zur Kunst* 105 (2017): 158–63.

Diepgen, Eberhard. "Halbjahresbilanz des Berliner Senats." Press conference. June 28, 1993. AdK, TiW 1043.

Doggett, Peter. *There's a Riot Going On: Revolutionaries, Rock Stars and the Rise and Fall of '60s Counter-Culture.* Edinburgh: Canongate, 2009.

Draxler, Helmut, Alexander Karschnia, Hans-Thies Lehmann, and Geert Lovink. "Phantasma und Politik #1." Hebbel am Ufer, Berlin, February 27, 2013.

Eisler, Hanns. "Bertolt Brecht and Music." In *Brecht, As They Knew Him*, edited by Hubert Witt, translated by John Peet, 93–95. New York: International Publishers, 1974.

Ellrich, Hartmut. *Das Berliner Schloss Geschichte und Wiederaufbau.* Petersberg: Imhof, 2008.

Elswit, Kate. "Berlin . . . Your Dance Partner Is Death." *TDR: The Drama Review* 53, no. 1 (2009): 73–92.

Esslin, Martin. *Brecht, a Choice of Evils: A Critical Study of the Man, His Work, and His Opinions.* 4th rev. ed. London: Methuen, 1984.

Everding, August. "Nein, So geht das nicht!" Lecture presented at "Grossveranstaltung—Solidarität der deutschen Theater mit den Staatlichen Schauspielbühnen," Schiller Theater, Berlin, June 27, 1993. AdK, TiW 1230.

Fischer-Lichte, Erika. *The Transformative Power of Performance: A New Aesthetics.* Translated by Saskya Iris Jain. New York: Routledge, 2008.

———. "Zur Einleitung." In *Transformationen: Theater der neunziger Jahre*, edited by Erika Fischer-Lichte, Doris Kolesch, and Christel Weiler, 7–11. Berlin: Theater der Zeit, 1999.

Fişek, Emine. *Aesthetic Citizenship: Immigration and Theater in Twenty-First-Century Paris.* Evanston, IL: Northwestern University Press, 2017.

Flierl, Thomas, and Hermann Parzinger, eds. *Humboldt-Forum Berlin—Das Projekt / The Project.* Berlin: Theater der Zeit, 2009.

Foellmer, Susanne. *Valeska Gert: Fragmente einer Avantgardistin in Tanz und Schauspiel der 1920er Jahre.* Bielefeld: Transcript Verlag, 2006.

Foerster-Baldenius, Benjamin. Interview by author. Berlin, February 16, 2012.

Förderverein Berliner Schloss. *Das Schloss? Eine Ausstellung über die Mitte Berlins.* Edited by Kristin Feireiss and Wilhelm von Boddien. Translated by Annette Wiethüchter. Berlin: Ernst & Sohn, 1993.

Fukuyama, Francis. *The End of History and the Last Man.* New York: Free Press, 1992.

Fülle, Henning. *Freies Theater: Die Modernisierung der deutschen Theaterlandschaft (1960–2010).* Berlin: Theater der Zeit, 2016.

———. "Freies Theater—Worüber reden wir eigentlich?" *Kulturpolitische Mitteilungen* 147, no. 4 (2014): 27–30.

———. "A Theatre for Postmodernity in Western European Theatrescapes." In *Independent Theatre in Contemporary Europe: Structures—Aesthetics—Cultural Policy*, edited by Manfred Brauneck and ITI Germany, 275–320. Bielefeld: Transcript Verlag, 2017.

Gert, Valeska. *Ich bin eine Hexe: Kaleidoskop meines Lebens*. Munich: Schneekluth, 1968.

Giles, Steve. *Bertolt Brecht and Critical Theory: Marxism, Modernity and the "Threepenny" Lawsuit*. Bern: P. Lang, 1997.

Göbel, Hanna Katharina. *The Re-Use of Urban Ruins: Atmospheric Inquiries of the City*. New York: Routledge, 2015.

Goethe-Institut. "Frank Castorf." www.goethe.de/kue/the/reg/reg/ag/cas/enindex.htm. Archived at https://perma.cc/3EFP-A2BV.

Goethe, Johann Wolfgang von. *Faust, Part 1*. Translated by A. S. Kline. https://www.poetryintranslation.com/PITBR/German/FaustIProl.php#Prelude_On_Stage. Archived at https://perma.cc/P2BG-GWZA.

Goethe, Johann Wolfgang von, and Frank Castorf. *Faust*. Regiebuch. Volksbühne am Rosa-Luxemburg-Platz, Berlin, premiered March 3, 2017. AdK, VB 3589.

Gough, Maria. "Paris, Capital of the Soviet Avant-Garde." *October* 101 (2002): 53–83.

Harvie, Jen. *Fair Play: Art, Performance and Neoliberalism*. Houndmills, Basingstoke, UK: Palgrave Macmillan, 2013.

Haselbach, Dieter, Stephan Opitz, Armin Klein, and Pius Knüsel. *Der Kulturinfarkt: Von Allem zu viel und überall das Gleiche*. Munich: Albrecht Knaus Verlag, 2012.

Haubrich, Rainer, ed. *Das Neue Berliner Schloss: Von der Hohenzollernresidenz zum Humboldt-Forum*. Berlin: Nicolai, 2012.

Heller, Mareike, ed. *No Humboldt 21! Dekoloniale Einwände gegen das Humboldt-Forum*. Berlin: AfricAvenir International, 2017.

Hennet, Anna-Inés. *Die Berliner Schlossplatzdebatte im Spiegel der Presse*. Berlin: Braun, 2005.

Hindemith, Paul. "Gemeinschaft für Musik." In *Aufsätze, Vorträge, Reden*, edited by Giselher Schubert, 8. Zürich: Atlantis-Musikbuch-Verlag, 1994.

———. "Introduction to Hindemith's Piano Score." In *Collected Plays: Three*, by Bertolt Brecht, edited by John Willett, 326–28. London: Bloomsbury Methuen Drama, 1997.

Hinton, Stephen. *The Idea of Gebrauchsmusik: A Study of Musical Aesthetics in the Weimar Republic (1919–1933) with Particular Reference to the Works of Paul Hindemith*. New York: Garland, 1989.

———. *Weill's Musical Theater: Stages of Reform*. Berkeley: University of California Press, 2012.

Holfelder, Moritz. *Palast der Republik: Aufstieg und Fall eines symbolischen Gebäudes*. Berlin: Christoph Links Verlag, 2008.

Holm, Andrej. "Berlin's Gentrification Mainstream." In *The Berlin Reader: A Compendium on Urban Change and Activism*, edited by Matthias Bernt, Britta Grell, and Andrej Holm, 173–87. Bielefeld: Transcript Verlag, 2013.

Holm, Andrej, and Armin Kuhn. "Squatting and Urban Renewal: The Interaction of Squatter Movements and Strategies of Urban Restructuring in Berlin." *International Journal of Urban and Regional Research* 35, no. 3 (2011): 644–58.

Honegger, Gitta. "Gossip, Ghosts, and Memory: *Mother Courage* and the Forging of the Berliner Ensemble." *TDR: The Drama Review* 52, no. 4 (2008): 98–117.

Hughes, David Ashley. "Notes on the German Theatre Crisis." *TDR: The Drama Review* 51, no. 4 (2007): 133–55.

Huyssen, Andreas. *Present Pasts: Urban Palimpsests and the Politics of Memory*. Stanford, CA: Stanford University Press, 2003.

Invisible Committee. *The Coming Insurrection*. Los Angeles: Semiotext(e), 2009.

Irmer, Thomas, and Harald Müller, eds. *Zehn Jahre Volksbühne: Intendanz Frank Castorf*. Berlin: Theater der Zeit, 2003.

Jackson, Shannon. "Just-in-Time: Performance and the Aesthetics of Precarity." *TDR: The Drama Review* 56, no. 4 (2012): 10–31.

———. *Social Works: Performing Art, Supporting Publics*. New York: Routledge, 2011.

———. "*Touchable Stories* and the Performance of Infrastructural Memory." In *Remembering: Oral History Performance*, edited by Della Pollock, 45–66. New York: Palgrave Macmillan, 2005.

———. "Working Publics." *Performance Research* 16, no. 2 (2011): 8–13.

Jameson, Fredric. "On 'Cultural Studies.'" *Social Text*, no. 34 (1993): 17–52.

Jarosinski, Eric. "Architectural Symbolism and the Rhetoric of Transparency: A Berlin Ghost Story." *Journal of Urban History* 29, no. 1 (2002): 62–77.

Jennings, Andrew. *The New Lords of the Rings: Olympic Corruption and How to Buy Gold Medals*. London: Pocket Books, 1996.

Johnson, Philip, and Mark Wigley. *Deconstructivist Architecture*. Exhibition catalog. New York: Museum of Modern Art, 1988.

Joseph, Miranda. *Against the Romance of Community*. Minneapolis: University of Minnesota Press, 2002.

Kaiser, Sebastian, and Carl Hegemann. "Faust: The Masculine Must Pass." Translated by Bettina Seifried. https://volksbuehne.adk.de/praxis/en/faust/index.html. Archived at https://perma.cc/8JPJ-Q4M5.

Karschnia, Alexander. "Cultural Counterrevolution Gaining Ground." November 2011. http://www.nettime.org/Lists-Archives/nettime-l-1111/msg00125.html. Archived at https://perma.cc/7LAB-D5BU.

———. "Für ein freies und d.h. freies freies Theater!" October 30, 2013. http://www.andco.de/media/fuer-ein-freies-und-d-h-freies-freies-theater. Archived at https://perma.cc/CV46-DNFK.

———. Interview by author. Berlin, October 11, 2013.

———. "(Post-)Performerism as a Way of Life oder das Theater der Produktion des Lebens." In *Politisch Theater machen: Neue Artikulationsformen des Politischen in den darstellenden Künsten*, edited by Jan Deck and Angelika Sieburg, 85–106. Bielefeld: Transcript Verlag, 2011.

Karschnia, Alexander, Nicola Nord, and Joachim Robbrecht&Co. "Occupy History." In program for *Der (kommende) Aufstand nach Friedrich Schiller*, Hebbel am Ufer, Berlin, February 2013.

Kelleher, Joe. *Theatre and Politics*. New York: Palgrave Macmillan, 2009.

Keller, Anthony. "The Tomato Revolution." *Journal of Arts Management and Law* 13, no. 1 (1983): 170–76.

Klapsch, Thorsten. *Palast der Republik*. Mannheim: Ed. Panorama, 2010.

Klaus, Völker, ed. *Beckett in Berlin: Zum 80. Geburtstag*. Berlin: Edition Hentrich, Frölich & Kaufmann, 1986.

Knebusch, Hans-Christoph. "Schillers Tod: Ein bürgerliches Trauerspiel?" 3sat. September 4, 1993. Video recording. AdK, TiW 1034, AVM 33.8254.

Knöss-Grillitsch, Elke. Interview by author. Berlin, February 24, 2012.

Knowles, Ric. *Performing the Intercultural City*. Ann Arbor: University of Michigan Press, 2017.

Koalition der Freien Szene. "Arbeitstitel: 'Bye Bye Berlin?'" https://www.koalition -der-freien-szene-berlin.de/2013/05/25/arbeitstitel-bye-bye-berlin. Archived at https://perma.cc/E76H-9X4F.

———. "Das erste Jahr Rot-Rot-Grün—eine ernüchternde Bilanz für die Freie Szene." December 21, 2017. http://www.koalition-der-freien-szene-berlin.de /2017/12/21/das-erste-jahr-rot-rot-gruen-eine-ernuechternde-bilanz-fuer-die -freie-szene. Archived at https://perma.cc/XDS3-7CW9.

———. "Freie Szene stärken! Geist ist noch flüchtiger als Kapital—haltet ihn fest." August 19, 2013. http://www.koalition-der-freien-szene-berlin.de/2013 /08/19/freie-szene-staerken-geist-ist-noch-fluechtiger-als-kapital-haltet-ihn -fest. Archived at https://perma.cc/VUB2-PSVQ.

———. "Hintergrund zum Berliner Kulturhaushalt." May 27, 2013. Indeed, Butler and Jackson's reworking. Archived at https://perma.cc/53GM-ZQU5.

———. "Über die Koalition der freien Szene aller Künste." August 21, 2017. http:// www.koalition-der-freien-szene-berlin.de/2017/08/21/ueber-die-koalition-der -freien-szene-aller-kuenste. Archived at https://perma.cc/2H4K-KG5R.

———. "Welcome to the Independent Art Coalition." May 1, 2013. http://www .koalition-der-freien-szene-berlin.de/2013/05/01/independent-art-coalition. Archived at https://perma.cc/M5X3-DWED.

Kolarevic, Branko, and Ali M. Malkawi. *Performative Architecture: Beyond Instrumentality*. New York: Spon Press, 2005.

Koshar, Rudy. *From Monuments to Traces: Artifacts of German Memory, 1870– 1990*. Berkeley: University of California Press, 2000.

Krabiel, Klaus-Dieter. *Brechts Lehrstücke: Entstehung und Entwicklung eines Spieltyps*. Stuttgart: J. B. Metzler, 1993.

———. "Spieltypus Lehrstück: Zum aktuellen Stand der Diskussion." In *Bertolt Brecht I*, edited by Heinz Ludwig Arnold and Jan Knopf, 41–52. Munich: Text+Kritik, 2006.

Krätke, Stefan. "City of Talents? Berlin's Regional Economy, Socio-Spatial Fabric and 'Worst Practice' Urban Governance." *International Journal of Urban and Regional Research* 28, no. 3 (2004): 511–29.

Krempl-Klieeisen, Sophie, ed. Volkspalast. Untitled program. August–September 2004.

Kuftinec, Sonja. "[Walking through a] Ghost Town: Cultural Hauntologie in Mostar, Bosnia-Herzegovina or Mostar—a Performance Review." *Text and Performance Quarterly* 18, no. 2 (1998): 81–95.

Kuhrmann, Anke. *Der Palast der Republik: Geschichte und Bedeutung des Ost-Berliner Parlaments- und Kulturhauses.* Petersberg: Imhof, 2006.

Kumar, Ashok, Dalia Gebrial, Adam Elliott-Cooper, and Shruti Iyer. "Marxist Interventions into Contemporary Debates." In "Identity Politics," special issue, *Historical Materialism* 26, no. 2, (2018): 3–20.

Ladd, Brian. *The Ghosts of Berlin: Confronting German History in the Urban Landscape.* Chicago: University of Chicago Press, 1997.

Landry, Olivia. "On the Politics of Love and Trans-Migrant Theater in Germany." *TSQ: Transgender Studies Quarterly* 5, no. 1 (2018): 30–48.

———. "Rethinking Migration: The Intervention of Theater." In "Forum: Migration Studies," *German Quarterly* 90, no. 2 (2017): 222–24.

———. *Theatre of Anger: Radical Transnational Performance in Contemporary Berlin.* Toronto: University of Toronto Press, 2021.

Laudenbach, Peter. "Die freie Szene in Berlin ist ein Wirtschaftsfaktor." *tip Berlin,* August 14, 2013.

———. "Die freie Szene Berlins will endlich bessere Finanzierung." *tip Berlin,* August 29, 2013.

Leeder, Karen, ed. "From Stasiland to Ostalgie: The GDR Twenty Years After." Special issue, *Oxford German Studies* 38, no. 3 (2009).

Lehmann, Andreas. "Hindemiths *Lehrstück.*" *Hindemith Jahrbuch / Annales Hindemith* 11 (1982): 36–76.

Lehmann, Hans-Thies. "Ästhetik des Aufstands? Grenzgänge zwischen Politik und Kunst in den neuen sozialen Bewegungen." Lecture presented at Foreign Affairs Festival, Berliner Festspiele, Berlin, Germany, October 16, 2012.

———. *Postdramatic Theatre.* Translated by Karen Jürs-Munby. New York: Routledge, 2006.

———. *Postdramatisches Theater.* Frankfurt am Main: Verlag der Autoren, 1999.

Lehmann, Hans-Thies, Karen Jürs-Munby, and Elinor Fuchs. "Lost in Translation?" *TDR: The Drama Review* 52, no. 4 (2008): 13–20.

Lehmann, Hans-Thies, and Helmut Lethen. "Ein Vorschlag zur Güte. Zu doppelten Polarität der Lehrstücke." In *Auf Anregung Bertolt Brechts: Lehrstücke mit Schülern, Arbeitern, Theaterleuten,* edited by Reiner Steinweg, 302–18. Frankfurt: Suhrkamp, 1978.

Lewis, Justin, and Toby Miller, eds. *Critical Cultural Policy Studies: A Reader.* Oxford: Wiley-Blackwell, 2003.

Libeskind, Daniel. "Between the Lines: The Jewish Museum, Berlin." *Research in Phenomenology* 22 (1992): 82–87.

———. "Deconstructing the Call to Order." In *Berlin,* edited by Alan Balfour, 35–37. London: Academy Editions, 1995.

———. "Trauma." In *Image and Remembrance: Representation and the Holocaust,* edited by Shelley Hornstein and Florence Jacobowitz, 43–58. Bloomington: Indiana University Press, 2003.

Linzer, Martin. "Entrée." *Theater der Zeit* (August–September 1993): 1.

———. "Thoughts on a Walking Corpse: The Berliner Ensemble Five Years after the 'Wende.'" *Brecht Yearbook* 21 (1996): 289–300.

Löfgren, Isabel. "Collateral Damage: Cultural Politics in the Age of Cultural Depression." *Paletten Art Journal* 284–85 (September 2011): n.p.

Lovink, Geert, and Ned Rossiter. "Dawn of the Organised Networks." *Fibre-culture Journal* 5 (2005). http://journal.fibreculture.org/issue5/lovink_rossiter.html. Archived at https://perma.cc/KB43-EAU9.

———. "Urgent Aphorisms: Notes on Organized Networks for the Connected Multitudes." In *Managing Media Work*, edited by Mark Deuze, 279–90. Thousand Oaks, CA: SAGE, 2011.

Lütticken, Sven. "Art as Immoral Institution." *Texte zur Kunst*, October 3, 2017. https://www.textezurkunst.de/articles/sven-lutticken-volksbuhne-occupation/?highlight=art%20as%20immoral%20institution. Archived at https://perma.cc/Z25Y-WAY2.

Lux, Joachim. "Wie dem Menschen die Haare wachsen: Ein Gespräch mit Frank Castorf." In program for *Hamlet* by William Shakespeare. Schauspiel Köln, Cologne, March 1989.

Lyon, James K. "Brecht in Postwar Germany: Dissident Conformist, Cultural Icon, Literary Dictator." In *Brecht Unbound*, edited by James K. Lyon and Hans-Peter Breuer, 76–88. London: Associated University Presses, 1995.

Marx, Karl. *The Eighteenth Brumaire of Louis Bonaparte*. Marx/Engels Internet Archive, 1999. https://www.marxists.org/archive/marx/works/1852/18th-brumaire/ch01.htm. Archived at https://perma.cc/6GPS-XL8U.

Mathews, Stanley. *From Agit-Prop to Free Space: The Architecture of Cedric Price*. London: Black Dog Publishing, 2007.

Mattis, Léon de. "What Is Communisation?" *SIC—International Journal for Communisation* 1 (2011): 11–28.

Matzke, Annemarie. "Jenseits des freien Theaters." *Nachtkritik*, November 21, 2012. http://nachtkritik.de/index.php?view=article&id=7472%3Ahildesheimer-thesen-v-n. Archived at https://perma.cc/4R66-VY2N.

Matzke, Annemarie, Christel Weiler, and Isa Wortelkamp, eds. *Das Buch von der angewandten Theaterwissenschaft*. Berlin: Alexander Verlag, 2012.

McGuigan, Jim. *Rethinking Cultural Policy*. Maidenhead, UK: Open University Press, 2004.

McKinnie, Michael. *City Stages: Theatre and Urban Space in a Global City*. Toronto: University of Toronto Press, 2007.

McRobbie, Angela. "All the World's a Stage, Screen or Magazine: When Culture Is the Logic of Late Capitalism." *Media, Culture and Society* 18 (1996): 335–42.

Merschmeier, Michael. "Jetzt wird es ernst. Das kann ja heiter werden: Ein Theater heute-Gespräch." *Theater Heute Jahrbuch* (1993): 52–60.

Merx, Sigrid. "The Argument for Autonomy: The Missing Link in the Discursive Arena." *Teorija koja hoda (Walking Theory)* 20 (2012): 22–30.

Mickley, Ellen, Annalie Schoen, and Lutz Jürgens, eds. *Internationale Expertenkommission—Historische Mitte Berlin: Abschlussbericht*. Berlin: Bundesministerium für Verkehr, Bau- und Wohnungswesen—Senatsverwaltung für Stadtentwicklung, 2002.

Miller, Hillary. *Drop Dead: Performance in Crisis, 1970s New York*. Evanston, IL: Northwestern University Press, 2016.

Miller, Toby. "Leavis to Beaver: Culture with Power, Culture as Policy." In *Technologies of Truth: Cultural Citizenship and the Popular Media*, 64–98. Minneapolis: University of Minnesota Press, 1998.

Miller, Toby, and George Yúdice. *Cultural Policy.* Thousand Oaks, CA: SAGE Publications, 2002.

Misselwitz, Philipp, Hans Ulrich Obrist, and Philipp Oswalt, eds. *Fun Palace 200x—Der Berliner Schlossplatz: Abriss, Neubau oder Grüne Wiese?* Berlin: Martin Schmitz Verlag, 2005.

Mitarbeiter der Staatlichen Schauspielbühnen Berlin, Die. "Wir spielen weiter— Wir werden dieses Theater nicht verlassen." Resolution. June 23, 1993. AdK, TiW 1227.

"Mit Frank Castorf sprach Frank Raddatz." *Theater der Zeit* (August–September 1993): 19–24.

Mueller, Roswitha. *Bertolt Brecht and the Theory of Media.* Lincoln: University of Nebraska Press, 1989.

Müller-Schöll, Nikolaus. "Brechts 'Sterbelehre.'" In *Ende, Grenze, Schluss? Brecht und der Tod,* edited by Stephen Brockmann, Mathias Mayer, and Jürgen Hillesheim, 23–35. Würzburg: Königshausen & Neumann, 2008.

Mumford, Meg. "Brecht Studies Stanislavski: Just a Tactical Move?" *New Theatre Quarterly* 11, no. 43 (1995): 241–58.

Nagel, Ivan. *Streitschriften: Politik, Kulturpolitik, Theaterpolitik 1957–2001.* Berlin: Siedler, 2001.

Nagel, Ivan, Friedrich Dieckmann, Michael Merschmeier, and Henning Rischbieter. "Überlegungen zur Situation der Berliner Theater." Berlin, April 6, 1991. AdK, TiW 1755.

Nägele, Rainer. "Brecht's Theater of Cruelty." In *Reading after Freud: Essays on Goethe, Hölderlin, Habermas, Nietzsche, Brecht, Celan, and Freud,* 111–34. New York: Columbia University Press, 1987.

Neilson, Brett, and Ned Rossiter. "From Precarity to Precariousness and Back Again: Labour, Life and Unstable Networks." *Fibreculture Journal* 5 (2005). http://five.fibreculturejournal.org/fcj-022-from-precarity-to-precariousness -and-back-again-labour-life-and-unstable-networks. Archived at https://perma .cc/BJM8-3KHM.

———. "Precarity as a Political Concept, or, Fordism as Exception." *Theory, Culture and Society* 25, nos. 7–8 (2008): 51–72.

———. "Towards a Political Anthropology of New Institutional Forms." *Ephemera: Theory and Politics in Organization* 6, no. 4 (2006): 393–410.

Ng, Julia. "The Museum, the Street, and the Virtual Landscape of Berlin." In *Urban Space and Cityscapes: Perspectives from Modern and Contemporary Culture,* edited by Christoph Lindner, 137–54. New York: Routledge, 2006.

Nierop, Henk van. "A Beggars' Banquet: The Compromise of the Nobility and the Politics of Inversion." *European History Quarterly* 21, no. 4 (1991): 419–43.

No Humboldt 21! "Stop the Planned Construction of the Humboldt Forum in the Berlin Palace!" http://www.no-humboldt21.de/resolution/english. Archived at https://perma.cc/C3FR-5TGB.

Novy, Johannes. "'Berlin Does Not Love You': Notes on Berlin's 'Tourism Controversy' and Its Discontents." In *The Berlin Reader: A Compendium on Urban Change and Activism,* edited by Matthias Bernt, Britta Grell, and Andrej Holm, 223–37. Bielefeld: Transcript Verlag, 2013.

Noys, Benjamin. "The Aesthetics of Communization." Lecture presented at Xero, Kline & Coma Gallery, London, May 11, 2013.

————, ed. *Communization and Its Discontents: Contestation, Critique, and Contemporary Struggles*. New York: Autonomedia, 2012.

Nyong'o, Tavia. "Situating Precarity between the Body and the Commons." *Women and Performance: A Journal of Feminist Theory* 23, no. 2 (2013): 157–61.

O'Regan, Tom. "(Mis)Taking Policy: Notes on the Cultural Policy Debate." In *Australian Cultural Studies: A Reader*, edited by John Frow and Meaghan Morris, 192–206. Chicago: University of Illinois Press, 1993.

Osborne, Peter. "'Whoever Speaks of Culture Speaks of Administration as Well.' " *Cultural Studies* 20, no. 1 (2006): 33–47.

Ostermeier, Thomas. "Die Zukunft des Theaters." In "Zukunft der Literatur," special issue, *Text+Kritik Sonderband* 5, no. 13 (2013): 42–50.

Oswalt, Philipp, Klaus Overmeyer, and Philipp Misselwitz, eds. *Urban Catalyst: The Power of Temporary Use*. Berlin: DOM Publishers, 2014.

Overmeyer, Klaus. *Urban Pioneers: Temporary Use and Urban Development in Berlin*. Berlin: Jovis, 2007.

Paul, Arno, and Martha Humphreys. "The West German Theatre Miracle: A Structural Analysis." *TDR: The Drama Review* 24, no. 1 (1980): 3–24.

Personalrat der Staatlichen Schauspielbühnen Berlin. "Anschlag auf die Deutsche Kulturlandschaft—Heute wir, morgen Ihr!" Public call (Aufruf des Personalrats an alle Personal- und Betriebsräte der deutschen Theater). June 23, 1993. AdK, TiW 1227.

Peymann, Claus. Open letter to Michael Müller. April 1, 2015. https://www.nachtkritik.de/images/stories/pdf/Offener_Brief_Claus_Peymann_Michael_Muller.pdf. Archived at https://perma.cc/C5VT-LCLU.

Phelan, Peggy. *Unmarked: The Politics of Performance*. New York: Routledge, 1993.

Philpotts, Matthew. *The Margins of Dictatorship: Assent and Dissent in the Work of Günter Eich and Bertolt Brecht*. Oxford: Lang, 2003.

"Precarity Talk: A Virtual Roundtable with Lauren Berlant, Judith Butler, Bojana Cvejić, Isabell Lorey, Jasbir Puar, and Ana Vujanović." *TDR: The Drama Review* 56, no. 4 (2012): 163–77.

Preuss, Joachim Werner. "Die Staatlichen Schauspielbühnen sollen geschlossen werden." Theaterredaktion. Sender Freies Berlin. June 27, 1993. Transcript. AdK, TiW 1003.

Price, Cedric, and Joan Littlewood. "The Fun Palace." *TDR: The Drama Review* 12, no. 3 (1968): 127–34.

Rakow, Christian. "Warum hört der Streit nicht auf?" *Nachtkritik*, September 19, 2017. https://www.nachtkritik.de/index.php?option=com_content&view=article&id=14413:debatte-um-die-berliner-volksbuehne&catid=101&Itemid=84. Archived at https://perma.cc/HLM9-CBZE.

Rancière, Jacques. *The Emancipated Spectator*. Translated by Gregory Elliott. London: Verso, 2009.

Rayner, Alice. *Ghosts: Death's Double and the Phenomena of Theatre*. Minneapolis: University of Minnesota Press, 2006.

Reifarth, Gert. "Fostering Cultural Schizophrenia: East German Theatres Re-create the GDR." In *Theatre in the Berlin Republic: German Drama since Reunification*, edited by Denise Varney, 229–66. Berlin: Peter Lang, 2008.

Richardson, Michael D. *Revolutionary Theater and the Classical Heritage: Inheritance and Appropriation from Weimar to the GDR.* Oxford: P. Lang, 2007.

Ridout, Nicholas. *Passionate Amateurs: Theatre, Communism, and Love.* Ann Arbor: University of Michigan Press, 2013.

Ridout, Nicholas, and Rebecca Schneider. "Precarity and Performance: An Introduction." *TDR: The Drama Review* 56, no. 4 (2012): 5–9.

Roloff-Momin, Ulrich. *Zuletzt: Kultur.* Berlin: Aufbau-Verlag, 1997.

Rossiter, Ned. *Organized Networks: Media Theory, Creative Labour, New Institutions.* Amsterdam: Institute of Network Cultures, 2006.

Rubin, Don, Péter Nagy, and Philippe Rouyer. *The World Encyclopedia of Contemporary Theatre.* Vol. 1. New York: Routledge, 1994.

Salter, Chris. *Entangled: Technology and the Transformation of Performance.* Cambridge, MA: MIT Press, 2010.

———. "Forgetting, Erasure, and the Cry of the Billy Goat: Berlin Theatre Five Years After." *Performing Arts Journal* 18, no. 1 (1996): 18–28.

———. "The *Kulturstaat* in the Time of Empire: Notes on Germany Thirteen Years After." *Performing Arts Journal* 26, no. 2 (2004): 1–15.

Sandler, Daniela. *Counterpreservation: Architectural Decay in Berlin since 1989.* Ithaca, NY: Cornell University Press, 2016.

Scharfenberg, Ute. "Überlegungen und Fragestellungen zur Fortsetzung der künstlerischen Arbeit des Berliner Ensemble nach der politischen Wende." Lecture presented at "Why Theater? Choices for a New Century: An International Conference and Theatre Festival," University of Toronto, November 1–4, 1995. AdK, TiW 612.

Schechter, Joel. "Brecht's Clowns: *Man Is Man* and After." In *The Cambridge Companion to Brecht*, edited by Peter Thomson and Glendyr Sacks, 68–78. Cambridge: Cambridge University Press, 1994.

Scheinhammer-Schmid, Ulrich. "'Schmeiss die Beine vom Arsch': Bertolt Brecht und der Totentanz." In *Ende, Grenze, Schluss? Brecht und der Tod*, edited by Stephen Brockmann, Mathias Mayer, and Jürgen Hillesheim, 98–120. Würzburg: Königshausen and Neumann, 2008.

Schiller, Friedrich. *"Don Carlos" and "Mary Stuart."* Translated by Hilary Collier Sy-Quia and Peter Oswald. Oxford: Oxford University Press, 1999.

———. *History of the Revolt of the United Netherlands.* Translated by E. B. Eastwick and A. J. W. Morrison. New York: Anthological Society, 1901.

———. *On the Aesthetic Education of Man: In a Series of Letters.* Edited and translated by Elizabeth M. Wilkinson and L. A. Willoughby. Oxford: Clarendon Press, 1982.

Schirmer, Lothar. "Das Ende kommt immer plötzlich: Theater zwischen Kultur und Event." In *"Damit die Zeit nicht stehenbleibt": Theater in Berlin nach 1945—Teil 4: Nach der Wende*, edited by Stiftung Stadtmuseum Berlin, 10–17. Berlin: Henschel, 2003.

Schneider, Rebecca. "Archives: Performance Remains." *Performance Research* 6, no. 2 (2001): 100–8.

———. "It Seems as If . . . I Am Dead: Zombie Capitalism and Theatrical Labor." *TDR: The Drama Review* 56, no. 4 (2012): 150–62.

———. *Performing Remains: Art and War in Times of Theatrical Reenactment.* New York: Routledge, 2011.

Schölling, Traute. "On with the Show? The Transition to Post-Socialist Theatre in Eastern Germany." Translated by Marc Silberman. *Theatre Journal* 45, no. 1 (1993): 21–33.

Schug, Alexander, ed. *Palast der Republik: Politischer Diskurs und private Erinnerung.* Berlin: Berliner Wissenschafts-Verlag, 2007.

Schütt, Hans-Dieter, and Frank Castorf. *Die Erotik des Verrats: Gespräche mit Frank Castorf.* Berlin: Dietz, 1996.

Schütt, Hans-Dieter, and Kirsten Hehmeyer. *Castorfs Volksbühne: Schöne Bilder vom hässlichen Leben.* With Andreas Kämper. Berlin: Schwarzkopf & Schwarzkopf, 1999.

Scribner, Charity. *Requiem for Communism.* Cambridge, MA: MIT Press, 2003.

Senat von Berlin, Der. "Senatsbeschluss Nr. 3528/93." Berlin, June 22, 1993.

Sharifi, Azadeh. "Multilingualism and Postmigrant Theatre in Germany." *Modern Drama* 61, no. 3 (2018): 328–51.

Sieg, Katrin. "Black Virgins: Sexuality and the Democratic Body in Europe." *New German Critique* 37, no. 1 (2010): 147–85.

———. "Class of 1989: Who Made Good and Who Dropped Out of German History? Postmigrant Documentary Theater in Berlin." In *The German Wall: Fallout in Europe,* edited by Marc Silberman, 165–83. New York: Palgrave Macmillan, 2011.

Staatliche Schauspielbühnen Berlin. "Einnahmen und Ausgaben der Staatlichen Schauspielbühnen Berlin 1992–1994." Vorabdruck zur Beratung im Abgeordnetenhaus. September 1993. AdK, TiW 1260.

———. "Entwurf zur strukturellen Veränderung." Proposal. August 23, 1993. AdK, TiW 1195.

———. Petition (Vorlage für Unterschriftenliste). June 23, 1993. AdK, TiW 1227.

———. "Positionen—Theaterkultur und Theatermodelle: Eine Strukturdebatte am Schiller Theater." Programmzettel zur Veranstaltungsreihe im Foyer des Schiller-Theaters. August 19–September 2, 1993. AdK, TiW 1197.

Staatliche Zentralverwaltung für Statistik. *Statistisches Jahrbuch der Deutschen Demokratischen Republik 1989, 34. Jahrgang.* Berlin: Rudolf Haufe Verlag, 1990.

Steiner, Uwe. *Walter Benjamin: An Introduction to His Work and Thought.* Translated by Michael Winkler. Chicago: University of Chicago Press, 2010.

Steinweg, Reiner. *Das Lehrstück: Brechts Theorie einer politisch-ästhetischen Erziehung.* Stuttgart: J. B. Metzler, 1972.

———. "Re-Konstruktion, Irrtum, Entwicklung oder Denken fürs Museum: Eine Antwort auf Klaus Krabiel." *Brecht Yearbook / Das Brecht-Jahrbuch* 20 (1995): 217–37.

Sterling, Bruce. "The Dark Age Netherlands." *Wired,* June 28, 2011. http://www.wired.com/2011/06/the-dark-age-netherlands. Archived at https://perma.cc/P7PN-BHH2.

Stewart, Lizzie. "Black Virgins, Close Encounters: Re-Examining the 'Semi-Documentary' in Postmigrant Theatre." In *In der Welt der Proteste und Umwälzungen: Deutschland und die Türkei,* edited by Seyda Ozil, Michael Hofmann, and Yasemin Dayioglu-Yücel, 81–102. Göttingen: V&R Unipress, 2015.

———. "Postmigrant Theatre: The Ballhaus Naunynstraße Takes on Sexual Nationalism." *Journal of Aesthetics and Culture* 9, no. 2 (2017): 56–68.

————. *Staging New German Realities: Turkish-German Scripts of Postmigration*. Houndmills, Basingstoke, UK: Palgrave Macmillan, forthcoming.

Steyerl, Hito. "Art as Occupation: Claims for an Autonomy of Life." *e-flux* 30 (December 2011). https://www.e-flux.com/journal/30/68140/art-as-occupation-claims-for-an-autonomy-of-life. Archived at https://perma.cc/ARF4-CG5A.

Strom, Elizabeth A. *Building the New Berlin: The Politics of Urban Development in Germany's Capital City*. Lanham, MD: Lexington Books, 2001.

Syme, Holger Schott. "A Theatre without Actors." *Theatre Survey* 59, no. 2 (2018): 265–75.

Taruskin, Richard. *The Danger of Music and Other Anti-Utopian Essays*. Berkeley: University of California Press, 2009.

Taylor, Diana. "Dancing with Diana: A Study in Hauntology." *TDR: The Drama Review* 43, no. 1 (1999): 59–78.

Tenner, Conrad. *Der Palast der Republik: Bilder und Geschichten*. Berlin: Das Neue Berlin, 2009.

Theaterleitung, Ensemble, und Belegschaft der Staatlichen Schauspielbühnen Berlin. Open invitation to the "Protestveranstaltung." June 23, 1993. AdK, TiW 1227.

Thompson, Peter. "'Die Unheimliche Heimat': The GDR and the Dialectics of Home." *Oxford German Studies* 38, no. 3 (2009): 278–87.

Till, Karen E. *The New Berlin: Memory, Politics, Place*. Minneapolis: University of Minnesota Press, 2005.

Tinius, Jonas. "Between Professional Precariousness and Creative Self-Organization: The Free Performing Arts Scene in Germany." In *Mobile Autonomy: Exercises in Artists' Self-Organisation*, edited by Nico Dockx and Pascal Gielen, 171–93. Amsterdam: Valiz, 2015.

Tracy, James D. *The Founding of the Dutch Republic: War, Finance, and Politics in Holland, 1572–1588*. Oxford: Oxford University Press, 2008.

Ulrich, Andreas. *Palast der Republik: Ein Rückblick / A Retrospective*. Munich: Prestel, 2006.

Völker, Klaus. "Brecht Today: Classic or Challenge." *Theatre Journal* 39, no. 4 (1987): 425–33.

"Volksbühne Staff on Chris Dercon: We Fear Job Cuts and Liquidation." *e-flux conversations*, June 2016. https://conversations.e-flux.com/t/volksbuhne-staff-on-chris-dercon-we-fear-job-cuts-and-liquidation/3911. Archived at https://perma.cc/2FGK-2J96.

Ward, Simon. "Material, Image, Sign: On the Value of Memory Traces in Public Space." In *Memory Traces: 1989 and the Question of German Cultural Identity*, edited by Silke Arnold-de Simine, 281–308. Oxford: P. Lang, 2005.

Waterfeld, Sarah. "B6112—Art after All: The Alleged Occupation of the Volksbühne am Rosa-Luxemburg-Platz." *Theatre Survey* 59, no. 2 (2018): 276–81.

————. Interview by author. Berlin, May 11, 2018.

Webber, Andrew J. *Berlin in the Twentieth Century: A Cultural Topography*. Cambridge: Cambridge University Press, 2008.

Weber, Carl. "Crossing the Footbridge Again; or, A Semi-Sentimental Journey." *Theatre Journal* 45, no. 1 (1993): 75–89.

————. "German Theatre: Between the Past and the Future." *Performing Arts Journal* 13, no. 1 (1991): 43–59.

———. "Periods of Precarious Adjustment: Some Notes on the Theater's Situation at the Beginning and after the End of the Socialist German State." *Contemporary Theatre Review* 4, no. 2 (1995): 23–36.

Weinstock, Jeffrey Andrew. "Introduction: The Spectral Turn." In *Spectral America: Phantoms and the National Imagination*, edited by Jeffrey Andrew Weinstock, 3–17. Madison: University of Wisconsin Press, 2004.

"Weiterspielen im Schiller trotz Schliessungsbeschluss." *Abendschau*. Sender Freies Berlin. July 2, 1993. AdK, TiW 1028, AVM 33.8243.

White, John J. *Bertolt Brecht's Dramatic Theory*. Rochester, NY: Camden House, 2004.

Wigley, Mark. *The Architecture of Deconstruction: Derrida's Haunt*. Cambridge, MA: MIT Press, 1993.

Wildermann, Patrick. "Interview zu Der(kommende) Aufstand im HAU." *tip Berlin*, February 26, 2013.

Wilmer, S. E. "Decentralisation and Cultural Democracy." In *Theatre Worlds in Motion: Structures, Politics and Developments in the Countries of Western Europe*, edited by H. van Maanen and S. E. Wilmer, 17–36. Amsterdam: Rodopi, 1998.

Wilzopolski, Siegfried. "Famous or Dead? The Volksbühne Theater under Frank Castorf" ("Berühmt oder tot? Die Volksbühne unter Frank Castorf"). Lecture presented at "Why Theater? Choices for a New Century: An International Conference and Theatre Festival," University of Toronto, November 1–4, 1995. AdK, Schriften-DK 152.

Wise, Michael Z. *Capital Dilemma: Germany's Search for a New Architecture of Democracy*. New York: Princeton Architectural Press, 1998.

Wizisla, Erdmut. *Walter Benjamin and Bertolt Brecht: The Story of a Friendship*. Translated by Christine Shuttleworth. New Haven, CT: Yale University Press, 2009.

Woolf, Brandon. "Towards a Paradoxically Parallaxical Postdramatic Politics?" In *Postdramatic Theatre and the Political: International Perspectives on Contemporary Performance*, edited by Karen Jürs-Munby, Jerome Carroll, and Steve Giles, 31–46. London: Bloomsbury Methuen, 2013.

Wright, Elizabeth. *Postmodern Brecht: A Re-Presentation*. New York: Routledge, 1989.

Wyss, Monika. *Brecht in der Kritik: Rezensionen aller Brecht-Uraufführungen sowie ausgewählter Deutsch- und fremdsprachiger Premieren: Eine Dokumentation*. Munich: Kindler Verlag, 1977.

Ybarra, Patricia. *Latinx Theater in the Times of Neoliberalism*. Evanston, IL: Northwestern University Press, 2018.

Yúdice, George. *The Expediency of Culture: Uses of Culture in the Global Era*. Durham, NC: Duke University Press, 2003.

Zolchow, Sabine. "The Island of Berlin." In *Theatre in the Berlin Republic: German Drama since Reunification*, edited by Denise Varney, 55–80. Berlin: Peter Lang, 2008.

Page numbers in italic indicate figures.